Global Latin(o) Americanos

Transoceanic Diasporas
and Regional Migrations

Global Latin(o) Americanos

Transoceanic Diasporas and Regional Migrations

EDITED BY
MARK OVERMYER-VELÁZQUEZ
University of Connecticut

ENRIQUE SEPÚLVEDA III
University of Saint Joseph, Connecticut

New York   Oxford
OXFORD UNIVERSITY PRESS

Oxford University Press is a department of the University of Oxford.
It furthers the University's objective of excellence in research, scholarship,
and education by publishing worldwide. Oxford is a registered trademark
of Oxford zUniversity Press in the UK and certain other countries.

Published in the United States of America by Oxford University Press
198 Madison Avenue, New York, NY 10016, United States of America.

For titles covered by Section 112 of the US Higher Education
Opportunity Act, please visit www.oup.com/us/he for the
latest information about pricing and alternate formats.

Library of Congress Cataloging-in-Publication Data

Names: Overmyer-Velázquez, Mark, editor. | Sepúlveda, Enrique, editor.
Title: Global Latin(o) Americanos : transoceanic diasporas and regional
    migrations / edited by Mark Overmyer-Velazquez, University of Connecticut &
    Enrique Sepulveda III, University of Saint Joseph, Connecticut.
Description: New York : Oxford University Press, 2018. | Includes
    bibliographical references.
Identifiers: LCCN 2016042407 | ISBN 9780199389698 (pbk.)
Subjects: LCSH: Latin America--Emigration and immigration. | Latin
    Americans--Foreign countries. | Latin America--Migrations. |
    Immigrants--Latin America. | Transnationalism.
Classification: LCC JV7398 .G55 2018 | DDC 304.8098--dc23 LC record
    available at https://lccn.loc.gov/2016042407

9 8 7 6 5 4 3 2 1

Printed by Sheridan United States of America

CONTENTS

TRANSOCEANIC DIASPORAS

PREFACE

Human mobility is a defining characteristic of our world today. Migrants comprise 1 billion of the globe's 7 billion people—with approximately 214 million international migrants and 740 million internal migrants. Historic flows from the Global South to the North have been met in equal volume by south-to-south movement.[1] Migration directly impacts and shapes the lives of individuals, communities, businesses, and local and national economies, creating systems of socioeconomic interdependence. In particular, migrant remittances make a fundamental contribution to many developing countries' gross domestic products, or GDPs.[2]

Latin America and the Caribbean have long been important destinations for global migrants. In recent years, however, they have also become sites of emigration. After four and a half centuries of immigration to Latin America and the Caribbean, starting with the arrival of Europeans, Africans, and Asians to the Americas during the colonial period, the flow of migrants has changed direction. In the decades following World War II, economic growth and liberalized immigration policies in Europe and Asia, and demographic expansion and repressive regimes in Latin America and the Caribbean contributed to a period of intensified migration. Internal migration developed from rural to urban areas, especially to the capitals and metropolises of Latin America. In the 1970s, migration flows grew between countries in the region and to the United States and Canada. Toward the end of the twentieth century and with the increasingly muscular US state security and border militarization following September 11, 2001, emigrants looked to resettle in Europe and Asia. In his introductory chapter in this volume, Douglas Massey carefully details the history of Latin American emigration and provides current demographic data on the global migration of Latin Americans.

By the end of the first decade of the twenty-first century, the contribution of Latin America and the Caribbean to international migration amounted to over 32 million people, or 15% of the world's international migrants. Although most have headed north of the Rio Grande/Bravo and Miami, in the past decade Latin

American and Caribbean migrants have travelled to new destinations—both within the hemisphere and to countries in Europe and Asia—at greater rates than to the United States.[3]

The diversity of these origins and destinations has not received balanced treatment.[4] Studies of US-bound migration have dominated the literature, reinforcing the sense of dependence, domination, and attraction exercised by the United States over the whole region. Although significant research has been conducted examining the flow of transoceanic market capital, the growing globalization of Latin American migration to non-US destinations requires a comprehensive overview. *Global Latin(o) Americanos: Transoceanic Diasporas and Regional Migrations* shifts the analytical lens away from US-dominant interpretations to document and examine the growing flow between and within destinations in the Global South and across the Pacific and Atlantic oceans. By demonstrating the ways in which people in the Global South participate in and negotiate globalization, this volume fosters a decentered, hemispheric, and transoceanic approach that enriches and broadens our theoretical conversations and substantive knowledge about Latin American and Caribbean migration.

The original, interdisciplinary studies in *Global Latin(o) Americanos* provide a critical examination of Latin American and Caribbean migrations to non-US destinations. Following two introductory chapters that situate the topic in its historical, academic, and sociodemographic contexts, the volume's authors focus on two broad migratory circuits originating in Latin America and the Caribbean: intraregional and transoceanic. Chapters on intraregional migration examine three different migratory trajectories within Latin America and the Caribbean. In addition to the relocation of workers from one country to another (e.g., Peruvian domestic workers to Chile), the volume explores the histories of temporary or seasonal cross-border migrants (e.g., Haitians harvesting sugar cane in the Dominican Republic) and transmigrants transiting through countries en route to a final destination (e.g., Guatemalans travelling to the United States via Mexico). The studies of transoceanic migration analyze both transatlantic flows to destinations such as Spain and Israel and trans-Pacific flows to Japan. Factors determining transoceanic migration include colonial ties and proactive immigration policies that privilege historical ethnic connections to Latin American descendants. A concluding chapter builds on the introductions by Massey and García to assess critical themes examined throughout the volume's case studies and to consider how migrants themselves live and are defined as global Latin(o) Americanos.

Global Latin(o) Americanos contributes to a growing literature that examines the flow of Latin American and Caribbean migrants to non-US destinations and, by building on theories of diasporic citizenship, advances our understanding of transnational practices and identities of global Latin(o) American immigrant communities outside of the United States. Although most studies have focused on individual bi- or transnational cases (e.g., Casillas 2011; Dandler 2012), the phenomenon requires a broad overview of this important migratory trend. *Global Latin(o) Americanos* also adds to studies that analyze recent shifts in migration from the Global South that have brought new or former inhabitants to countries in need of temporary workers (e.g., Silverstein 2005; Vora 2008; Willen 2007).[5] As Martinez explains in his chapter, given its formidable, hegemonic role, the United States cannot be excluded from this analysis as it continues to bear responsibility in shaping immigration in Latin America, even if migrants are not traveling to US destinations, as is the case with Haitians in the Dominican Republic.

As María Cristina García points out, this volume draws on the work of scholars, such as José Saldívar, who call for a "remapping" of American Studies through a discourse of "border thinking" that challenges us "to reimagine the nation as a site within many 'cognitive maps' in which the nation-state is not congruent with cultural identity" (p. ix) (Saldívar 1997). Expanding on this critique, *Global Latin(o) Americanos* reorients both Latina/o Studies outside of a (North) American locus and Latin American and Caribbean Studies beyond the hemisphere, integrating and decentering traditional ethnic and area studies approaches.

Our use of the term "Global Latin(o) Americanos" places people of Latin American and Caribbean origin in comparative, transnational, and global perspectives with particular emphasis on migrants moving to and living in non-US destinations.[6] Like its two stem words, "Global Latin(o) Americanos" is an ambiguous term with no specific national, ethnic, or racial signification. Yet, by combining the terms Latina/o (traditionally: people of Latin American and Caribbean origin in the United States) and Latin American in a bilingual fusion, we aim to disrupt national conventions and underscore the processual, dynamic, and transborder nature of migration. Furthermore, the hybrid term also signals the importance of bringing together different transnational case studies of Latin American migrants into comparative analysis. In stark contrast with migrants in other host countries, Latinos in the United States are predominantly of Mexican origin[7] and highly vulnerable to criminalization and deportation. As Massey points out, "this contrast alone cautions against generalizing about Latino identity and Latino integration from the experience of the United States" (p. 14). Placing this volume's case studies into conversation with one another allows for a deeper and more nuanced understanding of Latin American migrations. In our concluding chapter, we examine in further detail how migrants, scholars, business marketers, and government officials have understood and identified Latina/os and Latin Americans in various global contexts.

The work in *Global Latin(o) Americanos* addresses and reframes a central problem of our time: from the challenge of incorporating immigrants into Western societies and economies, which too often frames immigrants as "the problem," to the challenge of redefining citizenship in an era of globalization, which positions immigrants as uniquely poised to teach us about what this means.[8] How Latin(o) American immigrants respond and exercise agency under familiar and unfamiliar global conditions is of critical importance on a number of fronts, not least of which is the health of democratic societies and the diverse expressions of citizenship across the Latin American diaspora. Global Latin(o) Americanos and their new destinations provide important contexts for studying these issues.

The volume's chapters shed light on constructions of diasporic identities and the historical forces and movements that undergird them as well as illustrating for us the various and complex conceptions of membership, belonging, and citizenship. These studies examine the emergence of new ways of social and political participation that migrants coconstruct in their new national homes. Moreover, these chapters challenge us to decenter traditional subjects of study and locations of knowledge production. Lastly, these essays index for us possible topics for future study.

******

Our own personal and academic experiences as members of the Global Latin(o) Americano diaspora have shaped how we approached this book. With deep family ties to the Chicano/Mexicano community, we started our journey as Latinos in the United States. Formally educated in US academic institutions with training in Latino and Latin American Studies, we have studied and written about US Latina/o and Latin American experiences. However, after a time living as academic immigrants outside of the Greater Mexico-United States, in places like Madrid, Spain; San Salvador, El Salvador; and Santiago, Chile, our perspectives shifted and globalized. Working with and living in Latin American and Caribbean immigrant communities outside of the United States further challenged us to decenter our nation-centered orientations. Encounters with self-proclaimed "Latina/os" in places as far-flung as Jordan, Italy, Canada, and Israel have made us reconsider not only dominant usage of the term but also, and more important, to ask how migrants in those places have managed life in the diaspora. Outside of an academic home in traditional US Latina/o (ethnic) and Latin American and Caribbean (area) Studies, we hope the exciting and complex studies in this volume will provide new points of departure and arrival for scholars searching to locate the global experience of Latin(o) Americanos. Moreover, we hope that this work contributes in positive ways to the experience of Global Latin(o) Americanos who, despite often living lives of displacement, vulnerability, and marginalization, find innovative ways to secure rights for themselves while establishing new homes and communities and new forms of Latinidad.

Our work on this project has connected us with Latin(o) Americana/o and other scholars from around the world. We have been very fortunate to learn from these friends and colleagues as we deepened our understanding of our topic's local particularities and global comparisons. Mark thanks go to the faculty and staff at the Pontificia Universidad Católica de Chile's Instituto de Historia, especially Patricio Bernedo, Fernando Purcell, Claudio Rolle, Jaime Valenzuela, Javiera Müller, and Marisol Vidal. At the PUC, Mark benefited greatly from discussions with the graduate students in his seminar, "Historia de la migración en las Américas." Liliana Montesino and Sergio Palleres were of invaluable assistance with the collections at the Biblioteca Nacional de Chile, as was the archival staff with the press files at the Fundación Vicaría de la Solidaridad. Carolina Bank Muñoz aided his search for scholarship on Chile's labor history. His *hermano chileno*, David Preiss, helped him to get to Chile in the first place, and the Fulbright Foundation funded and assisted his visit. The comments and suggestions by *colegas* at three conferences helped to make this a better book: Latina/o Century: Path Breakers and New Directions in Latina/o Studies, Dartmouth College; Rethinking Space in Latin American History, Yale University; and *Aquí y Allá*: Migrations in Latin American Labor History, Duke University. Ongoing support from Ray Craib, Rick López, Merilee Grindle, Evelyn Hu-Dehart, María Cristina García, Gil Joseph and Silvia Spitta has been invaluable in advancing his work and situating it within broader currents in Latino and Latin American Studies. At the University of Connecticut, colleagues in the History Department and at El Instituto: Institute of Latina/o, Caribbean & Latin American Studies continue to provide Mark with much appreciated, vibrant intellectual homes. In particular, Anne Gebelein and Anne Theriault have been wonderful collaborators at El Instituto. In the midst of this multi- and transnational collaborative project, sharing ideas and work with his *compadre*, Enrique Sepúlveda, over the past years has been an exciting and treasured learning experience. As with all his academic journeys, they begin and end with family. Jordi, Sarai, Maceo y Adan: gracias por su apoyo, inspiración, paciencia y cariño infinito.

Enrique would like to thank the many colleagues, activists, educators, and young people in El Salvador for helping him understand the complex post–civil war context and the profound transnational migration experiences of *Salvadoreños* in Guatemala, Mexico, and the United States. Special heartfelt thanks to the Fe y Alegría education team, Dr. José Luis Benitez at the Universidad Centroamericana Simeón Cañas, and Haydee Díaz in San Salvador. Enrique also gives special thanks to colleagues at the Universidad Autónoma de Madrid (UAM) in Spain: Marta Morgade, Javier González Patiño, and especially David Poveda, for their intellectual, institutional, and social collaboration and solidarity. David was especially instrumental in securing multiple invaluable contacts and scholarly opportunities in both the city of Madrid and at the UAM, not to mention the many opportunities for our families to come together to eat and play. Enrique would also like to thank his *compadre* Mark for his *acompañamiento*, in every sense of the word, on this exciting project and beyond. ¡Muchas gracias a todos! A special thanks goes to Enrique's mom, Romelia R. Sepúlveda, who, many moons ago, crossed *El Rio Bravo* to give birth to him on US soil and who later taught him Spanish literacy as he struggled with learning English in a California grade school. Her love, vision, and commitment to their migrating family continue to anchor him. His wife and transnational soulmate, Dr. Andrea Dyrness, is the one responsible for taking him abroad to experience other Latinidades, first to El Salvador as an international elections observer and then to Spain as coresearchers. Her love, faith, and thirst for social justice enrich him profoundly. To his wonderful little globetrotting daughter, Sofía, whose own life lessons of displacement and questioning of identity through her child's eyes have added deeper layers of understanding to what it means to live and love in mobility.

Together, Mark and Enrique thank James A. Garza, Evan R. Ward, Gregory S. Crider, Emily Wakild, Amy Lutz, Patrice Olsen, Benjamin Nobbs-Thiessen, and one anonymous reviewer for their extremely helpful advice and Brian Wheel at Oxford University Press for his creativity, encouragement, and guidance throughout this process. Charles Cavaliere took over the editing midcourse and has done an admirable job navigating the project to completion. Herself a Transatlantic Spanish migrant with roots in Latin America, Irene Cuesta's cover art beautifully and provocatively engages the themes of *(des) encuentro* that migrants experience in their transborder journeys. Elizabeth Mahan has greatly improved a number of chapters with her elegant and detailed wordsmithing. Versions of the chapters by Armony, Sandoval-García, Margolis, Raijaman and Kemp, and Vior as well as the Preface and Conclusion appeared in the October 2015 edition of the *LASA Forum*. Finally, all of the authors of the volume deserve enormous praise and appreciation for their valuable contributions and support in this collaborative project.

Global Latin(o) Americanos is dedicated to the migrants themselves who have crossed regional and transoceanic borders, forging new paths for their themselves, their families, and the many countries to which they belong.

CONTRIBUTORS

Victor Armony is Director of the Laboratoire interdisciplinaire d'études latino-américaines (LIELA) and Professor of Sociology at Université du Québec à Montréal (UQAM). He is the former editor in chief of the *Canadian Journal of Latin American and Caribbean Studies* (2004–2011) and a former analyst for Radio Canada International's Spanish language section (2009–2012). He has published in English, French, Spanish, and German on ethnic diversity, immigration, and integration in Canada. In 2010–2013, he held a grant from the Social Sciences and Humanities Research Council to describe Québec's Latin American population, and in 2011–2012 he studied the Latino population in the United States as a Fulbright Visiting Research Chair. He is currently the Co-director of the recently created RELAM, the interuniversity Latin American studies network of Montreal.

Rodolfo Casillas R. is Senior Professor and Researcher at FLACSO Mexico. Professor Casillas has conducted extensive research on Central American undocumented migration through Mexico's southern border. His research interests include the study of the conditions of unrecognized refugees, international transmigration through Mexico, Central American migrant children, humanitarian networks and migration, human smuggling, and sex and human trafficking. He is the author of four books on human trafficking in México as well as of multiple articles and reports (over 100) on the conditions of Central American migrants traveling through Mexico. His most recent work explores the role of organized crime in the smuggling of undocumented immigrants in Mexico. He is currently working on a volume on violence and migration. (www.rodolfocasillasr.org)

Andrea Dyrness is Associate Professor of Educational Studies at Trinity College, Connecticut. She teaches in the areas of international and urban education, and her research addresses the relationship between education, cultural identity, and citizenship in societies affected by transnational migration. She has conducted research with transnational Latino communities in California, El Salvador, and Spain. Andrea received her BA in Anthropology and Educational Studies from Brown University and her MA and PhD in Social and Cultural Studies in Education from the University of California at Berkeley, and was a Fulbright Fellow in El Salvador. She is the author of *Mothers United: An Immigrant Struggle for Socially Just Education* (University of Minnesota Press, 2011).

María Cristina García is the Howard A. Newman Professor of American Studies in the Department of History at Cornell University, where she teaches courses on twentieth-century US history, immigration and refugee history, and Latino history. She also holds a joint appointment in Cornell's Latino Studies Program and served as the program's director from 2000 to 2003. She is the author of *Seeking Refuge: Central American Migration to Mexico, the United States, and Canada* and *Havana USA: Cuban Exiles and Cuban Americans in South Florida*, both published by the University of California Press. A third book project, *Refuge in Post-Cold War America*, is currently in press. García is President of the Immigration and Ethnic History Society (2015–2018) and a former Fellow at the Woodrow Wilson International Center for Scholars in Washington DC (2013–2014).

Adriana Kemp is a political sociologist at the Department of Sociology and Anthropology, Tel-Aviv University. Her research focuses on intersections between labor migration, citizenship, and civil society. Kemp is the coauthor (with Rebeca Raijman) of a book on *Migrants and Workers: The Political Economy of Labor Migration in Israel* (Van Leer Institute and Hakibbutz Hameuchad Press, 2008). Her publications appeared in *International Migration Review, Gender and Society, Ethnic and Racial Studies, Political Geography,* and *International Journal of Urban and Regional Review,* among others. Her research on the legal mobilization of migrant workers' rights (with N. Kfir) is forthcoming in *Critical Sociology, Law and Society Review,* and *Social Problems.* She has recently completed with Rebeca Raijman a research on political and public attitudes on illegality in migration, funded by the Israeli Ministry of Science and Culture. Kemp carried out consultancy work for the OECD and chaired the board of directors of the Association for Civil Rights in Israel, the largest human rights Israeli NGO.

Maxine L. Margolis is Professor Emerita of Anthropology at the University of Florida and Adjunct Senior Research Scholar at the Institute for Latin American Studies, Columbia University. She is the author or editor of eight books, including *Little Brazil: An Ethnography of Brazilian Immigrants in New York City* (Princeton University Press, 1994) published in Portuguese as *Little Brazil: Imigrantes Brasileiros em Nova York* (Editora Papirus,

1994), *True to Her Nature: Changing Advice to American Women* (Waveland, 2000), *An Invisible Minority: Brazilians in New York City* (revised 2nd edition, University Press of Florida, 2009), and *Goodbye, Brazil: Emigrés from the Land of Soccer and Samba* (University of Wisconsin Press, 2013), which was also published in Portuguese as *Goodbye, Brazil: Emigrantes Brasileiros no Mundo* (Editora Contexto, 2013). Dr. Margolis was elected to the American Academy of Arts and Sciences in 2009 and was awarded the Lifetime Contribution Award by the Brazilian Studies Association in 2014.

Samuel Martínez is a cultural anthropologist who teaches in the programs in Anthropology and Latin American Studies at the University of Connecticut. He is the author of two ethnographic monographs and several peer-reviewed articles on the migration and labor and minority rights of Haitian nationals and people of Haitian ancestry in the Dominican Republic. He is also editor of a contributory volume, *International Migration and Human Rights* (University of California Press, 2009). In his current research and writing he brings critical scrutiny to northern human rights solidarity with Haitian-ancestry people in the Dominican Republic, 1978 to 2015.

Douglas S. Massey is the Henry G. Bryant Professor of Sociology and Public Affairs at Princeton University. He is the coauthor of *Beyond Smoke and Mirrors: Mexican Immigration in an Age of Economic Integration* (2002) and *Brokered Boundaries: Creating Immigrant Identity in Anti-Immigrant Times* (2010), both published by the Russell Sage Foundation. He is the former President of the American Sociological Association, the Population Association of America, and the American Academy of Political and Social Science and an elected member of the American Academy of Arts and Sciences, the National Academy of Sciences, and the American Philosophical Society. He currently codirects the Mexican Migration Project with longtime colleague Jorge Durand.

Mark Overmyer-Velázquez is the founding Director of El Instituto: Institute of Latina/o, Caribbean & Latin American Studies and Associate Professor of History at the University of Connecticut. His first book, *Visions of the Emerald City: Modernity, Tradition and the Formation of Porfirian Oaxaca, Mexico* (Duke, 2006; Spanish translation, 2010), won the New England Council on Latin American Studies Best Book Award. He completed the volume, *Beyond la Frontera: The History of Mexico-U.S. Migration* (Oxford, 2011), while on fellowship as the Peggy Rockefeller Visiting Scholar at Harvard University. This current project emerged from his work as a Fulbright Scholar examining the history of Peruvian migrants in Chile. Former cochair of the Latina/o Studies Section of the Latin American Studies Association, he also edited the two volume, *Latino America: State by State* (Greenwood, 2008), which addresses the historical significance of the growing Latin(o) American population throughout the United States.

Rebeca Raijman is Associate Professor in the Department of Sociology and Anthropology at the University of Haifa, Israel. She received her PhD in Sociology from the University of Chicago. Her research focuses on international migration (in Israel, Europe, and the United States) with special emphasis on migrants' modes of incorporation into host societies (labor market outcomes, identity, and language acquisition). She conducted a comprehensive research project regarding the emergence on new migrant ethnic minorities in Israel, the sociopolitical organization of undocumented migrant communities, and the politics and policy of labor migration in Israel. The results of this investigation have been published in *"Workers" and "Foreigners": The Political Economy of Labor Migration in Israel* (Jerusalem: Van-Leer Instituteand Kibbutz Hamehuhad, in Hebrew and coauthored with Adriana Kemp, 2007). Her new book, *South African Jews in Israel: Assimilation in a Multigenerational Perspective* (University of Nebraska Press) is forthcoming in February 2016.

Luis Roniger is Reynolds Professor of Latin American Studies, Politics and International Affairs at Wake Forest University; and a professor emeritus of Sociology and Anthropology at Hebrew University of Jerusalem. A comparative political sociologist, his work focuses on the interface between politics, society, and public culture. He is on the international board of academic journals published in Argentina, Colombia, Mexico, Spain, Israel, and the United Kingdom; and has published over 160 academic articles and 18 books. Among his books are *The Legacy of Human-Rights Violations in the Southern Cone* (Oxford University Press, 1999, with Mario Sznajder, also in Spanish and Portuguese); *The Politics of Exile in Latin America* (Cambridge University Press, 2009, with Sznajder); *Transnational Politics in Central America* (University Press of Florida, 2011); and *Destierro y exilio en América Latina: Nuevos estudios y aproximaciones teóricas* (Editorial Universitaria de Buenos Aires, 2014).

Carlos Sandoval-García is a professor in the Media Studies School and the Institute for Social Sciences both at the University of Costa Rica. He obtained his PhD in Cultural Studies at the University of Birmingham, United Kingdom. His books published in English include *Threatening Others. Nicaraguans and the Formation of National Identities in Costa Rica* (Ohio University Press, 2004), *Shattering Myths on Immigration and Emigration in Costa Rica* (Lexington Books, 2011) and *Exclusion and Forced Migration in Central America* (Palgrave Pivot, 2016). Currently he is editor of the journal *Anuario de Estudios Centroamericanos* and is active in a number of networks of solidarity regarding migrants' rights in Costa Rica.

Enrique Sepúlveda III is Associate Professor in the School of Education at University of Saint Joseph in West Hartford, Connecticut. He is the son of Mexican migrant workers and in his early career worked as a bilingual teacher and school principal in the California central valley. He has conducted research projects in communities and schools heavily impacted by global migration in northern California, San Salvador, El Salvador, and Madrid, Spain. His research examines how Latino migrants negotiate global migration, citizenship, and belonging within schools and communities in both sending and receiving contexts. He has published in the *Harvard Educational Review* Special Issue on "Immigration, Youth, and Education" (81, no. 3, Fall 2011) and in the Spring volume of 2015 titled "Education and the Production of Diasporic Citizens in El Salvador."

Eduardo J. Vior is a freelance journalist who works in Buenos Aires (Argentina) and writes for several newspapers and magazines about international politics. He is also Associated Researcher in the Faculty of Philosophy and Literature at the University of Buenos Aires, where he studies the political participation of immigrated communities. His first book, *Migraciones internacionales y ciudadanía democrática* (Saarbrücken, Germany, 2012), reexamines his fieldwork in Germany, Brazil, and Argentina. He has also contributed to several books in Germany, Argentina, Brazil, and the United States, as well as to social science journals and conferences. The current project emerged from a paper presented in September 2013 at the 12th Argentinian Conference of Population Studies in Bahia Blanca. He also coordinates research projects at the universities of Magdeburg (Germany), La Matanza, and Río Negro (Argentina), as well at the UNILA (Brazil).

NOTES

1. For a review of current scholarship on global migrant flows, see Davide Pero and John Solomos, *Migrant Politics and Mobilisation: Exclusion, Engagements, Incorporation* (New York: Routledge, 2013).
2. "International remittance flows through official channels to developing countries in 2012 reached approximately USD 401 billion, three times the amount of total aid flows from OECD donors in 2011," in "IOM Position on the Post-2015 United Nations Development Agenda" (International Organization for Migration, 2015). See also "International Migration 2013: Migrants by Origin and Destination," United Nations Populations Facts, accessed on July 14, 2015, http://www.un.org/en/ga/68/meetings /migration/pdf/International%20Migration%202013_Migrants%20by%20 origin%20and%20destination.pdf.
3. United Nations, Website of United Nations Department of Economic and Social Affairs Population Division: International Migration (New York: United Nations, 2015). http://www.un.org/en/development/desa/population/migration/data/estimates2 /estimatesorigin.shtml
4. We are responding to the call by scholars such as Marcelo Suárez-Orozco, who writes, "While there is a general consensus that migration from Latin America is changing the Americas and the world beyond, there is little systematic empirical, conceptual, and theoretical work examining the Exodo in an interdisciplinary, comparative, and regional framework." In "Some Thoughts on Migration Studies and the Latin American Éxodo," *Latin American Studies Association Forum* 37, no. 1 (2006): 3.
5. A handful of recent collections, employing specific methodological or national perspectives, have approached the study of new migratory destinations for people from Latin Americans and the Caribbean. One recent example, Katharine M. Donato et al., "Continental Divides: International Migration in the Americas," *Annals of the American Academy of Political and Social Science* 630 (2010) establishes a common framework of data, methods, and theories that compares well-established studies of Mexican migration to the United States with the migratory patterns of other countries in the Americas. Other collected volumes focus on specific receiving countries (England: McIlwaine 2011; see also Garcia 2006 and Masanet 2010) or sending countries (Brazil: Margolis 2013; see also Fusco 2006 and Paerregaard 2009). None offers

a comprehensive, aggregate exploration of the topic that compares and contrasts the multiple reasons for migration to and then integration in non-US destinations.

6. In addition to including people from the Caribbean, we use "Global Latin(o) Americanos" as a shorthand meant to encompass Latina/o/@/xs of all subject positions and racial, ethnic, gender, and sexuality orientations. Furthermore, we recognize that the term "Latin America" is itself a fiction, concocted in the nineteenth century either by European elites to impose colonial dominance on the New World (Walter Mignolo, *The Idea of Latin America* [Malden, MA: Blackwell, 2005] or by Latin American elites to resist US and European imperialism Michel Gobat, "The Invention of Latin America: A Transnational History of Anti-imperialism, Democracy, and Race," *The American Historical Review* 118, no. 5 [2013]: 1345–1375).

7. Although the majority of Latina/os in the US are of Mexican origin (64% in 2012), the US Latina/o population in general is of diverse national and regional origins and is dispersed throughout the United States. (In 2012, other major groups included 9.4% of Puerto Rican background, 3.8% Salvadoran, 3.7% Cuban, 3.1% Dominican, and 2.3% Guatemalan). "Facts for Features," United States Census, accessed August 8, 2015, http://www.census.gov/newsroom/facts-for-features/2014/cb14-ff22.html. For additional details, see Mark Overmyer-Velázquez, ed., *Latino America: State-by-State* (Westport, CT: Greenwood Press, 2008).

8. Thanks to Dr. Andrea Dyrness for the idea in sentence and phrasing.

FOREWORD

María Cristina García

In her 2006 essay, "Nuestra América: Latino History as United States History," Vicki Ruiz examined three defining moments in US history—1848, 1898, and 1948—when Latinos were meaningful actors but summarily excluded from narratives of these historical events. Ruiz called for a reconsideration and reincorporation of these historical actors into the national narrative:

> Contrary to the popular media depictions of Latinos as people who arrived the day before yesterday, there exists a rich layering of nationalities, generations, and experiences. I seek a fuller recounting of this history, encompassing both transhemispheric and community perspectives. Nuestra América *es* historia Americana. Our America *is* American history.[1]

Like Ruiz, many scholars of the field now called "Latino Studies" have called for comparative and transhemispheric perspectives, for if Latino history and culture are integral to the history and culture of the United States, it is also integral to the history and culture of Latin America, the Caribbean, and increasingly, other parts of the globe. Some, like cultural theorist José David Saldívar, have called for a "remapping" of American Studies, in general, for the nation-state is not congruent with cultural identity. Geopolitical borders are not "natural"; they force the people of the Americas to separate themselves, and it is through migration that new possibilities for contact and exchange emerge. For Saldívar, the US-Mexico borderlands, in particular, offer "a paradigm of crossing, circulation, material mixing, and resistance"; and its history contests the uneven power relations between two nations, and the "violent mappings and representations of empire."[2]

Despite decades of exciting multidisciplinary scholarship on a wide range of Latino experiences, however, the field of Latino Studies—like American Studies, in general—remains associated primarily with the United States. The scholarship is written almost exclusively in English and requires readers to have a proficiency in English. The Latino subject is analyzed and scrutinized through an American (US) lens. Even when colleges and universities position Latino Studies within Latin American area studies programs (products of Cold War US academia), the US experience is privileged. Latin America and the Caribbean are viewed *from* the United States; the Latino actor is a dislocated actor, who relates to the country of ancestry from his or her position as an exile, immigrant, refugee, asylum-seeker, or *transmigrante.*

The scholarship's centering on the US experience is due partly to the rapid growth in (im)migration to the United States since the Immigration Act of 1965. In 2010, the US Census Bureau reported that 50.5 million people, or 16% of the general population, were of "Hispanic" or "Latino" origin—up from 14.5 million in 1980.[3] If one included the residents of the Commonwealth of Puerto Rico, the numbers increased to 54.3 million. The undocumented and/or victims of trafficking brought the tally of Latin American and Caribbean-origin people closer to 65 million.

But numbers are only part of the story. The centering of the US experience in the study of migration also has much to do with the historical moment out of which the field of Latino Studies emerged. During the civil rights struggles of the 1960s and 1970s, underrepresented populations called for a decolonization of knowledge as part of the political project that called for greater participation in the social, political, and economic life of the country. Activists targeted those institutions and practices responsible for the production and circulation of information—colleges and universities; archives, journals, and presses; school boards and curriculum; the news and popular media. The academic fields of Chicano/a and Puerto Rican Studies that emerged from these civil rights struggles were, at their core, social justice projects: they liberated those marginalized and made them the focus of intellectual inquiry they inserted into US historical narratives and literary canons those who had been made to disappear.

By the 1990s, a new generation of Latino students and scholars—children of the post-1965 migration from Latin America—had further enriched our understanding of the complexity of the "Latino" experience by examining not only the ways race, ethnicity, and class affected integration and assimilation but also how Latin American/Caribbean peoples transcend national boundaries through their political, cultural, and economic lives and relationships. The new "Latino Studies" was a field framed by, and in dialogue with, the theoretical insights developed by scholars of feminism, sexuality, race, postcoloniality, and postoccidentalism.

Emerging parallel to this US-centered scholarship on "Latino/as" was another body of multidisciplinary scholarship on Latin American/Caribbean peoples—much of it published outside the United States, in languages other than English—which examined migratory experiences in other national and regional contexts. In so doing, these scholars further "remapped" American Studies/ Latino Studies, examining and contesting power relations across geographies (as well as in academia itself), and expanding the conceptual and geographical boundaries of these fields.

Mark Overmyer-Velázquez and Enrique Sepúlveda have done us a great service in introducing us to a sample of the most recent scholarship on "Latino" (im)migrant populations *outside* the United States: migration that is intraregional but also transoceanic. Despite popular discourses, not all Latin American/ Caribbean migrants migrate to the US—nor want to. Nor is the United States the only hub or node through which migrations cross and intersect. The source countries, migratory circuits, and destinations are many: some routes are well established or cyclical, developed over the course of generations, and even centuries; others are fairly new—even unexpected—developments that demonstrate how state policies and economic institutions affect the character and flow of migration, and privilege some groups over others. Yet other migrations could be considered a return to ancestral homelands. Collectively, all these experiences highlight the linkages and interdependencies between countries, regions, and localities over time.

In expanding the geographic and conceptual boundaries of Latino (im)migration history, the authors offer an empirical basis for thinking about a wide range of questions, and they expand the possibilities for comparison and synthesis. What do the experiences of the global Latino (im)migrant population reveal about the construction of identity, citizenship, and political engagement? What do they reveal about the role gender, race, kinship, networks, and associations play in shaping migratory flows, and integration and assimilation in destination countries? Does ecology always determine whether the migration will be overland or overseas? What parallels and/or conclusions can be drawn about the role of the state, and the construction of political, legal, and nationalist borders? What can we learn through the comparative study of commercial markets, the structuring of labor, and the economic lives of workers? What does comparison reveal about the context of reception as well as about individual agency? Do particular circumstances in the source and destination countries always hinder—or accelerate—migration?

Ultimately, this volume points to the need for more case studies, and for a continued historical grounding of empirical data. The temptation is to conclude that the post-1970s migratory flows are a new phenomenon, entirely attributed to the modern iterations of globalization; but this perspective downplays the long history of movement within the Americas as enslaved, indentured, and free peoples relocated by force or by choice when political borders were redefined and political regimes supplanted; when trade routes were established and natural resources exploited; when dreams and opportunities beckoned individuals, families, and communities to move elsewhere. Unfortunately, it is not just migrants who are "uprooted" as Dirk Hoerder reminds us, but historical memory. Migrants have always moved through a wide range of cultural spaces; their trajectories have always been translocal, transregional, and transnational.[4] Whether migration is seasonal/temporary or permanent, it always exemplifies global connectivity, and (im)migrants are—and have always been—characters on international as well as local and national stages.

This intellectual project underscores the need to do comparative and synthetic work, understanding at once the particularities of migratory experience but also the persistent commonalities. It encourages us to engage with and question notions of territoriality and the nation, location and dislocation, the subaltern and the hegemonic, *Latinidad* and *Americanidad*. The volume answers Ruiz's call for a fuller recounting of the history of Latin American/Caribbean peoples that incorporates transhemispheric and community perspectives; and the volume "remaps" the *Americano* experience, as Saldívar encouraged us to do, to include a wide range of cultural and political spaces.

Ultimately, however, the project should also ask us to consider the rights of workers and the responsibilities of states to those workers. The trafficking of labor, the exploitation of women and children, the lack of environmental and workplace safeguards, the failure of states to offer workers a living wage—these are but a few of the challenges of our age.

I am excited by the work that Overmyer-Velázquez and Sepúlveda have compiled for us in this anthology. I look forward to the intellectual work that is yet to come.

NOTES

1. The article was a revised version of the presidential address Ruiz delivered to the convention of the Organization of American Historians (OAH) on April 22, 2006. Vicki L. Ruiz, "Nuestra América: Latino history as United States History," *Journal of American History,* 93(3), 655–672. Retrieved from http://search.proquest.com/docview /224881182?accountid=10267.
2. José David Saldívar, *Border Matters: Remapping American Cultural Studies.* Berkeley: University of California Press, 1997, 13.
3. U.S. Census, "The Hispanic Population: 2010." http://2010.census.gov/2010cesus/data.
4. Dirk Hoerder, "Transformations over Time or Sudden Change:Historical Perspectives on Mass Migrations and Human Lives," *Comparative Population Studies* 37, n. 1–2 (May. 2012): 213–227. Retrieved at: http://www.comparativepopulationstudies.de /index.php/CPoS/article/view/75.

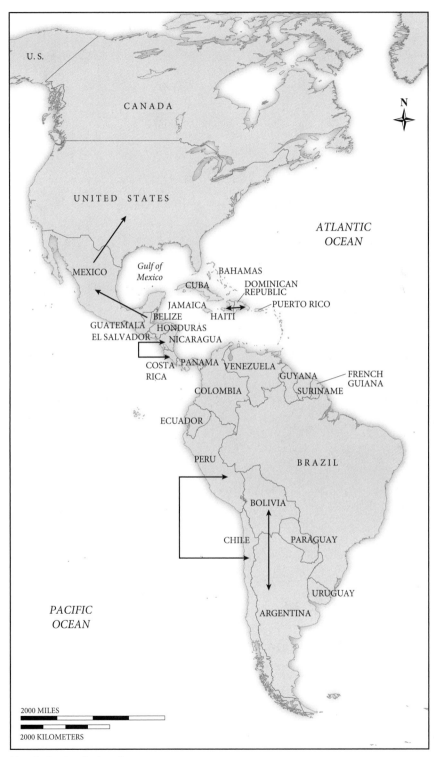

Map A Regional migrations.

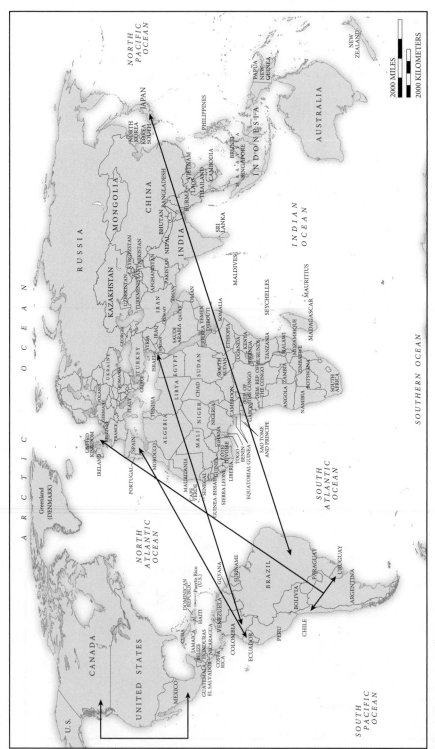

Map B Transoceanic diasporas.

Global Latin(o) Americanos

Transoceanic Diasporas
and Regional Migrations

The Origins and Future of Global Latinos

DOUGLAS S. MASSEY

Immigration has always been central to the social and cultural dynamics of Latin America, but only recently has emigration from the region created a new set of Latino populations in a diverse set of nations around the world. During the colonial period, of course, Latin America was primarily a region of immigration, though Spain and Portugal both sought to block immigration from other European nations so as to safeguard social and political control in their own colonies. As a result, the inflows from Europe were rather modest up until independence.[1] Of far greater consequence was the mass importation of slaves during the colonial era, which ultimately brought some 1.7 million Africans into Spanish America and 3.9 million into Brazil, thus creating a distinctive mix of European and African elements in societies around the Caribbean.[2]

It was only after independence that Latin American governments adopted policies to encourage mass immigration from Europe, usually as part of a deliberate project to "whiten" and thus "modernize" the fledgling nations.[3] In most cases, these Europeanization projects met with limited success. Only Argentina and Brazil emerged as countries of mass European immigration during the nineteenth century. By 1900 the foreign percentage stood at 7% in Brazil and 30% in Argentina.[4] European immigration to the Americas was curtailed in 1914 by the outbreak of World War I, and after a short revival in the 1920s it faltered once again during the Great Depression of the 1930s. After World War II, Argentina did reemerge as a country of immigration, though at this point most migrants came from neighboring countries in Latin America rather than Europe.[5]

The migration of Europeans and the importation of Africans (and in some cases Asians) into Latin America generated a diverse set of national and subnational identities reflecting different histories of conquest, colonization, slavery, and settlement; but the mixing within nations did not produce "Latino" identities per se. Such identities only emerged when Latin Americans began to migrate outside the region and interact at points of destination in culturally distinct set-tings. As immigrants, Latin Americans naturally brought into the host society their different national identities. Faced with the common challenge of integrat-ing within an alien and sometimes hostile context of reception, Latino immi-grants often drew upon shared linguistic and cultural resources to create a new pan-ethnic identity that had meaning for both immigrants and natives. In their analysis of Latin American immigrants in the northeastern United States, for example, Massey and Sánchez found that a shared Latino identity emerged rather quickly and naturally among Latin Americans after arrival, with shared experi-ences of exclusion, discrimination, and exploitation and common problems of adaptation creating a sense of solidarity among formerly disparate nationalities.[6] As this volume shows, however, today Latino identities are not only being forged in the United States but around the world, and to comprehend Latino identities in the twenty-first century, one must appreciate the origins and destinations of those who migrated outside the region for new lives as immigrants abroad.

A BRIEF HISTORY OF LATIN AMERICAN EMIGRATION

The first Latin American nation to experience large-scale emigration was Mexico, which began sending migrants to the United States around the turn of the twentieth century, when US-financed railroads penetrated into the Mexican interior from the north.[7] Along with the rail lines came US labor recruiters seeking to replace workers recently banned by the Chinese Exclusion Acts and the Gentleman's Agreement with Japan.[8] Immigration from Mexico expanded when the US gov-ernment implemented its own labor recruitment program during World War I and subsequently surged to record levels in the 1920s, when restrictive quotas curtailed European immigration and Mexicans sought opportunities north of the border to make up for shortfalls in an economy still recovering from violent revolution.[9]

This first era of mass immigration from Mexico came to an abrupt end with the onset of the Great Depression and the organization of mass deportation cam-paigns in the United States during the 1930s, when 469,000 Mexicans were forc-ibly expelled from the United States.[10] The second era of Mexican migration began in 1942 when the United States and Mexico negotiated a binational treaty known as the Bracero Accord, which gave temporary visas to Mexican workers for short-term labor north of the border.[11] Although originally viewed as a tem-porary wartime measure, the Bracero Program was extended and expanded through the 1950s before winding down in the early 1960s. Over the 22 years of its existence, it brought in close to 5 million temporary workers and reignited mass immigration from Mexico. At the program's height in the late 1950s, some 450,000 temporary workers and 50,000 permanent residents were entering the United States each year.[12]

The cancellation of the Bracero Program coincided with the passage of amendments to the Immigration and Nationality Act that imposed the first-ever numerical limits on immigration from the Western Hemisphere. Between the late 1950s and the late 1970s Mexico consequently went from access to an unlimited number of permanent resident visas and 450,000 temporary worker visas to just 20,000 residence visas and no worker visas.[13] The elimination of opportunities for legal entry ushered in the third era of mass migration, as flows established during the Bracero era reestablished themselves under undocumented auspices.[14] Despite the shift from documented to undocumented status, however, the movement of Mexican migrants remained heavily circular through 1985, with 85% of undocumented entries being offset by departures.[15]

The current era of Mexican migration began with the passage of the Immigration Reform and Control Act in 1986, which initiated a militarization of the Mexico–US border that steadily increased the costs and risks of undocumented entry, prompting migrants to remain longer in the north rather than returning home to face the gauntlet of enforcement resources on a future border crossing.[16] The increase in border enforcement paradoxically had no effect on the likelihood of either undocumented departure or unauthorized entry to the United States, however; but as trips lengthened, families increasingly began to reunite north of the border and rates of return migration plummeted. Given steady rates of undocumented in-migration and falling rates of out-migration, the ultimate effect of the border militarization was to increase net unauthorized migration and accelerate undocumented population growth.[17] As a result, the undocumented population rose from 1.9 million in 1988 to 12 million in 2008.[18]

Until 1940, the potential for the emergence of a pan-ethnic Latino identity in the United States was limited by the fact that the vast majority of Latin Americans living in the United States were of Mexican origin. Beginning in World War II, however, immigrants from Mexico were joined increasingly by waves of migrants from other regions of Latin America. The first to arrive were from Puerto Rico, and the mainland population of Puerto Rican origin grew from around 70,000 in 1940 to 1.43 million in 1970. Out-migration grew as the island shifted from an agrarian to an industrial economy and displaced rural dwellers responded to strong labor demand emanating from northeastern US cities such as New York and Philadelphia.[19]

Mass migration from the island came to an end around 1970, and after that date the population of Puerto Rican origin grew mainly through natural increase, reaching 4.68 million persons in 2010, only 1.4 million of whom were island-born. During the 1960s, Puerto Ricans were joined by new streams of migrants from Cuba and the Dominican Republic who were escaping Cold War–era turmoil in their homelands. The success of the Cuban Revolution in 1959 spurred the mass exodus of the entrepreneurial, professional, and middle classes in subsequent decades,[20] and after 1980 these more privileged migrants were joined by others from the lower middle class and working class.[21]

Mass emigration from the Dominican Republic likewise stemmed from political upheavals associated with Cold War politics. It began during the US occupation of Santo Domingo in 1965, when the US ambassador made legal residence visas generously available to students and intellectuals to get them out of the country and away from politics.[22] From 1980 to 2010, some 674,000 Cubans and 939,000 Dominicans entered the United States as legal immigrants and as of 2010 the number of persons of Cuban and Dominican origin stood at 1.79 million and 1.41 million, respectively.[23]

Mass migration from Central America to the United States began around 1980 and was also a product of the Cold War. After the success of the Sandinista Revolution in 1979, the Reagan Administration intervened militarily and politically in the region, funding and training a clandestine army known as the Contras to topple the Sandinistas while supporting military and paramilitary operations to suppress leftist insurgencies in El Salvador, Guatemala, and Honduras. Although the ensuing violence and economic dislocations generated large flows of refugees to the United States from all four countries, only Nicaraguans were welcomed and granted easy access to legal permanent residence, given that they were fleeing a left-wing regime supported by Russia. In other Central American nations with right-wing governments allied with the United States, refugees were compelled to enter the United States without authorization.[24]

Emigration to the United States from South America began in the 1980s when international lenders based in Washington, DC, imposed structural adjustment policies on Latin American nations in response to the debt crisis of 1982, which ushered in a "lost decade" of stagnant economic growth, structural adjustment, and labor displacement.[25] In some nations, out-migration also stemmed from rising civil violence, as in Colombia.[26] From 1980 to 2010, legal immigration from South America to the United states totaled around 1.7 million persons, with the largest contributors being Colombia (518,000), Peru (320,000), Ecuador (251,000), Brazil (201,000), Venezuela (133,000), and Argentina (100,000). In addition to these legal immigrants, Ecuador sent a net of some 110,000 undocumented migrants to the United States.[27]

Unlike Mexico and Central America, however, during the 1980s and 1990s a large number of migrants from South America also began leaving for Europe, with the largest number going to Spain, but with sizeable inflows also entering Italy, Britain, Germany, Portugal, and France.[28] A significant share of those coming from Argentina and Brazil were able to take advantage of European immigrant roots to reclaim Spanish, Portuguese, Italian, or German nationality, thus obtaining passports that enabled them to migrate throughout Europe as EU citizens.[29] Since the advent of the economic crisis in 2008, however, Latin American migration to Europe, and particularly to Spain and Portugal, has slowed and for some immigrant groups reversed.[30]

ORIGINS AND DESTINATIONS OF THE LATINO DIASPORA

In sum, since the mid-twentieth century out-migration from Latin America has expanded and diversified to bring Latinos not only into the United States but throughout the world. Figure I.1 draws on data from the United Nations,

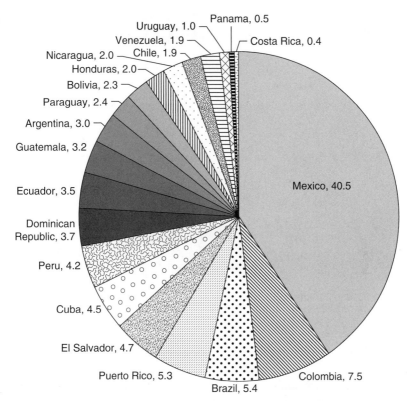

Figure I.1 National origins of 32.6 million global Latinos in 2013.

which tabulated the population of international migrants by origin and destination in 2013.[31] From those data I was able to determine the origin of the 32.6 million Latin American emigrants who lived outside the country of their birth in that year. As the figure clearly shows, among Latin American emigrants today, Mexicans are by far the largest group, making up 40.5% of all emigrants. The next closest origin country is Colombia at 7.5%, followed by Brazil (5.4%), Puerto Rico (5.3%), El Salvador (4.7%), and Cuba (4.5%). Next in order are Peru (4.2%), the Dominican Republic (3.7%), Guatemala (3.2%), and Argentina (3%). Relatively few Latino emigrants come from Costa Rica (0.4%), Panama (0.5%), or Uruguay (1%). Between Argentina at 3% and Uruguay at 1% lie Paraguay (2.4%), Bolivia (2.3%), Honduras (2%), Nicaragua (2%), Venezuela (1.9%), and Chile (1.9%).

Of the 32.6 million Latin American emigrants in 2013, 4.6 million (around 14%) simply moved from one Latin American nation to another. Although these flows are interesting topics for study in their own right, these migrants are not likely to be seen or view themselves as "Latinos," but as nationals of their countries of birth. In Argentina, for example, Paraguayans are categorized according to their national identity as Paraguayans while Bolivians remain Bolivians, and

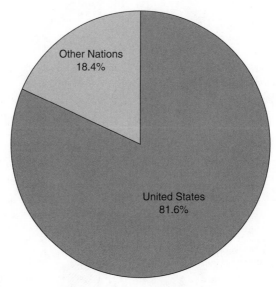

Figure I.2 Geographic distribution of 35.6 million global Latinos.

the two groups are generally not grouped together conceptually as Latinos. From this point on, therefore, I focus on the 28 million Latin American emigrants who moved outside the region to other parts of the world. Figure I.2 shows that for such migrants the United States remains by far the most important receiving nation, accounting for 82% of all Latinos living outside their country of birth. Although Latino migration may have globalized, therefore, the United States still remains the leading context for the social construction of Latino identity. A major reason for US dominance in the global distribution of Latinos, of course, is the fact that Mexico is by far the most important sending country and the vast majority of Mexicans emigrate to the United States.

To move beyond US dominance as a home for global Latinos, Figure I.3 refines the analysis by showing the distribution of the 9.3 million Latinos who settled in destinations other than the United States. Perhaps unsurprisingly Spain is the most important non-US destination, accounting for around 24% of the non-US Latino diaspora. The three next most important destinations are Italy (6.8% of the diaspora), Japan (4.8%), and Canada (4.1%). The shares drop off rapidly after Canada, however. Portugal and France each account for 1.8% of the diaspora; China comes in at 1.5%, and Australia and New Zealand together account for 1.4%, whereas Germany and the United Kingdom each make up just 1.3% of the total. Together, all of the foregoing account for roughly half (48.7%) of all non-US emigrants. The remainder are scattered in very small numbers across thirty-eight different countries (with one exception, all with emigrant populations below 100,000 persons).

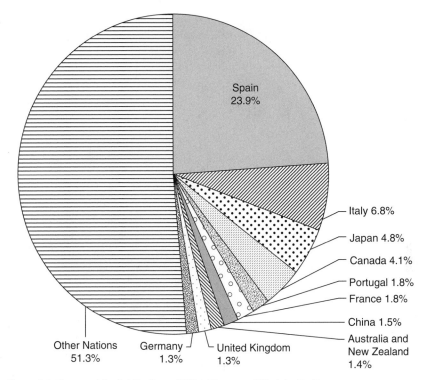

Figure I.3 Geographic distribution of 9.3 million non-US global Latinos.

LATINO NATIONALITIES IN COUNTRIES
OF DESTINATION

In general, the potential for the formation of a pan-ethnic Latino identity is greatest when the Latino population is large and diverse, representing a wide variety of different national origins in significant numbers. Latino identity formation is also enhanced by a greater cultural and linguistic distance between the destination country and Latin America, greater exposure to processes of exclusion and discrimination, and greater economic exploitation at the hands of natives—in other words, a hostile context of reception.[32] Here I examine the size and diversity of Latino populations in the most important receiving nations, leaving research on the various contexts of reception to future investigators.

Figure I.4 begins with the United States, showing the distribution by national origin of its 22.8 million Latino immigrants in 2013. As already noted, by far the largest share of Latino immigrants in the United States come from Mexico. Whereas 56.7% of Latino migrants are Mexican, the next largest source is Puerto Rico at 7.4%, followed by El Salvador (6%), Cuba (5.3%), and the Dominican Republic (4.2%). Next, in descending order, are Colombia (3.2%), Honduras (2.4%),

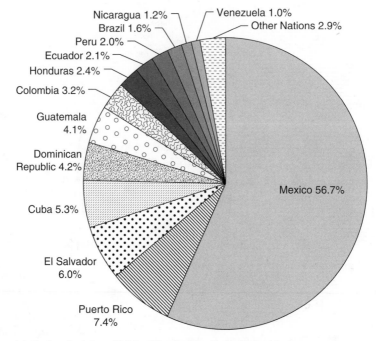

Figure I.4 National origins of 22.8 million Latinos in the United States.

Ecuador (2.1%), Peru (2%), Brazil (1.6%), Nicaragua (1.2%), and Venezuela (1%), leaving the final 2.9% to be scattered among Argentina, Bolivia, Chile, Costa Rica, Panama, Uruguay, and Paraguay. Reflecting the realities of geography and history, therefore, 88% of Latino immigrants in the United States hail from Mexico, Central America, or the Caribbean, with relatively few coming from South America, and then the principal senders are Colombia, Ecuador, and Peru.

Prior to 1970, the category "Latino" was rarely employed among Latinos themselves nor with non-Hispanic whites in common discourse. At that time, the Latino population was composed primarily of Mexicans in the southwest United States, Puerto Ricans in the northeast United States, and Cubans in Miami, Florida, and these groups tended to self-identify in terms of their national origins. The only place where the three groups met and interacted in significant numbers was Chicago, Illinois, and even there Cubans were quite sparsely represented. In 1970, however, Hispanics joined together to demand the inclusion of a pan-ethnic identifier on the US Census. After initially resisting, the Census Bureau finally agreed to place the identifier on a 5% sample of those enumerated in that year, and from 1980 onward it has been included as a 100% item answered by all respondents to each decennial census.

Since 1970 Latinos or Hispanics have become widely recognized as a social category in the United States, and societal conditions have evolved to overcome differences between the various national identities and create a broader Latino identity, one that complements but does not replace specific national identities.[33] Latino identity has solidified and consolidated for several reasons. First, nativist hostility toward Latino immigrants has steadily increased with the rise of a Latino Threat Narrative in the public sphere[34] and the emergence of a full-blown white backlash[35] that helps to sustain a record number of annual deportations.[36] Second, during the 1990s immigration shifted from being a regional to a nation-wide phenomenon with the emergence of new immigrant destinations throughout the fifty states, bringing diverse national origins together in new and old receiving communities.[37] Third, the degree of economic exploitation and discrimination increased after the criminalization of undocumented hiring in 1986 and the simultaneous growth of a large undocumented population, which undermined the wages and working conditions of Latinos generally, not just those without documents.[38] Finally, levels of residential segregation have risen among Latinos over recent decades, especially among those lacking documents.[39]

Figure I.5 examines the national origin distribution of Latino immigrants living in the five most important destination countries after the United States. According to the United Nations, in 2013 some 2.2 million Latino immigrants lived in Spain, with 630,000 in Italy, 441,000 in Japan, 381,000 in Canada, and 169,000 in Portugal. In terms of size and diversity, there is clearly some potential for the formation of a Latino identity in Spain, where no single national origin dominates. The largest single Latino immigrant group consists of Ecuadorians (20.3%), followed by Colombia (16.2%), Argentines (12.1%), Peruvians (8.6%), Bolivians (8.3%), and Cubans (5.2%). Compared to the United States, relatively few migrants come from Central America or Mexico and most are from South America (around 82%).

At this point, it is not clear whether a broad social category of "Latino" will emerge in Spain, with Latin American immigrants identifying in pan-ethnic terms rather than according to national origin. The linguistic and cultural distance between Spaniards and immigrants from former Spanish colonies is relatively small, and large-scale migration only dates from the late 1980s; accordingly, the second generation is still quite young and research on it has only just begun.[40] Moreover, although Latin Americans have suffered disproportionately from the severe Spanish recession, they do not appear to have been subjected to categorical exploitation.[41] Although the ethnic slur "sudaca" is sometimes applied to Latin Americans, especially those of indigenous origin, Latinos seem to be tolerated far more than Muslim immigrants from North Africa; and thanks to successive legalization programs, the vast majority of Latino immigrants are documented.[42]

Of the remaining countries in Figure I.5, two others—Italy and Canada—also evince a diverse array of national origins, increasing the potential for the emergence of a pan-ethnic Latino identity. Although Canada has a long tradition of research on immigrant integration, little has focused on Latinos, given that they represent a relatively small share of the Canadian immigrant population (around 5% according to UN data). Although Chapter 9 in this volume offers a first glimpse of Canada's Latinos, the jury is still out on the direction Latino identity formation might take. Foreseeing the future of Latino identity is complicated by the fact in

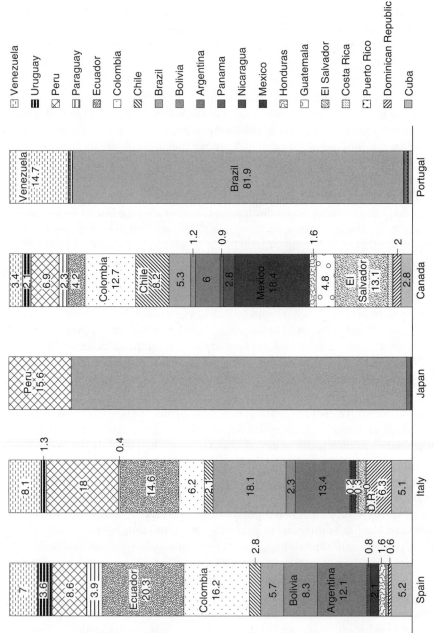

Figure I.5 National origins of Latinos in the top-five non-US destinations.

10

Canada that there there two contexts of reception—one Anglophone and the other Francophone—though both Quebec and English Canada subscribe to a common policy of tolerance and multiculturalism, which mitigates against the formation of a reactive identity. In addition, although Canada has a small Mexican guest worker program,[43] the large majority of its Latino immigrants entered either as political exiles in the 1970s and 1980s or as skilled immigrants in recent years. As a result, the population is predominantly middle class and virtually all are documented; and in Canada a Latino threat narrative never emerged, sparking no backlash and certainly no mass deportations, unlike its southern neighbor.

Much less is known about the context of reception for Latinos in Italy. As in Canada, they comprise a relatively small share of the total immigrant population (around 11%); and even though Italy is currently in the midst of a rather intense anti-immigrant reaction, the xenophobia is focused more on the very poor migrants from Africa and the Middle East who are now attempting to enter Europe in large numbers by crossing the Mediterranean in rickety, overloaded boats. In addition, nearly a third of all Latinos living in Italy are from Brazil or Argentina, and many of these people are likely of Italian ancestry and were able to enter the country on Italian passports after reclaiming Italian nationality through a parent or grandparent.[44] Pope Francis is but one example of many Argentines of Italian origin currently living in Italy.

The other two countries in Figure I.5, Japan and Portugal, are notable for the dominance of Brazil among their Latino populations—83% in Japan and 82% in Portugal. The mass migration of Brazilians to Portugal is hardly surprising given the common language; and a significant share of immigrants from the second major source country, Venezuela (15% of all Latinos) are also quite likely to be of Brazilian or Portuguese origin, descendant from migrants who entered Venezuela during the years of the oil boom when jobs were plentiful and wages high. Such people are probably more likely to be seen and self-identified as Brazilians in their host countries rather than Latinos.

In contrast to Portugal, the second major origin group in Japan is from Peru. Both Brazilian and Peruvian immigrants to Japan are quite likely to be of Japanese origin themselves, descendant from labor migrants who emigrated during the first half of the twentieth century.[45] Although Peruvian migrants to Japan experience less socioeconomic mobility than those to the United States,[46] it is unclear whether this fact indicates a high level of discrimination against Japanese-origin Latinos—indeed, they hold a privileged position in Japan's immigration system. Moreover, at this point little is known about the degree of interaction between Brazilian and Peruvian immigrants in Japan, which is critical for developing a common identity as Latinos.

Finally, Figure I.6 shows the national origins of immigrants living in the five next largest non-US destinations, including 165,000 Latino immigrants in France, 137,000 in China, 132,000 in Australia and New Zealand, 125,000 in the United Kingdom, and 121,000 in Germany. It is immediately apparent that Brazil is the largest source country for immigrants in four of these five nations. Interestingly,

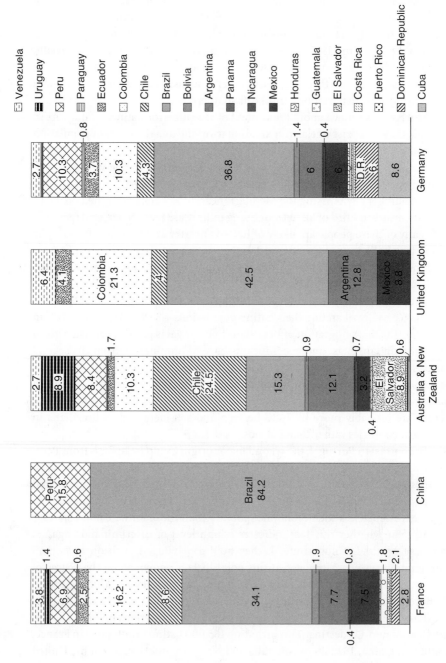

Figure I.6 National origins of Latinos in the next five largest non-US destinations.

the national origins of Latino migrants to China are nearly identical to those of Japan: 84% Brazilian and 16% Peruvian. How this parallel outcome came about is unknown, but one possibility is step migration to Japan from Brazil and Peru, followed by subsequent migration from Japan to China in response to its booming economy. Brazilians also constitute the largest single group of Latino immigrants in the United Kingdom (42.5%), Germany (36.8%), and France (34.1), suggesting the importance of Brazil as a diasporic nation, but little is known about the reasons behind this outcome. In Australia and New Zealand the largest national origin group is from Chile (24.5%), but Brazil is second at 15.3%. In the end, information about the situation of Latino immigrants in any of these five countries is exceedingly scarce, making it difficult even to speculate about the state of Latino identity or the degree of Latino integration within the various host societies.

FUTURE RESEARCH ON GLOBAL LATINOS

As this introduction has pointed out, the globalization of Latinos is quite recent and has only just been recognized by scholars as a topic for productive study. Hence, the work presented in the current volume is but the first step in a much larger agenda of comparative research. Here I have undertaken a preliminary survey of where global Latinos come from and where they go in order to identify potential locations for fruitful research in the coming years. Although here I have described the current composition of global Latinos in leading receiving nations, work done by future researchers is necessary to specify the historical background and current contexts of reception for Latinos in different destination nations around the world.

As we have seen, by far the largest sending country in Latin America is Mexico, and the largest receiving nation outside the region is the United States. Although the overwhelming majority of Mexican emigrants go to the United States and a majority of Latino emigrants in that country are of Mexican origin, the US Latino immigrant population has steadily diversified since the mid-twentieth century and a pan-ethnic Latino "identity" has clearly emerged, despite the fact that almost 90% of Latino immigrants come from a handful of nearby nations in Central America (Mexico, Guatemala, Honduras, El Salvador, and Nicaragua) and the Caribbean (Cuba, the Dominican Republic, and Puerto Rico). In contrast, with some notable exceptions, other destinations draw on a greater diversity of Latin American sources and generally evince a much greater representation by nations in South America.

The principal exceptions with respect to the rule of diversity within non-US countries of destination are Portugal, Japan, and China. Portugal draws migrants almost exclusively from Brazil and Venezuela, and these people are typically either native Portuguese speakers or descendants of earlier Portuguese migrants to Latin America. Japan and China draw their Latino migrants almost entirely from Brazil and Peru. In the case of Japan, migrants are likely to be overwhelmingly themselves of Japanese origin; but next to nothing is known about Latino immigrants in China. Thus, as in China, Japan, and Portugal, Latinos in the

United States are unusual in being dominated by migrants from a single country (Mexico) and a few specific regions (the Caribbean and Central America).

Compared to other host nations, especially those in Europe, the United States is also unusual in the degree to which Latino migrants are formally excluded from social, economic, and political integration and subject to repressive pressures from the state. A historically complex and highly differentiated population, at present a majority of all immigrants of Mexican (57%), Guatemalan (62%), Honduran (63%), and Salvadoran origin (51%), present in the United States are unauthorized and deportations are running at 420,000 per year.[47] In Spain, the second most important destination country, the vast majority of Latino immigrants are authorized and very few are deported. This contrast alone cautions against generalizing about Latino identity and Latino integration from the experience of the United States, which offers an unusually hostile context of reception, both compared to earlier periods in the 1960s and 1970s and relative to other immigrant receiving societies today.

NOTES

1. David FitzGerald and David Cook-Martín, *Culling the Masses: The Democratic Origins of Racist Immigration Policy in the Americas* (Cambridge, MA: Harvard University Press, 2014).

2. Herbert S. Klein, *The Atlantic Slave Trade* (Cambridge: Cambridge University Press, 1999).

3. Edward E. Telles, *Race in Another America: The Significance of Skin Color in Brazil* (Princeton, NJ: Princeton University Press, 2004); Edward E. Telles, *Pigmentocracies: Ethnicity, Race, and Color in Latin America* (Chapel Hill: University of North Carolina Press, 2014).

4. FitizGerald and Cook-Martin, *Culling the Masses*, 37.

5. Douglas S. Massey, Joaquín Arango, Graeme Hugo, Ali Kouaouci, Adela Pellegrino, and J. Edward Taylor, *Worlds in Motion: International Migration at the End of the Millennium* (Oxford: Oxford University Press, 1998).

6. Douglas S. Massey and Magaly Sánchez R., *Brokered Boundaries: Creating Immigrant Identity in Anti-Immigrant Times* (New York: Russell Sage Foundation, 2010).

7. Lawrence A. Cardoso, *Mexican Emigration to the United States, 1897–1931: Socio-Economic Patterns* (Tucson: University of Arizona Press, 1980).

8. Douglas S. Massey, Jorge Durand, and Nolane J. Malone, *Beyond Smoke and Mirrors: Mexican Immigration in an Era of Economic Integration* (New York: Russell Sage Foundation, 2002).

9. Cardoso, *Mexican Emigration to the United States, 1897–1931*.

10. Francisco E. Balderrama and Raymond Rodríguez, *Decade of Betrayal: Mexican Repatriation in the 1930s* (Albuquerque: University of Arizona Press, 1995); Abraham Hoffman, *Unwanted Mexican Americans in the Great Depression: Repatriation Pressures, 1929–1939* (Tucson: University of Arizona Press, 1974).

11. Kitty Calavita, *Inside the State: The Bracero Program, Immigration, and the I.N.S.* (New York: Routledge, 1992).

12. Douglas S. Massey and Karen A. Pren, "Unintended Consequences of US Immigration Policy: Explaining the Post-1965 Surge from Latin America," *Population and Development Review* 38, no. 1 (2012): 1–29.
13. Massey and Pren, "Unintended Consequences."
14. Massey, Durand, and Malone, *Beyond Smoke and Mirrors.*
15. Douglas S. Massey and Audrey Singer, "New Estimates of Undocumented Mexican Migration and the Probability of Apprehension," *Demography* 32 (1985): 203–213.
16. Douglas S. Massey, Jorge Durand, and Karen A. Pren, "Explaining Undocumented Migration," *International Migration Review* 48, no. 4 (2014): 1028–1106; Douglas S. Massey, Jorge Durand, and Karen A. Pren, "Border Enforcement and Return Migration by Documented and Undocumented Mexicans," *Journal of Ethnic and Migration Studies* 41, no. 7 (2015): 1015–1040.
17. Massey, Durand, and Malone, *Beyond Smoke and Mirrors.*
18. Ruth E. Wassam, *Unauthorized Aliens Residing in the United States: Estimates Since 1986* (Washington, DC: Congressional Research Service, 2011).
19. Edna Acosta-Belen and Carlos E. Santiago, *Puerto Ricans in the United States: A Contemporary Portrait* (Boulder, CO: Lynne Rienner, 2006).
20. Alejandro Portes and Robert L. Bach, *Latin Journey: Cuban and Mexican Immigrants in the United States* (Berkeley: University of California Press, 1985).
21. Alejandro Portes and Alex Stepick, *City on the Edge: The Transformation of Miami* (Berkeley: University of California Press, 1993).
22. Fernando Riosmena, "Policy Shocks: On the Legal Auspices of Latin America–U.S. Migration," *Annals of the American Academy of Political and Social Science* 630 (2010): 270–293.
23. Sharon R. Ennis, Merarys Ríos-Vargas, and Nora G. Albert, *2010 Census Briefs: The Hispanic Population 2010* (Washington, DC: US Bureau of the Census, 2010).
24. Jennifer H. Lundquist and Douglas S. Massey, "Politics or Economics? International Migration During the Nicaraguan Contra War," *Journal of Latin American Studies* 37 (2015): 29–53; Massey, Durand, and Pren, "Explaining Undocumented Migration."
25. Douglas S. Massey and Chiara Capoferro, "Sálvese Quien Pueda: Structural Adjustment and Emigration from Lima." *Annals of the American Academy of Political and Social Science* 606 (2006): 116–127.
26. Carolina Silva and Douglas S. Massey, "Violence, Networks, and International Migration from Colombia," *International Migration*, doi: 10.1111/imig.12169/.
27. Michael Hoefer, Nancy Rytina, and Bryan C. Baker, *Estimates of the Unauthorized Immigrant Population Residing in the United States: January 2010* (Washington, DC: Office of Immigration Statistics, US Department of Homeland Security).
28. Beatriz Padilla and Joao Peixoto, *Latin American Immigration to Southern Europe* (Washington, DC: Migration Information Source, 2007).
29. Jorge Durand and Douglas S. Massey, "New World Orders: Continuities and Changes in Latin American Migration," *Annals of the American Academy of Political and Social Science* 630, no. 1 (2010): 20–52.
30. María Aysa-Lastra and Lorenzo Cachón, *Immigrant Vulnerability and Resilience: Comparative Perspectives on Latin American Immigrants During the Great Recession* (New York: Springer, 2015).
31. United Nations, Website of United Nations Department of Economic and Social Affairs Population Division: International Migration (New York: United Nations, 2015).

http://www.un.org/en/development/desa/population/migration/data/estimates2/estimatesorigin.shtml

32. Alejandro Portes and Rubén G. Rumbaut, *Immigrant America: A Portrait* (Berkeley: University of California Press, 2014); Massey and Sánchez, *Brokered Boundaries*.

33. Massey and Sánchez, *Brokered Boundaries*.

34. Leo R. Chavez, *Covering Immigration: Population Images and the Politics of the Nation* (Berkeley: University of California Press, 2001); Leo R. Chavez, *The Latino Threat: Constructing Immigrants, Citizens, and the Nation* (Stanford, CA: Stanford University Press, 2008).

35. Marisa Abrajano and Zoltan L. Hajnal, *White Backlash: Immigration, Race, and American Politics Hardcover* (Princeton, NJ: Princeton University Press, 2015).

36. Douglas S. Massey, *New Faces in New Places: The New Geography of American Immigration* (New York: Russell Sage Foundation, 2008).

37. Daniel Kanstroom, *Aftermath: Deportation Law and the New American Diaspora* (New York: Oxford University Press, 2014).

38. Douglas S. Massey and Kerstin Gentsch, "Labor Market Outcomes for Legal Mexican Immigrants under the New Regime of Immigration Enforcement," *Social Science Quarterly* 92, no. 3 (2011): 875–893; Douglas S. Massey and Kerstin Gentsch, "Undocumented Migration and the Wages of Mexican Immigrants in the United States," *International Migration Review* 48, no. 2 (2014): 482–499.

39. Jacob S. Rugh and Douglas S. Massey, "Segregation in Post-Civil Rights America: Stalled Integration or End of the Segregated Century?" *The DuBois Review: Social Science Research on Race* 11, no. 2 (2014): 202–232; Matthew Halland and Jonathan Stringfield, "Undocumented Migration and the Segregation of Mexican Immigrants in New Destinations," *Social Science Research* 47, no. 1 (2014): 61–78.

40. Alejandro Portes, Rosa Aparicio, William Haller, and Erik Vickstrom, "Moving Ahead in Madrid: Aspirations and Expectations in the Spanish Second Generation," *International Migration Review* 44, no. 4 (2010): 767–801, 1010.

41. Aysa-Lastra and Cachón, *Immigrant Vulnerability and Resilience: Comparative Perspectives on Latin American Immigrants During the Great Recession*.

42. Douglas S. Massey, "Preface: The Great Divide between Spain and the United States," preface to *Immigrant Vulnerability and Resilience: Comparative Perspectives on Latin American Immigrants During the Great Recession,* eds. María Aysa-Lastra and Lorenzo Cachón (New York: Springer, 2015), i–iv.

43. Douglas S. Massey and Amelia E. Brown. "New Migration Streams Between Mexico and Canada." *Migraciones Internactionales* 6, no. 1 (2011): 119–144.

44. Durand and Massey, "New World Orders."

45. Ayumi Takenaka, "How Ethnic Minorities Experience Social Mobility in Japan: An Ethnographic Study of Peruvian Migrants," in *Social Class in Contemporary Japan: Structures, Sorting and Strategies*, eds. Hiroshi Ishida and David H. Slater (Oxford: Routledge, 2009), 221–238.

46. Ayumi Takenaka and Karsten Paerregaard, "How Contexts of Reception Matter: Comparing Peruvian Migrants' Economic Trajectories in Japan and the US," *International Migration* 53, no. 2 (2015): 236–249.

47. Douglas S. Massey, "The Real Hispanic Challenge," *Pathways Magazine*, Special Issue on "Hispanics in America: A Report Card on Poverty, Mobility, and Assimilation," Winter (2015): 3–7. For a detailed examination of the complex and differentiated history of Latinos in the United States, see David Gutiérrez, *The Columbia History of Latinos in the United States Since 1960* (New York: Columbia University Press, 2004).

CHAPTER 1

Out of the Fires

Peruvian Migrants in Post-Pinochet Chile

MARK OVERMYER-VELÁZQUEZ

The fires that burned in Santiago's bombed presidential palace on September 11, 1973, have cast a long shadow into present-day Chile. On that September day a military coup overthrew democratically elected President Salvador Allende and initiated an authoritarian dictatorship that would endure until 1990. Although many scholars have documented the political and economic consequences of the event, the theme of immigration and its regulation by the state has been largely ignored. Following the coup, Chile's military government enacted immigration legislation that severely restricted the rights and movement of individuals entering and within its national space. The Pinochet regime positioned unwanted domestic and transnational labor migrants as "dangerous elements" in an attempt to simultaneously keep people perceived to be politically threatening outside the borders while redefining the nation within them. As a result, a repressive state system forced thousands of its citizens into global exile. The Chilean government's actions following the coup can help explain how at times of national crisis politicians turn to immigration to reassert notions of national sovereignty and delineate membership in the imagined community.[1]

This chapter examines how the related emergence of Chile's Pinochet-era economic and immigration legislation was shaped by a long history of racist policies that privileged white European immigration while subordinating perceived nonwhite migrants. With a focus on Chile's recent wave of Peruvian immigration, this study also analyzes the country's histories and historiographies of immigration, racialization, and nation-state formation. With Chile's "democratic opening" following the end of Pinochet's military dictatorship, large numbers of Peruvian migrants began crossing the country's narrow northern border in search of work primarily in the capital, Santiago.[2] This unprecedented wave of spontaneous (versus targeted or strategic) immigration largely from Peru has forced Chileans to reconsider their ethnoracial definition of the nation and their relationship with others. To safeguard and maintain a neoliberal economic regime that has required large supplies of cheap labor, the Chilean government enacted and continued to enforce legislation that placed immigrants into positions of illegality and vulnerability.

The last national decennial census of 2012 registered a 200% increase in Chile's documented Peruvian population over the previous decade.[3] According to the 2012 decennial census, 339,536 documented foreigners lived in Chile, or 2% of the total population. In 2012, the Peruvian population accounted for 30.5% of that total with 103,624 people, the majority of whom were female.[4] Although only a small percentage of Chile's total population, the unprecedented surge of migration represents the largest absolute number of migrants in the country's history. In turn, the novelty of this data has fueled speculation about the potentially negative consequences of these high numbers of migrants.[5]

In the midst of the Cold War, US-trained Chilean economists seized the 1973 regime change as an opportunity to implement neoliberal economic strategies of privatization and deregulation that would eventually take hold as the country's dominant economic model. Those strategies would have enduring consequences for Chile's working-class immigrants. Paul Drake argues, "As the paragon of neoliberalism in Latin America, Chile is the crucial test case for the consequences of those market-driven policies for the working class. It has been hailed as the shining example not only for Latin America but also for other parts of the world."[6] The development of neoliberal policies and international free trade agreements in Chile shaped economic priorities that privileged and protected markets over labor or corporate profits over workers' rights.[7]

Two years after the coup, the government of Augusto Pinochet passed the 1975 Ley de Extranjería (Foreigner or Alien Status Law), which delineated various immigrant categories as well as functions of the office that regulated the entrance, residence, control, and expulsion of foreigners.[8] Still in effect today, the 1975 law functioned as a central mechanism of control in Chile's hardening security state. While the Pinochet administration utilized the act to prevent entrance of "subversive" and "dangerous" elements identified along political and ideological lines (predominantly suspected supporters of Allende and labor and student leaders), it also contributed to a new migratory period in Chile's history that from 1973 to 1990 witnessed more than 500,000 Chileans (out of a total population of 10–13 million) voluntarily or forcibly fleeing the country into exile around the world.

The peoples in what currently are Chile and Peru share a long and complex history dating from the colonial period when Chile was essentially a political and economic appendage of the powerful Viceroyalty of Peru, headquartered in Lima. In the nineteenth century, the War of the Pacific (1879–1883) continued the country's colonial relationship, but this time it was Chile that subordinated Peru as it occupied its northern neighbor and annexed a portion of its territory. That encounter built upon existing mutual constructions of racial discrimination that persist to this day. Today, the border Chile shares with Peru provides it access to a steady source of inexpensive labor for its growing economy. As a result, Peruvians currently account for Chile's largest immigrant population.

Chile asserts a national mythology of exceptionalism regionally, promoting its uniqueness among countries in Latin America. In the dominant national narrative that gained force during the period of the dictatorship, Chile projects a European, non-Latin heritage that—eliding its mestizo roots—is racially distinct from its Latin American and Caribbean counterparts. Chile's invented narrative has helped to shape its enduring relationship with immigrants and immigration.

Contributing to the "internationalization of the history of Chile,"[9] this study weaves together elements from a broad literature that includes research in Chilean, US, and foreign relations history, migration, human rights, and American, Latin American, and US Latino studies with a hemispheric orientation. Drawing on a strategically eclectic mix of sources, including archival material (government reports and legislation), oral history interviews, census records, human rights reports, newspaper articles, and television commercials, this study adds to the work of Peter Winn and others that examines the consequences of neoliberalism in the years during and after the Pinochet dictatorship. The chapter situates those economic and political changes in the context of Chile's recent transition from a migrant-sending to a migrant-receiving country as part of the independent country's two hundred years of immigration history and related racist policies.[10]

I divide this chapter into four historical and historiographical sections concerning Chile's migratory present and past. I begin with an exploration of Chile and Peru's historical colonial relationship to one another and how the subsequent formation of national racial types has shaped immigration attitudes and policies. Following that I place the recent immigration and its legislation in the broader historical context of Chilean immigration and include an analysis of immigration studies in Chile's historiography as an aspect of the production of the country's national narrative. I then explain how the immigration legislation that emerged after September 11, 1973, has impacted the Peruvian immigrant community in Chile. Finally, I turn to a summary and examination of Peru's "Quinto Suyo" in Chile, a designation of Peru's emigrant community, placing it in the context of other regional South American migratory trajectories.[11]

COLONIALISM, RACE, AND NATIONAL IDENTITIES

> There exists a contradiction between the idea that each
> nation-state can truly represent only one ethnos and the
> reality that all nation-states historically involve the amalga-
> mation of many identities. Even where long-standing
> identities have been forgotten or buried, the combination of
> migration and mass mediation assures their reconstruction
> on a new scale and at larger levels. Incidentally, this is why the
> politics of remembering and forgetting (and thus of history

and historiography) is so central to the ethnicist battles tied
up with nationalism.
— Appadurai, *Modernity at Large*, 1996

I'm a Chilean, I'm from here, from Chile, yo soy chileno, yo
soy chileno!
— "Chile es tuyo," Servicio Nacional de Turismo Chile, 2011

In what seemed like an anachronistic message orchestrated by nineteenth-century
white supremacist immigration promoters, in 2011 Chile's National Tourist Service launched a new advertising campaign, "Chile Is Yours," apparently advocating the marriage of Chileans with white North American travelers (see Fig. 1.1).
Riddled with class, gender, and racial stereotypes, the video spot portrays a
young couple talking with one another against the backdrop of the Torres del
Paine National Park, a major tourist destination in the country's southern Patagonia region. Speaking in English with subtitles provided, the allegedly North
American woman (her accent betrays a Scandinavian origin) confesses to her
Chilean companion that she laments having to return to New York City, but she
has learned that if she were to marry a Chilean man she could remain in the
country. Almost hysterical, the young man eagerly responds that he is Chilean, "I
am Chilean . . . yo soy chileno!" The frame then changes to a series of still images
plotting an ebullient, imagined future progression of matrimony, pregnancy, and
white progeny.[12]

The government's racially homogenous, heteronormative rendering of transnational sociability in the commercial adheres well to Chile's normative immigration narrative discussed earlier as it reasserts its globally marketed image as a
racially white nation.[13] In a country where tourist visas are one of the only

Figure 1.1 "Chile es tuyo": ". . . and if I marry him I could stay here forever."

methods that growing Peruvian and other nonwhite immigrants can utilize to legally enter the country, the state-sponsored advertisement is indicative of historically entrenched notions of race, immigration, and US-bound ideals of class.[14]

This section explores Chile and Peru's historical colonial relationship to one another and the subsequent mutual formation of national racial types that have shaped current immigration attitudes and policies between the two countries.[15] Coincident with the establishment of race-based immigration policies were the mutually constitutive construction of an immigrant other and, as Muñoz states, "an ideal of a white homogeneous national community that highlights its European ancestry and has traditionally denied both its indigenous roots and has excluded other minority groups."[16] Immigration in Chile's past and present has forced a reconsideration and rearticulation of the national self. In the words of one Chilean sociologist, recent spontaneous Peruvian immigration has challenged Chileans to "confront [their] mestizo identity and take [them] back to that which [they] try to forget."[17]

Chile's defeat of Peru and subsequent territorial expansion after the War of the Pacific (1879–1883) further developed the two countries' reciprocal constructions of racial discrimination that persist to this day.[18] Chile's racial orientation toward Latin Americans in general and Peruvians in particular emerged from colonial-era histories. The "dialectic of the negation of the other" in Chile initially developed with the colonial European subjugation of indigenous peoples and continued in the nineteenth century with the marginalization of the immigrant-other.[19] In the War of the Pacific, Chile defeated Peruvian and Bolivian allies and acquired a vast amount of mineral-rich land. Chile's annexation of Bolivian and Peruvian territory fueled mutual animosities and enhanced Chilean constructions of racial difference.[20] Additionally, as the esteemed Chilean historian Mario Góngora has argued, the War "consolidated in Chile the notion of the nation-state."[21] Territorial tensions between Chile and its northern neighbors persisted through the twentieth century. Although negotiators in Chile and Peru attempted to find resolutions to these antagonisms, political nationalists on both sides succeeded in sabotaging agreements.[22]

Racial constructions emerging from the War of the Pacific were part of larger discourses in nineteenth- and twentieth-century Chile. Government officials who advocated for a prescription of racial "improvement" through white European immigration did so in the context of prevalent notions of Chilean exceptionalism that had been shaped by European ideologies such as the romantic idea of a national Volkgeist and Social Darwinism. Both notions placed emphasis more on the national community's racial and ethnic base than its geographic circumscription.[23] Throughout the period, immigration officials referred to the work of Argentine political theorist Juan Bautista Alberdi (who had spent most of his life exiled in Chile), as a touchstone for their policies. Books, pamphlets, and reports on immigration often framed their arguments around Alberdi's famous phrase, "To govern is to populate," which continued: "in the sense that to populate is to educate, improve, civilize, enrich, and to spontaneously and rapidly enlarge as has happened in the United States."[24] Alberdi's endorsement of immigration's "civilizing" properties resonated with the writings of Vicente Pérez Rosales and in official reports such as one from 1872 that urged the government to establish an office to promote European migration where "contact with the best principles of progress has elevated the European spirit to a considerable level."[25] Thirty years later, the 1904 publication of Nicolás Palacios's *Raza chilena* proved an influential example of the era's persistent racialist thinking.[26] Palacios conjured a national racial narrative of a country populated by a mixture of noble Aruacanian Indians and Spaniards with predominantly Germanic bloodlines. As a result of these unique origins, the "Chilean race," Palacios argued, "is not Latin." Arguing for the superiority of Chileans, Palacio stated, "Latin peoples do not get on well with Chileans, because we are not of the same nature and therefore they do not understand us."[27] Palacio's ideas continued well in to the century, echoed in Sergio Cavallo Hederra's 1945 report: "I have observed that there are certain races that resist mixing with others, above all when engaged in a colonizing mission . . . Chile can pride itself on the fact that . . . it possesses a homogenous white race."[28]

These racist attitudes were put into practice with immigration policies in the twentieth century that discriminated against Arab, Chinese, and Jewish newcomers, offering them none of the protection and assistance provided to targeted white European settlers.[29] One turn-of-the-century commentator carefully ranked both European and non-European immigrants, arguing, for example, that although "Chinese and Kurds" were bad for mixing with Chileans, they were efficient laborers.[30]

The War of the Pacific and racialist thinking from the colonial past continue to haunt Chile–Peru relations and influence attitudes among citizens of both countries. While discussing Peruvian attitudes toward Chileans, a recent immigrant living in Santiago, Erika S., pointed to her schooling in Lima and the lessons learned about the War of the Pacific. "They taught us," Erika exclaimed, "that Chileans were treacherous (traicioneros) and not to be trusted."[31] In his work, Paz Milet argues that the War generated a series of colonizer/colonized-related images in both countries that has "helped to construct a negative perception of the other."[32] As recent as the 2011 presidential electoral season, Peru has witnessed a resurgence of this tension. In a press statement, the soon-to-be elected Ollanta Humala, signaling ongoing abuse of migrants, warned Chile's President Sebastián Piñera (2010-2014) that "Chileans would be treated in the same manner in Peru as Peruvians are in Chile."[33]

The myth of racial homogeneity and the expression of Chile's exceptional position as the region's non-Latin country continue today.[34] "Chilean elites have long attempted to differentiate Chile from neighboring Peru and Bolivia on the basis of racial superiority, a contrast," Mahler and Staab aver, "that still lingers in language about Chile's European heritage, its lack of *tropicalismo* and its whiteness or racial homogeneity compared to its neighbors."[35] Or as a group of Chilean students recently and ironically remarked, "Chileans are not Latin Lovers; we are the opposite of Carmen Miranda!"[36] Unlike Argentine immigrants that can pass as lighter skinned Chileans, the growing number of Peruvians are visibly noticeable, especially in urban areas with large immigrant concentrations. This visibility and frequent media representation as "dangerous elements" in Chilean society distort the fact that they constitute a relatively small percentage of Chile's total population.[37]

Chile's Peruvians have been tied to two additional negative national discourses, those of indigenousness and illegality. Peruvians in Chile have been discursively linked to the country's Mapuche and other indigenous populations, rendering them as atavistic obstacles to progress.[38] As Javiera Barandiarán writes of recent Bolivian immigrants to Chile, "the attribution of race to Bolivians and its simultaneous denial to Chileans reflects a deep, uncontested assumption in Chile that equates race with being indigenous, and being indigenous as a problem that exists only in poorer countries like Bolivia."[39] Chile's indigenous population largely has been either silenced or denigrated in the country's official narrative. In an early example of this attitude, a 1903 government report reported that "one of the largest challenges of colonization [in Chile] is the indigenous population. Despite efforts to the contrary, the indigenous remains savage. Neither cities, nor the railroad, nor schools, nor religious practices have been able to civilize them. . . . We must flood the southern provinces with foreign colonists, confusing the Indians and leaving them lost in an ocean of culture like fish in the sea."[40]

Additionally, media reports have associated unscheduled immigrants and Peruvians in particular with the concept of illegality.[41] For example, a sensationalist television news show in Chile, "En la mira," in 2011 ran an extended program allegedly examining the increase in the country's population. As the title, "Silent Invasion," reveals, for the most part the program crudely portrayed Peruvian and other immigrants as a contagion-ridden population, prone to violence and social depravity.[42] This type of representation has been exacerbated by the absence of the legal category for immigrant laborers in Chilean immigration law.

HISTORY AND HISTORIOGRAPHY OF CHILEAN IMMIGRATION

Chile has not been a country of immigrants as in Argentina, Brazil, Venezuela, or the United States.
—Stefoni Espinoza, "Inmigración peruana en Chile," 2003

The speed and extent of the process of globalization during the last decades has made clear the impossibility of conceiving of economic, social, political, and cultural phenomena that shape the history of countries merely utilizing a national framework of analysis.
—Purcell and Riquelme, *Ampliando miradas*, 2009

The recent wave of Peruvian migration is part of Chile's larger history of migration. Despite the common refrain that Chile "has not been a country of immigrants," its politicians have had an enduring preoccupation with the subject and promoted legislation that attempted to encourage targeted immigration. Furthermore, Chilean elites have strategically referenced their ties to Western European immigration as a marker of their privileged status. For most of the nineteenth and twentieth centuries Chilean politicians promoted the idea and practice of attracting a largely white, European immigration as an important source of economic and racial modernity. As such, Chile's dominant historical immigrant narrative—unlike the (albeit problematic) embrace of mestizaje or race mixing in other Latin American countries—resembles elements of the US assimilationist, white supremacist model that emerged during the Cold War and celebrates the integration of white European populations while excluding racial minorities.[43] In this section I examine the history and historiography of migration in Chile and argue that the absence of an engagement with a transnational perspective on migration that includes the histories of non-European migrants such as Peruvians ignores vital elements in Chile's definition of the nation.

Although never a major destination for migrants like its eastern neighbors, Argentina and Brazil (since the mid-nineteenth-century foreign-born have averaged between 1% and 2% of the total population), immigration has played an influential role in Chile's history since colonial times. The country's migratory past can be roughly divided into five broad stages: the colonial-era arrival of predominantly Spanish colonists and neighboring Andean migrants (with a trace of slaves from Africa); the postindependence nineteenth- and early twentieth-century efforts to promote strategic immigration of white Europeans; the unregulated arrival of Syrian, Lebanese, Palestinian, and then later Spanish exiles in the first half of the twentieth century; the mass emigration of up to 500,000 citizens during the military dictatorship; and the post-Pinochet-era rapid growth of immigrants from neighboring South American countries, principally from Peru, Argentina, and Bolivia.

During and following the wars against Spanish colonists starting in 1810, Chilean government officials worked quickly to shape the emerging nation, turning to foreign immigration as one way to modernize and consolidate the newly independent country.[44] To document this persistent effort, here I focus on the formative second stage of immigration and review some of the milestones of Chile's nineteenth- and twentieth-century immigration legislation. The overall situation that politicians hoped to address with this legislation was that Chile was underpopulated, had vast tracts of rich agricultural land, and ample areas that they considered required colonization. Chile's politicians hoped the legislation could fill the country's "empty" spaces by populating them with "civilized" settlers that would in turn work the vast quantities of fertile agricultural land.[45]

In the earliest example of many immigration initiatives of the nineteenth century, in 1811 the future national leader Bernardo O'Higgins proposed a program to attract English and Swiss colonists to Chile. Eight years later in his first official immigration policy as Supreme Director, O'Higgins commissioned an administrator to manage immigration and offer free passage and support for migrants bringing skills and machinery. In 1824, the government passed the country's first immigration law, offering territorial and financial guarantees to mainly German and English immigrants dedicated to agricultural production or establishing new industries. The government passed a succession of over ten similar laws from the mid-nineteenth to early twentieth century. Also starting in the mid-nineteenth century, immigration agents established themselves in countries such as Germany, resulting in the arrival of thousands of settlers to Chile's southern regions. Between 1883 and 1895, over 31,000 northern Europeans settled in the southern colonies of Llanquihue and Valdivia. In the late nineteenth century, in addition to new laws, the government established new bureaucracies and offices to promote and manage European immigration. Collier and Sater point out that "the influence of foreigners was out of all proportion to their numbers." In the nineteenth and early twentieth centuries, European and North American migrants established businesses, industrial dynasties, and major agricultural enterprises, leaving "a permanent mark on the country."[46]

Non-European migrants, such as Arabs (fleeing from the Ottoman Empire: Syria, Palestine, and Lebanon) and Asians, also arrived during the turn of the century, but they were largely rejected and discriminated against by Chileans who viewed them as both culturally inferior and an economic threat to the ruling class. Similar discriminatory attitudes persisted in legislation into the twentieth century. Fearing an influx of undesirable refugees following World War I, policymakers restricted the entry of foreigners in 1918, and as a result the number of new immigrants in Chile fell to an all-time low.[47]

In the years following World War II and into the 1960s, the government established a series of commissions, offices, studies, and decrees to resurrect some of the nineteenth-century efforts encouraging strategic European immigration of industrialists and agriculturalists. For example, in 1945 and again in 1953, provisions of two government decrees stipulated that "a direct result of immigration would be population increase, technological improvement, and the perfection of the biological conditions of the [Chilean] race." To institutionalize these renewed efforts, in 1954 the government created the Department of Immigration as part of the Ministry of Foreign Relations. The department established the category "immigration" to mean a foreigner who entered into the country with the intention to work. The category would later fall into disuse. Chile's long postindependence period of immigration came to an end with the 1973 military coup and the radical change to a country of net emigration. Built on the country's long legislative history, the restrictive 1975 immigration law added a new chapter to Chile's migratory narrative that continues to shape immigrant policies toward Peruvian and other migrants today.

More closely resembling Arab immigration from earlier in the century, Peruvian migration to Chile does not fit well into Chile's standard historical narrative or literature. With a focus on nation-bound narratives and the arrival of

European colonists, unscheduled Peruvian migration unsettles Chile's history and historiography, disrupting the conceit of national unity. Necessarily involving the histories of more than one country, the study of transnational migration requires a transnational approach.[48] As Purcell and Riquelme point out, "since its consolidation as an academic discipline in the 19th century, Chile's historiography has constituted 'the nation' as an almost natural category of analysis."[49] The case of Chile, they argue, is not unique to Latin America where politically motivated historiographies maintain a national focus and reduce "other nations [to] either real or potential threats."[50] Yet in the historical literature in general, recent immigration is absent as is mention of the context and implications of the 1975 Alien Status Law. In a kind of nostalgic frame reminiscent of the United States, Chile's written history accounts of immigration are relegated to the arrival of white ethnics in the nineteenth and early twentieth centuries.[51]

Reflecting the defensive nature of the 1975 immigration law, the military regime viewed migration—especially the flight into exile of hundreds of thousands of supposed dissidents—as a threat to the nation's security. Since 1990 the study of non-European origin migration has developed at academic institutions, albeit at a slow pace.[52] In the late 1990s, nonhistorians began publishing valuable social scientific studies concerning interregional migration, focusing on topics such as demographics, policies, labor, social and cultural integration, discrimination, health, education, and children.[53] Still missing, however, has been a broader historical examination of the intersecting processes of racialization, immigration, and nation formation.

OUT OF THE FIRES: LEGISLATIVE RESPONSES TO NATIONAL CRISES

> Despite the changes that have been made to the Alien Status Law under democratic governments, the spirit of it [since the Pinochet era] continues to have an element of police control that views foreigners as potential threats to national security, and ignores the fundamental social and humanitarian aspects of migration.
> —Riquelme and Alarcón, "El peso de la historia: inmigración peruana en Chile," 2008

Recent Peruvian immigrants to Chile have had to confront Pinochet-era immigration policies that treat them and other immigrants as potential threats to the nation and force them into positions of illegality and vulnerability. The post–September 11, 1973 immigration policies in Chile were implemented as aggressive responses to shocks to the country's new neoliberal economic system. Although more severely restrictive than previous immigration regulation in Chile's history, the new laws were not a radical departure from a historical framework, which consistently sought to regulate and control immigrants. Chile's enduring immigration laws have crafted racist, exclusionist immigration policies with the intent to "improve and civilize" the country.[54]

Chile's current immigration laws have proved inadequate for processing and regulating the new immigrant arrivals. The 1975 Alien Status Law (Law Decree N° 1.094), slightly altered by the 1984 Alien Status Regulation (Supreme Decree N° 597), continues in force today without significant modification.[55] While the Pinochet regime permitted greater market access to foreign corporations and currencies, the same was not true to foreigners in general. With a focus on preventing the entrance of "dangerous elements" or terrorists, the 1975 law omitted a category for immigrant laborers and granted visas only for tourists and temporary or permanent residents. During the period, conservative commentators reporting on the 1975 and 1984 laws merely summarized their contents, underscoring their importance as legal measures to prohibit the entrance of unwanted foreigners.[56] Recent critics have focused on the 1975 law's section 15 of article 3 and its prohibition on the entrance of certain aliens as indicative of the general arbitrary nature of the law:

> Whosoever spreads or disseminates by word or in writing or in any other way, any doctrines that are aimed at destroying or altering, through violence, law and order in the country or its government; people accused of being or reputed to be agitators or activists of such doctrines and, in general, whosoever acts in such a way that qualifies under Chilean law as being in breach of external security, national sovereignty, internal security or public law and order in Chile and whosoever undertakes any acts which are contrary to the country's interests or which represent a danger for the State.[57]

This section and the law in general lack specific instructions on exactly how to determine if an entering individual is guilty of these or other acts. This imprecision and absence of due process allows immigration officials (and others with related enforcement powers) to rely on their own discretion to determine an immigrant's status and whether or not to permit entrance. Provisions for immigrant rights and social integration assistance by the state are conspicuously absent from the 1975 law, which is instead oriented toward security and control in the form of distribution of visas and fines.

Commenting during an interview from his improvised legal clinic on Avenida Catedral next to the Plaza de Armas, Peruvian immigrant rights activist Víctor Paiba Cossios intoned with conviction that "The government of Chile knows that illegals do not exist! The migrants that do exist are those that find themselves in an irregular migratory status due to the arbitrary closing of the [Peru-Chile] border." Commenting on the capricious behavior of the city's *caribineros*, Paiba Cossios continued, indicating that racially motivated random spot checks occur regularly among Peruvian day laborers waiting for employment, because they "do not satisfy the requirements of being tall, blond, and blue eyed."[58]

For Peruvians in the contemporary period, the majority of whom enter as laborers, there is no legal category that recognizes their status in Chile. Instead, they need to cross the border either as undocumented immigrants or acquire a 3-month tourist visa and then search for employment and obtain a contract. After securing employment, immigrants can apply for a temporary residence permit that is only valid as long as they remain employed. This initial lack of status and dependency on a labor contract means that employers wield an arbitrary power of control over immigrant workers. In turn, immigrant employees often choose to suffer abuses rather than lose their positions, since contract cancellation forces them into a vulnerable legal vacuum. As a result, vulnerability and illegality are hallmarks of Chile's current law. Politicians have begun to try to exploit the law's vagueness. In one case from 2009, Cristián Espejo, a Santiago congressional candidate for the right-wing Independent Democrat Union Party (Unión Democrata Independiente), argued that "Peruvians staying illegally in Chile should be deported." Although he was quick to add that his suggestions were neither about "xenophobia nor extreme nationalism," he emphasized that Peruvians were uniquely responsible for leading criminal gangs and abusing social services meant for Chilean citizens.[59]

The law's arbitrary nature also impacts children, the most vulnerable members of the immigrant community. Chilean law continues to deny nationality to the growing number of children born in Chile to "irregular immigrants" (without visa), impeding their access to social services that protect their economic and social rights.[60] In clear violation of international law and the 1960 Convention Relating to the Status of Stateless Persons, the right of *jus solis*[61] is denied to many immigrant children who instead must rely on a type of "*jus visa*."[62]

Despite the assumption that with the return to democratic rule in Chile and governance by the left-leaning Concertación party would improve the rights of the country's vulnerable immigrants, only short-term and palliative efforts have been made such as the granting of amnesty to irregular immigrants in 1998 and 2007.[63] The first presidency of Michelle Bachelet gave immigrant rights activists new hope that government policies would be changed in their favor. Unfortunately, despite the creation of the Council on Migratory Policy and including new legislative initiatives in her administration's plans, no proposal was ever presented to congress. A former political refugee herself, during her first term, Bachelet paid more attention to the rights of Chileans in exile and refugees in Chile, helping to pass the Law for the Protection of Refugees in 2008. President Sebastian Piñera also paid little attention to immigration reform.

Peruvian and other working-class immigrants in Chile should be added to the ill-fated list of what Peter Winn calls the "victims of the Chilean miracle." The lasting inattention to real immigration reform in Chile is a result of government priorities that privilege market expansion over workers' rights. Winn makes the point that

> More than a decade of democracy and center-left governments has not altered neoliberalism's fundamentally negative impact on Chilean workers. In fact, viewed in historical perspective as part of the Pinochet era, the neoliberal democracy of the Concertación consolidated the neoliberal "revolution" that

Pinochet began. It did this by conferring democratic legitimacy on the decrees that Pinochet had imposed by dictatorial fiat and by embracing and even extending many of his policy shifts.[64]

Whereas "denationalized" global business immigrants from places like the United States, Europe, and Australia frequently receive every courtesy to work and settle in Chile, Peruvian and other laborers struggle to obtain employment contracts and residence visas.[65]

EL QUINTO SUYO: RECENT PERUVIAN MIGRATION TO CHILE

In the last days of May 2011, eager supporters of Peruvian presidential hopeful Keiko Fujimori paraded through the streets surrounding Santiago's main square, the Plaza de Armas, strategically distributing thousands of pamphlets to members of the Peruvian immigrant community.[66] The trademark Keiko-orange flyers projected a simple message: a vote for Ms. Fujimori would improve the lives of the Quinto Suyo, the growing Peruvian community abroad. Promising increased savings and efficiency with the transmission of remittances to their home country, improved consular services, and even a congressional seat to represent Peruvians abroad, Ms. Fujimori was pulling out all the stops in advance of the June 5, 2011, second-round election against her left-wing opponent, Ollanta Humala.[67]

Keiko Fujimori's politicking on foreign soil was a bid to the then 62,000 eligible Peruvian voters in Chile, 90% of whom live in Santiago.[68] As part of a larger global and regional migratory trend, in the last two decades Chile has become an emerging corridor of migration in Latin America.[69] Peruvian migration to Chile is one example of long-standing intraregional migrations between South American countries. Initiating in the early nineteenth century when nations were just beginning to solidify their borders, migrants crossed from one South American country to another with relative ease. Largely because of the high costs of transportation and communication, most migrants remained within the region. As borders hardened and dictatorial regimes in the 1970s imposed restrictions on movement, the flow of working-class migrants slowed (while thousands fled in exile). In the first decades of the twenty-first century, regional economic integration and liberalized migration policies have facilitated a renewed flow of migrants throughout the region. Nevertheless, the foreign-born population from neighboring South American countries represents only a small percentage of the host country's total population, most well under 5%.[70]

This recent regional South American migration has yielded a range of worker types and destinations. Most migrants have traveled to major urban centers like Rio de Janiero to find work and settle. Like the Peruvian-dominated female domestic workers in Santiago, other nation-specific working-class migrants occupy a particular occupational niche, including Bolivian construction workers in Buenos Aires and Colombian day laborers in Caracas. To a much smaller degree, relatively higher salaries in Argentina and Chile attract professional migrants.[71]

Today, Peruvians in Chile—primarily in Santiago—work as *nanas*, or female domestic workers. Prior to the 1990s, most domestic workers were of Chilean origin and many of those were members of the country's indigenous Mapuche community. In that decade, the growth of export agriculture and the fishing industry in Chile's South opened up new employment opportunities for Mapuche women, who in turn opted to stay in their own communities rather than migrate north to Santiago. The 1990s also witnessed the growth of professional opportunities for middle-class Chilean women. That change, combined with a lack of state-subsidized childcare, created a need for *nanas* that would ultimately be filled by Peruvian women. Staab and Maher suggest that replacing Mapuche women with Peruvian women for domestic work also allowed Chilean employers to perpetuate a subordinated, pliant, racialized workforce in contrast with increasingly rights-demanding Chilean servants. In addition to their status as a racial-other, Peruvians also suffer from the insecurity of being international immigrants with little rights protection.[72]

A number of binational factors in the past two decades have contributed to the recent rise in Peruvian migration to Chile, most centering on disparities in economic and political stability, violence, and the advantage of proximity; disincentives to migrate to the United States, Europe, and Japan also added to the reasons for new migratory destinations.

The Chilean Context

Chile's current period of both emigration and immigration differs significantly from previous ones. Whereas the period of Chile's military dictatorship witnessed the emigration of hundreds of thousands of its citizens into forced and voluntary exile, the transition to democracy and accompanying political stability and economic advancement in the 1990s initiated Chile's shift from a migrant-sending to a migrant-receiving country.[73] Starting with the presidency of Patricio Aylwin in 1990, Chile began the vexing process of reinstating a democratic system of government while maintaining many legal and administrative structures in force during the Pinochet years. Indeed, into the 1990s Pinochet retained control of the military and then, enabled by the new Constitution, became "lifetime senator" in 1998.[74] Additionally, most elements of the 1980 Constitution continued as well as the 1975 immigration law. The legacy of the Pinochet years within the larger historical context of Chilean migration shaped Chile's response to Peruvian immigrants in recent decades.

The emerging political landscape in the 1990s was supported by and intimately linked to an average gross domestic product (GDP) growth rate of 7.7%.[75] Continuing the neoliberal economic priorities of the Pinochet era, the Concertación governments in the 1990s (a coalition of center-left parties in power until 2010) tied politics to an aggressive strategy that included a focus on export, opening the economy to international investment, eliminating trade barriers, privatizing state industries, devaluing currency, and replacing universal social services with private programs targeting particularly needy sectors. By the end of the decade a quick succession of trade agreements were signed with Canada (1997), the European Union (2003), and the United States (2003). Staab and Hill view the country's transition to democracy in global economic terms and part of the latest stage in nation-state formation: "The contemporary national identity project in Chile might be seen partly as an externally oriented marketing strategy on a global stage."[76] Chile's rank in the Human Development Index, a measure of several factors, including income, education, inequality, and health, steadily increased over the past two decades and became the highest of all countries in Latin America.[77] It is this prosperity that caused one Peruvian migrant, Sonia C., to underscore the conspicuous difference in material wealth between herself and visiting family from Peru: "We have a television in each bedroom . . . and when we have visitors [from Peru] they always say, 'you're a millionaire!'"

Yet Chile's emergence as an economic "tiger" in the 1990s, the Latin American equivalent to its East Asian counterparts, produced ambivalent results that would directly affect immigration policies in the ensuing decades. As geographer Solange Muñoz explains:

> Since 1990, Chile has been considered extremely successful both economically and politically. . . . In some ways, Santiago resembles that of a global city, like New York or Paris. However, despite Chile's move toward a more modern, global economy, it remains a somewhat closed society, that in many ways continues to grapple with its past and present in relation to concepts such as national identity both internally and in relation to the other countries of the region and the rest of the world.[78]

Along with a triumphant sense of success (*exitismo*) that accompanied the country's increasing economic privatization came cultural disillusionment among other sectors of society who viewed the accelerated global marketing of Chile and promotion of the "consumer and the quest for individual self-actualization" as a narcissistic attack on a more humble national self-image.[79] The flood of credit cards, supermarkets, and mega malls underscored the country's positioning as a center for capitalist investment. Although the economy grew and the rate of poverty fell, income distribution and hyperconcentration of wealth resulted in one of the world's highest levels of inequality.[80] Both Pinochetistas and Concertacionistas claimed ownership over the country's economic successes, one as a legacy of its policies, the other as a sign of a successful break from the past.[81] Regardless of which claim emerged victorious, both demanded that social policies such as immigration reform "would not upset the rules of the market-driven economic game, particularly the investment and export motors that assured high growth and a satisfied business sector."[82] Despite some half-hearted attempts over the decades to update immigration structures, Chilean politicians have determined that low-income foreign workers were drawn to and indirectly supported the neoliberal economic system they hoped to maintain. Favoring economic investment and a culture of privatization, the government relegated immigration policy to the backseat of national affairs. Chile's neoliberal transformation "undermined the concept of citizenship by transforming social rights (like education, health care, and social security) into individual problems."[83]

The Peruvian Context

> A friend [said] that Chile is a "country of wonders that welcomes you with open arms. That there was ample work and incredible salaries, that there were so many McDonalds . . . and malls all over the place, automatic teller machines where you can take out money simply by sticking in a little card, that it was like being in the U.S.!"
>
> —"Carta abierta," Juan Radrigán, 2004

Keiko Fujimori's courting of Peruvian migrant votes in 2011 was an ironic gesture, considering that her father, Alberto Fujimori, was in part responsible for the out-migration of thousands of his fellow citizens during his presidency from 1990 to 2000. Fujimori's neoliberal economic policies, meant to arrest the rampant economic inflation underway from a decade before, only further exacerbated the problem. According to economist Oscar Dancourt, Peru's dollarization of the banking system and capital liberalization combined with poor fiscal leadership failed to protect the country from adverse external shocks and contributed to the failure of the country's version of neoliberalism.[84] Health, education, and living conditions all deteriorated during his terms, which concluded with 54% of the population living below the poverty line. Accused of corruption and human rights violations, Alberto Fujimori went into self-imposed exile in Japan in 2000 and was eventually convicted and imprisoned after returning to Peru.

This political and economic chaos was made all the worse by the violence of protracted guerilla warfare, rapid urbanization, and climatologic destruction.[85] The end of a four-decade-long urban population explosion in Lima coincided with the devastating effects of the El Niño current in 1982. Since 1940 Lima's population had risen from 645,000 to 4.6 million inhabitants in 1980 and grew to 8.7 million in 2008. These demographic and infrastructural pressures on social services and the economy contributed to Peru's political and economic instability.[86] Furthermore, during this same period of demographic growth, Peru and Chile increasingly integrated their economies into regional market alliances. Although the focus in agreements such as MERCOSUR (Southern Common Market; Peru and Chile are Associate Members) is on the flow of goods and not people, corporate interests—while far from the influential level in the United States—are increasingly playing a role in regional migration in South America.[87]

As a consequence of these past two decades of volatility, Peru has become a nation of emigrants with more than 10% of its population currently living abroad.[88] Although the majority of Peruvian emigrants reside in the United States, following the restrictive and punitive legislation that emerged after

September 11, 2001, a growing number has turned to neighboring countries such as Chile, where growing labor demands, proximity, and relative ease of entrance support migration flows.[89] Echoing the earlier epigraph from Chilean playwright Juan Radrigán, Emilia M., a Peruvian residing in Santiago, recounted how her hopes to migrate to the United States were dashed after 9/11 and beyond: "I hoped things would change with Obama," she confessed, "but things remain the same and are even more dangerous [for migrants in the United States]."[90] Along with Mexico, whose migrants travel primarily to the United States, Peru has one of the highest levels of emigration in Latin America. However, whereas Mexicans have been migrating to the United States in high numbers for well over a century, large-scale Peruvian migration to Chile is a recent phenomenon and thus deserves special attention.[91]

AFTERWORD

In 2011, as the world watched hundreds of thousands of Chilean students march in protest against failing secondary and postsecondary school systems, Peruvian and other vulnerable migrants had little recourse to challenge a system they too inherited from the years of the Pinochet dictatorship. Immigration and academic reforms in the late 1970s and 80s both were part of the dictatorial government's new economic and social programs. As Peter Winn explains, Chile's version of neoliberalism took on a particularly virulent strain, a "highly ideological version that made it a vehicle for an aggressive attack on Chile's workers and the labor rights they had acquired during decades of struggle."[92] Chile's "return to democracy" has yielded little gain for Peruvian workers, and it has instead perpetuated the country's enduring racialized immigrant narrative.

As Chile's relationship with redemocratization develops into the new millennium, it continues to confront both the haunting of its Pinochet-era past and recent popular challenges to that enduring system of rule. With her return to the presidency in March of 2014, Michelle Bachelet promised to craft legislation and constitutional reforms that shift the focus from "security and controlling immigrant labor" to "inclusion, regional integration, and rights." Although it will be difficult to pass through a divided congress, if enacted, these reforms would be radical revisions to the Pinochet-era document.[93]

Since 2005, new waves of Peruvians migrants are showing signs of permanence in Chile, moving away from what often has been seen as a temporary status. Like their counterparts in other parts of the globe, in increasing numbers Peruvians in Chile are attempting to integrate into their host society. A 2014 study demonstrates that nearly 38% of Peruvians are transitioning to permanent status in Chile, many of them intermarrying and building binational families.[94]

With the possibility of new constitutional reforms, a renewed activist community, and a growing and shifting immigrant population, Chileans will need to reconsider their ethnoracial definition of citizenship, the nation, and their relationship with others.

NOTES

1. Although not focused on immigration reform, Naomi Klein's work illustrates the larger phenomenon of "shock capitalism": when government and corporate leaders, working together, take advantage of social, political, and environmental crises to promote free trade and other neoliberal policies. *The Shock Doctrine: The Rise of Disaster Capitalism* (New York: Metropolitan Books, 2007). For non–Latin American examples of government responses to the "shock" of increased immigration see, Wayne A. Cornelius et al., *Controlling Immigration: A Global Perspective* (Stanford, CA: Stanford University Press, second edition, 2004); Christopher Rudolph, *National Security and Immigration: Policy Development in the United States and Western Europe Since 1945* (Stanford, CA: Stanford University Press, 2006).

2. The vast majority (approximately 80%) of Peruvian migrants reside in and around Greater Metropolitan Santiago. Other concentrations of Peruvian migrants can be found in the north in Arica, Iquique, and Antofagasta with smaller amounts in the country's southern regions. Ricardo A Jiménez Ayala, "Algo está cambiando: globalización, migración y ciudadanía en las asociaciones de peruanos en Chile" (Santiago: Impresos Gotelli, 2005).

3. Departamento de Extranjería y Migración, Chile, Censo Nacional 2012. Carolina Stefoni, "La migración en la agenda chileno-peruana. Un camino por construir," in *Nuestros vecinos*, eds. Mario Artaza and Paz Milet (Santiago: RIL Editores/Universidad de Chile, 2007). During the period of Alberto Fujimori's presidency, many Peruvians arrived as political refugees. However, refugees currently do not make up a substantial number of Peru's immigrants to Chile. In 2009 the Departamento de Extranjería y Migración only registered one refugee arrival from Peru (most came from Colombia). *Informe anual Departamento de Extranjería y Migración, Ministerio del Interior*, 2009.

4. Argentines came second with 57,019. Over 57% of Peruvian immigrants in Chile were women in 2011, most attracted to the burgeoning demand in domestic work. For additional studies on Peruvian female migrants, see Kristen Hill Mahler and Silke Staab, "Nanny Politics: The Dilemmas of Working Women's Empowerment in Santiago, Chile," *International Feminist Journal of Politics* 7, no. 1 (2005): 71–88.; Centro de Encuentros Cultura y Mujer, *Migraciones, globalización, y género en Argentina y Chile* (Chile: Fundación Instituto de la Mujer, 2005).

5. Jorge Martínez Pizarro, *El encanto de los datos: Sociodemográfica de la inmigración en Chile según el censo de 2002* (Santiago: Naciones Unidas, 2003).

6. Paul Drake, foreword to *Victims of the Chilean Miracle: Workers and Neoliberalism in the Pinochet Era, 1973–2002* by Peter Winn (Durham, NC: Duke University Press, 2006), xi.

7. For studies on labor and neoliberal economic policies in Chile, see Louise Haaugh, "The Emperor's New Clothes: Labor Reform and Social Democratization in Chile," *Studies in Comparative International Development* 37, no. 1 (2002): 86–115; José Cademartori, "The Chilean Neoliberal Model Enters into Crisis," *Latin American Perspectives* 30, no. 5 (2003): 79–88; Patricio Escobar and Camelia LeBert, "The New Labor Market: The Effects of the Neoliberal Experiment in Chile," *Latin American Perspectives* 30, no. 5 (2003): 70–78; John Lear and Joseph Collins, "Working in Chile's Free Market," *Latin American Perspectives* 22, no. 1 (1995): 10–29; Francisco Zapata, "The Chilean Labor Movement under Salvador Allende: 1970–1973," *Latin American Perspectives* 3, no. 1 (1976): 85–97.

8. Unless otherwise indicated, all translations are by the author.
9. Fernando Purcell and Alfredo Riquelme, eds., *Ampliando miradas: Chile y su historia en un tiempo global* (Santiago: RIL editores, 2009), 13.
10. Winn, *Victims of the Chilean Miracle: Workers and Neoliberalism in the Pinochet Era, 1973–2002*, 2.
11. "Quinto Suyo" means "the Fifth Region," a reference to the Quechua term for the Inka empire, Tawantinsuyu, "The Four Regions." See Ulla Berg, "El Quinto Suyo: Contemporary Nation Building and the Political Economy of Emigration in Peru," *Latin American Perspectives* 37 (2010): 121.
12. "Chile es tuyo," Servicio Nacion de Turismo, accessed June 6, 2011, http://www.chileestuyo.cl/ or https://www.youtube.com/watch?v=8XwJfvlaxP4.
13. Doreen Massey, "A Place Called Home?" *New Formations* 17 (1992): 3–15. Mahler and Staab argue further that "In order to win the trust of foreign business and political authorities in the First World, the Chilean state and business interests have constructed a national image for international consumption." Silke Staab and Kristen Hill Maher, "The Dual Discourse about Peruvian Domestic Workers in Santiago de Chile: Class, Race, and a Nationalist Project," *Latin American Politics and Society* 48, no. 1 (2006): 106. For an excellent review of recent work on race in contemporary Chile, see Javeria Barandiarán, "Researching Race in Chile," *Latin America Research Review* 47, no. 1 (2012): 161–176.
14. In the early days of Chile's tourist industry, government officials promoted the southern Patagonia region along racio-nationalist lines, often labeling the southern zone as "la Suiza chilena": a place of exquisite natural beauty, but one already discovered and civilized. Rodrigo Booth, "El paisaje aquí tiene un encanto fresco y poético: Las bellezas del sur de Chile y la construcción de la nación turística," *Revista de historia iberoamericana* 3, no. 1 (2010): 10–32.
15. See the detailed discussion on this topic and on "neoliberal multiculturalism" in Patricia Richards, *Race and the Chilean Miracle: Neoliberalism, Democracy and Indigenous Rights* (Pittsburgh: University of Pittsburgh Press, 2013).
16. Muñoz, "Peruvian Migration to Chile: Challenges for National Identity, Human Rights and Social Policy," 6. Works that have helped to sustain that myth include Hebe Clementi, *La frontera en América. Vol. 3 América del Sur* (Buenos Aires: Leviatán, 1987); Álvaro Jara, *Guerra y sociedad en Chile* (Santiago: Editorial Universitaria, 1971); Francisco Antonio Encina, *Historia de Chile* (Santiago: Editorial Nascimento, 1949); Magnus Mörner, *El mestizaje en la historia de Ibero-América* (Stockholm: School of Economics, 1960).
17. Carolina Stefoni, "Inmigración y ciudadanía: la formación de comunidades peruanas en Santiago y la emergencia de nuevos ciudadanos," in *El Quinto Suyo, Transnacionalidad y formaciones diaspóricas en la migración peruana*, eds. Ulla Berg and Karsten Paerregaard (Lima: Instituto de Estudios Peruanos, 2005).
18. The previous War of the Confederation (1836–1839) between a Peruvian-Bolivian alliance and Chile (and independently Argentina), although less thoroughly studied in this regard, should also be considered in terms of Chile and Peru's mutual racial formation. Distinct from the War of the Pacific, however, the war concluded not with the annexation of Peruvian and Bolivian territory, but with the dissolution of the confederacy. For a unique treatment of the War of the Confederation's role in Chile's formation of a national self, see Gabriel Cid Rodríguez, "Guerra y conciencia nacional: la guerra contra la confederación en el imaginario chileno, 1836–1888" (PhD diss.,

Instituto de Historia, Pontificia Universidad Católica de Chile, 2009). Also see Carlos Donoso and Jaime Rosenblitt, eds., *Guerra, región y nación: La Confederación Perú-Boliviana, 1836–1839* (Santiago: Centro de Investigaciones Diego Barros Aran/Universidad Andrés Bello, 2009).

19. Ximena Zavala San Martín and Claudia Rojas Venegas, "Globalización, procesos migratorios y estado en Chile," in *Migraciones, globalización y género en Argentina y Chile*, eds. Cristina Cacopardo et al. (Movimiento Por Emancipación de la Mujer MEMCH – Chile, 2005), 150–191.

20. William Skuban, *Lines in the Sand: Nationalism and Identity on the Peruvian-Chilean Frontier* (Albuquerque: University of New Mexico Press, 2011). Skuban also discusses the simultaneous related development of Peruvian racial stereotypes of Chileans and Peruvians themselves, 77–86; Ericka Beckman, "The Creolization of Imperial Reason: Chilean State Racism in the War of the Pacific," *Journal of Latin American Studies* 18, no. 1 (2009): 73–90.

21. Mario Góngora, *Ensayo Histórico sobre la noción de Estado en Chile en los siglos XIX y XX* (Santiago: Editorial Universitaria, 1981). See also, Eduardo Cavieres and Cristóbal Alijovín de Losada, *Chile-Perú, Perú-Chile: 1820–1920. Desarrollos Políticos, Económicos y Culturales* (Valparaíso: Ediciones Universitarias de Valparaíso, 2005).

22. Skuban, *Lines in the Sand: Nationalism and Identity on the Peruvian-Chilean Frontier*, 219–223.

23. Sylvia Dummer Sheel, "Los desafíos de escenificar el 'alma nacional': Chile en la Exposición Iberoamericana de Sevilla, 1929," *Historia Crítica* 42 (2010): 84–111.

24. Juan Bautista Alberdi, "Bases y puntos de partida para lo organización de la República Argentina" (Valparaíso: 1852).

25. Luis de la Cuadra Luque, *Necesidad de la emigración europea a Chile: algunas consideraciones sobre su importancia, utilidad i la urgencia de formar una sociedad anónima con este objeto* (Santiago: Impr. Chilena, 1872).

26. For a discussion of the enduring influence of Palacios and the *Raza chilena*, see Patrick Barr-Melej, *Reforming Chile: Cultural Politics, Nationalism, and the Rise of the Middle Class* (Chapel Hill: University of North Carolina Press, 2001) and Sandra McGee Deutsch, *Las Derechas: The Extreme Right in Argentina, Brazil, and Chile, 1890–1939* (Stanford, CA: Stanford University Press, 1999).

27. Nicolás Palacios, *Raza chilena: Libro escrito por un chileno i para los chilenos* (Valparaíso: Imprenta de Gustavo Schäfer, 1904), 5.

28. Sergio Carvallo Hederra, *El problema de la inmigración en Chile y algunos países sudamericanos* (Santiago: La Universidad de Chile, 1945). In the following year a university debate generated much of the same urgency to populate the country with European capitalists that would in turn "enrich the biological qualities of [the Chilean] race." Acción Cívica y Cultural (Santiago, Chile), *Conclusiones de la Acción Cívica y Cultural sobre "Nuestro problema Humano y la Inmigración,"* Tema debatido en un foro público en la Universidad de Chile, 1946.

29. Antonia Rebolledo Hernández, "La 'turcofobia'. Discriminación antiárabe en Chile. 1900–1950." *Historia* 28: 249–272; Cano Christiny et al., "Conocer para legislar y hacer política: los desafíos de Chile ante un nuevo escenario migratorio."

30. Félix del Campo, *La inmigración europea en Chile: Como servicio del Estado* (Valparaíso: Lit. e Impr. Moderna, 1910). See a similar ranking system from nearly thirty years earlier in De la Cuadra Luque, *Necesidad de la emigración europea a Chile:*

Algunas consideraciones sobre su importancia, utilidad i la urgencia de formar una sociedad anónima con este objeto.

31. Interview with Erika S. (Santiago, Chile, February 20, 2011).

32. Paz Milet, "Chile-Perú: Las dos caras de un espejo," *Revista de Ciencia Política* 24, no. 2 (2004). See also Jorge Riquelme Rivera and Gonzalo Alarcón Muñoz, "El peso de la historia—inmigración peruana en Chile," *Polis* 7, no. 20 (2008): 299–310.

33. Maximiliano Sbarbi Osuna, "Crecen las migraciones internas en Sudamérica" *Observador Global*, accessed on May 2, 2011. http://observadorglobal.com/crecen -las-migraciones-internas-en-sudamerica-n21018.html. Despite the signing of the Chile-Peru Social Integration Council in 2006, the two countries continue to revisit old conflicts. In January of 2014, the International Court of Justice ruled in favor of Peru concerning a dispute over maritime boundaries in the border between both countries that emerged from the War of the Pacific and then treaties in the 1950s. http://www.icj-cij.org/docket/files/137/17842.pdf

34. In their article, Doña-Reveco and Levinson noted that the 2007 *Latinobarómetro* study "ranked Chile 15 out of 18 Latin American countries on openness to migration, with only about one-third of those surveyed (35%) agreeing that foreigners should have the same rights as natives. When asked about "race" or ethnic group and class, the percentages were even lower: only 13% of Chileans agreed with bringing foreigners with a similar race or ethnic group to that of the majority of the country. The same study states that only 10% of Chilean agreed with bringing a lot of people from poorer countries."

35. Mahler and Staab, "Nanny Politics." The authors' main argument centers around the fact that racial discrimination is particularly pronounced along gendered lines; see also Jorge Larraín, *Identidad Chilena* (Santiago: LOM ediciones, 2001).

36. Credit for this statement goes to Andrés Kalawski Isla, Pontificia Universidad Católica de Chile.

37. Martínez Pizarro, *El encanto de los datos: Sociodemográfica de la inmigración en Chile según el censo de 2002*, 9–10.

38. Nora Barrientos, "Políticas públicas e identidades étnicas: la corporación nacional de desarrollo indígena," in *¿Hay patria que defender? La identidad nacional frente a la globalización* by Centro de Estudios para el Desarrollo (Santiago: Ediciones del Segundo Centenario, 2000).

39. Barandiarán, "Researching Race in Chile," 169.

40. No author, *Servicios de Colonización Inmigración: colonización—tierras fiscales, defensa fiscal indígenas* (Santiago: Impr. y Enc. Bandera, 1903).

41. Carolina Stefoni, "Inmigración en Chile. Nuevos desafíos," in *Impactos y desafíos de las crisis internacionales*, Facultad Latinoamericana de Ciencias Sociales (FLACSO), ed. (Santiago, Chile 2002), 241–265; Nicolas De Genova, "The Legal Production of Mexican/Migrant 'Illegality,'" *Latino Studies* 2 (2004): 160–185.

42. Chile Visión Television (CHV), "En la mira," "Invasión silenciosa." Aired on June 22, 2011.

43. The mainstream US "melting pot" immigrant narratives gained force among sociologists (specifically with the Chicago School's assimilationist paradigm) in the aftermath of World War II in contradistinction first to Nazi and fascist policies of racial purity and then to the perceived threat of increasingly empowered nonwhite groups during the civil rights era. For studies examining the construction of immigrant histories and historiographies in the United States, see Matthew Frye Jacobson,

Whiteness of a Different Color: European Immigrants and the Alchemy of Race (Cambridge, MA: Harvard University Press, 1999); Donna R. Gabaccia, "Is Everywhere Nowhere? Nomads, Nations, and the Immigrant Paradigm of United States History," *The Journal of American History* 86, no. 3 (1999): 1115–1134; David A. Gerber, "Forming a Transnational Narrative: New Perspectives on European Migrations to the United States," *The History Teacher* 35, no. 1 (2001): 61–78; Andreas Wimmer and Nina Glick Schiller, "Methodological Nationalism and Beyond: Nation-State Building Migration and the Social Science," *Global Networks* 2, no. 4 (2002): 301–334; Barry Goldberg, "Historical Reflections on Transnationalism, Race, and the American Immigrant Saga," *Annals of the New York Academy of Sciences* 645 (1992): 201–215.

44. I draw on the following sources for this section: Félix del Campo, *La inmigración europea en Chile: Como servicio del Estado* (Valparaíso: Lit. e Impr. Moderna, 1910); Vicente Pérez Rosales, *Emigración, Inmigración y Colonización* (Santiago: Impr. de Julio Belin, 1854); Collier and Sater, *A History of Chile, 1808–2002*; María Verónica Cano Christiny et al., "Conocer para legislar y hacer política: los desafíos de Chile ante un nuevo escenario migratorio" (Santiago: Centro Latinoamericano y Caribeño de Demografía (CELADE) – División de Población de la CEPAL, 2009); Jorge Martínez Pizarro, "Exigencias y posibilidades para políticas de población y migración internacional. El contexto latinoamericano y el caso de Chile" (Santiago: Centro Latinoamericano y Caribeño de Demografía (CELADE) – División de Población de la CEPAL, 2002); Lorenzo Agar, "Inmigrantes en Chile, un desafío para la interculturalidad," *Novamérica* 115 (2007); Jean Pierre Blancpain, "Francia y los franceses en Chile 1700–1980" (Chile: Hachette, Ediciones Pedagógicas Chilenas [EPC], Editorial Universitaria, 1987); Jean Pierre Blancpain, "Los alemanes en Chile 1816–1945" (Santiago: Hachette, Ediciones Pedagógicas Chilenas [EPC], Editorial Universitaria, 1985); Lucas Bonacic-Doric, *Historia de los yugoslavos en Magallanes* (Chile: Imprenta La Nacional); Baldomero Estrada, *Presencia italiana en Chile* (Valparaíso: Ediciones Universitarias de Valparaíso, 2005); Enrique Fernández, "La emigración francesa en Chile, 1875–1914: Entre integración social y mantenimiento de la especificidad," *Amérique Latine Histoire et Mémoire* (2006); Gilberto Harris, *Emigrantes e inmigrantes en Chile, 1810–1915. Nuevos aportes y notas revisionistas* (Valparaíso: Universidad de Playa Ancha, 2001); Carmen Norambuena, "Política y legislación inmigratoria en Chile, 1830–1920," Cuadernos de Humanidades, *10, Historia* – Serie 3, Departamento de Historia, Facultad de Humanidades, Santiago de Chile, Universidad Santiago de Chile, 1990; Cristián Doña and Amanda Levinson, "Chile: Moving Towards a Migration Policy," accessed June 3, 2011. http://www.migrationinformation.org/Feature/display.cfm?ID=199

45. Collier and Sater, *A History of Chile, 1808–2002*, 94.

46. Collier and Sater, *A History of Chile, 1808–2002*, 94. In 1914, foreigners owned 49% of all industry in Chile. Teresa Rodríguez, Las migraciones internacionales en Chile, Buenos Aires, Secretaría General de la OEA, 1982; see also Norambuena, "Política y legislación inmigratoria en Chile, 1830–1920."

47. Doña-Reveco and Amanda Levinson, "The Chilean State and the Search for a New Migration Policy."

48. For a discussion of the use of the transnational frame in labor history, see the chapters by French et al. in *Workers Across the Americas: The Transnational Turn in Labor History*, ed. Leon Fink (New York: Oxford University Press, 2011).

49. Purcell and Riquelme, *Ampliando miradas: Chile y su historia en un tiempo global,* 10. Their work builds on recent studies that examine the "tyranny of the national" in national historical literatures. For example, see Gérard Noiriel, *La Tyrannie du nacional. Le droit d'asile en Europe (1793–1993)* (Paris: Calman-Levy, 1991); Thomas Bender, *Rethinking American History in a Global Age* (Berkeley: University of California Press, 2002); George Iggers and Edward Wang, *A Global History of Modern Historiography* (Harlow, UK: Pearsons-Longman, 2008); Joaquín Fermandois, *Mundo y fin de mundo: Chile en la política mundial, 1900–2004* (Santiago: Ediciones Universidad Católica de Chile, 2005); Alfredo Riquelme and Michelle León, *Globalización: Historia y actualidad* (Santiago: Ministerio de Educación de Chile, 2003).

50. Purcell and Riquelme, *Ampliando miradas: Chile y su historia en un tiempo global,* 12.

51. The nearly comprehensive digest, *Historiografía chilena: Fichero bibliográfico, 1959–1996* (Santiago: Instituto de Historia, Pontífica Universidad Católica de Chile, 2000) records works on Chilean history published in Chile and abroad between 1959 and 1996. Of the ninety-four publications listed in the category "History of Immigration and Colonization," only one pertains to the history of non-European immigration to Chile (Japanese). The overwhelming majority of studies focus on German, Italian, and Spanish immigration histories. As further indication of this historiographic omission, in his two-volume review of the Chilean historiography, Cristian Gazmuri omits immigration as a category of analysis, examining only the concept of the frontier with reference to works such as Mario Góngora's *Vagabundaje y sociedad fronteriza.* Cristian Gazmuri, *Historia de la Historiografía chilena (1842–1970)* (Santiago: Editorial Taurus y Centro de Investigaciones Barros Arana, 2006).

52. Martínez Pizarro, *El encanto de los datos: Sociodemográfica de la inmigración en Chile según el censo de 2002.*

53. In "Conocer para legislar y hacer política," 23–25, Cano Christiny et al. provide a comprehensive list of recent immigration studies, with increasing focus on Peruvian immigration after 2000.

54. Aside from a temporary growth of immigrants from Korea, during the dictatorship, the number of foreign-born in Chile reached a historic low of 84,000, only 0.75% of the country's total population. Cristián Doña-Reveco and Amanda Levinson, "The Chilean State and the Search for a New Migration Policy" *Ignire-Centro de Estudio Política Pública* (2012): 67–90. See also Alberto Vargas del Campo, "Hacia una Política de Inmigración. Los inmigrantes económicos: Criterios para su elegibilidad," *Revista Diplomacia* 73 (1997).

55. See analysis of 1984 law in the report, "Nuevo reglamento de extranjería," Departamento jurídico de la Vicaria de la Solidaridad. Documento 002129.

56. My review of several mainstream periodicals from these periods revealed consistent and limited responses to the 1975 and 1984 laws. The title of one article in *La Tercera de la hora* (November 25, 1984) was an example of the overall reaction to the legislation: "Law Prohibits Entrance of Foreign Agitators to Chile, also to [Gun and Drug] Traffickers." A review of the opposition press in the well-organized press clippings collection at the Fundación Vicaría de la Solidaridad revealed very little commentary on the Alien Status laws. This is not entirely surprising since most opposition periodicals focused their attention on the country's growing exile population and the slim possibility of their return and reinstatement of civil rights.

57. Ministerio de Relaciones Exteriores, República of Chile, "Decree Law N° 1,094 of 1975," accessed on February 4, 2011. http://www.extranjeria.gov.cl/filesapp/ley_reglamento_ingles.pdf

58. Interview with Víctor Paiba Cossios (Santiago: March 20, 2011). Santiago's most outspoken immigrant activist, Paiba Cossios has himself faced deportation and self-publishes a monthly newsletter, "La voz del inmigrante."

59. La Tercera, "Christian Espejo: 'Muchos peruanos lideran bandas de delincuentes'," accessed on June 13, 2011. http://latercera.com/contenido/674_190106_9.shtml

60. Tania Vásquez, "La migración peruana a Chile: el crecimiento de la comunidad binacional peruano-chilena," *Revista Argumentos* 8, no. 1 (2014).

61. Also known as "birthright citizenship," *jus solis* grants citizenship or nationality to any individual born in the territory of a given nation.

62. Informe Anual sobre Derechos Humanos en Chile, 2010. http://www.derechoshumanos .udp.cl/archivo/informe-anual/, 238. Chile is a signatory of the 1960 Convention.

63. Under the government of Eduardo Frei, the 1998 amnesty benefitted approximately 23,000 foreigners, 21,000 of which were Peruvian. The 2007 amnesty similarly granted 32,000 Peruvians new visas out of a total 45,000.

64. Winn, *Victims of the Chilean Miracle: Workers and Neoliberalism in the Pinochet Era, 1973–2002*, 11.

65. For a discussion of the global mobility capital and labor among business elites, see Saskia Sassen, *The Mobility of Labor and Capital: A Study in International Investment and Labor Flow* (Cambridge: Cambridge University Press, 1988). On denationalized elites and agendas, see Saskia Sassen, ed., *Global Networks, Linked Cities* (New York: Routledge, 2002).

66. My thanks go to Daniela Serra and Andrés Kalawski for obtaining a pamphlet for me. The Plaza de Armas is also known as "la pequeña Lima" due to its function in Santiago as a public gathering space for Peruvian immigrants.
Election campaigning abroad has long been a familiar strategy to many of the millions of Latin American and Caribbean descendent people living in the United States. For an excellent study, see Michael Jones-Correa, "Under Two Flags: Dual Nationality in Latin America and Its Consequences for Naturalization in the United States," *International Migration Review* 35, no. 4 (2001): 997–1029.

67. As one measure of the importance of Peru's migrant community to their country of origin, in 2008 Peruvian migrants from around the world sent home remittances worth US$2.96 billion, more than the combined value of the country's foreign direct investment and official development assistance, tourism revenues, and agricultural exports. Berg, "El Quinto Suyo," 123.

68. "Unos 62.000 peruanos en Chile pueden votar hoy en las elecciones de su país," *Que Es?* accessed on May 20, 2011. http://www.que.es/ultimas-noticias/espana /201104101952-unos-62.000-peruanos-chile-pueden-efe.html; Berg, "El Quinto Suyo." Peruvian migrants have a long history of settlement in Chile. During the colonial period Peruvian migrants in large numbers worked in Chile, principally in Santiago. Jaime Valenzuela Márquez, "Inmigrantes en busca de identidad: Los indios *cuzcos* de Santiago de Chile, entre clasificación colonial y estrategia social," in *América colonial: Denominaciones, clasificaciones e identidades*, eds. Alejandra Araya Espinoza and Jaime Valenzuela Márquez (Santiago: RIL, 2010); Jaime Valenzuela Márquez, "Indígenas andinos en Chile colonial: Inmigración, inserción espacial, integración económica y movilidad social," *Revista de Indias* 70, no. 250 (2010): 749–778.

In the early part of the twentieth century, along with Bolivians, Peruvians represented one of the largest national groups in the country. Simon Collier and William Stater, *A History of Chile, 1808–2002* (Cambridge: Cambridge University Press, 2004), 172.

69. Peruvian migration to Chile is part of a larger regional trend in Latin America in which populations not only emigrate to the United States and Western Europe, but to neighboring countries within the region. The United Nations estimates that in 2010 the 7,480,267 migrants from Latin American and the Caribbean accounted for the 213,943,812 worldwide total. United Nations, Department of Economic and Social Affairs, Population Division, *Trends in International Migrant Stock: The 2008 Revision* (2009).

70. Jorge Durand and Douglas S. Massey, "New World Orders: Continuities and Changes in Latin American Migration," *ANNALS, AAPSS* 630 (2010): 20–52.

71. Durand and Massey, "New World Orders: Continuities and Changes in Latin American Migration."

72. Silke Staab and Kristen Hill Maher, "The Dual Discourse about Peruvian Domestic Workers in Santiago de Chile: Class, Race, and a Nationalist Project," *Latin American Politics and Society* 48, no. 1 (2006): 87–116. For studies on the history of Mapuche and indigenous populations in Chile, see Patricia Richards, *Race and the Chilean Miracle: Neoliberalism, Democracy and Indigenous Rights* (Pittsburgh: University of Pittsburgh Press, 2013). See also Jose Bengoa, ed., *La memoria olvidada: Historia de los pueblos indígenas de Chile* (Santiago: Cuadernos Bicentenario, 2004).

73. María Florencia Jensen Solivellas, "Inmigrantes en Chile: la exclusión vista desde la política migratoria chilena," paper presented at *El III Congreso de la Asociación Latinoamericana de Población, ALAP*, Córdoba, Argentina, 2008. The 2005 INE-DICOEX index registered approximately 700,000 Chileans resident abroad for economic, political, and personal reasons. Instituto Nacional de Estadísticas y Dirección para la Comunidad de Chilenos en el Exterior (INE-DICOEX), Registro de chilenos en el exterior: Dónde viven, cuántos son y qué hacen los chilenos en el exterior, Santiago de Chile, 2005.

74. Steve Stern, *Reckoning with Pinochet: The Memory Question in Democratic Chile, 1989–2006* (Durham, NC: Duke University Press, 2010), 212.

75. Stern, *Reckoning with Pinochet: The Memory Question in Democratic Chile, 1989–2006*, 177. Kathy Araujo et al. cite an average growth rate of 5.5% for the entire decade. *Migrantes andinas en Chile: El caso de la migración peruana* (Santiago: Fundación Instituto de la Mujer, 2002). See also Winn, *Victims of the Chilean Miracle: Workers and Neoliberalism in the Pinochet Era, 1973–2002*.

76. Levels of direct foreign investment increased rapidly from 1990 ($661 million) to 1999 ($9,221 million). Staab and Hill, "The Dual Discourse about Peruvian Domestic Workers in Santiago de Chile: Class, Race, and a Nationalist Project," 106.

77. Out of 169 countries, Chile ranked 45, Peru, 63. United Nations, "Human Development Reports," accessed on May 24, 2011. http://hdr.undp.org/en/. See also Dante Contreras, "Distribución del ingreso en Chile: Nueve hechos y algunos mitos," *Perspectivas* 2, no. 2 (1999): 311–332; Ernesto Stein et al., *The Politics of Policies: Economic and Social Progress in Latin America* (Washington, DC: Inter-American Development Bank, 2006).

78. Solange Muñoz, "Peruvian Migration to Chile: Challenges for National Identity, Human Rights and Social Policy" (Santiago: CLASPO Report, 2005), 1–2.

79. Stern, *Reckoning with Pinochet: The Memory Question in Democratic Chile, 1989–2006*, 176–184.

80. Andrés Zahler Torres, "¿En qué país vivimos los chilenos?" *Opinión*, accessed June 25, 2011. http://ciperchile.cl/2011/06/06/%C2%BFen-que-pais-vivimos-los-chilenos/

81. For an overview of Pinochet's aggressive neoliberal transformation of Chile's economy model after the Chicago School of Economics, see Collier and Stater, *A History of Chile, 1808–2002*, 364–376; and continued similar economic policies under the post-1990 Concertación governments, 394 ff.

82. Collier and Stater, *A History of Chile, 1808–2002*, 182 and 184.

83. Javier Couso, "Chile: The End of Privatopia?" *Berkeley Review of Latin American Studies* (2013), accessed on July 8, 2014, http://clas.berkeley.edu/research/chile-end-privatopia.

84. Oscar Dancourt, "Neoliberal Reforms and Macroeconomic Policy in Peru," *CEPAL Review* 67 (1999): 51–73.

85. Araujo et al., *Migrantes andinas en Chile: El caso de la migración peruana*

86. Jürgen Golte and Norma Adams, *Los caballos de Troya de los invasores: Estrategias campesinas en la conquista de la Gran Lima* (Lima: Instituto de Estudios Peruanos, 1987); Peru Instituto Nacional de Estadística e Informática, 2008, accessed on May 25, 2011, http://www.inei.gob.pe/

87. Peru is the third largest market for Chilean capital after Brazil and Argentina, with over $10 billion invested over the past twenty years. *La Tercera*, "Inversiones chilenas en Perú," June 6, 2011.

88. Ayumi Takenaka et al., "Peruvian Migration in a Global Context," and Jorge Durand, "The Peruvian Diaspora: Portrait of a Migratory Process," both in *Latin American Perspectives* 37, no. 121 (2010).

89. Similar restrictions have been implemented in Spain, Italy, and Japan, the other top destinations for Peru's migrants. Ulla Berg and Carla Tamagno, "El Quinto Suyo from above and from below: State Agency and Transnational Political Practices among Peruvian Migrants in the US and Europe," *Latino Studies* 4, no. 3 (2006): 258–281.

90. Interview with Emilia M. (May 23, 2011).

91. Takenaka et al., "Peruvian Migration in a Global Context."

92. Winn, *Victims of the Chilean Miracle: Workers and Neoliberalism in the Pinochet Era, 1973–2002*, 3.

93. Eilis O'Neill, "How Will Chile's President-Elect Bachelet Tackle Immigration Reform?" *The Christian Science Monitor*, December 16, 2013, accessed on July 7, 2014. http://www.alaskadispatch.com/article/20131216/how-will-chiles-president-elect-bachelet-tackle-immigration-reform

94. Tania Vásquez, "La migración peruana a Chile: El crecimiento de la comunidad binacional peruano-chilena," *Revista Argumentos* 8, no. 1 (2014).

CHAPTER 2

Bolivians in Buenos Aires

Human Rights, Immigration, and Democratic Participation

EDUARDO J. VIOR

Argentina belongs to a group of countries whose population has increased mainly through immigration from abroad since the mid-nineteenth century.[1] Between 1850 and 1950, most immigrants came from Southern and Eastern Europe as well as from Lebanon. However, over the past 60 years, people coming from the neighboring countries in South America have taken the lead. Some of them have mixed with the local population; a few have become rich. However, only those wealthy immigrants who adopted the lifestyle of the Argentinian elite have been recognized as "equals" in the eyes of Argentinian society.[2] Yet economic success alone has not yielded the same rights as those held by native Argentines.

This is especially the experience of Bolivian immigrants, who have arrived over the last 50 years. What distinguishes them is their ability to work hard and long hours, and their ambition of upward social mobility, but they get too little recognition. Why has this been the case? Many Bolivians who work the land in semirural areas surrounding most Argentinian cities have experienced a considerable economic ascent and, in some ways, social acknowledgment in the communities where they live through pressure on and negotiations with the local elites. On the contrary, some of their countrymen who are active in the garment industry in the City of Buenos Aires and its suburbs have achieved the same economic success, but they have not been publically recognized. What is more, most of the people working in this branch of the textile industry are brutally exploited in sweatshops, and they are only seen or heard in the public sphere when serious accidents occur and people die.[3]

It could be argued that this is the fate of all immigrants. Nevertheless, there are different "classes" of migrants all over the world depending on the reigning political, economic, and cultural systems of the host countries but also in terms of their color, origin, education, and, naturally, their wealth. In most countries these differences are sanctioned by the legal system, but in Argentina the protection of human rights, together with regional agreements and the legal system, guarantees South American citizens free entry to the country. In addition, Argentine law endows all registered immigrants with the same civic, economic, social, and cultural rights that are already granted to nationals. In some districts they also enjoy political rights. Notwithstanding, state officials and public opinion differ between "desirable" and "undesirable" immigrants, mainly according to their skin color. Therefore, it is evident that, although Argentina's legal system grants many rights to immigrants, the racial and cultural prejudices predominating in the country justify the treatment of some immigrant communities as belonging to a "second-class" population and their confinement in ethnic and cultural enclaves. This has resulted in the effective exclusion of the immigrants and their descendants from the public sphere and agenda. Immigrants are virtually invisible in the processes of formulating and implementing public policies. This exclusion and lack of visibility have had very serious effects on how Argentinians and immigrant communities live together.

At the beginning of the twentieth century in Argentina, Italians, Spaniards, Jews, and Arabs were subjected to similar discrimination. However, they succeeded in achieving some kind of political and cultural recognition. Why has it been so difficult, then, for Bolivian immigrants to receive social acknowledgment today? This is a nontrivial question, because the ongoing existence of these discriminated enclaves restrains the development of Argentine citizenship.[4] This chapter analyzes the "objective" and "subjective" conditions limiting the access of the Bolivian community in the City of Buenos Aires to Argentinian citizenship.[5] As this chapter aims to clarify the existing relationship between political rights and cultural and ethnic constructions, it begins with an examination of an intercultural approach to citizenship.

THE INTERCULTURAL APPROACH TO CITIZENSHIP

Human Rights and Questions of Universality

Mainstream political science usually considers immigrant communities, especially immigrants from non-Western countries, as unable to build democratic representation and organizations, unless they adopt Western values, norms, and symbols.[6] If the host country is also non-European, then the problem seems unsolvable. Behind this pessimism lie hidden ethnocentric assumptions about the values, norms, and symbols needed for the development of democratic citizenship.[7]

In the United States, Canada, and Western Europe, from the beginning of migration studies at the University of Chicago in the 1920s until the 1970s, an assimilationist paradigm prevailed, supporting the acculturation of immigrants, trying to make them "normal" citizens of the host countries.[8] Linguistic homogenization and the military service (mainly the participation of immigrants and their descendants in both world wars) were the most important instruments for achieving this goal.

Simultaneously, the liberal and democratic revolutions and reforms that expanded civic and political rights from the 1830s onward achieved this goal on the basis of a contradictory assumption: the foundations of civic and political rights are the universal and common rights of all adult men, but these rights apply only if all citizens share the same duties of loyalty to their homeland and state (or king). Thus, the universality of these rights depends on the power of states with specific cultural forms.

The Universal Declaration of Human Rights (1948) subordinated national allegiance to the universality of human rights. Nevertheless, until the mid-1970s, since there was not an international authority capable of enforcing the validity of these rights, their application depended on the goodwill of the state. Although the main democratic countries had already included human rights in their constitutional and legal systems,[9] the strong national framework within which the rights were guaranteed shaped the way in which subaltern groups—including immigrants and their descendants—could participate in political life.[10]

A multilateral international stage was built on the framework of the Helsinki process from 1975 onward. This scenario successfully combined respect for national self-determination with the universal validity of human rights. Simultaneously, from the 1970s onward, the reception of Thomas H. Marshall's reflections on citizenship[11] changed the perspective of political theory on this subject. Rather than a concession of the state, citizenship increasingly became a subjective right people had to demand from their respective states. At the same time, feminist theory and the upheaval of ethnic and cultural minorities in Western Europe, Canada, and the United States highlighted gender and ethnic differences and inequalities.

Considering that these differences give rise to different perceptions of the world and different abilities to construct narratives about oneself and the surrounding world, multiculturalist authors have attempted, since the early 1980s, to combine the constitutional and legal frameworks of liberal democracies with the recognition of the cultural specificities of ethnic minorities and immigrant groups.[12] Although it is not possible to reproduce here the complex discussion on multiculturalism,[13] the author of this chapter acknowledges the importance Charles Taylor assigns to recognition as the basis and mechanism for identity building.[14] Problematic identity building is always linked to a nonachieved or truncated recognition. As a result, the barriers immigrant groups face as they attempt to act independently in the host society are always related to the difficulties this society has in recognizing the newcomers.[15] Therefore, identity-building processes always have a relational character. Controversy arises, however, about the characterization of the relation between cultures. Is this relationship equal or unequal? Furthermore, if the relationship is unequal, is this inequality contingent or necessary?

Universal Rights and the Recognition of Identity:
The Intercultural Approach

Intercultural authors have frequently pointed out the normative locus that constitutional and political bases of power have in multiculturalist thinking. Multiculturalist authors usually underline that democratic states should guarantee the right of cultural minorities to live according to their own customs, to practice their religions, and to educate their children following their own moral principles and specific habits. However, this guarantee depends on their allegiance to the ethical, economic, and juridical foundations of the political order. Intercultural authors, on the contrary, criticize this condition as a reinforcement of the dominance of white elites behind the mask of tolerance.[16]

The intercultural perspective is based on a discursive and historical reconstruction of the theory of human rights.[17] The definitions of human rights commonly applied by international organizations agree that they are universal, innate, inalienable, and inseparable,[18] but there is no common understanding of what universality means.[19]

The intercultural approach to human rights allows the elucidation of the political implications of the human right to migrate. Human beings have always moved around the world. All peoples and nations have their origin in migration, and, if human rights are inherent to human beings, they carry with them all human rights wherever they move. This fact is indirectly acknowledged by the international documents on human rights, insofar as they recognize the right of all citizens to circulate freely through their home countries and to abandon them. However, since the whole world is composed of countries, the right to abandon the home country necessarily implies the right to enter another one, bearing all human rights, including political rights. The effectiveness of the right to political participation, however, depends on the arrangements each nation-state has made to govern itself, and on the agreements between the host cultures and the immigrant ones.

A key assumption of interculturalist migration theory maintains that the links between the majority population and immigrants are structurally asymmetric.[20] Except in the settler colonies of the nineteenth century,[21] the unequal development of the world system had already set the framework for migratory movements under strongly unequal conditions.[22] Socioeconomic differences and racial constructions inside the nations and between them also determine the submission of immigrants through the legitimating reference that leading elites make to the national image.[23] Insofar as the immigrant group reproduces this devaluation of the image of itself, it loses its capacity to narrate its own history and, consequently, to present itself to other social partners. In this way, the communication channels between—and within—the immigrant group, on the one hand, and the state and the majority, on the other, became obstructed.

As a result, communities formed by immigrants can only participate freely and autonomously in the democratic systems within the host states if the host state and the society, on the one hand, and the immigrant minority, on the other, engage in a permanent intercultural dialogue. To be authentically intercultural, this dialogue must proceed from the recognition of the equal value of all participants and the disposition of both sides to deal with the changes their encounter fosters. The scene and the subject of this dialogue can both be termed "emerging intercultural citizenship"[24]: the political space for democratic conflict and negotiation between the dominant and subordinate cultures, and as the sum of all citizens interchanging meanings and demands between cultures.

The question of how the members of subordinate cultures represent themselves remains unanswered. Some European studies and the author's own research[25] underline the role of "intercultural mediators," those persons and/or groups belonging mostly to the subordinate cultures, who are able to "translate" the necessities and demands of these subaltern peoples in the codes of the dominant culture.[26] When the "translation" process begins, a communication sphere between both sides takes form, which enables the circulation of information, meanings, and persons from one side to another. In these "contact zones,"[27] the meanings produced by both sides mutually interpenetrate. As a result of this crossing, both cultures modify themselves and each other. At a political-theoretical level, this means that no political system remains unchanged if it coexists with an important immigrant community living under its jurisdiction. Whether the participants want it or not, the multifaceted contacts between both sides distort all existing rules for the interplay among dominance and legitimation. The study of the meaning-building processes in these "meeting spaces," and the role that intercultural mediators play in them, is therefore fundamental to understanding the (possible) modifications of the political game.

THE HISTORY OF IMMIGRATION TO ARGENTINA

Argentina's independence from Spain in 1816 started 50 years of civil war over the control of revenue from the port of Buenos Aires.[28] In 1880, General Julio A. Roca unified elites, establishing a cohesive oligarchy and putting an end to the civil wars. The new Argentinian state encouraged European immigration with the aim of "whitening" the country. Between 1881 and 1914, a total of 4.2 million immigrants arrived, including Italians, Spaniards, French from the southern regions, Jews from Eastern Europe, and Christian and Muslim Arabs from Syria and Lebanon.[29]

Three combined processes during this period conditioned the building of a neocolonial Argentina. First, the bureaucratized army that resulted from the war against Paraguay (1865–1870), and the 1879 conquest of Patagonia, guaranteed the unity of the oligarchy and shaped the later transition to mass democracy under President Hipólito Yrigoyen (1916–1922 and 1928–1930).[30] Second, low prices for meat exported to Great Britain[31] intensified concentration of land ownership, allowing ranchers to maintain their high profit margins through economies of scale.[32] As a complement to this concentration process, the farms' leasing system hampered the development of a rural middle class.[33] Third, the combination of these economic and political trends, the oligarchy's racist treatment of the subjugated Indians and some European immigrants,[34] and its intellectual dependency on Europe[35] gave rise to a free-riding mentality and a cult of appearances, which, even today, hamper productive investments.

In 1854, the City of Buenos Aires had a population of 90,000 inhabitants, which rose to 670,000 by 1895.[36] In 1914, immigrants represented 30% of the total population of Argentina.[37] In the capital itself, this group made up between 60% and 80% of the total population. In 1914, the number of immigrants reached its highest historical level, constituting 30% of the whole population (7.9 million people).[38]

The economic recession in Argentina after the 1929 crisis put an end to massive European immigration.[39] Shortly after World War II, however, following Peron's industrialization efforts (1946–1955), Argentina attracted qualified immigrants from Central and Eastern Europe, in addition to the traditional Spaniards and Italians.[40]

Since the 1950s, immigration has come mainly from the bordering countries. Between 1950 and 1980, Paraguayans fleeing the Stroessner dictatorship and poverty represented between 40% and 65% of this flow.[41] Brazil, Bolivia, Chile, Peru, and Uruguay also supplied migrants until the 1990s. Even though this regional migration never accounted for more than 3% of the total population, since the 1960s it has been larger than immigration from nonbordering countries.

Until the 1960s, circular migration across the borders was a normal practice. Up to the 1990s, labor migration from bordering countries mainly reflected demands for seasonal workers as well as those in housekeeping, construction, and commerce.

From the mid-1970s to the beginning of the 1980s, that is, the period of military dictatorship (1976–1983), many Argentinians emigrated to other Latin American countries, as well as to the United States, Canada, and Spain. Between the 1990s and the 2000s a large number of skilled workers and professionals also left the country, but they began to come back after 2003, as the economy improved.[42]

Since the beginning of human settlement in Argentina's present territory, there have been strong links between its northwestern regions and the Andean highlands, which currently belong to Bolivia, and, by the 1960s, seasonal workers from the Bolivian highlands had become ubiquitous in the Argentinian northwest. As the regional production that sustained these provinces failed during this decade, Bolivian workers moved to the cities in the central and eastern part of the country, where they found jobs in the construction industry and in agriculture.[43] After the introduction of neoliberalism in Bolivia, in 1985, a second wave of migrants came from the mines and the textile industry of the La Paz Department to Buenos Aires and began to work in the textile and garment industries.[44] During the 1990s, 150,000 Peruvians also came to Argentina, fleeing the civil war in their country and settling mainly in Buenos Aires.[45]

LEGAL FRAMEWORK GOVERNING
INTERNATIONAL MIGRATION

In 1994, Argentina's National Constitution was reformed. However, legislators avoided modifying the first chapter and section 25 in particular, maintaining provisions that encouraged immigration from Europe. The privilege to immigrate was not modified until 2004 with the establishment of the new Migration Act 25,871/2004,[46] in which Article 4 proclaims the human right to migration:

> The right to migration is a fundamental and inalienable human right which is guaranteed by the Argentine Republic on the basis of the principles of equality and universality.

Argentina was the first country in the world to establish this right as a part of its legal framework (Uruguay followed in 2008). The Argentine Act establishes rights and obligations of foreigners, specifies conditions for entry and residence in Argentina, and incorporates provisions regarding nationals abroad. Modifying the reception criteria established in the Constitution, it prioritizes people from the MERCOSUR countries.[47] The corresponding Regulatory Decree 616 was issued in April 2010.

The 2004 Migration Act reaffirms equal access of migrants to social services, public assets, health, education, justice, work, employment, and social security. It sets up the right of immigrants to be informed regarding their rights and obligations, and it provides them the possibility to participate or to be consulted on decisions related to the life and management of the communities in which they reside. It also establishes the right to family reunification, guarantees access to education and health, regardless of migration status, and it prohibits the expulsion of immigrants without a warrant. From the beginning, however, the implementation of this law has been resisted by many immigration officials and members of the intelligence and security agencies who fear the loss of control over Argentina's population.

Undoubtedly, Argentina's migration policy, together with Uruguay's, is the most progressive in the Americas. These South American immigrants have the same civic, social, and economic rights as citizens, and all immigrants get their documents as quickly as nationals. Immigrants are also eligible for the same grants as poor Argentinians, and they have the right to send their children to the same public schools as Argentinians do. Immigrants are also entitled to receive the same obligatory vaccines as Argentinian children. However, the Argentinian immigration policy ends here. No systematic efforts have been made to harmonize the work of the state agencies charged with incorporating immigrants and their descendants into Argentine society, or to increase the awareness of officials about the cultural particularities of the newcomers. Except for some isolated cases, neither businesses nor trade unions have developed special initiatives for foreign workers. Nor do the police or other security agencies have the cultural abilities needed to deal adequately with groups with different cultural backgrounds.

The immediate effect of these lapses is the effective exclusion of the immigrants and their descendants from the public sphere and agenda. Immigrants are virtually invisible in the processes of formulating and implementing public policies. This lack of vision has very serious effects on how Argentinians and immigrant communities live together.

BOLIVIANS IN ARGENTINA

Since the first settlements in the central and southern Andean region, people have moved between the northern highlands and the southern lowlands. From the sixteenth to the beginning of the nineteenth century, the current territories of Argentina and Bolivia were united in the same colonial district. This unity was broken during the independence wars (1810–1818), because the Spanish army controlled the territory north of the Humahuaca Ravine until the liberation of the Altiplano in 1824. When the government of Buenos Aires waived its rights to these areas, Bolivia became independent.[48]

From its foundation to the nationalist revolution of 1952, the Bolivian Republic was controlled by oligarchic elites. As long as the rural areas were subject to quasi-feudal conditions, they could retain a large part of their population, but when peasants obtained property titles, thanks to the Revolution, they began to push out the spillover population. Because the border with Argentina was not clearly marked, the circulation of Bolivian seasonal workers between both countries was common, but the crisis of the regional economies in northern Argentina in the middle of the 1960s pushed the Bolivian workers to central and eastern Argentinian towns, where they began to work in construction, agriculture, and other labor-intensive industries, as well as manufacturing.[49]

As the 1998 economic recession in Argentina began, unemployment affected immigrants first, but, thanks to their associative networks and their practice of not saving money in banks, they withstood the crisis better than other groups.[50]

THE BOLIVIAN COMMUNITY
IN THE CITY OF BUENOS AIRES

The City
The Metropolitan Area of Buenos Aires (AMBA) is a maze of overlapping jurisdictions. On the one side, there is the City of Buenos Aires, Argentina's Federal District, where almost 3 million people live. On the other side, there are twenty municipal districts that belong to the Province of Buenos Aires, with more than 10 million inhabitants.[51] As the City of Buenos Aires only became autonomous in 1996, after the reform of the Constitution in 1994, many of the powers and prerogatives of the local government are still concentrated in the central state.

Since the civil-military dictatorship (1976–1983), the metropolitan region has been strongly fragmented between the North (rich) and South (poor). Whereas the upper middle class resides in gated communities along the northern and western motorways, the middle and lower middle classes concentrate in the commercial and service centers of the main regional cities, and the low-income groups live far from the centers. Most jobs are concentrated in the City of Buenos Aires, which doubles its daytime population.

Inside the City, approximately 170,000 people live in twenty shantytowns. Some 150,000 live in very precarious conditions in hotels and guesthouses. Between the censuses of 2001 and 2010, real estate speculation forced many people to migrate outside the city or inside it, from the northern to the western and southern communities. So, while the total population of the City dropped slightly in this period, communities 7, 8, and 9 (see Figure 2.1) have increased their population.[52] As a highly topical, specialized report states:

> In the Autonomous City of Buenos Aires, 173,721 households (more than a half million "*porteños*"[53]) have housing problems, because they live in precarious

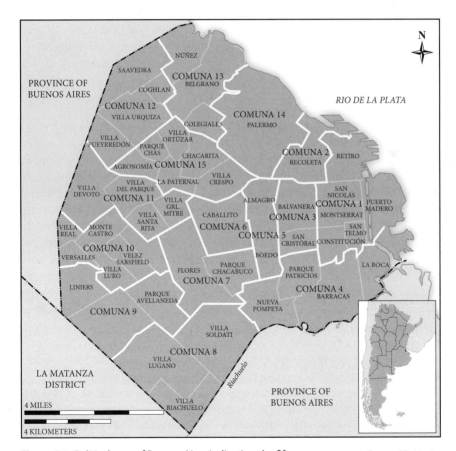

Figure 2.1 Political map of Buenos Aires indicating the fifteen communes. Source: Ministerio de Educación de la Nación–Mapoteca. Available at http://mapoteca.educ.ar/files/index.html.1.5.html

buildings or because of overcrowding. Despite this housing deficit, 24% of the houses in the city are empty, i.e. about 341 thousand dwellings.[54]

Since 1999, *porteños* have elected their own mayor.[55] The last mayor of Buenos Aires was Mauricio Macri (born 1959). From 2005 until 2007, after a long period as president of Boca Juniors soccer club (1995–2007), where he built a still influential network of soccer hooligans,[56] businessmen, politicians, and senior police officers, Marci represented the City of Buenos Aires in the Lower House of Congress and held his office from 2007 to 2015. He was reelected in 2011 for a second term as mayor. His party, the Republican Proposal (PRO, following the Spanish acronym) is conservative. Following neoliberal principles,[57] Macri's strategy for urban development was based on the delimitation within the city of specific districts for certain categories of economic activity.[58] Although Macri developed several urban projects, the jobs they create were largely destined for well-educated middle- and upper-class Argentines; they had no effect on the creation of employment for unskilled workers, and they also increased property speculation. A well-oiled electoral machine ensures the support of even the poorest residents. Notwithstanding, in the election of Macri's Chief of Staff, Horacio Rodríguez Larreta, as the city's new mayor on July 19, 2015, the PRO obtained only 3 percentage points over their opponent, Martín Lousteau, who represented a broad middle right–middle left alliance. This result was interpreted by several political analysts as a sign of the fatigue of many people belonging to the middle and lower classes after 8 years of a PRO government.

Bolivian Migration

According to the latest National Population Census,[59] 345,272 Bolivians live in Argentina, making Bolivians the second largest immigrant group, immediately behind Paraguayans. The Bolivian community grew steadily between 1980 and 2010, but since then immigration has stopped, and in the last few years many Bolivians have gone back to their homeland. Many of them also rotate seasonally between both countries, making it very difficult to estimate how many Bolivians live continuously in Argentina. The real dimension of this community is greater than what is reflected by census numbers (approximately 1.3 million people), because many immigrants have taken Argentinian citizenship, others were not counted in the censuses, and most children who were born in Argentina[60] to Bolivian parents (although they are Argentinian citizens) remain attached to their community of origin.

Just over 55% of the Bolivian population in Argentina lives in the Metropolitan Area of Buenos Aires (AMBA, according to its Spanish abbreviation).[61] This high concentration can be explained by the conjunction within the AMBA of two different economic activities with a strong Bolivian presence: the garment industry in the city and its immediate southwestern neighborhoods, and agriculture in the southwestern and southern semirural peripheries of the region.

As described earlier, two successive immigration waves between the 1960s and the 1990s created the Bolivian community in Argentina. The first one came from Bolivia's southern departments and was composed mainly of creole or mestizo speakers of Spanish and/or Quechua. Mainly from peasant backgrounds, they generally work in the agricultural economy or in the construction industry.[62] The second wave of immigrants came from the department of La Paz. They speak mainly the indigenous language Aymara, work in the garment industry, and live primarily in the western areas of the AMBA. There are very few communication channels between these two groups.

The Bolivian Community

Since the arrival of the first Bolivians to the AMBA, they have gathered in certain shantytowns on the basis of both their kinship networks and the connections they keep with their regions of origin. As occurred under the dictatorship (1976–1983), the government of the City of Buenos Aires has brutally evicted the residents of several slums. The Bolivian immigrants in the so-called Barrio Charrúa resisted this displacement.[63] This successful experience further helped them build a strong territorial identity within the city. Since 1985, after the closure of the tin mines in Bolivia, many residents of department (state) of La Paz also moved to the AMBA.

The Bolivian community lives in a small corner of the southwest of the City,[64] in the slums surrounding the city to the east and south, and in a large urban corridor that originates in the neighboring district of La Matanza in the west, enters Buenos Aires City from the west and southwest, and winds through communities 7, 8 and 9, with some side branches toward community 4 (see Fig. 2.1). In effect, the Bolivian community occupies the section of Avenida Avellaneda situated between the Flores and Floresta quarters, an area that since the beginning of this century has become the center of the country's clothing industry. In this quarter, shoppers from all over converge. Many retailers, but also the general public, buy in this shopping mile. The adjacent streets are filled with warehouses and workshops (many of which are unregistered).

This reality is imperfectly supported by the census data.[65] According to the last Population Census, in 2010, 345,272 Bolivians lived in the City of Buenos Aires (C.A.B.A.), 76,609 of whom were born in Bolivia.[66] Two-thirds of the population born in Bolivia and who now live in the City of Buenos Aires inhabit the three west and southwest communities 7, 8, and 9.[67] As indicated earlier, this figure must be doubled, raising the population of the community of Bolivian origin in the C.A.B.A. to around 150,000. Most of this population has been residing in the City of Buenos Aires for a long time.[68]

The Communitarian Internalization of the "Chinese Pressure"

Bolivian workers in Argentina experience labor exploitation and physical violence everywhere they work. At the same time, however, most people working in the garment industry assume that being exploited is a transitory situation that they hope to overcome as soon as they can open their own workshops. That only few workers achieve this goal raises a question about the motivation for so many people to continue tolerating such extreme exploitation. This contradiction between the shared perception of the labor situation and the individual perception of one's own situation particularly catches the eye in field research.[69] Resolving this contradiction would make it easier to understand why this community does not seem to care about having strong political representatives to advocate for improving their living conditions.

Labor exploitation and slave labor emerged in Argentina's garment industry at the end of the twentieth century in the context of the worldwide trade liberalization that began in the mid-1990s. At that time, the Argentinian garment industry could not compete with the so-called Chinese pressure.[70] The extremely low labor costs in China and its aggressive export policy forced the transition to "nonvertical" production methods.[71] The dominant garment enterprises have retained control over design, marketing, image, molding, and tailoring tasks, and outsourced garment making, ironing, and finishing to intermediary workshops and facilitators, which, in turn, subcontract to home workers or to other workshops, and so on.[72] Workshop owners, distributors, and wholesalers account for 80% of the sector's entire earnings.[73]

As the entrepreneurs in all links of the production chain improve their profit rates by keeping wages low and transferring the investments in fixed capital to the last subcontractors,[74] there is very little motivation to invest in innovative technologies. In the City of Buenos Aires, real estate speculation and the legal restrictions on the licensing of commercial and industrial premises, to which garment workshops must adhere, are also noteworthy, as they date back to the last dictatorship.[75] Therefore, as transport and logistics are considerable cost points, and distributors seek quick access to the Avenida Avellaneda shopping mile, the west and southwest districts of the City are full of illegal sweatshops that pay steep bribes to inspectors and police officers who allow them to operate.

As soon as workers learn their trades and how the garment market works, they try to get the money to set up their own workshops and begin to exploit their own family members and/or other workers.[76] These practices allow an abusive social environment to arise and expand.[77] Police investigators[78] have estimated that about 15% of this sector of the garment industry works on the basis of slavery. Notwithstanding, slavery is not entrenched in Buenos Aires. Soon after their arrival in the city, the workers initially deceived by the recruiters in Bolivia begin to understand their situation. Some of them are allowed to go out on Sundays, when they make contact with other workers, or sometimes the sweatshop simply shuts its doors or moves to another location because of real estate speculation, and the workers become free. The Argentine legal system and the profusion of associations and organizations among the Bolivian workers in Buenos Aires offer many chances to escape slavery.[79]

Due to the conditions in these sweatshops, it is very difficult to get reliable official statistics. According to credible estimates, in the City of Buenos Aires there are approximately 5,000 garment workshops.[80] In the whole country, there may be 10,000. Following Adúriz's estimates, only 20% of the garment production is carried out in licensed establishments.[81]

Since 2003, the governments of Néstor Kirchner and Cristina Fernández had often intervened against slave labor, which has been included as a criminal offense in the Argentine Traffic Act 26,842/2013. Kirchner and Fernández promoted the organization of textile and garment cooperatives comprising a few hundred workers, but this has not eliminated illegality or slavery.[82] For its part, the government of the City of Buenos Aires has failed, since 2007, to prosecute exploitation and slave labor, perhaps for personal reasons.[83]

The entire labor and production system operating in garment workshops is supported by the collusion between city government, organized traffickers who mislead workers from Bolivia, and corrupt police. Further assistance comes from the numerous small radio stations broadcasting in Quechua and Aymara in the western quarters of Buenos Aires, which are regularly heard in the factories and workshops urging workers to mistrust "the Argentinians" (meaning, primarily, state officials) who aim to "close their workplaces." However, the enormous profit margins and the expansion of mass consumption promoted by the Kirchner and Fernández administrations induced Korean, Bolivian, and Argentinian entrepreneurs to keep working illegally and the workers to accept harsh working conditions, hoping someday to become bosses themselves.

UPDATING THE GHETTO

The Bolivian community in the City of Buenos Aires has become considerably politicized in recent years. The group identifies itself passionately with the indigenous and peasant movement in Bolivia, embodied in the figure of former President Evo Morales (1998–2016). However, this general political identification with the Morales government has resulted neither in better intracommunitarian political articulation nor in greater, more effective participation of the community in Argentinian politics.[84] The previously mentioned patronage and corrupt traits of the Argentinian political system, the limitations of the Argentinian migration policy, and the hegemony of an "obstructive" communitarian leadership (discussed later) are the main causes for this lack of articulation between demand and interest. This situation is determined by many causes. The representation of the Bolivian community is very difficult because of the irregular status of many immigrants, personal struggles between the community leaders, and the tendency of the majority of the latter to confuse their associative representation with their private business affairs.

The Federation of Bolivian Civic Associations in Argentina (FACBOL in Spanish), the umbrella organization representing most groups and associations of the community, was founded in 1995.[85] FACBOL claims to represent the community as a whole, but, according to a well-informed and deeply analytical broadcast report, the intertwining of its leaders with the sweatshop owners and the personal interests of these communitarian representatives has led to harsh clashes among them in recent years.[86] In the same report, Juan Carlos Estrada Vásquez, a Bolivian immigrant who worked years ago in illegal workshops (and who now edits the biweekly newspaper *El Visor Boliviano*), identifies FACBOL as the link between the Bolivian community and the group surrounding Mauricio Macri. "Alfredo Ayala is behind this entity. He is the president of the Bolivian Federative Civic Association (ACIFEBOL in Spanish), the greatest single member organization in FACBOL, and FACBOL's president, too, but in fact he is a multifunctional businessman and politician, who links legal and illegal business with the PRO-party."[87]

Thanks to Alfredo Ayala's mediation, the network of entrepreneurs controlling the garment industry in Buenos Aires has built firm and lasting ties with the city's political elite.[88] He uses his connections in politics, business, and policy to usurp the community's representation and build a network of power that controls a vast urban territory.[89] This group has two main political goals: (1) to achieve a downward adjustment of the standards and norms for the authorization of industrial premises and (2) to prevent the workers from organizing themselves.[90] This patron–client network represents an important endorsement of conservative dominance in Buenos Aires. Moreover, this hegemony is continuously reproduced by the majority of workers, who look up to Ayala as their model.

The complexity of structural conditions and hegemonic effects, in which the informal garment sector plays an active part, demands reconsideration of the question of the necessity of autonomous representation of the workers in the garment industry in the City of Buenos Aires. How far is this indispensable? Two propositions may elucidate the question: (a) only the free and equal articulation of these workers with other political and social organizations aimed at improving the living conditions of the popular groups can help Bolivian immigrants overcome overexploitation; and (b) if they do not organize themselves, nobody will do it for them.

The structural conditions in the garment industry and the prejudice predominating among workers and small entrepreneurs prevent the autonomous articulation of Bolivian immigrants with the mainstream society. For its part, the national government is inconsequential and has too little power to impose a reform of the labor market in Buenos Aires. The community's own intelligentsia has only weak links to the political organizations of the mainstream society and almost no connections with the workers in the garment sector. The combination of the obstructive role Ayala plays and the tenuous ties binding Bolivian intellectuals and activists to the majority of their co-nationals perhaps better explains the difficulties this community faces in expressing itself politically.

CONCLUSIONS: AN INTERCULTURAL APPROACH TO THE POLITICAL PARTICIPATION OF IMMIGRANTS

It is very difficult for Bolivian immigrants in Buenos Aires to improve their life conditions. Lack of recognition and representation perpetuate their exploitation. Even those who achieve economic success get no social recognition. This de facto apartheid reinforces the patronage bonds linking their obstructive leadership and the community elite upward to the City's elite and downward to their own clients. This authoritarian structure deepens ghetto construction and exploitation. Also complicit in this situation are the structures of the garment industry and the corrupt linkage between the City's elite and the immigrant community's current representatives. The lack of open communication channels among the community's own intellectuals, workers, and small business owners, on the one hand, and the social majority, on the other, plays its part too. The absence of a transversal migration policy in Argentina also contributes to ghetto building.

The exploitation of the workers in the garment industry is inherent to the political and economic system, and it reinforces the system's worst features. The lack of autonomous representation of the people working in the garment industry hinders further development of the democratic system, limiting the variety of groups that can participate effectively in it and distorting political competition through recourse to illegal means and criminally obtained money.

When the author first discovered the central role that "intercultural mediators"[91] play in the "contact zone" between host societies and immigrant communities, he had an exclusively positive view of it, but after having studied Alfredo Ayala and his group, his initial perception had to be modified. Two types of "intercultural mediator" can then be proposed:

- The "enabling mediators," who mostly belong to the subaltern community, identify the community's demands for rights and interests, include them in a coherent discourse, and translate it to the language and codes of the mainstream society and its state, with the intention of negotiating their implementation. The enabling mediator can be a single person or a group.
- "Obstructive mediators" are persons or groups who monopolize the relations between the state and the majority, on the one hand, and the ethnic and cultural minority, on the other, blocking the communication channels between both sides. Obstructive mediators convincingly fuse their perception of the needs of the subordinate community with their own particular interests, and they impose this combination as the agenda of the negotiations with the political system. They often appeal to a vague communitarian imaginary, presenting it as opposed to the image they build of the host country.

This second type of mediation currently prevails within the Bolivian community working in the garment industry in the City of Buenos Aires, and it is reinforced by the city's mayor and his associates. The mutual misperceptions help Buenos Aires's elite and community leadership to avoid political and economic competition in their respective arenas.

Depending on the origin of the political demands, theoretical and empirical studies of the political participation of communities that arise from immigration distinguish three types of political mobilization and/or participation:

a) Through individual ascent and assimilation to the patterns of the host country's hegemonic political culture. In immigrant communities this path is only open for some representatives of the middle classes, and it does not usually benefit the community as a whole.

b) Through communitarian mobilization for concrete demands. This type of mobilization is only possible in parliamentary systems and/or in political systems with strong cultural cleavages.

c) Through the adoption of the cleavages of the home country in the host nation. This type of mobilization and participation prevailed among the immigrants in Central and Northern Europe from the 1960s to the 1980s. Insofar as their home countries have built democratic systems and many immigrants have returned home, this type of political participation has lost importance. However, for those immigrant communities that have re-mained in the host countries, the failure of the political systems to recog-nize the elites arising from these communities has pushed them to embrace ghetto images and conduct.[92] This political enclosure promotes, among their children and grandchildren, the idealization of the home country, culture, or religion of their grandparents, and it prompts the adoption of ethnic and/or religious imaginaries.

Nowhere in Europe or North America are there intercultural political systems, in the sense that this chapter has argued for, but some successful local experiences of communitarian self-government in Western Europe suggest that it is possible to move beyond the limits of the national state. If regional integration processes convert monocentric, sovereign states into pluricentric confederative entities based on the right to free movement with multifaceted identification images, circular migration may become normal. The capacity of all parties involved to harmonize their requirements and to implement an ongoing, common policy aimed at broadening and deepening democracy is the main component of an "emerging intercultural citizenship."

NOTES

1. Australia, Canada, New Zealand, the United States, and Uruguay are also included in this group.
2. "Recognition" was first introduced in the social sciences by Charles Taylor (Charles Taylor and Amy Gutmann, *Multiculturalism: Examining the Politics of Recognition* [Princeton, NJ: Princeton University Press, 1994]) as a key category for the study of intercultural relations in pluricultural societies. As the author of this contribution has already explained in early works (Eduardo J. Vior, *Migraciones internacionales y ciudadanía democrática: Influencias de las comunidades de origen inmigrante sobre el desarrollo político en Alemania, Argentina y Brasil* [Saarbrücken: Editorial Aca-démica Española, 2012], 20–24), "recognition" refers here to an effect on the domi-nant discourse of the perception of a cultural minority constructed as "different." "Recognition" can be thus spoken of when ruling elites and the social majority are compelled to address their relationship to cultural minorities as an issue concerning the whole society.

3. Due to the precarious working conditions of sweatshops in the garment industry, there are often accidents. Most remain unnoticed by the media, but some particularly serious incidents enjoy public interest, like the 2006 fire in Luis Viale Street in the City of Buenos Aires, where eight people died and, more recently (April 27, 2015), in Páez Street, where two children lost their lives in a basement fire. The way in which the media cover such events, however, is extremely sensationalist, treating the workers in the garment industry exclusively as "victims" and not as people who act on their own behalf, who have needs and demands, and who are involved in the complex social and cultural framework of the immigrant enclave.

4. Rogers Brubaker, ed., *Immigration and the Politics of Citizenship in Europe and North America* (Boston: Boston University Press, 1989); Roberto Herrera Carassou, *La perspectiva teórica en el estudio de las migraciones* (México: Siglo XXI, 2006); Ruud Koopmans, "Partizipation der Migranten, Staatsbürgerschaft und Demokratie: Nationale und lokale Perspektiven," in *Strategien der Integration*, M. Pröhl and H. Hartmann, eds., 103–111 (Gütersloh: Bertelsmann, 2003); Ruud Koopmans and Paul Statham, "Migration and Ethnic Relations as a Field of Political Contention: An Opportunity Structure Approach," in *Challenging Immigration and Ethnic Relations Politics*, R. Koopmans and P. Statham, eds., 13–56 (Oxford: Oxford University Press, 2000); Ana M. López Sala, "Derechos de ciudadanía y estratificación cívica en sociedades de inmigración," in *Una discusión sobre la universalidad de los derechos humanos y la inmigración*, Ignacio Campoy, ed., 129–151 (Madrid: Dykinson/Universidad Carlos III, 2006); Douglas S. Massey, Joaquín Arango, Hugo Graeme, Ali Kouaouci, Adela Pellegrino, and J. Edward Taylor, "Teorías de migración internacional: una revisión y aproximación," *ReDCE* 10 (2008): 435–478; Ricard Zapata Barrero, *Ciudadanía e interculturalidad* (Barcelona: Anthropos, 2001).

5. These terms refer to the economic, social, and political conditions that influence the possibility for immigrants to participate in politics and government, as well as the ideological and psychological dispositions of people who have immigrated, which determine their capacity to organize themselves and to present their demands before the state.

6. This was the unanimous answer the author of this contribution received in 2002, as he began to do research on "Democratic Initiatives in the Political Education of Muslim Youth in Germany" (Valerja Manjuk, Stoyanka Manolcheva, and Eduardo J. Vior, "The Politics of Otherness—Constructing the Autonomy of Political Subjects in the Migrant Minorities as a Way of Reforming Western European Democracies," in *Rethinking Non-Discrimination and Minority Rights*, M. Scheinin and R. Toivanen, eds., 135–154 (Helsinki/Berlin: Åbo Akademi University/Institute for Human Rights, 2004); Valerja Manjuk, Stoyanka Manolcheva, and Eduardo J. Vior, "Bestandsaufnahme demokratischer Initiativen in der politischen Bildungsarbeit mit muslimischen Jugendlichen in Deutschland—Ein Forschungsbericht," in *Extremismus in Deutschland*, Bundesministerium des Innern, ed., 316–337 (Berlin: Bundesministerium des Innern, 2004). All the German scholars consulted stated that "it is impossible to have a democratic Muslim education."

7. Norberto Bobbio, Antonio de Cabo and Gerardo Pisarello. *Teoría general de la política* (Madrid: Trotta, 2009); David Easton, "An Approach to the Analysis of Political Systems," *World Politics* 9, no. 3 (1957): 383–400; Harold J. Laski, *Liberty in The Modern State* (New York: Harper & Brothers, 2014); Giovanni Sartori, *La política: lógica*

y método en las ciencias sociales, Marcos Lara, trans. (México D.F.: Fondo de Cultura Económica, 1996).

8. Petrus Han, *Soziologie der Migration: Erklärungsmodelle, Fakten, Politische Konsequenzen, Perspektiven* (Stuttgart: Lucius & Lucius, 2000), 38–62.

9. Antônio A. Cançado Trindade, "La interdependencia de todos los derechos humanos. Obstáculos y desafíos en la implementación de los derechos humanos," Instituto Interamericano de Derechos Humanos, 1999, accessed on September 27, 2004 (http://www.iidh.ed.cr/BibliotecaWeb); Danielle Annoni, Antonio Augusto Cançado Trindade, et al., *Os novos conceitos do novo direito internacional: cidadania, democracia e direitos humanos* (Rio de Janeiro: América Jurídica, 2002).

10. Giovanni Sartori, *La sociedad multiétnica—Pluralismo, multiculturalismo y extranjeros* (Madrid: Taurus, 2001), 103–105.

11. Thomas H. Marshall and Tom B. Bottomore, *Ciudadanía y clase social* (Madrid: Alianza, 2007).

12. Will Kymlicka, *Multiculturalism: Success, Failure, and the Future* (Washington, DC: Migration Policy Institute, 2012); Taylor and Gutmann, *Multiculturalism: Examining the Politics of Recognition*.

13. Yasmeen Abu-Laban, "Liberalism, Multiculturalism and the Problem of Essentialism," *Citizenship Studies* 6, no. 4 (2002): 459–482; Alcira B. Bonilla, "Ética y multiculturalismo," in *Segunda Muestra Nacional de Filosofía,"La recuperación del sujeto a partir de la construcción de la identidad,"* M. Lobosco, ed., 20–27 (Buenos Aires: Universidad de Buenos Aires, Ciclo Básico Común., 2004); Paul Dixon, "Is Consociational Theory the Answer to Global Conflict? From the Netherlands to Northern Ireland and Iraq," *Political Studies Review* 9 (2011): 309–322; Marc Leman, *Canadian Multiculturalism* (Ottawa: Library of Parliament, Parlamentary Information and Research Service, 1999); Antônio Sidekum, "Multiculturalismo: Desafíos para la educación en América Latina," *Polylog. Foro para filosofía intercultural*, 2003, accessed on September 28, 2004 (http://them.polylog.org/4/asa-es.htm).

14. Taylor and Gutmann, *Multiculturalism: Examining the Politics of Recognition*; Gérard Bouchard and Charles Taylor, "Fonder l'avenir Le temps de la conciliation. Rappor," *Commission de consultatation sur les pratiques d'accommodement reliées aux différences culturelles*, 2008, accessed on June 27, 2009 (http://collections.banq.qc.ca/ark:/52327/bs66285).

15. Brubaker, *Immigration and the Politics of Citizenship in Europe and North America*; Herrera Carassou, *La perspectiva teórica en el estudio de las migraciones*; Manjuk, Manolcheva and Vior, "The Politics of Otherness—Constructing the Autonomy of Political Subjects in the Migrant Minorities as a Way of Reforming Western European Democracies"; Manjuk, Manolcheva, and Vior, "Bestandsaufnahme demokratischer Initiativen in der politischen Bildungsarbeit mit muslimischen Jugendlichen in Deutschland—Ein Forschungsbericht"; Massey, Arango, Graeme, Kouaouci, Pellegrino, and Taylor, "Teorías de migración internacional: una revisión y aproximación"; Karl Schlögel, *Planet der Nomaden* (Berlin: Wjs-Verlag, 2006); Vior, *Migraciones internacionales y ciudadanía democrática: influencias de las comunidades de origen inmigrante sobre el desarrollo político en Alemania, Argentina y Brasil*.

16. Charles Taylor and Amy Gutmann, *Multiculturalism: Examining the Politics of Recognition*. Princeton, NJ: Princeton University Press, 1994; Alcira B. Bonilla, "Ética y multiculturalismo." In *Segunda Muestra Nacional de Filosofía, "La recuperación del sujeto a partir de la construcción de la identidad,"* edited by M. Lobosco, 20–27.

Buenos Aires: Universidad de Buenos Aires, Ciclo Básico Común, 2004.; Will Kymlicka, *Multiculturalism: Success, Failure, and the Future.* Washington: Migration Policy Institute, 2012.

17. For its substance it also relies on a relational view of culture, as argued by Geertz in Clifford Geertz, *The Interpretation of Cultures: Selected Essays* (New York: Basic Books, 1973).

18. Karl-P. Fritzsche, *Menschenrechte: Eine Einführung mit Dokumenten* (Padeborn: Ferdinand Schöningh and UTB, 2004); United Nations Organization (UNO), *Universal Declaration of the Human Rights* (UDHR), 1948, http://www.un.org/en /documents/udhr/. For example, under the title "What Are Human Rights?" the official site of the Office of the UN's High Commissioner for Human Rights (http:// www.ohchr.org/EN/Issues/Pages/WhatareHumanRights.aspx) characterizes them as "Universal and inalienable," "Interdependent and indivisible," "Equal and non-discriminatory," and "Both rights and obligations." This is the classification used by all international organizations. Trindade, "La interdependencia de todos los derechos humanos. Obstáculos y desafíos en la implementación de los derechos humanos."

19. In the mainstream perspective, universality lies in the worldwide spread of the rights codified in laws and declarations issued in England, the United States, and France during the eighteenth century, without changing the original form and style (Jakob Schissler, "Menschenrechte zwischen Univesalismus und Kulturrelativismus," in *Der Bürger im Staat*, 26–30 [Stuttgart: Landeszentrale für Politische Bildung Baden-Württemberg, 2005[). In their critique, interculturalists point out that this view attributes the idea of human dignity only to one culture and exclusively to modern times (Raúl Fornet Betancourt, *Crítica intercultural de la filosofía* [Madrid: Trotta, 2004]). This approach also makes the acknowledgment of rights strongly dependent on the compliance of the political contract between the sovereign and the citizen, that is, the effectiveness of human rights relies unilaterally on the framework of the national state. This contradicts, however, a wealth of historical findings that demonstrate that all human communities everywhere and at any time have developed shared notions of human dignity and of the human right to resist oppression. Therefore, it is preferable to speak of "the multiple universality" of human rights from the earliest times of mankind and all over the world (Alcira B. Bonilla, "Autonomía moral entre limones y colectivos: Las "mamacitas" bolivianas en Buenos Aires," in *Un continente en movimiento: Migraciones en América Latina*, I. Wehr. Frankfurt, ed., 143–158 [Madrid: Vervuert/Iberoamericana, 2005]; Alcira Bonilla, "La filosofía intercultural como traducción racional," 2006 [http://www.ddhhmigraciones.com. ar/publicaciones/publicacioneshome.htm]; Alcira Bonilla, "Ética, mundo de la vida y migración," in *Sociedad y Mundo de la Vida a la luz del pensamiento Fenomenológico-Hermenéutica actual*, R. Salas Astrain, ed., 27–58 [Santiago de Chile: EUCSH, 2007]; Eduardo J. Vior, "Migración y derechos humanos desde una perspectiva intercultural," in *Migración e interculturalidad. Desafíos teológicos y filosóficos*, R. Fornet-Betancourt, ed., 109–117 [Aachen: Wissenschaftsverlag Mainz in Aachen, 2004]; Eduardo J. Vior, "Die politische Partizipation von Migranten stärkt die Demokratie—Fallstudie: die bolivianische Minderheit in Argentinien," in *¿Sin fronteras? Chancen und Probleme laeinamerikanischer Migration*, Lena Berger et al., eds., 49–72 [München: Martin-Meidenbauer-Verlag, 2007]). All human cultures have always had representations of values, norms, and symbols that are inherent in human dignity, but insofar as each culture has its own language, symbolic and imaginary, the representation of human

dignity and the place it has in each culture differ. On the other hand, the emancipating development of human rights has always coexisted with oppressive trends coming from ancestral fears and the expansionism of conquering nations. This means that oppression and emancipation are two omnipresent and conflicting trends in the history of human cultures. This clash is constitutive of human history, but it is always contingent and cannot be generalized. (Heiner Bielefeldt, *Philosophie der Menschenrechte: Grundlagen eines weltweiten Freiheitethos* [Darmstadt: Wissenschaftliche Buchgesellschaft, 1998]; Manfred Brocker, *Ethnozentrismus: Möglichkeiten und Grenzen des interkulturellen Dialogs* [Darmstadt: Primus, 1997]; Peter Dudy, *Menschenrechte zwischen Universalität und Partikularität: Eine interdisziplinäre Studie zu der Idee der Weltinnenpolitik* [Münster: Lit, 2002]; Raúl Fornet-Betancourt, *Menschenrechte im Streit zwischen Kulturpluralismus und Universalität* [Frankfurt a.M./London: IKO-Verlag für Interkulturelle Kommunikation, 2000]; Raúl Fornet-Betancourt and Hans-J. Sandkühler, *Begründungen und Wirkungen von Menschenrechten im Kontext der Globalisierung* [Frankfurt a.M./London: IKO-Verlag, 2001]; Georg Lohmann and Stephan Gosepath, eds., *Philosophie der Menschenrechte* [Frankfurt a.M.: Suhrkamp, 1998]).

20. At this point it may be useful to apply the decolonial perspective of the study of racism. See Walter Mignolo, Introduction to *Capitalismo y geopolítica del conocimiento*, Walter Mignolo, ed., 9–53 (Buenos Aires: del Signo, 2001) and Aníbal Quijano, "Colonialidad del poder, eurocentrismo y América Latina," in *La colonialidad del saber: Eurocentrismo y ciencias sociales – Perspectivas latinoamericanas*, E. Lander, ed., 219–264 (Buenos Aires: Ciccus/Clacso, 2011).

21. Argentina, Australia, Southern Brazil, Canada, New Zealand, South Africa, the United States, and Uruguay.

22. For the world-system approach in migration studies, see Albert Kraler and Christof Parnreiter, "Migration theoretisieren," *Prokla: Zeitschrift für eine kritische Sozialwissenschaft* 140, no. 35 (2005): 327–344 and Alejandro Portes and John Walton, *Labor, Class and the International System* (New York: Academic Press, 1981).

23. Alcira B. Bonilla, "Ética intercultural de los Derechos Humanos. Teoría y praxis de los derechos culturales," in *XI° Seminario Argentino Chileno y V° Seminario Cono Sur de Ciencias Sociales, Humanidades y Relaciones Internacionales 'A propósito de la integración. Las ciencias y las humanidades desde una perspectiva crítica latinoamericana* (Mendoza: Universidad Nacional de Cuyo, Centro de Estudios Trasandinos y Latinoamericanos, 2012); Alcira B. Bonilla and Eduardo J. Vior, "Mundo de la vida, ciudadanía y migraciones," *Cultura-Hombre-Sociedad. Revista CUHSO* 18, no. 1 (2009): 9–28; Eduardo J. Vior and M. del Carmen Cabezas, "Fundamentaciones pragmáticas y teóricas de la ciudadanía sudamericana," paper presented at the IV Jornadas sobre Debates Actuales de la Teoría Política Contemporánea, Buenos Aires, 2013; Marilena Chaui, *Cultura e Democracia: O Discurso Competente e Outras Falas* (São Paulo: Editora Moderna, 1981).

24. In Spanish, the term *"emergente"* connotes both "emergent" and "emergency." In this way the *ciudadanías interculturales emergentes* refers to forms of citizenship, simultaneously expressing a severe social emergency and the new ways of struggling for rights made possible by the intercultural approach to the democratic participation of subaltern groups in pluricultural societies. Alcira B. Bonilla, "El derecho humano a migrar y la transformación de la noción de ciudadanía," in *Transformaciones, prácticas sociales e identidad cultural*, R. Arué, B. Bazzano, and V. D'Andrea, eds., 773–788

(Tucumán: Universidad Nacional de Tucumán, 2008); Alcira B. Bonilla, "El mundo cotidiano de la vida y las ciudadanías interculturales emergentes," in *Alltagsleben: Ort des Austausch oder der neuen Kolonialisierung zwischen Nord und Süd*, R. Fornet-Betancourt, ed., 211–234 (Aachen: Wissenschaftsverlag Mainz, 2010); Alcira B. Bonilla, "Ciudadanías Interculturales Emergentes y vigencia de los Derechos Humanos," in *La Travesía de la Libertad ante el Bicentenario. IV Congreso Interoceánico de Estudios Latinoamericanos, X Seminario Argentino-Chileno, IV Seminario del Cono Sur de Ciencias Sociales, Humanidades y Relaciones Internacionales* (Mendoza: Universidad Nacional de Cuyo, Centro de Estudios Trasandinos y Latinoamericanos, 2010); Alcira B. Bonilla, "Ciudadanías Interculturales Emergentes," in *La ciudadanía en jaque. II. Problemas éticos políticos de prácticas conquistadoras de sujetos*, A. Bonilla and C. Cullen, eds., 7–38 (Buenos Aires: La Crujía, 2013).

25. Patricia Dreidemie and Eduardo J. Vior. "Indagaciones teórico-metodológicas sobre la construcción de ciudadanía cultural de comunidades de origen inmigrante en la Provincia de Río Negro (Argentina)." *Antíteses* 4, no. 7 (2011): 319–339. http://www.uel.br/revistas/uel/index.php/antiteses.

26. Manjuk, Manolcheva and Vior, "The Politics of Otherness—Constructing the Autonomy of Political Subjects in the Migrant Minorities as a Way of Reforming Western European Democracies"; Manjuk, Manolcheva, and Vior, "Bestandsaufnahme demokratischer Initiativen in der politischen Bildungsarbeit mit muslimischen Jugendlichen in Deutschland—Ein Forschungsbericht."

27. Mary Louise Pratt, *Ojos imperiales: literatura de viajes y transculturación* (Buenos Aires: FCE, 2011).

28. Due to the protectionist policy of the Spanish monarchy, from its foundation in 1580 until 1776, Buenos Aires did not have authority over its own port. Legal commerce with Spain flowed through Peru. From the beginning, however, the traders of Buenos Aires developed a strong smuggling route through Brazil, which brought them in contact first with the Dutch colony in Northern Brazil, and then with the British. In 1776, when King Charles III separated the Viceroyalty of the Rio de la Plata from Peru and made Buenos Aires its capital, the former smugglers became legal businessmen and began to appropriate the customs revenue. This was one of the most important causes of the civil wars between Buenos Aires and the interior provinces following Independence, at the beginning of the nineteenth century.

29. Fernando Devoto, *Historia de la inmigración en Argentina* (Buenos Aires: Sudamericana, 2004), 247.

30. Hipólito Yrigoyen (1853–1933) was Argentina's first freely elected president (1916–1922 and 1928–1930). His Radical Civic Union (Unión Cívica Radical, or UCR, in Spanish), at that time a reformist middle-class movement, is Argentina's oldest political party.

31. During the so-called Great Depression, between 1873 and 1896, low economic growth, low commodity prices, and the high concentration of financial capital prompted the exodus of millions of migrants from Europe to the Americas, South Africa, and Australia, and increased the indebtedness of the formally independent Latin American countries (Samir Amin, "Mundialización y financiarización," in *Los desafíos de la mundialización*, Samir Amin, ed., 127–145 [México: Siglo XXI, 1999], 139–140, and Alessandra Pescarolo, Luis Á. Fernández and Jaime Rierra R, *La gran depresión [1873-1896]* [Barcelona: Oikos-tau, 1991]).

32. Susana Bandieri, *Historia de la Patagonia* (Buenos Aires: Sudamericana, 2009), 223–239; David Rock, *Argentina 1516–1982 from Spanish Colonization to the Falklands War*

(Los Angeles: University of California Press, 1985). In 1876, the introduction of the first freezer vessels for the transportation of Argentinian meat to Great Britain also gave rise to cold storage facilities (mostly British owned) and modified meat production methods.

33. Many years later, in August 1912, after the so-called Alcorta Cry in the homonymous town in Santa Fe province, the foundation of the Argentinian Agrarian Federation (Federación Agraria Argentina, or FAA, in Spanish) offered protection to the small and midsized rural producers, leading to the emergence of a conservative middle class in the southern region of this province.

34. At the beginning of the twentieth century, the Argentinian elite adopted the "melting pot" myth from the United States, through which the fusion of white Argentinians and European immigrants would create and perpetuate a new "white" nationality, while Indians and Afro-Argentinians were relegated to the past. This model was introduced through the newly organized national school system, and several generations of Argentinians were thus educated until the beginning of the twenty-first century.

35. Until the middle of the twentieth century, the dominant Argentinian culture was highly imitative of British patterns in economics and of French models in politics, social sciences, and humanities.

36. Rock, *Argentina 1516–1982 from Spanish Colonization to the Falklands War*, 142.

37. Devoto, *Historia de la inmigración en Argentina*, 49.

38. Devoto, *Historia de la inmigración en Argentina*, 294; Organization of the American States (OAS), *International Migration in the Americas: Second Report of the Continuous Reporting System on International Migration in the Americas*, Washington, DC, 2012, accessed on September 9, 2013 (http://www.oecd.org/migration/48423814 .pdf), 65; Mario Rapoport, *Historia económica, política y social de la Argentina (1880–2003)* (Buenos Aires: Emecé, 2005), 53–58.

39. Marie-Ange Veganzones and Carlos Winograd, *Argentina en el siglo XX: crónica de un crecimiento annunciado* (Buenos Aires: Centro de Desarrollo, Organización para la Cooperación y Desarrollo Económicos, 1997), 52.

40. Peron aimed to attract entrepreneurs, engineers, and technicians who could contribute to the industrialization of the country. For this reason his government allowed both Nazi fugitives and Jewish refugees to immigrate (Nidia De Cristóforis, "El primer gobierno peronista y la llegada de inmigrantes españoles y exiliados republicanos a la Argentina," *Miradas en movimient* 7 [2012]: 4–25).

41. Roberto Benencia, "Apéndice: La inmigración limítrofe," in *Historia de la inmigración en Argentina*, F. Devoto, ed., 433–524 (Buenos Aires: Sudamericana, 2004), 439–446 and 454–457; Veganzones and Winograd, *Argentina en el siglo XX: Crónica de un crecimiento annunciado*, 52.

42. FEDEAR, *La inmigración argentina: Una cuestión de Historia e Identidad* (Alicante: Casa de las Américas, Colección Seminarios, 2009); Susana Novick, *Sur-Norte: Estudios sobre la emigración reciente de argentinos* (Buenos Aires: Catálogos/IIGG, 2007); Andrés Solimano, *Development Cycles, Political Regimes and International Migration: Argentina in the Twentieth Century* (Santiago: ECLAC, Economic Development Division, 2003), 5.

43. Benencia, "Apéndice: la inmigración limítrofe."

44. Benencia, "Apéndice: la inmigración limítrofe"; Sergio Caggiano, "Riesgos del devenir indígena en la migración desde Bolivia a Buenos Aires: Identidad, etnicidad y desigualdad," in *Amérique Latine Histoire et Mémoire. Les Cahiers ALHIM*, 2014,

accessed on February 15, 2015 (http://alhim.revues.org/4957); Guillermo Cantor, "Entramados de clase y nacionalidad: Capital social e incorporación política de migrantes bolivianos en Buenos Aires," *Migraciones Internacionales* 7, no. 1 (2013): 197–234; Alejandro Goldberg, "Trayectorias migratorias, itinerarios de salud y experiencias de participación política de mujeres migrantes bolivianas que trabajaron y vivieron en talleres textiles clandestinos del Área Metropolitana de Buenos Aires, Argentina," *Anuario Americanista Europeo* 11 (2013): 199–216; Paula D. Salgado, "El trabajo en la industria de la indumentaria: una aproximación a partir del caso argentino," in *Trabajo y Sociedad: Sociología del trabajo – Estudios culturales – Narrativas sociológicas y literarias* (Santiago del Estero, Verano, 2012), accessed on January 28, 2015 (http://www.unse.edu.ar/trabajoysociedad).

45. Santiago Canevaro, "Experiencias individuales y acción colectiva en contextos migratorios: el caso de los jóvenes peruanos y el ingreso a la Universidad de Buenos Aires," in *Migraciones regionales hacia la Argentina: Diferencia, desigualdad y derechos,* A. Grimson and E. Jelin, eds., 285–324 (Buenos Aires: Prometeo, 2006); Julia Castillo and Jorge Gurrieri, "El panorama de las migraciones limítrofes y del Perú en la Argentina en el inicio del siglo XXI," *Cuadernos Migratorios: El impacto de las migraciones en Argentina* 2 (2012): 17–50.

46. Barbara Hines, "The Right to Migrate as a Human Right: The Current Argentine Immigration Law," *Cornell International Law Journal* 43, no. 3 (2010): 472–511.

47. MERCOSUR (Mercado Común del Sur) was founded in 1991 by Argentina, Brazil, Paraguay, and Uruguay. In 2012 Venezuela joined the bloc and, in 2015, Bolivia also became a member. Through various association agreements, all South American countries (except Guyana and Suriname) are now associated with MERCOSUR. Therefore, all South Americans are permitted to travel and immigrate to Argentina.

48. Almost from the beginning of the Independence wars (1810–1818), the ambition of the Buenos Aires commercial and landowner elites to dominate the interior provinces led to a half-century-long civil war. In this context, the national executive was dissolved in 1820. This situation lasted until 1853, with a brief exception during 1826–1827.

49. Alejandro Grimson, "La migración boliviana en la Argentina. De la ciudadanía ausente a una mirada regional," in *Migrantes bolivianos en la Argentina y los Estados Unidos,* A. Grimson and E. Paz Soldán, eds., 13–52 (La Paz: Programa de las Naciones Unidas para el Desarrollo [PNUD], 2000), 16.

50. As developed by Castells (Manuel Castells, *La era de la información* [Madrid: Alianza, 1997]) and Gurak and Caces (Douglas T. Gurak and Fe Caces, *Migrant Networks: Mechanisms for Shaping Migrations and Their Sequelae* [Ithaca, NY: Dept. of Rural Sociology, 1989]), associative network refers to different types of noninstitutionalized associations through which many groups all over the world try to adapt themselves to the new conditions of the Third Industrial Revolution and neoliberal globalization. These networks may be based upon migrants, Mafia organizations, ethnic and cultural groups, religious communities, and so on. Benencia ("Los inmigrantes bolivianos en el mercado de trabajo de la horticultura en fresco en la Argentina") and Roberto Benencia and Marcela Geymonat ("Migración transnacional y redes sociales en la creación de territorios productivos en la Argentina: Río Cuarto, Córdoba," *Cuadernos de Desarrollo Rural* 55 [2005]: 9–28) employed this concept to describe and explain the organizational forms of Bolivian immigration in Argentina, in particular the system of connections transversally linking individuals, kinship groups, and communities of origin between Bolivia and several regions of Argentina.

51. Thomas Abbot, "The Two Worlds of Buenos Aires: Macri's Legacy of Inequality" (Washington, DC: Council on Hemispheric Affairs [COHA], 2014) (http://www.coha.org/the-two-worlds-of-buenos-aires-macris-legacy-of-inequality-2/)

52. The National Population Census of 2010 reported 2,890,151 inhabitants living in the City of Buenos Aires, 4.1% more than were registered by the Census 2001. Although Argentina's total population grew 11% between both censuses, the city experienced a decrease in the net population (INEC [Instituto Nacional de Estadística y Censos], *Indicadores Demográficos 2013*, San José: INEC, 2014).

53. Because of their proximity to the port of Buenos Aires, the natives of the City have been called *porteños* (from *puerto*, port) since the nineteenth century.

54. CESO, Centro de Estudios Económicos y Sociales, "La situación habitacional en la Ciudad de Buenos Aires," *Informe C.A.B.A. Nro. I.* 2015, accessed on February 23, 2015 (http://www.ceso.com.ar/tipo/producciones-ceso). Translated from the Spanish.

55. The City's own constitution allows foreigners living legally in the city to vote for the Mayor, the Legislature, and communal representatives, the so-called *comuneros*. Notwithstanding, very few immigrants have joined the special Electoral Register because of the many bureaucratic obstacles. As the vote is obligatory for Argentinians, they do not need to sign up, but foreigners wishing to vote must register.

56. Since the civil-military dictatorship, most soccer clubs are indirectly controlled by the wildest parts of their fans, the so-called *barrabravas*. With criminal contacts in the FIFA, player-representatives, police, politicians, and club officers, the clubs exert their power with harsh violence, aiming to obtain economic advantages, drugs, and privileges.

57. "Neoliberal" can be understood as the economic policy implemented throughout the Western world beginning in the 1970s (Víctor Barone, "Globalización y neoliberalismo: elementos de una crítica," *Consejo Latinoamericano de Ciencias Sociales [CLACSO], Documento de trabajo* 95 [1998]). This policy concept rests on the deregulation of economic relations, the priority given to financial capital over the other forms of capital, the emphasis put on supply to the detriment of demand, and the reduction of state functions to a minimum. The theoretical concept was elaborated by the Austrian philosopher Friedrich von Hayek and the economic theory by Milton Freedman. This doctrine was first implemented in Chile during Augusto Pinochet's dictatorship (1973–1990). Thereafter, it was also applied by other military dictatorships in South America. In Great Britain, it was put into practice by Margaret Thatcher (1979–1991), and in the United States, beginning in 1981, by President Ronald Reagan (1981–1989). The worldwide hegemony of neoliberalism led to the huge growth of finance capital all over the world but also to a relative reduction of industrial growth, weakening states as well as international organizations and making the world economy more likely to fall into reiterative crises. Argentina introduced neoliberal economics in two steps: first, under the civil-military dictatorship, between 1976 and 1983, and under President Carlos Menem (1989–1999). As a result of neoliberal policies, Argentina's foreign debt escalated so that in 2001 the country defaulted. From 2003 onward, President Néstor Kirchner modified the economic policy radically, reducing Argentine debt and protecting industry. Following the tenets of neoliberalism, the current government of Buenos Aires promotes the nonregulation of the housing market and public transport, the reduction of investments in public health care and education, the outsourcing of public services, increasing public indebtedness through foreign loans, and the repression of social and political protest.

58. Abbot, "The Two Worlds of Buenos Aires: Macri's Legacy of Inequality"; Romina Smith, "Distrito Tecnológico: Parque Patricios se Transforma: ya se radicaron 158 empresas," *Clarín*, September 8, 2013, accessed January 13, 2015 (http://www.clarin .com/ciudades/Parque-Patricios-transforma-radicaron-empresas_0_989301167.html).

59. Gobierno de la Ciudad de Buenos Aires (GCBA), *Censo Nacional 2010: Selección de cuadros de Población. Cuadros por comuna. Población total nacida en el extranjero por lugar de nacimiento, según sexo y grupo de edad. Año 2010*, accessed on September 10, 2013 (http://www.buenosaires.gob.ar/areas/hacienda/sis_estadistico/censo_datdef /cuadros_poblacion.php).

60. According to the law, they are Argentinians.

61. Not to be confused with the "CABA" (also C.A.B.A), the Spanish acronym for the Autonomous City of Buenos Aires; Castillo and Gurrieri, "El panorama de las migraciones limítrofes y del Perú en la Argentina en el inicio del siglo XXI," 22.

62. Roberto Benencia, "Los inmigrantes bolivianos en el mercado de trabajo de la horticultura en fresco en la Argentina," *Cuadernos migratorios* 2 (2012): 166.

63. Charrúa Street is a side road in southern Flores, in the current Commune 7. Up to the mid-1960s this was a marshy ground with no buildings. Bolivian families who came from the southwestern departments and whose men worked in the building industry settled there. Today this is an organized quarter, which still keeps the small passages through the city blocks. The celebration of the Virgin of Copacabana is carried out there in September.

64. Leopoldo Halperín Weisburd, *Precariedad y heterogeneidad del trabajo en la Ciudad de Buenos Aires* (Buenos Aires: Universidad de Buenos Aires, 2012).

65. Instituto nacional de Estadísticas y Censos (INDEC), *Censo Nacional de Población 2010*, accessed on September 9, 2013 (http://www.censo2010.indec.gov.ar/CuadrosDefinitivos /P1-P_Caba.pdf).

66. Instituto nacional de Estadísticas y Censos (INDEC), *Censo Nacional de Población 2010*.

67. Gobierno de la Ciudad de Buenos Aires (GCBA), *Censo Nacional 2010: Selección de cuadros de Población. Cuadros por comuna. Población total nacida en el extranjero por lugar de nacimiento, según sexo y grupo de edad. Año 2010*.

68. Romina Sánchez, "Aquí vivo y aquí quiero votar." *Noticias Urbanas*, July 13, 2013 (http://www.noticiasurbanas.com.ar/noticias/aqui-vivo-y-aqui-quiero-votar/).

69. Frances Holloway, "A City with a Hidden Textile Industry," *The Argentina Independent*, April 2, 2009, accessed on January 17, 2015 (http://www.argentinaindependent .com/socialissues/humanrights/a-city-with-a-hidden-textile-industry/).

70. Although space constraints make it impossible to consider critically the broad range of theories dealing with "immigrant economics," the argument presented here draws upon the main currents, among them Han, *Soziologie der Migration: Erklärungsmodelle, Fakten, Politische Konsequenzen, Perspektiven*, 239–258; Kraler and Parnreiter, "Migration theoretisieren," 332–240; Michael J. Piore, *Birds of Passage: Migrant Labor and Industrial Societies* (Cambridge: Cambridge University Press, 1979); Alejandro Portes, "Chapter 1: Economic Sociology and the Sociology of Immigration: A Conceptual Overview," in *The Economic Sociology of Immigration: Essays on Networks, Ethnicity, and Entrepreneurship*, A. Portes, ed., 1–41 (New York: Russel Sage Foundation, 1995); Alejandro Portes and Kenneth Wilson, "Immigrant Enclaves: An Analysis of the Labor Market Experiences of Cubans in Miami," *American Journal of Sociology* 86, no. 2 (1980): 295–319.

71. Textile Aspects of Argentina, 2013, accessed January 17, 2015 (http://www.textile -future.com/dynpg/print_text.php?lang=en&aid=978&showheader=N).

72. Isidro Adúriz, *La Industria Textil en Argentina. Su evolución y sus condiciones de trabajo* (Buenos Aires: INPADE, 2009).

73. Ariel Lieutier, *Esclavos: Los trabajadores costureros de la Ciudad de Buenos Aires* (Buenos Aires: Retórica, 2010), 49. Significantly, wholesale takes place mostly outside the formal circuits in La Salada (Latin America's greatest textile market, on the bank of the Matanza River, 10 kilometers west of the City of Buenos Aires' border with La Matanza, Sebastián Hacher, *Sangre salada: una feria en los márgenes* (Buenos Aires: Marea, 2011), at the Central Market of Buenos Aires (at the Ricchieri-motorway leading to Ezeiza-airport, in La Matanza-district), and in the 2-kilometer-long shopping mile along the Avellaneda Avenue. Especially in the wholesale sector, Bolivian traders confront the strong concurrence of Korean and Argentinian entrepreneurs— among them several orthodox Jews. Behind the Central Market, Korean businessmen are currently building a giant shopping center for textile products with about 22,000 stalls.

74. Salgado, "El trabajo en la industria de la indumentaria: una aproximación a partir del caso argentino."

75. The ruling Junta-designated mayor, Osvaldo Cacciatore (1976–1982), implemented an urban planning policy to deindustrialize the City, aiming to avoid the concentration of industrial workers and prevent the organization of trade unions and social agitation.

76. Juan Carlos Vásquez, *El Visor Boliviano*, CABA, March 3, 2015.

77. Adhering to communitarian Andean traditions, Bolivians are used to relying on kinship ties and reciprocal help to organize their labor units (*ayni* is the Aymara name of this institution); however, under the conditions of a nonregulated labor market, the misuse of this tradition hides brutal exploitation.

78. Deputy Inspector of the Argentinian Federal Police (PFA*), Non-identified by the Trafficking Squad of the Argentinian Federal Police (PFA)*, June 8, 2013.

79. Goldberg, "Trayectorias migratorias, itinerarios de salud y experiencias de participación política de mujeres migrantes bolivianas que trabajaron y vivieron en talleres textiles clandestinos del Área Metropolitana de Buenos Aires, Argentina."

80. José Zambrano Torrico, president of the recently founded Confederation of Small and Mid-size Bolivian Enterprises in Argentina (Conamype Bol-Ar is the Spanish acronym), in an interview with *El Visor Boliviano* (August, first fortnight, 2014, 11) (*El Visor Boliviano*, CABA, http://www.elvisorboliviano.com) estimated that, in Argentina, there are 100,000 Bolivian workshops in the garment industry, and that almost 3.7 million people are directly or indirectly employed in the sector. Because he did not show the data sources he used for his statement, it seems greatly exaggerated.

81. Adúriz, *La Industria Textil en Argentina. Su evolución y sus condiciones de trabajo.*

82. Fabio Bertranou, Luis Casanova, and Tomás Lukin, *La formalización laboral en Argentina: Avances recientes y el camino por recorrer*, 2013, accessed February 24, 2015 (http://www.ilo.org/wcmsp5/groups/public/---americas/---ro-lima/---ilo-buenos _aires/documents/publication/wcms_228768.pdf); Carlos Tomada, "El combate contra el trabajo esclavo," *Página/12*, March 26, 2013, accessed on February 24, 2015 (http://www.pagina12.com.ar/diario/elpais/1-216619-2013-03-26.html).

83. Juliana Awada, the wife of the Head of the City Government, is the owner of one of the most important clothing market brands, and she demonstrably buys from

sweatshops that foster slave labor (Lieutier, *Esclavos: Los trabajadores costureros de la Ciudad de Buenos Aires* and La Alameda Foundation, "Historia," 2015. (http://www.fundacionalameda.org/2011/06/historia.html).

84. Caggiano, "Riesgos del devenir indígena en la migración desde Bolivia a Buenos Aires: Identidad, etnicidad y desigualdad"; Cantor, "Entramados de clase y nacionalidad: Capital social e incorporación política de migrantes bolivianos en Buenos Aires"; Goldberg, "Trayectorias migratorias, itinerarios de salud y experiencias de participación política de mujeres migrantes bolivianas que trabajaron y vivieron en talleres textiles clandestinos del Área Metropolitana de Buenos Aires, Argentina"; Vanina Modolo, "Participación política de los migrantes. Reflexiones sobre la extensión de la ciudadanía en Argentina," *Revista Mexicana de Ciencias Políticas y Sociales* 59, no. 220 (2014): 349–370, accessed on February 6, 2015 (http://www.scielo.org.mx/pdf/rmcps/v59n220/v59n220a12.pdf); Cynthia Pizarro, " 'Ciudadanos bonaerenses-bolivianos': Activismo político binacional en una organización de inmigrantes bolivianos residentes en Argentina," *Revista Colombiana de Atropologia* 45, no. 2 (2009), accessed on February 6, 2015 (http://www.scielo.org.co/scielo.php?pid=S0486-65252009000200007&script=sci_arttext).

85. Buenos Aires Ciudad, *Derechos humanos y pluralismo cultural. Observatorio de colectividades*, 2013, accessed on September 10, 2013 (http://www.buenosaires.gob.ar/areas/secretaria_gral/colectividades/?secInterna=162&subSeccion=513&col=38).

86. González, Daniel. "Cómo opera la patota que protege a los talleres clandestinos de ropa," *Tiempo Argentino*, August 28, 2011, accessed on September 11, 2013 (http://tiempo.infonews.com/notas/como-opera-patota-que-protege-los-talleres-clandestinos-de-ropa). Interviews conducted by the author of this chapter with members of the Alameda Foundation, a Deputy Inspector of the Trafficking Squad of the Argentinian Federal Police (PFA), and H. Zunini, technical advisor at the Centro Demostrativo de la Indumentaria (CDI, Experimental Center for Clothing) in June 2013, and a long conversation with Mr. Vásquez in March 2015 confirm this scenario.

87. At the end of February 2015, the author of this chapter empirically confirmed Vásquez's assertions: in the middle of February, in the Mataderos quarter (in the west of the City), a Uruguayan kiosk owner killed a young man, Franco Zárate, apparently for no other reason than that he complained about the beer being too expensive. As the young man was very well known in his Bolivian group and loved by everyone, a massive protest arose among the local Bolivian community, and two street protests took place. The author also took part in a second meeting, on February 27, in downtown Buenos Aires, where he was very surprised to learn that even people criticizing Ayala's corrupt and illegal practices had, on this occasion, followed his leadership. González, "Cómo opera la patota que protege a los talleres clandestinos de ropa."

88. González, "Cómo opera la patota que protege a los talleres clandestinos de ropa"; Vásquez, *El Visor Boliviano.*

89. As Vásquez reports in Vásquez, Juan Carlos. *El Visor Boliviano*, by strengthening the ties within this entrepreneurial elite, and between it and their business partners, the City plays an important symbolic role in the patronage of the *morenadas*, the dance blocs that are ubiquitous in La Paz Carnival. *Morenos* means brown-skinned and the *morenadas* mimic the dances of African slaves during colonial times. According to Vásquez, however, participation in the current *morenadas* in Buenos Aires costs each dancer almost $20,000 (USD). Only the children of garment entrepreneurs can, therefore, hope to take part in these prestigious performances. Even more important

than the *bajadas* (the annual *morenadas* parade at the central Mayo Avenue) are the prior *recepciones* (receptions), that is, luxury parties in closed halls, to which the organizers invite their business and political contacts.

90. González, "Cómo opera la patota que protege a los talleres clandestinos de ropa."
91. Patricia Dreidemie and Eduardo J. Vior, "Indagaciones teórico-metodológicas sobre la construcción de ciudadanía cultural de comunidades de origen inmigrante en la Provincia de Río Negro (Argentina)," *Antíteses* 4, no. 7 (2011): 319–339 (http://www .uel.br/revistas/uel/index.php/antiteses).
92. For example, Maghrebis in France, South Asians and Africans in Great Britain, and Turks in Germany.

CHAPTER 3

Peripheral Migrants

Haiti–Dominican Republic Mobilities in Caribbean Context

SAMUEL MARTÍNEZ

The Dominican Republic shares the Caribbean island of Hispaniola with Haiti, a fact that conditions its relations not only with Haiti but with the rest of the world. One main stream of Dominican historiography holds that Dominicans' mistrust of Haiti dates to the colonial era, when the island was first divided into French and Spanish colonies.[1] The animosities of that era were subsequently confirmed and heightened as a result of the Dominicans' struggle for independence from Haiti, which followed two periods of Haitian domination. The first, when Haitian revolutionary Toussaint Louverture invaded the Spanish colony of Santo Domingo in 1801, brought it under Haitian rule and abolished slavery there. The second period, between 1822 and 1844, was when the island was united under Haitian government. Revisionists counter that Dominican anti-Haitian attitudes cannot be understood independently of European and North American hostility toward Haiti. The years following Dominican independence, in 1844, saw uncounted meetings with emissaries from "civilized" Western European and North American nations, which all brought Dominicans to realize that their aspirations to gain international acceptance would hinge on how loudly they rejected Haiti and its heritage of black rebellion.[2] Where both streams of historiography may coincide is in highlighting the particular intensity with which Dominicans grapple with the identity dilemmas attendant upon being both African-descendant and Hispanic and that these dilemmas have been heightened by the presence of not just a blacker neighbor to the west but also a racist colossus to the north.

Safer still is to say that Western governments, merchants, and business entrepreneurs have exerted an even more determinative influence than Haiti has on Dominican political, economic, and cultural life, these foreign agents having repeatedly played transformative roles in Dominican affairs in the years after independence from Haiti. Among the most lasting transformations imposed from overseas has been the Dominican Republic's dependence on seasonally imported migrant labor from Haiti for the yearly harvest of its sugar cane crop. Following the United States' military invasion and seizure of power in the Dominican Republic in 1916, a labor recruitment system was set up by the military occupation authorities, much like that to be denounced decades later as slavery by international human rights monitors, journalists, and social justice documentarians.[3] From these early decades of the twentieth century well into the 1990s, the bulk of sugar cane harvest labor was recruited from Haiti, whether on an officially approved or an informal basis, by Haitian Kreyòl-speaking sugar cane grower employees, termed *buscones* ("seekers," pronounced "booss-CONE-ess").

Each year, a small minority of these seasonal migrants has not returned to Haiti. Over a span of decades, the nonreturnees have gradually snowballed into the Dominican Republic's largest immigrant and minority group. A recent national survey of immigrants conducted by the official Dominican government statistical agency puts the number of "Haitian origin" people in the Dominican Republic at 668,144, of whom 209,912 are estimated to be Dominican-born people of Haitian parentage.[4] Despite sugar's central importance in the recent past, sugar production declined drastically over the 1990s, to a small fraction of what it was in the 1970s and early 1980s. It is also now likely that the majority of new immigrants from Haiti never set foot on a sugar plantation, the economic center of gravity of the host country having shifted over the 1990s and 2000s and toward service and tourism. Haitian ancestry peddlers have taken over whole segments of urban informal commerce previously dominated by ethnic Dominicans, while Dominicans of all backgrounds stretch the inflation-sapped value of their pesos by buying clothes, shoes, and accessories from Haitian sidewalk vendors. Although numerical estimates of their presence are lacking, Haitian itinerant merchants also appear to have extended their circuits of international trade in growing numbers to include Dominican frontier and urban markets, where they buy eggs, sugar, and other staples for resale at a profit in Haiti. The shakedowns and sexual violence to which this predominantly female group of merchants is subjected on the Dominican side of the border has become a new frontier of human rights concern.[5] Even as the focus of international human rights has effectively followed Haitian-ancestry people away from the sugar plantations, the rights struggles of Haitian nationals and Dominican citizens of Haitian ancestry remain as vital a topic of international scrutiny as ever. And following an extraordinary Dominican high court judgment of September 23, 2013, the questions surrounding Haitians' and Haitian-Dominicans' right claims are as salient as ever in Dominican media and politics. The evolving human rights story is inescapably central to this chapter's account of Haiti–Dominican Republic migration.

Even as the new immigrants come more often from urban rather than rural locales in Haiti and as their modes of integration into the Dominican economy are evolving, and even as much remains to be learned through field research among the new migrants, a look at the history and political economy of Haiti–Dominican Republic mobilities may reveal much about human geographical mobility within the wider Caribbean region. On Hispaniola, there is much that is unique in Caribbean context: an island divided by language and heritage; an international relationship between Haiti and the Dominican Republic of unsurpassed intensity and complexity; large and extraordinarily enduring mobilities of people, from Haiti to the Dominican Republic and back. Yet, looking to the underlying historical trends and international political economic forces, common points emerge with other places across the Caribbean region. In stepwise sequence, this chapter places particular importance on regional patterns that emerged during the slavery, postemancipation and post–World War II eras, to make sense of the size, endurance, and political inflammability of Haiti–Dominican Republic migration. The crucible from which today's mobilities flow is colonial racism or, more particularly, the African slave trade and the plantation industries that it supported. Yet, as is explained in the next section of this chapter, Afro-Caribbeans on the move continued to confront injustice in the generations following the end of chattel slavery. Thus, even as most ethically committed Europeans and North Americans may have felt that they had acquitted their moral obligations toward the Caribbean after winning the abolition of the slave trade, a largely unnoticed case for international social justice solidarity endured. Migration in the generations immediately following slave emancipation may be contextualized as a site of struggle in a larger battle for labor control versus effective freedom, pitting plantation elites against African-descendant peasants/rural proletarians. And as much as during the era of slavery, global responsibilities have stood out. Both in the era of slavery and afterwards, the western and eastern sides of Hispaniola have been asymmetrically integrated into global commodity supply chains; yet regardless of its unevenness, patterns of global market integration have always been major determinants of international migration.

Today's situation still responds to international political economic forces: even as the Dominican sugar empire crumbled, demand for cheaper and more easily disciplined Haitian immigrant labor survived, albeit under recognizably different political and economic conditions and in forms that are arguably better adapted to the more flexible capitalist enterprise encouraged by neoliberal reform. Recent legal changes affecting the residency and work status of Haitian immigrants and challenging the citizenship of Dominicans of Haitian ancestry may also be placed in global context, as responses to international human rights pressure. Both the political and economic restructuring led by the International Monetary Fund (IMF) and international human rights pressure can be read as the latest chapter in a story of global interventionism going back to the colonial era, placing direct and important pressures on human geographical mobility.

THE CARIBBEAN CONTEXT

A brief description of the postslavery context of the wider circum-Caribbean region is crucial to understanding the reasons why migrants began to move in large numbers from Haiti to the Dominican Republic, the circumstances under which the early migrants traveled, and the meanings of their travels for their own lives and the lives of others. Historically, the Dominican Republic contrasts with other migrant-hosting or migrant-sending islands and territories of the Caribbean. Even as slavery existed there, the Spanish colony of Santo Domingo was never the scene of the production of export crops on a large scale based on slave labor.[6] Before the Haitian Revolution and for decades afterward, the Spanish colony was sparsely populated and had a low global economic profile. Spanish Santo Domingo served as a port for the replenishment and repair of Spanish fleets, on their way between the Iberian Peninsula and mainland Spanish America.[7] Probably more lucratively, the colony supplied wood, livestock, and food staples to French Saint-Domingue, commodities vital to the survival of that slave labor–based export juggernaut.[8] While enslaved Africans and their descendants never comprised the greater part of Spanish Santo Domingo's population and its numbers of slave imports never rivaled those of French Saint-Domingue, neither should it be forgotten that the Spanish colony's lumber and cattle-raising enterprises depended on enslaved labor, too. Yet the Spanish colony was effectively a periphery of a French colonial periphery: it carried out an important but by no means irreplaceable role as a supplier of animal traction, building material, and subsistence foodstuffs to the French colony of Saint-Domingue. Whatever importance Santo Domingo held, then, was primarily rooted in its role in propping up the monocrop agriculture of French Saint-Domingue, Europe's most lucrative overseas colony of the eighteenth century.

Even bearing in mind Hispaniola's peculiar, divided colonial history, migration on Hispaniola, as in much of the rest of the Caribbean, would unfold in ways that bore the mark of industrial slavery's demographic distortions and political and economic inequalities. The migration of workers from Haiti that started in the early decades of the twentieth century shared at base a similar dialectic of consent and coercion as existed in neighboring colonies and former colonies of the Caribbean. As emancipation from slavery was won in island after island in a nearly century-long chain of events, starting with Haiti in 1804 and ending in Cuba in 1886, a first means for the newly freed to make good their hard-won freedom was to move away from the scenes of their former enslavement in search of greater economic opportunity elsewhere. As Bonham Richardson remarks concerning the Commonwealth Caribbean, "Migrating away for wages, although the earliest destinations were often other plantation islands, was an assertion of independence.[9] It was not a complete escape from the larger plantation sphere, but neither did it represent a docile willingness to accept local conditions dictated by former plantation masters."

Migration's two-fold character, in the decades following emancipation, was rooted in the circumstance that labor followed where foreign capital led. The emigrants left islands where foreign capital, from an antecedent domination of the economy, was stagnating or being withdrawn, and moved toward places into which capital had been freshly injected. Following emancipation in the British West Indies (1838), laborers began to travel by sailboat from smaller islands with obsolescent sugar industries, for better paid employment on the relatively thriving sugar plantations of Trinidad and British Guiana.[10] Beginning in the last quarter of the nineteenth century, steamship travel facilitated the circulation of labor throughout the Caribbean. This period saw the beginning of migration from Jamaica to banana plantations in Costa Rica as well as to the ill-fated French effort to build a Panama Canal. In common among all these displacements was that when Afro-Caribbean workers left home it moved labor and talent from their home islands to the territories that were their hosts, undercutting capital at home while bolstering it abroad.

The complete significance to the regional dynamic of control and resistance through geographical mobility cannot be appreciated without considering that the new arrivals were not just a scalable factor of production but also a politically vulnerable group. The migrants did not just increase the numerical supply of labor in the host societies but also provided employers with a more easily disciplined labor force. As strangers and nonnatives, the immigrants lacked the social contacts and employment alternatives that locally born workers had, and which might have made it possible for them to turn down work on unfavorable terms and bargain for better with large proprietors. Elsewhere in the Caribbean, still harsher constraints were suffered by another group of new immigrants, those who were shipped to the Caribbean as indentured workers from India, China, and Java. For the duration of their indentureships, those migrants had no choice but to accept the substandard wages and work conditions of the employers to which they were contractually bound.[11] The explicit rationale for the Spanish, French, Dutch, and British colonial authorities to pay for indentured immigration was to "replace" the former slaves, whom it was assumed would not respond to the offer of wages as they had to the threat of the whip. Similar reasoning sustained the decision of export entrepreneurs, in these territories and others, to pay for the recruitment of seasonal migrants from neighboring Caribbean islands. Dealing with the locals was always made easier by the presence of large numbers of imported and more coercible laborers. Not that the planter elite ever gave up trying to push the descendants of former slaves into work for large proprietors. Where regressive taxation and planter-contrived scarcity of agricultural land failed to press newly freed workers into wage labor, laws against "vagrancy" (broadly construed as acts of avoiding work for wages) were enacted in several Caribbean territories (including independent Haiti), the breaking of which was to be punished with forced labor.[12]

Whereas indentured Asian workers were to be the major population segment competing for work with the descendants of slaves in Trinidad and the Guianas, migrant Afro-Caribbeans, drawn from the descendants of former slaves in Haiti, Jamaica, and a host of smaller islands, would subsidize major increases in sugar exports in Cuba and the Dominican Republic. Gradations in the forms and levels of constraint are notable even as a shadow of coercion ran across all laborers' relationships with large proprietors: even local, volitional recruits felt the pressure of competition for jobs, be it with the indentured, with contract migrants, or with penal conscripts. Even as hunger replaced the lash as the main instrument of planter control, coercion remained a seemingly inextricable ingredient in sugar production.

That link would emerge early even in the development of industrial-scale sugar production in the Dominican Republic, where there was no recent pre-emancipation history of large-scale sugar production. Worker resistance to exploitation was pivotal. In the 1880s, cane cutters, drawn from Dominican peasant communities, opened up a new avenue of wage negotiation by holding out for payment by task rather than a fixed daily wage.[13] Because payment by task gave the worker a regular opportunity to haggle for higher wages, cane growers preferred to pay a fixed daily wage and to deploy cutters in closely supervised gangs. In the words of the prominent sugar industrialist, William Bass, payment by task involved not just "long and heated debate" but "a tacit recognition that the laborer is in a position to impose his demands on the owner."[14] In the minds of many plantation owners, all of the problems involved in recruiting harvest laborers from the local population had a single solution: to import cheaper and more easily disciplined labor from elsewhere. In 1893, leading sugar producers formed an association for the recruitment of workers from the Lesser Antilles, the Immigration Society of Macorís.[15] Not just wages but control was seen to be crucially important by growers. Thereafter, changes in the supply source of immigrant labor would facilitate every subsequent major shift in the prevailing system of sugar cane harvest labor.[16] By the nineteenth century's end, Dominican cane growers, using a mostly West Indian harvest labor force, broke worker resistance to ganged day labor in the cane harvest.[17] By this time also, mill owners had standardized their practice of issuing advances on monthly or semimonthly payments to workers via credit usable only at plantation stores.[18]

In the 1930s, Haitians had taken the place of West Indians as the backbone of the harvest labor force. The presence of this new labor force, with whom no prior understandings existed about terms of labor, facilitated cane growers' moves to cut costs. The growers not only lowered wages but also instituted piece-rate wages in place of ganged day labor.[19] Under the piece-rate wage system, the cane cutter would be paid only by how many tons of cane he cut, as measured at weigh stations in the fields.[20] From management's point of view, piece rates were a more efficient way of extracting labor, because each cutter's pay was calibrated directly to his output and because productivity could be maintained with many fewer supervisory personnel in the fields than were required than with the day labor gangs. From management's point of view, part of the beauty of piece rates was that field bosses neither had to push cane cutters to work early nor supervise them closely at work. As long as piece rates were set to pay barely enough for one substantial meal per day, the cutters would of their own accord work steadily and for long hours.

INTERNATIONAL RESPONSIBILITY

If the movement of capital out of senescent sugar properties and into new ones was one major shaper of postslavery migrations, then another was US neocolonialism. The United States is neither an unwitting consumer of unethically produced sugar nor an otherwise nonimplicated party in relation to today's Haitian rights crisis in the Dominican Republic. Instead, US government agencies and business corporations stand among the parties most directly responsible historically for having set large-scale immigration in motion from Haiti. Admittedly, Dominican sugar barons continued to profit from grossly underpaid Haitian labor, long after the end of the era of dollar diplomacy. Yet they need not be absolved in order to locate responsibility also with the US government and the US-based corporations and banks that came to dominate the sugar industry between the key dollar diplomacy years of 1894 (when US banks purchased the Dominican Republic's foreign debt) and 1930 (when US client Rafael Trujillo first took power in a military coup).

The already-mentioned recruitment of seasonal migrants in Haiti, involving the dispatch of company-paid *buscones* into the Haitian countryside, was instituted under US watch and for the benefit of US-based multinational sugar companies. Recruitment of Haitian workers along these lines was first done following the United States' military invasion and seizure of power on both sides of the island—in Haiti (1915–1934) and in the Dominican Republic (1916–1924)—and was initially regulated through US military government ordinances.[21] Not only did the mode of recruitment infringe workers' freedom to choose employers; it also resulted, as noted earlier, in the gradual accretion of a vulnerable population of Haitian nationals and Haitian-descendant Dominicans numbering in the hundreds of thousands. And US corporations were preeminent among the beneficiaries of this system of migrant labor exploitation later to be dubbed "Dominican sugar slavery."

Other negative human rights consequences for immigrant cane workers would flow from the early twentieth-century US military takeover of government in Haiti and the Dominican Republic. The establishment of national constabularies enabled dictators to impose absolute control in each country—Rafael Trujillo, in the Dominican Republic, from 1930 to 1961, and the Duvaliers, father and son, in Haiti, from 1957 to 1986.[22] These national constabularies also extended and entrenched the roles played by their respective governments in channeling Haitian labor toward Dominican sugar estates. The creation of the Guardia Nacional for the first time made policing the movements of Afro-Caribbean immigrants across Dominican national territory a practical possibility. It was only after the American occupation that Dominican police officers were first reported to be rounding up Haitian immigrants in non-sugar-producing areas of the Dominican Republic.[23] In 1937, Trujillo unleashed a display of barbarism unparalleled in the region, in the "*corte* (mowing down")" of Haitians living in the Dominican frontier region and northern Cibao Valley, in which over 10,000 Haitian men, women, and children were murdered, without warning or mercy, by Trujillo loyalists. It is not known just what Trujillo intended this atrocity to achieve politically.[24] Among the *corte*'s effects, however, was its enactment of a foundational fiction of Dominican national identity, in casting Haiti, and not the United States, as the main foreign threat to Dominican sovereignty.

Trujillo's anti-Haitian stance and his pledge to Dominicanize the sugar industry did not prevent him from reaching an accord with Haiti in 1952 for the recruitment of *braceros*. Whereas previously the two governments had regulated labor circulation separately under their own laws, with recruitment remaining largely privately organized, this accord placed it for the first time under an international treaty, giving the Haitian authorities responsibility for organizing one or more centers each year for issuing contracts to *braceros*.[25] Publicity given to the labor contract at the time of its signing may have been intended to give the appearance to concerned members of the public that the new labor scheme would be an improvement, by promising legal safeguards not available under the old system of recruitment through *buscones* (which continued to operate in parallel with the bilateral treaty). But by legally committing the *bracero* to work only for the employer who paid his passage from Haiti, the contract in effect handed the security forces a standing justification for forcibly relocating Haitian immigrants to the sugar plantations. Any undocumented Haitians found off estate grounds could be detained and shipped to a sugar estate, under the pretext that they had abandoned their contractually assigned places of work.

In the last decades of the twentieth century, the exact nature of coercion in the Dominican sugar cane fields became an international controversy. Human rights monitors and journalists highlighted migrant workers' testimony about being recruited through force or deception and then kept at gunpoint on the sugar plantations, to make the case that Dominican sugar is a slave-produced commodity. Academic researchers, by contrast, found little evidence of forced labor per se but made the case that Haitian *braceros* (seasonal migrant workers) are neither free nor slaves but suffer multiple economic and social constraints, centering on poverty, dearth of alternative employment, and anti-Haitian bias.[26] While deceptive labor recruitment was denounced repeatedly by human rights observers in the 1980s and 1990s, scholarly field studies of the era disputed the prevalence of deception—being rare to come across Haitian cane workers who spoke of having been duped but common to find *braceros* who had returned willingly, year after year, to the same *bateyes* (company-owned agricultural worker residential compounds, pronounced "bah-TAY-yess").[27]

Where there was agreement between activist and academic observers was on issues that human rights monitors relegated to the background. First, the growers and sugar mill owners were profiting handsomely in a challenging world market by avoiding making long-term investments in productivity because they could rely on seemingly unceasing supplies of labor from Haiti to accept starvation wages for brutalizing labor. The low cost and elastic supply of labor made it possible for growers to throw tens of thousands of manual workers at the harvest instead of spending money on mechanizing the cutting, lifting, loading, and hauling of the sugar cane. Second, intolerable human costs accompanied this undervaluation of Haitian labor, expenses being skimped also by providing neither protective gear for the cutters handling dangerously sharp machetes in the fields nor adequate health care, housing, or potable water in the *bateyes*. Even if forced labor allegations seemed questionable, then, pity had to flow toward an overworked, starved, sick, and hopeless sugar proletariat, wearing rags and living in dilapidated, mud-floored wooden barracks. And even as the most flagrantly coercive labor control practices have been abandoned, dreadful conditions of work and life for the few thousand remaining cane workers still constitute intolerable economic rights infringements.

Equally important have been the questions not asked. Into the communication gap between international human rights monitors and academic observers fell the opportunity to go beyond simple questions about whether the *braceros* are as a group slave or free. It remains an open question to this day what the coerced labor of an exceptional few cane workers might indicate about the superficially volitional terms of labor of the vast majority. Might the testimony, highlighted by international rights monitors, of recruitment by force and fraud be significant not as a representation of the typical experience of Haitian cane workers but as the extreme end of a coercion continuum?

In this connection, it is useful to bring into consideration a third body of perspectives on what I have elsewhere called the "onion of oppression."[28] Those perspectives derive from the practice of membership-based rights organizations, largely founded and staffed by Haitian immigrants and Dominicans of Haitian ancestry. These groups—the most prominent of which has been the Movimiento de Mujeres Domínico-Haitianas (Haitian-Dominican women's movement)— differ from international human rights monitor groups in focusing not just on the most obvious and flagrant abuses but seeking to pierce all the layers of injustice, exclusion, and abuse of oppression's onion—civil, political, economic, social, and cultural. What matters to these Dominican-based rights defenders is a broad spectrum agenda, including rights of legal residency for de facto resident immigrants, the right for all workers to organize trade unions freely, women's economic empowerment and right to sexual self-determination, and, above all, recognition that Dominican-born people of Haitian ancestry are Dominican citizens. Starting in the early 1980s but gaining prominence only in the 1990s, these groups arose independently of international human rights monitors' antislavery campaigning and framed the issues in more inclusive ways, representing not just the *braceros* but *batey* women, Haitian nationals living outside the sugar plantations and Dominicans of Haitian ancestry. In methods, too, these Dominican-based rights organizations broke new ground in seeking to build their constituency's ability to promote and defend its own rights, in order to avoid creating situations in which "everything is known by the lawyer, nothing is known by the client."[29]

In addition to the multidimensionality of the oppression, what should also stand beyond dispute is that much has changed from when I first lived in a *batey* for my dissertation research in 1985 and 1986. With a sharply downsized Dominican sugar industry requiring fewer migrant workers, the prevalence of recruitment via sugar company–paid *buscones* has diminished drastically; those migrants who still go on a yearly basis mostly pay their own way.[30] And it appears to be the case that no one is any longer held inside doors locked from the outside or blocked from leaving sugar plantations by company guards armed with shotguns. On the key question of whether the workers can walk away, a recent study sponsored by the US Department of Labor and the independent labor rights monitor group revealed that 99% of its more than 700 Haitian cane worker survey respondents felt that they can leave their *bateyes* at any moment.[31] Even *The Price of Sugar* video documentary, which in 2007 made the case that Haitian workers are held as slaves on Dominican plantations, inserts passing mention of the same changes. In the final third of its more than 90 minutes, the film reveals that central elements of its denunciations no longer hold: plantation guards, it is admitted, no longer carry firearms nor attempt to restrain workers from leaving plantation grounds.[32]

More will be said, in this chapter's next section, about the magnitude of these changes. Amid these, one constant is that the sugar *bateyes* remain a historical and symbolic baseline: the *bateyes* were the point of entry or birthplace of many who have since moved to other, non-sugar-producing zones; the *bateyes* symbolize for even more people the economic precariousness and rights deficits from which Haitian migrants and their offspring seek to ascend. From the *bateyes*, an unknown fraction, probably the majority of the settlers, has moved to non-sugar-producing villages and urban slums, a trickle turned flood after International Monetary Fund–mandated restructuring of the Dominican economy led to sugar production's precipitous decline during the 1990s.[33] The demographic, economic, and political situation is therefore more complex than conveyed by visual media reports that, after 2007, have augmented *The Price of Sugar*'s revival of the dormant allegation of Dominican sugar slavery.[34] Haitian descendants can now walk away from sugar plantations as easily as they walk onto them but fewer and fewer, as I explain in the next section of this chapter, can escape the shadow of the law and the bureaucracy. Rather than dwell on outdated forced labor allegations, then, it would be more accurate and more on target politically for international solidarity efforts to focus on emerging rights threats, through which exclusionism is being legalized, and prejudice, "modernized."

Still, some aspects of history are not so much erased as written over through the interventions of the living. Spanning the long arc of history, up to and beyond when allegations of Dominican sugar slavery first garnered front-page press attention in 1978, European and North American responsibility stands out. None of these developments would have been possible without either the powerful state security forces set up under US rule or without tacit US blessings for authoritarian solutions in its Latin American "backyard." Among the beneficiaries were US-, Canadian-, and Dominican-owned sugar mills, the shipping companies that exported the raw sugar, sugar refiners and merchandisers in the Canadian and Western European markets to which Dominican sugar was mainly exported prior to the Cuban Revolution, and the mainly US-based banks that invested in Dominican sugar. Many a detail could be added but the evidence is there: seen from the standpoint of the historical archive, US fingerprints are all over the scene of this crime.

RIGHTS STRUGGLES AND STATE RESPONSES

Momentarily leaving aside questions of global responsibility, it bears clarifying that, as a legacy of the history that I sketched earlier, the Haitian-Dominican rights struggle is a single movement but with two main lines. One line, that of "minority rights," is advanced by the Dominican-born descendants of Haitian immigrants, who seek acceptance as Dominican nationals on the basis of both their place of birth and the existence of an effective connection between them and the Dominican state (and their lack of connection with the Haitian state).[35] Rejection of this claim by the Dominican state has placed tens of thousands of Haitian-Dominicans at risk of statelessness. The other, "migrant rights" line, is pushed by the Haitian-born, who seek legal acceptance of their de facto permanent residence, only about one-tenth of whom possessing any legal permit to live in the Dominican Republic.[36] Both antiminority and antimigrant forms of exclusionism are targets of pro-rights social movement organizations, headed by Haitian-ancestry leaders as well as by Dominicans and expatriates.

Within the growing salience of minority rights and statelessness as organizing frames for Haitian rights struggles, particular attention has gravitated to the children and young adults whose valid aspirations to belong fully and realize their human potential now stand in danger of being stymied by agents of a Dominican state who say that the Dominican-born are neither Dominicans nor minority group members but Haitians and immigrants. Here, again, a bit of historical background is helpful to understanding today's crisis.

Obtaining Dominican citizenship has always been made difficult by anti-Haitian racism but was for decades facilitated by compliant civil registry officials. These local-level officials approved the issuance of tens of thousands of valid birth certificates to the Dominican-born children of Haitian nationals, even when the latter bore no proof of identity other than the "temporary" identity cards (*carnets temporeros* or *fichas*) issued to seasonal workers by the sugar companies upon arrival from Haiti.[37] Electoral politics and the creation of small pockets of grateful voters may have had much to do with it. Over the 1990s and 2000s, prospects for sugar's future went from buoyant to depressed, and official permissiveness was replaced by growing restrictiveness. By 1990, evidence had emerged that Dominican-born children of Haitian ancestry were being denied birth certificates under the pretext that the Dominican Constitution exempted the children of persons "in transit" from the jus soli right to Dominican nationality, even when their parents could prove that they had resided in the Dominican Republic for years.[38] By 1997, the rights advocacy group, Centro Cultural Domínico-Haitiano (CCDH, Haitian-Dominican Cultural Center), found a clear indication that increasing numbers of Haitian-Dominicans were having difficulty obtaining the legally required Dominican national identity card, the Cédula de Identidad y Electoral: an estimated 80% of Haitian-Dominicans over the age of 30 possessed a cédula but only 30% of those under 30 had this document.[39]

The denial of late registration birth certificates to Dilcia Yean and Violeta Bosico by the civil registry office in the sugar-producing town of Sabana Grande de Boyá, on March 5, 1997, set in motion litigation that culminated years later in a landmark Inter-American Court of Human Rights (IACHR) ruling invalidating the Dominican Republic's exclusion of Dominican-born people of Haitian ancestry from jus soli citizenship. Improvised rationales and protocols, on the spot, seemingly prejudiced determination of who was "Haitian," on the basis of last names and appearance rather than official documentation—in short, arbitrary exceptionalism rather than legal script—seemed to be the guiding principles when civil registry officials would unpredictably refuse basic identity documents to black applicants. During the *Yean and Bosico v. Dominican Republic* court proceedings, it became embarrassingly clear how messy the legal basis of official policy was, when government lawyers presented the Court at different times with distinct and incompatible lists of official criteria for issuing late registration of births.[40]

Yean and Bosico's legal representatives, the Inter-American Commission (which, if it refers a case to the Court, joins in arguing the petitioners' case),[41] as well as expert witnesses and friends of the court, presented an expansive case. Yean and Bosico were initially represented at the Inter-American Commission by MUDHA and lawyers from the International Human Rights Law Clinic of the University of California Berkeley. Their original petition cited the Dominican Republic for violating nine articles of the American Convention on Human Rights. Rights to a legal identity and a nationality were always the central issues, for without a birth certificate the girls' names and nationality would have been completely absent from any official register. But to index the gravity of these wrongs, the girls' representatives described a cascade of other rights infringements that would follow if the girls could not get birth certificates: their right of free mobility within the Dominican Republic would be endangered if they could not get the *cédula* that every Dominican is required by law to carry; their right to travel abroad would be invalidated by their inability to obtain a passport, and with it would go any possibility of seeking educational or job prospects internationally (as has led Dominicans to emigrate in their hundreds of thousands); registering for secondary and postsecondary schools would be precluded by their inability to present required legal identity documents; even opening a bank account or getting legally married would be impossible.

The case presented by the Dominican state's representatives consisted largely of procedural objections against the admissibility of the case at first and then of the evidence. The basis of the state's case was the unelaborated assertion that as a sovereign state the Dominican Republic has the right to set and interpret rules of citizenship as it pleases. The state also set a pattern that it would repeat in other cases that gained international attention, when years into the legal process it relented to giving Yean and Bosico their birth certificates and then tried to argue to the court that the case was exceptional and provided no grounds for making a ruling that would apply to Haitian descendants as a group.

The ruling of the Court, in turn, traced a middle ground, not troubling the precept that each state holds a sovereign right to set the broad contours of its citizenship rules, even as the Court found the Dominican state in contravention of both the country's own existing rules of citizenship and the international legal obligation to protect individuals' rights to a legal identity and a nationality. Conservative though it was, the Court's judgment also made detailed reference to the range and seriousness of the other rights infringements to which Yean and Bosico were being exposed, in support of the petitioners' claim to have suffered grievous harm as a result of the state's refusal to register their names and nationality. And the ruling highlighted that thousands of other Haitian-ancestry Dominicans were being wronged in like manner, and ordered the state to take sweeping corrective steps. Considering that the IACHR generally advances legal precedent incrementally and not by leaps, this ruling was about as decisive a victory as the plaintiffs could have expected.

Euphoria triggered by Yean and Bosico's victory in 2005 quickly faded. The Dominican government might issue birth certificates—or might not: one case, currently before the IACHR, revolves around the state's refusal to issue an official copy of a birth certificate to Emildo Bueno Oguis, a Haitian-ancestry Dominican who sought to assemble the legal documents needed to emigrate to join his US-citizen wife in the United States—but the state made it clear that, with birth certificates or not, it would continue denying Haitian-ancestry Dominicans citizenship. Just months before the IACHR judgment, a separate registry had already been set up for foreigners' children; foreign parents would henceforth be issued special pink-colored birth certificates that give their children no right to obtain the *cédula*. To date, state compliance with the Inter-American Court's judgment in Yean and Bosico has been limited to the redress prescribed by the Court to the claimants—issuing them birth certificates and identity documents and paying monetary reparations and legal fees—but has not taken the form of improved treatment being extended to other Haitian-Dominicans.

To the contrary, a climate of potential threat has come to shadow even those Haitian-Dominicans who have legally possessed citizenship, assimilated culturally and moved up the social ladder. For the first time, not just day laborers and informal sector workers but Haitian-ancestry people aspiring to enter the middle class have come into the crosshairs of newly legally mandated exclusionism. People who had passed unperceived into the mainstream are now being detected to be of Haitian ancestry, through inspection of their birth certificates by government officials, and are facing the prospect of exclusion from Dominican citizenship and its official protections and entitlements. It was not that these people had earlier "slipped under the radar" but that no "radar" formerly existed; now ensnaring these people are legal and bureaucratic instruments instituted from 2004 onward.

Particularly worrying are government moves to strip Dominican nationality retroactively from people who have had valid Dominican papers their whole lives. This has typically occurred when an applicant seeking to renew her/his *cédula* or obtain official replica documents for university enrolment or foreign travel is found through inspection of his or her birth certificate to be the off-spring of an undocumented immigrant.[42] Nationality stripping began even before the Dominican Constitution's amendments, blocking citizenship for children of undocumented immigrants, took effect in January 2010. The government claims this power under Section VII, Article 10 of the *Ley General de Migración*, which in 2004 made it official that anyone who is not a legal resident is, for the purposes of the law, "in transit," and hence that person's Dominican-born children excludable from birthright citizenship.[43] It is the government's contention also that this interpretation of the "in transit" exclusion from jus soli has been its official policy all along. In its Resolution 12 of 2007, the state organ that issues the *cédula* card, the Junta Central Electoral (JCE, Central Electoral Board) announced that it holds the prerogative to suspend any applicant's citizenship pending forensic investigation.[44] On the basis of this Resolución 12-07, thousands have been informed that their identity documents have been "provisionally suspended" and their right to Dominican citizenship put under investigation. Months and years on, few of these provisional suspensions have been definitively resolved, leaving the people thus affected in a legal limbo. Published figures of the number of Haitian descendants affected vary widely but estimates range into the five figures.[45] The number whose Dominican citizenship could potentially be revoked is even higher if we accept the finding of a recent survey by the Dominican National Statistics Office that there are almost a quarter of a million offspring of foreign-born parents living in the Dominican Republic, 86% of whom are of Haitian ancestry.[46]

In a judgment of extraordinary scope, the Dominican high court in September 2013 sustained the Resolución 12/07 in barring the issuance of official copies of birth certificates to "irregularly cedulized individuals."[47] The irregularly cedulized include anyone who appears in the civil registry as having been registered by a parent bearing an identity document other than the official *cédula*. What was unexpected was how far the court went beyond the challenge to the Resolución 12-07 put forward by the plaintiff, Juliana Deguis Pierre. In its Sentencia 168/13, the court ordered the JCE to make an inventory of all "foreigners" whose birth certificates have been entered into the nation's Civil Registry since 1929. The Ministries of Migration and of the Interior and Police were, in turn, to use this list of "irregularly inscribed foreigners" as the target population for a National Plan of Regularization of Illegal Aliens, as foreseen in the Ley General de Migración. The court also called upon the Presidency and Congress to craft legislation aimed at resolving the residency status of three groups: undocumented foreign nationals as well as two groups of Dominican-born offspring of nonresident foreigners, those inscribed as citizens in the Civil Registry and those lacking identity documents. The Tribunal left unexplained how Haitian descendants, once stripped of Dominican citizenship, are to regain a legal identity through Haitian citizenship in cases where the identity documents of parents or grandparents who left Haiti decades ago are practically irretrievable or never existed. Undetermined numbers thus stand at risk of becoming de jure stateless persons if denied Dominican citizenship because they have no means of claiming Haitian citizenship, either. The Dominican Republic is the only state with which most long-term resident Haitian nationals and Dominican-born Haitian descendants hold an effective connection, and for many it is the only state to which they hold any demonstrable connection at all.

As I write in mid-2014, all three steps ordered by the Tribunal Constitucional are under preparation. As expected, the JCE's arduous task of identifying all who are "irregularly inscribed" in the Civil Registry lags behind, with no certain completion date. A possible flaw in the whole scheme could materialize if the JCE keeps on indefinitely discovering irregularly cedulized individuals, setting the stage for future court battles if the JCE moves to strip such tardily identified individuals of their citizenship after the immigration status regularization deadlines have passed. It can be expected that, by the time this chapter is published, the deadlines for regularization will have passed and a further momentous decision necessitated about whether or not to extend the inscription period for either Haitian nationals or "irregularly cedulized" and non-birth-registered Dominicans.

On the administrative front, a first piece fell into place in November 2013, when Dominican President Danilo Medina published a National Plan of Regularization of unauthorized resident foreigners.[48] That plan became effective in early June 2014, with the opening of special registration stations in civil registry offices in twelve of the nation's thirty-two provinces.[49] With the implementation of the Regularization Plan in its early stages, suffice it to note that many undocumented Haitian immigrants will likely be unable to assemble the kinds of documents that the Plan requires to prove their eligibility. There is a continuum from the documented undocumented (who hold official Haitian identity documents but have no legal permit to reside in the Dominican Republic) to the undocumented undocumented (who have no papers from either country). Distinct advantage, in being able to prove their deservingness to stay as legal residents, is also held by those among the undocumented who can read, have formal sector employment, and own property. They will have easier access than the less advantaged to documents that attest to how long they have lived in the Dominican Republic, where they are employed, and what family ties they have. The fate of those in the lower half of the documented to undocumented continuum may hinge on whether the Haitian state can take special measures to issue official identity documents to the many who lack these.[50]

In May 2014, the Dominican Congress followed up on its obligations under the high court ruling with its Law 169-14, establishing a special protocol to affirm the Dominican citizenship of all those who have been granted official identity documents prior to 2007 on the basis of the registration of their birth on Dominican soil.[51] For those Dominican-born people whose names do not appear in the Civil Registry, the law also provides a path to legal residency and then citizenship, 2 years later. There is much that is surprisingly liberal in Law 169-14, even as it affirms a basic exclusionary principle, established in a 2009 amendment to the

Dominican Constitution, that the Dominican-born children of unauthorized immigrants will henceforth be denied birthright citizenship. Concerning Haitian descendants' right to jus soli nationality—the matter effectively dealt with by Law 169-14—observers on both the xenophobic Right and the liberal Left had understood the constitutional court's Sentencia 168/13 to be clear in confirming that the offspring of unauthorized immigrants would be stripped of citizenship. The Law 169-14 provides measures that run contrary to that aim, reasoning in its preamble that even people improperly registered were at no fault if civil registry officials committed an "error" in registering them at birth in the same manner as other Dominicans. The Law's preamble also cites the interest of the state in protecting a range of individual rights, including equality, human development, and nationality, as a rationale for granting Dominican nationality to the pre-2007 Dominican-born. That this concession is characterized as exceptional and that a 2007 end date is attached to eligibility for this exception are important boundaries that permit the Law's authors to juggle at least three political aims, first, remaining true to the letter of the Sentencia 168/13, second, mitigating the Sentencia's massive potential for social disruption and legal conflict, while, third, drawing a bright limit line, at the year 2007, past which no further Dominican-born children of undocumented Haitians will be accepted into the Dominican nation.

In the days after its passage, Law 169-14 appears to have appeased both liberals and xenophobes but pleased neither. Leading Dominican human rights organizations, including the Jesuit-led Centro Bonó (2014) and the Haitian rights network, the Red Jacques Viau, accepted the law as an important, if less than fully satisfying step forward and promised to cooperate with its implementation.[52] Amnesty International (2014) staked out higher moral ground, denouncing among other things both the law's failure to repudiate the Sentencia 168/13 and its requirement for the Dominican-born, whether inscribed in the Dominican civil registry or not, to go through a first step of registering as immigrants before they can apply for naturalization. A worry for rights liberals (but perhaps a consolation to anti-Haitian xenophobes) is the concessional and temporary character of the law's remedy and its failure to restore citizenship rights automatically to those whose citizenship seemed on the verge of being stripped by the Sentencia.

Even as the need to maintain constant attention will likely continue for years to come, it is not too soon to assess the impact of three decades of international human rights denunciations—from the Dominican sugar slavery allegations of 1978 through the campaign against statelessness of today—as well as subsequent advocacy for trade sanctions and litigation in the inter-American human rights system: What has international social justice solidarity won or lost for Haitian-ancestry Dominicans? The inevitable answer is that the international community has failed to bring the Dominican state into greater conformity with human rights norms even as its pressure has produced policy movement and not just static resistance.[53] In an essay originally published in 2005, sociologist Wilfredo Lozano[54] observed that the Dominican state "has in general defined its migration policies in a 'logic of absence,'" ceding control over migration to private entrepreneurs and the military but, he added, the country was facing "increased external pressures from the international system . . . not only to institutionally formalize its policies but do that in [conformity with] a human rights canon." The formalization of migration and minority rights policy foreseen by Lozano has taken place but has happened without bringing greater conformity with liberal norms. It is as if Dominican legislators and the administrations of three successive presidents, representing the two major Dominican political parties, took international advocates' strategic translation of Haitian rights claims into liberal constitutional terms and turned that on its head, by legally encoding exclusionism in an antiliberal sovereignty-rights nexus.[55] Starting with the General Migration Law of 2004, followed by the Resolución 12/07 in 2007 and the revision of the Dominican Constitution in 2010 to exclude the children of undocumented immigrants from eligibility for birthright citizenship, the basis of anti-Haitian exclusionism is shifting from custom and rude force to the law and public administration.

It is telling that the political debate about modifying the Constitution's jus soli citizenship rule began just weeks after the IACHR's verdict against the Dominican Republic in Yean and Bosico.[56] It is precisely *by* losing in international venues that anti-Haitian opinion has gained ground in Dominican politics at an accelerated pace over the 2000s.[57] Little in that contrarian strategy could have been planned. Yet the legitimacy of stridently nationalist anti-Haitian rhetoric has been augmented by a narrative which holds that the country is "under attack" not just from the silent infiltration of Haitian immigrants but also the outspoken contentiousness of international human rights activists. Seen from the perspective of the anti-immigrant trend in Dominican politics, part of the problem with representatives of the international community barking human rights orders from on high is how easily that position of moral superiority can be recast as a symptom of global arrogance.

CONCLUSION

Following the January 12, 2010, earthquake in Haiti, well-reasoned arguments were made that not just the Haitian state but northern governments shared the blame for this moderately strong quake having inflicted death in numbers massively out of proportion to those a similar strength event would have killed in other seismically prone areas of the world.[58] Questions, too, continue to swirl around the dereliction of duty involved when governments and peoples pledged billions of dollars to Haitian reconstruction with disappointing outcomes and the inexcusable misallocation of funds to underwriting a bourgeois lifestyle in Haiti for aid providers.[59] Can similar questions be raised about emigration from Haiti and, with it, the rights deficits being suffered by Haitian descendants in the Dominican Republic today?

In this chapter, I have drawn a historical sketch of how international interventions have shaped successive mobility regimes on Hispaniola, from colonialism, through US neocolonialism, to the present era of global governance through international financial institutions and human rights organizations. Extractivist models of development, which would later wreak terrible ecological damage, were effectively set in place in Saint-Domingue by its French colonists. Also in common with much of the Caribbean was the artificially dense peopling of the island to support slave labor–based plantation industries. Irresolvable disagreements surround the question of what or whom to blame for Haiti's postcolonial slide, from being after the Revolution one of the best poor person's countries in the Americas to being simply the poorest country of the Western Hemisphere. Was that an inevitable outcome of overpopulation? A product of its rulers' incompetence and venality? Or a result of disadvantages imposed on Haiti through the hostility of the world's slaveholding powers to an independent black republic? Clearer conclusions can be drawn about the genesis of emigration. As densely populated as Haiti and these other Caribbean islands were, putting thousands of seasonal labor migrants on the move required outside intervention, in the shape of labor recruitment and, in Haiti's case, bald infringement of its national sovereignty through the US military invasion and occupation of 1916 to 1934. If Haitians began traveling each year in their tens of thousands to Cuba and the Dominican Republic during those years, it probably had less to do with the hidden hand of the market than the heavy hand of the country's US military law givers and administrators. Of the latest chapter of global interventionism, led by the International Monetary Fund and a broad coalition of international human rights organizations, some good outcomes may be highlighted. Even as Haiti's economic growth has stagnated, the Dominican economy has been among the region's fastest growing since the early 1990s, albeit with a growing gap between haves and have-nots. As yet untallied human rights gains have also accrued from sugar's decline in that the nearly despotic grip of the sugar companies has been broken and that people of Haitian ancestry are now more visibly and broadly integrated into the Dominican economy. At the same time, international social justice solidarity is failing. Presenting evidence against the Dominican state in prosecutorial style—whether in actual courts or before the "court of world opinion"—has only moved the Dominican state to adopt forms of exclusionism that are farther reaching, more rigidly mandated by laws and more bureaucratically efficient than ever held before.

In insisting that migration from Haiti to the Dominican Republic cannot be explained independently of the actions of outside governments and corporations, the possibility exists of going beyond critique of actually existing human rights practice, to open questions similar to those debated after the earthquake about northern complicity and evasions of responsibility. Can northern states accurately be said to have supported resource stripping, authoritarian government, and rights-abusing schemes for plantation profit, at the cost of working Haitians' rights and lives? And if so, then does this complicity add up to prescriptive duties for the international community, this time in relation to the plight of Haitian descendants in neighboring Dominican Republic? Can a share of responsibility for Haitians emigrating in desperate conditions be traced to a "historical construction of vulnerability" similar to that said to have augmented the quake's toll?[60]

Unlike the quake, structural causality need not even be invoked to establish international historical responsibility vis-à-vis today's Haitian rights crisis in the Dominican Republic: the United States in particular is a *direct* author of human rights infringements as well as an indirect contributor to the conditions that are to blame for perpetuating these wrongs. If we accept this, then questions follow that are, if anything, even more uncomfortable than the questions raised about international responsibilities toward Haiti after the quake: Do the United States and the European Union states carry too many violent antecedents in Haiti and the Dominican Republic to act effectively as an impartial investigator, prosecutor, and judge of the Dominican Republic's infringements of Haitian descendants' rights? Are these foreign governments, in short, too morally compromised to pretend to argue for and, if necessary, impose greater norms compliance on a reluctant Santo Domingo? It may smack of idealism even to ask whether there are alternatives to human-rights-as-usual—alternatives which might be more horizontally dialogic than vertically power-played—yet what motivates the question is practical concern about the limits of human rights' dominant legal/retributive approaches. These limits are evident in the illiberal but increasingly legally and procedurally normative-appearing positions on Haitian rights, which the Dominican state has crafted in response to international human rights pressure. The price of confrontation via legal adversarial approaches has been a legalization, rigidification, and extension of anti-Haitian exclusionism, which formerly took largely customary forms and had only imprecise foundations in law. More important still, the price of confrontation has been paid by Haitian descendants, who, after three decades of denunciations, advocacy for trade sanctions, and litigation in the Inter-American human rights system, now face forms of exclusion from state protections that are further reaching and more clearly codified in law than before international activists took up their cause. Where idealism may be justified, then, is in persisting in asking in what ways the statelessness and migrant rights problems of today are the legacy of past movements of footloose core country capital, and how many dollars the use of underpaid Haitian labor has contributed to profits internationally. It seems fair to ask, in short, not just "Who is to blame?" but also "Who owes what to whom?"

NOTES

1. Anne Eller, "'All Would be Equal in the Effort': Santo Domingo's Italian Revolution, Independence, and Haiti, 1809–1822," *Journal of Early American History* 1, no. 2 (2011); Meindert Fennema and Troetje Loewenthal, *La construcción de raza y nación en la República Dominicana* (Santo Domingo: Editora Universitaria—UASD, 1987); Eugenio Matibag, *Haitian-Dominican Counterpoint: Nation, State, and Race on Hispaniola* (New York: Palgrave Macmillan, 2003).

2. Ginetta E. B. Candelario, *Black Behind the Ears: Dominican Racial Identity from Museums to Beauty Shops* (Durham, NC: Duke University Press, 2007); Silvio Torres Saillant, "The Tribulations of Blackness: Stages in Dominican Racial Identity," *Latin American Perspectives* 25, no. 3 (1998).

3. The first international denunciation was issued by the Migration Secretariat of the World Council of Churches, in 1978, but the report most often credited with first raising international awareness of the plight of Haitian workers in the Dominican Republic is that issued the following year by the Anti-Slavery Society (1979). The earliest reports, published by journalists and independent investigators (Maurice Lemoine, *Bitter Sugar: Slaves Today in the Caribbean*, trans. Andrea Johnston [Chicago: Banner Press, 1985]; Roger Plant, *Sugar and Modern Slavery: A Tale of Two Countries* [London: Zed Books, 1987]), international human rights monitor groups (World Council of Churches, Migration Secretariat 1978, 1980), and the ILO (1983), centered on sugar cane growers holding Haitian cane workers against their will and on a gamut of other abuses under a bilateral guest-worker treaty, which since 1952 had brought thousands of migrants as cane workers from Haiti each harvest season. That program ended with the fall of Haitian president Jean-Claude Duvalier in 1986, at which point the allegation of contemporary slavery was simply shifted to describe yet another set of wrongs, substantiated by migrants' testimony about the use of force and fraud in an older, parallel scheme of recruitment by company touts (Americas Watch, *A Troubled Year: Haitians in the Dominican Republic* [New York: Americas Watch and National Coalition for Haitian Refugees, 1992]; Lawyers Committee for Human Rights, *A Childhood Abducted: Children Cutting Sugar Cane in the Dominican Republic* [New York: Lawyers Committee for Human Rights, 1991]). After not having been the focus of any international fact finders for nearly 15 years, the Dominican sugar slavery allegation was revived through a wave of photo-essays, documentaries, and fictional films released in the late 2000s (Céline Anaya Gautier, *Esclaves au paradis* [La Roque d'Anthéron: Vents d'Ailleurs, 2007]; *The Price of Sugar*, dir. William Haney, 2007; New York: New Yorker Films; Claudio Del Punta, *Haïti Chérie*, film, directed by Claudio del Punta [Rome: Esperia Film – Arethusa Film, 2007]; *The Sugar Babies: The Plight of the Children of Agricultural Workers in the Sugar Industry of the Dominican Republic*, dir. Amy Serrano, 2007; Miami: Siren Studios; Alex Webb, "Bitter Toil: Haitian Sugar Workers in the Dominican Republic," in *Documenting Disposable People: Contemporary Global Slavery*, eds. Mark Sealy, Roger Malbert, and Alice Lobb, 138–151 [London: Hayward, 2008]).

4. ONE, *Primera encuesta nacional de inmigrantes en la República Dominicana, ENI-2012, Informe General* (Santo Domingo: Oficina Nacional de Estadística, ONE, 2013), 73.

5. Allison Petrozziello and Bridget Wooding, *Fanm nan Fwontye, Fanm Toupatou: Making Visible the Violence Against Haitian Migrant, In-Transit and Displaced Women on the Dominican-Haitian Border* (Santo Domingo: Colectiva Mujeres y Salud, Mujeres del Mundo, Observatory Migrants of the Caribbean (CIES-UNIBE), 2012).

6. Mervyn Ratekin, "The Early Sugar Industry in Española," *Hispanic American Historical Review* 34, no. 1 (1954).

7. Frank Moya Pons, *The Dominican Republic: A National History* (New Rochelle, NY: Hispaniola Books, 1995), 42–45.

8. Moya Pons, *The Dominican Republic*, ch. 4.

9. Bonham C. Richardson, *Caribbean Migrants: Environment and Survival on St. Kitts and Nevis* (Knoxville: University of Tennessee Press, 1983), 6.

10. Elizabeth M. Thomas-Hope, "The Establishment of a Migration Tradition: British West Indian Movements to the Hispanic Caribbean in the Century after

Emancipation," in *Caribbean Social Relations*, ed. Colin G. Clarke, 66–81 (Liverpool: Centre for Latin American Studies, University of Liverpool, 1978); Dawn I. Marshall, "The History of Caribbean Migrations: The Case of the West Indies," *Caribbean Review* 11, no. 1 (1982).

11. Aisha Khan, "Africa, Europe, and Asia in the Making of the 20th-century Caribbean," in *The Caribbean: A History of the Region and Its Peoples*, eds. Stephan Palmié and Francisco A. Scarano, 399–413 (Chicago: University of Chicago Press, 2011), 400.

12. Elizabeth Cooper, "The Conundrum of Race: Retooling Inequality," in *The Caribbean: A History of the Region and Its Peoples*, eds. Stephan Palmié and Francisco A. Scarano, 385–397 (Chicago: University of Chicago Press, 2011), 391.

13. José del Castillo, "The Formation of the Dominican Sugar Industry: From Competition to Monopoly, from National Semiproletariat to Foreign Proletariat," in *Between Slavery and Free Labor: The Spanish-Speaking Caribbean in the Nineteenth Century*, edited by Manuel Moreno Fraginals, Frank Moya Pons, and Stanley L. Engerman, 215–234 (Baltimore: Johns Hopkins University Press, 1985), 229–230.

14. del Castillo, "The Formation of the Dominican Sugar Industry," 230.

15. José del Castillo, *La inmigración de braceros azucareros en la República Dominicana, 1900–1930* (Santo Domingo: Centro Dominicano de Investigaciones Antropológicas (CENDIA)/Universidad Autónoma de Santo Domingo, 1978), 31–37.

16. Samuel Martínez, "From Hidden Hand to Heavy Hand: Sugar, the State, and Migrant Labor in Haiti and the Dominican Republic," *Latin American Research Review* 34, no. 1 (1999).

17. José del Castillo, "Azúcar y braceros: historia de un problema," *INAZUCAR* 6, no. 29 (1981): 44.

18. Harry Hoetink, *The Dominican People, 1850–1900: Notes for a Historical Sociology*, trans. Stephen K. Ault (Baltimore: Johns Hopkins University Press, 1982), 15.

19. Justino José del Orbe, *Mauricio Báez y la clase obrera* (Santo Domingo: Taller, 1981), 27, 30–31.

20. Piece-rate wages differed crucially—and unfavorably from the standpoint of most cane cutters—in that the standardized rate of remuneration did not take account of major differences between fields in how much cane they would yield, Catherine Le-Grand, "Informal Resistance on a Dominican Sugar Plantation During the Trujillo Dictatorship," *Hispanic American Historical Review* 74, no. 4 (1995). A "good" field held tall, heavy, straight cane; a "bad" field had cane that was stunted, thin, fallen, or choked with weeds. Under the older task system, these differences and more—including personal ties, the worker's negotiating ability and experience, and temporary scarcities of labor—could be taken into account as the pay for each task was negotiated with individual workers or work teams.

21. del Castillo, *La inmigración de braceros azucareros en la República Dominicana, 1900–1930*, 47–58.

22. Bruce J. Calder, *The Impact of Intervention: The Dominican Republic During the U.S. Occupation of 1916–1924* (Austin: University of Texas Press, 1984), 61–62.

23. Michiel Baud, "Sugar and Unfree Labour: Reflections on Labour Control in the Dominican Republic, 1870–1935," *Journal of Peasant Studies* 19, no. 2 (1992): 316.

24. Bernardo Vega, *Trujillo y Haití, Volumen I (1930–1937)* (Santo Domingo: Fundación Cultural Dominicana, 1988), Ch. 9 and 10.

25. Max Dorsinville, "Accord sur l'embauchage en Haïti et l'entrée en République Dominicaine des journaliers temporaires haïtiens," *Revue du Travail* 3 (1953): 108–114.

26. Samuel Martínez, "Indifference Within Indignation: Anthropology, Human Rights, and the Haitian Bracero," *American Anthropologist* 98, no. 1 (1996).

27. Americas Watch, *A Troubled Year: Haitians in the Dominican Republic* (New York: Americas Watch and National Coalition for Haitian Refugees, 1992); Lawyers Committee for Human Rights, *A Childhood Abducted: Children Cutting Sugar Cane in the Dominican Republic* (New York: Lawyers Committee for Human Rights, 1991).

28. Samuel Martínez, "The Onion of Oppression: Haitians in the Dominican Republic," in *Geographies of the Haitian Diaspora*, eds. Regine O. Jackson, 51–70 (New York: Routledge, 2011).

29. Wiktor Osiatyński, *Human Rights and Their Limits* (Cambridge: Cambridge University Press, 2009).

30. Verité, *Research on Indicators of Forced Labor in the Supply Chain of Sugar in the Dominican Republic*, 2012, 58–59. http://www.verite.org/sites/default/files/images/Research%20on%20Indicators%20of%20Forced%20Labor%20in%20the%20Dominican%20Republic%20Sugar%20Sector_9.18.pdf.

31. Verité, *Research on Indicators of Forced Labor in the Supply Chain of Sugar in the Dominican Republic*, 50.

32. *The Price of Sugar*, directed by William Haney, 2007; New York: New Yorker Films, minutes 69:55 through 70:25.

33. Rubén Silié, Carlos Segura, and Carlos Dore Cabral, *La nueva inmigración haitiana* (Santo Domingo: FLACSO, 2002); Franc Báez Evertsz and Wilfredo Lozano, "Los cambios de la inmigración haitiana y la polémica de sus cifras," *Revista Dominicana de Política Exterior* 1, no. 1 (2005): 95–98.

34. Anaya Gautier, *Esclaves au paradis*; *The Price of Sugar*; Claudio Del Punta, *Haïti Chérie*; *The Sugar Babies*; Webb, Bitter Toil.

35. Inter-American Court of Human Rights, "Case of the Yean and Bosico Children v. the Dominican Republic, Judgment of September 8, 2005," *Refugee Survey Quarterly* 25, no. 3 (2006): 119.

36. FLACSO, *Encuesta sobre inmigrantes haitianos en la República Dominicana: Resumen de resultados* (Santo Domingo: FLACSO-Secretaría General and Organización Internacional de Migraciones-OIM, 2004), 27.

37. Interview with MUDHA Staffers (Santo Domingo: May 22, 2002). Garcia, Michelle. "No Papers, No Rights." *Amnesty International Magazine*. 2006. http://www.amnestyusa.org/amnesty-magazine/fall-2006/no-papers-no-rights/page.do?id=1105216.

38. "Jus soli" is effectively synonymous with "birthright citizenship." Merriam-Webster, Dictionary Entry of "Jus soli," accessed at http://www.merriam-webster.com/dictionary/jus%20soli; Carmen Cedeño, "La nacionalidad de los descendientes de haitianos nacidos en la República Dominicana," in *La cuestión haitiana en Santo Domingo: Migración internacional, desarrollo y relaciones inter-estatales entre Haití y República Dominicana*, ed. Wilfredo Lozano, 137–143 (Santo Domingo: FLACSO-Programa República Dominicana and Centro Norte-Sur/Universidad de Miami, 1992), 139; Lawyers Committee for Human Rights, *A Childhood Abducted: Children Cutting Sugar Cane in the Dominican Republic* (New York: Lawyers Committee for Human Rights, 1991), 13–14.

39. CCDH (Centro Cultural Domínico-Haitiano), *Análisis de la situación de inmigrantes haitianos en la República Dominicana* (Santo Domingo: CCDH, 1997), 16.

40. Interview with Laurel Fletcher (New Haven, CT: February 4, 2005). Also, Genaro Rincón Miesse, the Dominican lawyer representing MUDHA at the IACHR proceedings, noted, "The civil status registrars do not apply these requirements consistently," registrars in districts where there are few Haitians being more permissive (Inter-American Court of Human Rights, "Case of the Yean and Bosico Children v. the Dominican Republic, Judgment of September 8, 2005," *Refugee Survey Quarterly* 25, no. 3 [2006]: 116).

41. The Inter-American Commission on Human Rights (the older of the two institutions of the Inter-American human rights system) has wide powers to investigate cases, publish findings, and request state compliance with preliminary measures, and it may be said effectively to function as a court of first instance for parties who cannot get justice in their own countries, but only the Inter-American Court (the newer body, which has heard contentious cases only since the mid-1980s) has the power to adjudicate and issue binding decisions in cases brought before the Inter-American system (Laurence Burgogue-Larsen and Amaya Úbeda de Torres, *The Inter-American Court of Human Rights: Case Law and Commentary*, trans. Rosalind Greenstein (Oxford: Oxford University Press, 2011); Jo M. Pasqualucci, *The Practice and Procedure of the Inter-American Court of Human Rights* (Cambridge: Cambridge University Press, 2003).

42. Garcia, 21.

43. República Dominicana, "Ley General de Migración, No. 285-04," *Gaceta Oficial* 10291, August 27, 2004, 5-46, http://www.seip.gob.do/Portals/0/docs/Migracion/ley.pdf, 22; David C. Baluarte, "Inter-American Justice Comes to the Dominican Republic: An Island Shakes as Human Rights and Sovereignty Clash," *American University Human Rights Brief* 13, no. 2 (2006): 28.

44. Interview with Sonia Pierre (Bloomfield: March 6, 2009); see also the video, "Resolución 12-07 ¿Qué es?" accessed at http://www.youtube.com/watch?v=Rukj6D1Oxvs.

45. RECONICI.DO, "Resumen preliminar de la investigación sobre personas afectadas por la Resolución 12/07," 2011, http://www.reconoci.do/images/stories/documentos/resumen-preliminar.pdf.

46. ONE, *Primera encuesta nacional de inmigrantes en la República Dominicana*, 75.

47. República Dominicana, Tribunal Constitucional, "Sentencia TC/0168/13," 2013, 99–100, http://noticiasmicrojuris.files.wordpress.com/2013/10/sentenciatc0168-13-c.pdf.

48. República Dominicana, Oficina de la Presidencia, "Decreto No. 327-13," 2013. http://www.consultoria.gov.do/spaw2/uploads/files/Decreto%20327-13.pdf.

49. Agencia EFE, "Entra en vigencia el plan dominicano para regular extranjeros," 2014, accessed June 2. http://feeds.univision.com/feeds/article/2014-06-02/entra-en-vigencia-el-plan.

50. The Haitian government, with the support of the UN Refugee Agency and the European Union, has in the recent past sent out mobile units to issue birth certificates and passports to Haitian nationals living in sugar-producing areas. See Carmen Matos, "Haití expide documentos a sus ciudadanos el el país," *Hoy*, September 15, 2012. http://hoy.com.do/haiti-expide-documentos-a-sus-ciudadanos-en-el-pais/.

51. República Dominicana, Congreso Nacional, "Ley No.169-14," 2014, http://www.consultoria.gov.do/spaw2/uploads/files/Ley%20No.%20169-14.pdf.

52. Agencia EFE, "Entra en vigencia el plan dominicano para regular extranjeros," 2014, accessed June 2, 2012. http://feeds.univision.com/feeds/article/2014-06-02/entra-en-vigencia-el-plan.

53. Samuel Martínez, "The Price of Confrontation: International Retributive Justice and the Struggle for Haitian-Dominican Rights," in *The Uses and Misuses of Human Rights: A Critical Approach to Advocacy*, eds. George Andreopoulos and Zehra Arat, 89–115 (New York: Palgrave, 2014).

54. Author's translation of Wilfredo Lozano, *La paradoja de las migraciones: El estado dominicano frente a la inmigración haitiana* (Santo Domingo: Editorial UNIBE, Facultad Latinoamericana de Ciencias Sociales, Servicio Jesuita de Refujiados y Migrantes, 2008), 131.

55. Kamari Maxine Clarke, *Fictions of Justice: The International Criminal Court and the Challenge of Legal Pluralism in Sub-Saharan Africa* (Cambridge: Cambridge University Press, 2009), 236.

56. Baluarte, "Inter-American Justice Comes to the Dominican Republic," 28.

57. Samuel Martínez, "The Price of Confrontation: International Retributive Justice and the Struggle for Haitian-Dominican Rights," in *The Uses and Misuses of Human Rights: A Critical Approach to Advocacy*, eds. George Andreopoulos and Zehra Arat, 89–115 (New York: Palgrave, 2014).

58. Sidney W. Mintz, "Whitewashing Haiti's History," *Boston Review*, January 22, 2010. http://www.bostonreview.net/world/whitewashing-haiti%E2%80%99s-history; Anthony Oliver-Smith, "Haiti and the Historical Construction of Disasters," *NACLA Report on the Americas* 43, no. 3 (2010).

59. Mark Schuller, *Killing with Kindness: Haiti, International Aid, and NGOs* (Piscataway, NJ: Rutgers University Press, 2012), Ch. 5.

60. Oliver-Smith, "Haiti and the Historical Construction of Disasters," 32.

CHAPTER 4

Nicaraguan Immigration to Costa Rica

Tendencies, Policies, and Politics

CARLOS SANDOVAL-GARCÍA

Like migration from Haiti, Bolivia, and Guatemala to the Dominican Republic, Argentina, and Mexico, respectively, Nicaraguan migration to Costa Rica is a major case of south-to-south migration in Latin America.[1] It takes place in Central America, a region where both intraregional and extraregional migration is a structural dimension of everyday life. Demographers estimate that between 12% and 14% of Central Americans live in a country different from their country of birth. Military conflicts, economic inequalities, and, more recently, violence are among the main factors that expel Central Americans from their countries of birth.[2]

Although the 2011 census confirms that Nicaraguan migration to Costa Rica shows a slow decrease (about 6% of Costa Rica's total population), discrimination continues to be an everyday experience for Nicaraguans in Costa Rica.[3] Images of immigration, most of them derogatory, are present in conversations, emails, and digital social networks, and expressions such as "No sea Nica" (Don't be Nica) or "Parecés de La Carpio" (You seem to come from La Carpio, an impoverished and criminalized community where about half of the population is from Nicaragua) inscribe hostility in everyday life.

Although Nicaraguan migrants are vital to most sectors of the old and new export-based economy for which Costa Rica is known abroad, not to mention the infrastructure that has made the tourism boom possible, they find it hard to make their voices heard in the public square. Because Nicaraguans perceive themselves as unwanted foreigners, they do not feel authorized to speak out about their rights or their contributions, economic and otherwise, to Costa Rican society. This chapter illustrates how Costa Rican hostility and xenophobia toward Nicaraguans, and the internalized fear and silence that these instill, have contributed to a social and political environment that sows marginality and prevents migrants' political participation and inclusion.

I organize this chapter into five sections. The first summarizes some of the major periods of Nicaraguan immigration to Costa Rica. The second describes the imageries deployed to represent the Nicaraguan as a threatening other. The third section reflects on the current Immigration Law in Costa Rica, its promise of integration and the ways in which legality produces the irregularity that it aims to overcome. Of particular interest are the Immigration Law, which changed twice during the early twenty-first century, and a reform proposal submitted to the Legislative Assembly in the year 2013. The fourth section presents advocacy initiatives regarding immigrants' access to health care and education, in particular an initiative that made undocumented youths eligible to apply for places at the Instituto Nacional de Aprendizaje (INA), a national institution that provides technical education. I also discuss a "white paper" whose aim was to end undocumented pregnant women's access to health care through the Caja Costarricense de Seguro Social (CCSS), the public health system. The last section of the chapter reflects on the challenges immigration and discrimination pose to social science research that aims to be public, not purely academic, and explores ways to promote recognition of rights. Overall, this chapter suggests that representations and public policies regarding immigration in Costa Rica during the past 30 years need to be located in a broader context of institutional and ideological changes that have been taking place in the country and have given rise to a more unequal society.

HISTORICIZING NICARAGUAN IMMIGRATION

Immigration from Nicaragua to Costa Rica has been occurring since independence from Spain in 1821. Toward the end of the nineteenth century, the expansion of coffee plantations in Nicaragua dislocated peasants, who then sought job opportunities created by the building of the Panama Canal. Many of them worked in Costa Rica on the construction of the railway to the Atlantic and, later, on the banana plantations being developed in that country. Novels in the social realist tradition, considered classics of Costa Rican literature, re-created their lived experience in Costa Rica.[4] Nicaraguans were also active during the Costa Rican Civil War of 1948.[5] The winning leader, José Figueres Ferrer, looked for ways to undermine the Somoza dictatorship that ruled Nicaragua from 1936 to 1979. In turn, Anastasio Somoza, the latest member of the dynasty, sought to defeat Figueres Ferrer. In short, political animosities have been present through the years and constitute the context under which Nicaraguan immigration to Costa Rica is usually portrayed.

Toward the end of the war against Somoza's dictatorship (1934–1979) most of Costa Rican society supported the Sandinistas' upheaval. Soon after the Sandinista Revolution brought down the Somoza regime in 1979, the Reagan Administration began its financial support of military and political adversaries of the Sandinistas. In response, the Sandinistas felt compelled to establish the Patriotic Military Service, a compulsory military recruitment program, which prompted the immigration of thousands of families to Costa Rica, to avoid the conscription of their children into the army. The Reagan Administration (1981–1989) framed the conflict against the Sandinista government in Cold War terms and viewed the Sandinistas as "communists." This rhetoric resonated well with the strong anticommunist ethos that dominated Costa Rican political culture for decades.[6] Under the influence of anticommunism rhetoric, support for the Sandinistas diminished drastically.

In the 1990 Nicaraguan general elections, a year after the fall of the Berlin Wall, Violeta Barrios de Chamorro defeated Daniel Ortega, the Sandinista presidential candidate, who expected to be re-elected. Chamorro's victory meant the end of the military conflict in Nicaragua and, simultaneously, began a period characterized by neoliberal policies that privatized public institutions and eliminated subsidies, resulting in a considerable increase in unemployment.[7] Thus, political change in Nicaragua took place in a context defined by the legitimization of neoliberal policies in Central America, which, during the last 30 years, have transformed economies and the land, pushing millions of people from their countries of birth, especially because of the dismantling of local economies based on agriculture.

These measures, together with Hurricane Mitch in 1989, aggravated the living conditions of hundreds of thousands of Nicaraguans and forced them to leave their country. Most members of upper middle classes who left Nicaragua hoped to relocate in the United States, and Brown and Patten (2013) estimate that about 400,000 of them did so.[8] Meanwhile, the popular classes, initially from urban areas and later from rural regions, crossed the Costa Rican border.

Barrios's victory in the context of neoliberal Central American and the end of communism in Europe, symbolized by the fall of the Berlin Wall, undermined the association of the Sandinista Revolution with communism. Meanwhile, the departure of Nicaraguans for Costa Rica increased. A political consequence of this shift is that Costa Ricans began to view Nicaraguans more as migrants than as communists whether or not they were Sandinistas, and as cultural outsiders because they were migrants.

This brief account of political developments must also consider the territorial dimension. The very definition of the border between Nicaragua and Costa Rica, as with many such disputes in Latin America, has sparked political controversy since the beginning of independence.[9] Both states looked to the imperial powers of the time, Britain, France, and the then-emerging United States, seeking political and financial support to build a canal, envisioned as part of the San River, a project that eventually came to fruition with the building of the Panama Canal.[10] The very same definition of borders remains an issue today, and it is now under review by the International Court of Justice in The Hague. Although both Nicaragua and Costa Rica claim that its definition of the border is based on geographical and political evidence, conflicts around borders are much more disputed in the capitals than in the border communities themselves, which are characterized by chronic poverty on both sides.[11] Meanwhile, the Nicaragua government, under Daniel Ortega (president since 2007 and now serving his second consecutive term), has signed a contract with Chinese investors who, presumably, will manage the construction of the long-envisioned San River canal. Imperial powers still play a key role in the definition of what matters in the Central American isthmus.

FRAMING THE THREATENING OTHER

According to popular xenophobic sentiments, notorious in everyday conversations in Costa Rica, there are at least three main ways of representing Nicaraguans: they are "too many," they are violent and produce insecurity, and they take jobs in public works that should go to Costa Ricans.

The 2000 population census estimated that Nicaraguans who live in Costa Rica represent around 226,374 (5.9%) of the total inhabitants. Eleven years later, in 2011, the population census reported Nicaraguans to number 287,766, or 6.6% of the total population.[12] Over the course of a decade (2000–2011), while there was a 27.1% absolute rise in the number of Nicaraguans living in Costa Rica, there was only a very slight increase in their share (0.9%). This figure is much lower than the increase reported between the census carried out in 1984 and the 2000 census, which was 4.1%.

Although commonplace hostility toward Nicaraguans regards them as "too many," they actually play a key role within the demographic transition that is taking place in Costa Rica, which is characterized by an increase in life expectancy and a decrease in the fertility rate. Men's life expectancy is approximately 76.7 years, and women's life expectancy is about 81.6 years. Meanwhile, the fertility rate decreased from 2.12 in 2003 to 1.76 in 2013,[13] an important variation that will have long-term repercussions on the establishment of the economically active population and pensions systems, to mention only two. Indeed, the fertility rate would be even lower if migrants from Nicaragua were not having children in Costa Rica. The "demographic bonus" provided by Nicaraguan migrants and their children is beginning to diminish, although the Costa Rican imaginary does not seem to register this change. Figure 4.1 shows this transition.

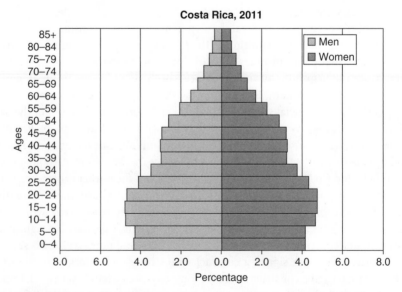

Figure 4.1a 2011 Costa Rican–born population. Source: Roger Bonilla and Carlos Sandoval, "Aspectos sociodemográficos de la migración nicaragüense en Costa Rica, según el Censo 2011," in Costa Rica a la Luz del Censo, San José, 2014, 267.

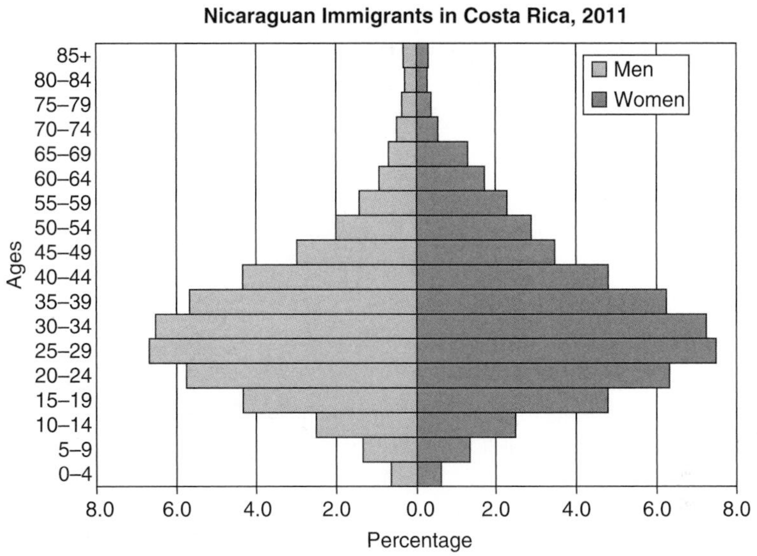

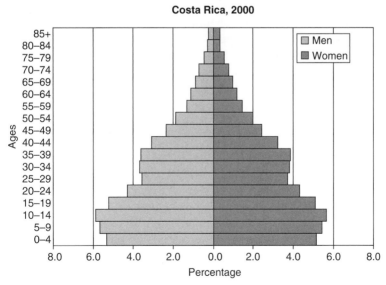

Figure 4.1b 2011 Nicaraguan migrants. Source: Roger Bonilla and Carlos Sandoval, "Aspectos sociodemográficos de la migración nicaragüense en Costa Rica, según el Censo 2011," in Costa Rica a la Luz del Censo, San José, 2014, 267.

Figure 4.1c 2000 Costa Rican–born population. Source: Roger Bonilla and Carlos Sandoval, "Aspectos sociodemográficos de la migración nicaragüense en Costa Rica, según el Censo 2011," in Costa Rica a la Luz del Censo, San José, 2014, 267.

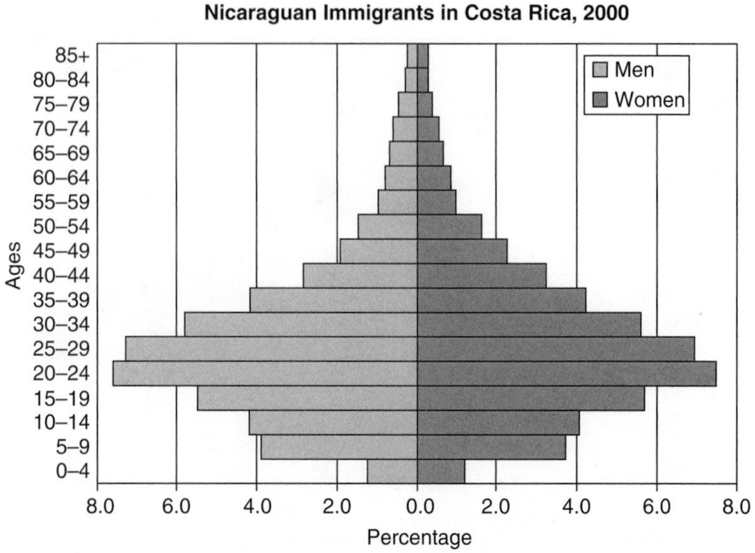

Nicaraguan Immigrants in Costa Rica, 2000

Figure 4.1d 2000 Nicaraguan migrants. Source: Roger Bonilla and Carlos Sandoval, "Aspectos so-ciodemográficos de la migración nicaragüense en Costa Rica, según el Censo 2011," in Costa Rica a la Luz del Censo, San José, 2014, 267.

Regarding violence, Costa Rica reports one of the lowest rates of homicides (the indicator usually deployed for analysis of violence) in Latin America, but it exhibits one of the highest senses of insecurity. Violence rates in Costa Rica are not comparable with indicators of the so-called North Triangle of Central America, which includes Guatemala, Honduras, and El Salvador. Whereas Costa Rican authorities report 8.8 homicides per 100,000 inhabitants, in Honduras the figure is 79. Tegucigalpa and San Pedro Sula, the main Honduran cities, are two of the cities with the highest proportion of homicides worldwide.[14]

Researchers have addressed the contrast between levels of violence and the sense of insecurity in Costa Rica from a variety of perspectives. One possible explanation of this paradox is that violence rates have been rising in Costa Rica. This is true particularly for crimes against property, which is not surprising in a country where inequality has been increasing such that it is currently the fifth most unequal in Latin America. It is also true for crimes associated with illicit substances, whose consumption has also increased, especially because their transport through Central American territory makes them more available within the region. A second explanation builds upon the prevailing discourses that criminalize poverty by associating law breaking with certain places, and viewing migrants as the main transgressors. These two broad generalizations are often present in the media and seem to constitute a sort of discursive structure,[15] which is then used to make sense of news media reports.

Media representations on immigration usually frame immigration as a problem that must be controlled. Overall, whereas political change in Costa Rican society has oriented its institutions toward a quasi-social democratic welfare state,[16]cultural policy—the sphere to which the media belongs—advocated conservative perspectives. This is a major paradox of Costa Rican society: while key institutions made access to key services (e.g., insurance, health, electricity, telecommunications, and higher education were among the key sectors) possible for large groups of people, media and other institutions related to the cultural sector were left behind.[17]

Between 2010 and 2013, criminality rates have decreased. Homicides went from 11.5 per 100,000 inhabitants in 2010 to 8.8 in 2013. Crimes against property diminished 9% in the beginning of the year 2012. Perception of insecurity also fell from 48.6% to 30%, but it is still considered the main problem of the country.[18] During 2014, the number of homicides seems to have increased, but, interestingly, this does not seem to be related to Nicaraguans but rather to disputes between small groups who seek to control distribution of illicit drugs within impoverished communities. Since most of victims and offenders are Costa Ricans, nationality has not become an issue.

A third kind of imagery views the weakening of public services like education, health, and housing as a consequence of aid given to Nicaraguans migrants. An alternative view would suggest that Costa Rican society has experienced a change in its style of development, currently characterized by the legitimacy of neoliberal policies, which has diversified the economy but also increased inequality. Economic policies have configured an export-based economy that has diversified production of goods and increased markets. Under this economic pattern, economic growth has not meant equity. While the proportion of the population living below the poverty line remains at about 20%, inequality has risen considerably. A new methodology applied to estimating income distribution reported that the Gini coefficient is about 0.54.[19]

Health provision is a case in point. Data provided by the 2011 census show that the percentage of Nicaraguans who belong to the economically active population is higher than that of Costa Ricans in the same condition (51.4 and 43.2, respectively), which confirms the long-term consequences of the demographic change. Measures of affiliation with the public health system, or Caja Costarricense de Seguro Social (CCSS), are also relevant. The percentage of Nicaraguans who are affiliated with the CCSS through their jobs is higher than that of Costa Ricans in the same condition (27.4 and 22.6, respectively). However, the percentage of Nicaraguans who get access to health care through their relatives (known as family insurance) is much lower than that of their Costa Ricans counterparts (22.8 and 41.4, respectively).[20] Table 4.1 presents a more detailed description of these patterns.

The census does not provide evidence of why Nicaraguans do not include their relatives in their family insurance. A number of possible factors may explain this absence. One is lack of information about the rights of relatives regarding affiliation with the public health system. Second, since migrants are mainly of an age at which health care is not a major issue, many do not think about including family members. Third, relatives may be undocumented, which would make them ineligible to affiliate. Last, but not least, patriarchal culture may prevent men from including their partners. All of these factors require further research.[21]

TABLE 4.1   Types of Insurance: Costa Rica, 2000 and 2011.

	2000		2011	
	Costa Ricans	Nicaraguan Migrants	Costa Ricans	Nicaraguan Migrants
Types of insurance	%	%	%	%
Paid work	18.5	22.6	22.3	27.4
Self-employment	6.6	4.6	8.7	9.6
Retired	4.1	1.2	6.1	1.7
Family insurance	44.8	24.1	41.4	22.8
State insurance	8.7	7.1	7.9	3.0
Others	0.7	0.7	0.7	0.6
Without insurance	16.6	39.8	12.9	34.8
Total	100.0	100.0	100.0	100.0

Source: Bonilla and Sandoval, "Aspectos sociodemográficos de la migración nicaragüense en Costa Rica, según el Censo 2011," 274.

A weak public sphere limits reflection on the ways in which neoliberal policies have undermined key institutions of Costa Rican society.[22] In this context, fantasies about the nation frequently replace debates about an inclusive society. Anti-immigrant hostility, often fueled by the media, has been the raw material of exclusionary fantasies about nation. In turn, this same anti-immigrant hostility aims to contain and make bearable the anxiety generated by the uncertainty over weakening institutions and the imaginaries about Nicaraguan migrants.[23]

Paradoxically, though considered "threatening others," Nicaraguans are indispensable to neoliberal economic development. The agriculture-based economy that produces "new" commodities like watermelons, oranges, melons, and mangoes, as well as the traditional coffee and bananas, depends on Nicaraguan men and women. Ironically, production and processing of the traditional and new tropical fruits that Costa Rica exports to the world are in the hands of migrants. The case of the construction sector is similar, since Nicaraguans have become indispensable for building the infrastructure that has made the tourist boom possible, especially in the Pacific coast region.

Unfortunately, neither academic research nor nongovernmental organizations (NGOs) have been able to estimate the economic contribution of Nicaraguans in terms, for example, of the Gross Internal Product. The erasure of migrants' economic contributions might be due to their absence from the media and everyday conversations. Lack of recognition of the Nicaraguan community renders migrants invisible and erases their economic contributions from the public imagination. Instead, the media frame most discussions in terms of the economic costs of migrants. Prevailing discourses denote Nicaraguan immigration as a "cost" and a drain upon resources, paying scant attention to its contribution in a number of key economic activities. In short, as noted, absences, such as Nicaraguans' contribution to the Costa Rica economy, make it even more difficult to acknowledge how much Costa Rican society depends on the migrant labor force.[24]

The popular representation of Nicaraguans as violent and lawless conflicts with the roles some of them play in tempering the insecurity that is often considered Costa Rica's main social problem. Private security companies often recruit Nicaraguan guards to protect property, and Nicaraguan women perform a great deal of (poorly) paid domestic work, in particular, caring for Costa Rica's middle-class children and elderly people. These Nicaraguan migrants usually leave their own children at home or bring them to Costa Rica to take care of other people's children. In short, those who many in Costa Rica consider violent are, at the same time, responsible for the protection and support of life. Nicaraguan domestic workers, construction workers, and private security guards generally live in highly criminalized neighborhoods or shantytowns. Ironically, those who live in such settings are responsible for the production and reproduction of life in the respected neighborhoods, which include gated communities.

Underscoring this irony, Costa Rica's soccer team turned in an outstanding performance in the World Cup Games, in Brazil in 2014, thanks in part to a goal scored by Oscar Duarte in the opening game against Uruguay (which Costa Rica won). Duarte was born in Nicaragua and migrated to Costa Rica at the age of 5. His World Cup goal inscribed immigration within a national celebration. For a moment, as in the case of carnival, distinctions between who belongs to the nation and who does not were blurred. Duarte's goal existed in a discursive space beyond national boundaries, but as in carnival, the euphoria did not last very long. Despite Costa Rica's self-representation as a peaceful and democratic society, Nicaraguan migrants, the main foreign-born community in the country, continue to be portrayed in derogatory terms as violent and threatening outsiders.[25]

IMMIGRATION LAW PRODUCES IRREGULARITY

In July 2009, Costa Rica's Legislative Assembly passed the current General Law of Migration and Alien Affairs (No. 8,764), which went into effect in March 2010.[26] In general, this law eliminates a good part of the vocabulary linked to security that abounded in the earlier law, replacing it with the discourse of human rights, alluding to multiple international agreements ratified and in effect in Costa Rica. The human rights frame bestowed important legitimacy upon the new law. The new law combines this framing with specific provisions that make the regularization of the migratory process even more cumbersome and grants competencies, such as to extend detentions for more than 24 hours, to the executive branch that, according to the Constitution, properly belong to the judicial branch.

Participation in the public social security system is one of the new requirements for a migrant beginning the regularization process (articles 7.7, 78.3, and 97). A consequence of this new requirement is that the responsibility for securing insurance falls on the workers, not their employers. The law also establishes a series of payments to extend or otherwise change migratory status. For example, persons categorized as tourists must pay US$100 to prolong their stay in the country (article 90). Those wishing to change their migratory category must, in addition to meeting the requirements to obtain the new status, pay US$200 (articles 96 and 125) unless they leave the country to re-enter on a visa, in which case they must begin residency proceedings again, which costs US$30.

High costs impede regularization of status. In fact, one of the grounds for cancelling a person's permanent residency is failure to renew documentation within 3 months of its expiry date (article 129.10). To this must be added that for every month of irregular status in Costa Rican territory, one must pay a US$100 fine or, "by default, the person's entry will be prohibited for a period equivalent to triple the time of his/her irregular residence" (article 33.3). The insurance requirement, added to the severity of the fines, has increased nondocumentation. A report on regularization requests presented to the General Direction of Migration and Alien Affairs (DGME) reveals that there was a decrease of almost 50% in new permanent visa applications between 2010 and 2011.[27] In other words, the law's promise of regularization is far from being fulfilled.

During the second half of 2012, the DGME announced a number of temporary measures that make some of the requirements for legal residence more flexible. This announcement coincided with the recognition of the Apostille Convention, which establishes that when a state recognizes documents executed by another state, such documents need not be certified by the consular authorities of the country where they will be submitted. Currently, Nicaraguans applying for residency in Costa Rica can obtain their documents at the Nicaraguan consulate in Costa Rica. Long queues at the Nicaraguan consulate seem to confirm migrants' willingness to become legal residents. However, expensive paperwork deters them from applying for residency. A major challenge for the current government of Costa Rica is to recognize that the costs of residency reduce the possibility of recognition of migrants' duties and rights.

A second set of provisions in the law refers to the powers granted to agencies with authority over migration. The Migration Police may detain migrants for 24 hours, but articles 12 and 31.5a and 5b empower the DGME director to authorize extension of detention without specifying a limit. This power to impose indeterminate detentions appears to conflict with article 37 of the Political Constitution of Costa Rica, which reserves this power for a judicial authority. The provision in article 16 of the existing Law of Migration and Alien Affairs that "the Professional Migration Police will investigate the trading and trafficking in persons, as well as any infraction of a migratory nature" must be understood in the same sense. The administrative police appear to have been given the power to apprehend suspected illegal migrants, but to do so to investigate cases would usurp a power of the judicial branch, as established in article 153 of the Political Constitution.[28]

From a wider perspective, the discretion granted to Costa Rican administrative authorities coincides with changes in the legislation of a large number of countries. These have eroded several aspects of the rule of law by granting greater discretion to police and undermining the presumption of innocence and the separation of powers.[29] In the migratory sphere in Costa Rica and elsewhere, changes are taking place whose nature and consequences could be far-reaching.

The General Law of Migration and Alien Affairs is open to challenge in the Constitutional Court on the grounds of unconstitutionality and because some of its provisions contravene international agreements to which Costa Rica is a signatory. Scholar-activists argue, for example, that some of the requirements, costs, and fines the law establishes violate the principles of reasonableness and proportionality which underpin the rule of law, and that the powers assigned to the DGME and the Migration Police violate the principle of independence of the branches of government.[30]

For scholar-activists, challenging the law involves not only systematizing some of the criticisms of the existing legislation but also building a persuasive case that justice and citizens' rights should prevail regardless of nationality. Based on this concern, the team that worked on the project "Advancing the Rights of Migrant Women in Latin America and the Caribbean" invited colleagues working in NGOs and churches to reflect on the scope of the law and the possibilities for engaging in advocacy. In the framework of these initiatives, they delivered a document outlining their main concerns to the then-director of the DGME, suggesting, for example, that the charges for obtaining documents remain the same but that the documents be valid for longer. In response to this initiative, the DGME agreed to extend the validity of residence permits from 1 to 2 years at first issue and to 3 or 4 years for revalidations, as verified by article 56 of the Regulations of Alien Affairs, published in the official daily, *La Gaceta*, in January 2011.

A second stage of the work consisted of convening a group that met over a longer period for a more careful reflection on the law and on the possibilities of preparing a writ of unconstitutionality. In September 2011, they submitted a final version of the writ to the Constitutional Court, which, in April 2012, partially admitted it. Overall, the Court admitted the claims against those articles in which the distinctions between the judicial and executive powers were blurred, but it did not accept that high costs were a matter of constitutional law. In December 2012, the Constitutional Court dismissed the case, arguing the State is not obliged to comply with international law.[31] This was a major disappointment.

If one compares the response when the 2006 migration law went into effect with what happened with the General Law of Migration and Alien Affairs, an important difference emerges. Scholar-activist responses to the 2010 law reveal greater collective critical effort and capacity to produce detailed and informed analysis. In fact, in 2006, the possibility of writing a writ of unconstitutionality was unthinkable. Now the possibility of working together with colleagues from the social sciences and law represents a substantive step forward.

In 2013, the government agreed to postpone the application of the fines of US$100 for each month that a person failed to renew her resident visa. A year later, however, the likelihood of these fines was again a matter of concern. Advocacy efforts took place in a new political context because, for the first time in modern Costa Rican history, a nontraditional political party, Partido Acción

Ciudadana (PAC), won the presidential election. It was a major surprise because, a year before, no one envisioned such a possibility.

The PAC began its term with huge electoral support and a wide variety of expectations, including the possibility of changing migration policies. However, no major changes took place during the first months of the new government. The director of the DGME remains the same and the fines, postponed by the last government, went into effect in August 2014. The current Deputy Ministry of Government, Ms. Carmen Muñoz, who is responsible for migration policies, was a member of Legislative Assembly during the last government. As a legislator, she co-submitted a proposal to reform the Immigration Law that emphasized that the costs make it harder for migrants to get residency visas. Ironically, as Deputy Minister, she agreed to charge the fines. So, despite the efforts made by organizations and activists, the new authorities do not appear ready to modify migration policies.

WHEN RETAINING RIGHTS IS A CHALLENGE

An estimation based mainly on community work might suggest that about a third of Nicaraguan migrants do not have regular status in Costa Rica. Most of them, about two-thirds, have the requirements for applying for a residence, which are to have a child born in Costa Rica or being partner of a resident or a Costa Rican. However, most migrants with irregular status do not have the money for all the paperwork in the application process. Those with irregular migrant status are primarily women and children. Most often, within families, men are first to seek to regularize their migrant status, because they must look for jobs. Women heads of households who are responsible for children usually cannot afford the payment for the residency application.[32]

Children without residency may study in state education institutions, and they have access to health care, but they need to show a valid identification document, either a passport or an identity card provided by the Nicaraguan consulate. Women face more restrictions. If they are in an irregular status, they cannot access health care, including essential preventive tests, such as cervical screening. Additionally, they do not have access to contraception, which means they usually give birth to more children than they wished to have.[33]

The United Nations Convention on the Rights of the Child has been a resource for the legitimization of children's rights. However, international agreements, such the Convention on the Elimination of All Forms of Discrimination Against Women (CEDAW), which was adopted by the United Nations in 1979, has had little effect on women migrants' rights. Thus, it is not surprising that no more than 15% of paid domestic workers in Costa Rica, many of them Nicaraguans, have social security rights and, in consequence, a right to retirement.

In this context, the team of the project Advancing the Rights of Migrant Women in Latin American and the Caribbean, supported by the International Development Research Centre (IDRC) of Canada, prepared a proposal to allow women in irregular migratory status the possibility to access health care.

The goal was to assure their right to contraception and preventive reproductive care. Prior to this, women did not have access to health services except in emergencies or during pregnancy. Because Costa Rica has ratified CEDAW, providing access to these services is mandatory. The challenge is how to make international law enforceable at a national level.

This initiative faced difficult times. First, just before submitting the proposal to the authorities, a number of financial and administrative difficulties at the CCSS (Caja Costarricense de Seguro Social) were revealed by the media, which made it politically improbable that health care would be offered to nondocumented women. The Minister of Health even suggested that caring for migrants was one of the factors that caused the financial crisis.[34] Second, a new border dispute between Nicaragua and Costa Rica made the initiative even less feasible.[35] The media represented the border conflict as a confrontation between societies, and in 2010 Costa Rican flags were placed on houses and automobiles to underscore the identification of the population with the position of then-President Laura Chinchilla. The new President, Luis Guillermo Solís, invited all other Central American presidents to the inauguration of his administration, except the President of Nicaragua, Daniel Ortega. His decision confirmed that Costa Rica's nationalist rhetoric was unlikely to diminish anytime soon.

Even worse, in 2013, while the border conflict evolved, the CCSS drafted a mandatory resolution stating that pregnant women in irregular migration status would not have routine access to health care. The document stated, "pregnant women with an irregular migratory status only may access healthcare in case of emergencies."[36] In effect, undocumented migrant women would not have access to pre- and postnatal care. Such a decision had been under consideration for a number of months, but it was available soon before it was going to be made public. The Ombudsman of that time, Ms. Ofelia Taitelbaum, agreed to meet with representatives of universities, NGOs, and religious networks to discuss the matter. She was familiar with the details of the issue and quoted correspondence in which the Ombudsman requested criteria from the CCSS's Legal Department.[37]

Two mid-level authorities at the CCSS—the State Coverage Department and the Legal Department—had conflicting views. Whereas the State Coverage Department aimed to stop women's access to health care, the Legal Department insisted that providing service was compulsory (Should deleted sentenced be footnoted?). After summarizing a number of mandatory resolutions regarding access to care, the main conclusion from CCSS's Legal Department was that pregnant women (Costa Ricans or not) must receive prenatal and postnatal health services. The recommendation also established that the Costa Rican State must bear the costs.[38] Finally, the decision of proscribing health provision to undocumented pregnant women was rescinded, and they may now access health care while they are pregnant. Once they give birth, however, they are unable to use the public health system for health services, and the risk of unwanted children returns. To my knowledge, this is the most radical decision that limits migrants' access to public health services.

From a broader perspective, the linkage between migration, gender, and sexuality is key in terms of rights.[39] However, the task of advancing rights is not easy. In fact, rather than extending rights, advocacy initiatives often aim simply to retain rights jeopardized by exclusionary institutional decisions. Assuming this defensive position may not seem to be a big step forward, but in a context defined by neoliberal politics and policies, it is a highly demanding one, especially because it requires constant vigilance to prevent major steps backward, while at the same time deploying diverse strategies and resources to contest exclusionary policies.

Advocacy around access to health care faces a major challenge associated with the weakness of the CCSS. Views that explain the decline of CCSS's services and infrastructure as the result of services granted to migrants overshadow its underfunding, corruption, and bureaucracy. In such a context, the defense of public health services, even from the Left, often takes a nationalist tone, which complicates both defending the public health system and arguing for inclusive access. Viewing "public" through a nationalist lens usually pushes toward exclusion.

The experience of the association Merienda and Zapatos (Snack and Shoes), of which I am cofounder, that works with children and youth who run the risk of being expelled from formal education, made clear that migrant children's access to technical education is also a contested issue. The Instituto Nacional de Aprendizaje (National Apprenticeship Institute, INA) is an autonomous public institution that provides free applied technical education with the goal of increasing the possibilities of getting paid, formal work.

For many years, the INA accepted applicants who did not have regular migratory status, but its entry requirements changed to disqualify youths with irregular migratory status. According to INA's official position, the change reflected the guidelines provided by the DGME toward the end of the 1990s. I requested an interview with the Executive President of INA, Dr. Olman Segura, who had been Rector of the Universidad Nacional, a state-funded higher education institution, and later became Minister of Labor, but he declined, noting that he was busy. He did provide the following statement via an email sent on August 20, 2012:

> The INA legislation allows us to bring professional training to Costa Ricans and naturalized foreigners [sic]. We do not offer it to foreigners, not only because of legal restrictions but also because we do not have the capacity to receive the thousands of applicants who already live in the country as well as those who might be attracted [from Nicaragua] by such decision.[40]

Dr. Segura states that being "nationalized" was a precondition for a foreigner seeking a place at the INA, and he expresses his concern that accepting students with irregular migrant status might increase migration from Nicaragua. In fact, Dr. Segura mischaracterized the INA's entry requirements, which state that foreigners must be legal residents, which is different from being "nationalized." Segura also notes the "pull effect," suggesting that access to education would increase migration flows. His assumption does not follow the 2011 census, which revealed that migration was declining, as mentioned earlier.

The Deputy Technical President of INA explained in a letter why youths without residency could not gain entry to the institution. The letter cites "legal security," which was understood to require following Immigration Legislation, which cannot be transgressed.[41] It means that foreign youths must hold legal residency before they may obtain a place at INA. In another letter, signed in 2013, the Technical Director[42] appeals to the "principle of legality," which signifies the mandatory rule to follow positive law. As lawyer Raquel Zuñiga perceptively notes, the very same "principle of legality" mandates that INA administrators abide by international law, including the United Nations Convention on the Rights of the Child and Costa Rican legislation regarding childhood and adolescence, both of which make clear that minors have no limits on their to access to their fundamental right to education.[43] However, in this context, national legislation trumps "legality" and duties overshadow rights.

Framing undocumented migrant children's access to education in terms of "legal security" and the "principle of legality" makes clear that INA's authorities were not in a position to compromise. Their statements came out at the same time that health services for pregnant migrant women became a possibility, and these two major difficulties drove the effort to get support from the Ombudsman, who has made important declarations regarding controversial disputes in recent years.

The Ombudsman agreed that rejecting migrants' access to both health care and technical education infringed upon fundamental rights, and he urged the staff at the Ombudsman office to speed up the procedures in order to protect theses fundamental rights. This was especially relevant because the Director of Childhood at the Ombudsman's office knew of the INA case and had scarcely advanced a single initiative. The Ombudsman arranged a meeting that brought together INA's Executive President, the Director of the DGME, and members of grassroots organizations who have been promoting the case.[44] During the meeting, INA's new Executive President, Francisco Marín, who had replaced Dr. Segura months before, agreed that INA had to align its procedures with child rights legislation. The call from the Ombudsman received media attention from La Nación, the newspaper of record in Costa Rica, which demanded attention by INA authorities.[45]

In response, INA established a working committee to draft a resolution to the problem, which was signed by the Ombudsman, the Director of DGME, and the INA's Executive President at the beginning of May 2014. This case confirms how reactive institutions are when it comes to recognizing rights in practical terms. The establishment of formal rights, in this case as spelled out in the Código de la Niñez y la Adolescencia, does not guarantee their application. INA did not develop a strategy to make the change in admission policies visible among the migrant community policies. Even though the INA has sufficient resources (in 2013 it did not use about a third of its total budget), it has not taken the initiative to publicize the changes.

Overall, advocacy related to the CCSS and INA uses possibilities made available by the State to reclaim rights that State institutions do not recognize as such.

Advocates face the challenge of criticizing existing institutional procedures while they use the very same procedures to argue for recognition of migrants' rights. Note that these cases do not aim to gain new rights but to preserve existing ones. In this context, the liberal State, often criticized for its identification with the views and interests of the powerful classes, must now justify policies that attempt to erode rights that have never been universal. The two cases discussed herein show that public servants who are supposedly responsible for protecting migrants' rights are generally resistant to change, mainly motivated by hostility and even xenophobia. Hostility is rarely overt, but rather appears as a sort of "inferential racism," which Stuart Hall defines as unquestioned assumptions that "enable racist statements to be formulated without ever bringing into awareness the racist predicates on which the statements are grounded."[46] Thus, hostility and xenophobia toward migrants speak through other languages and discourses. For example, in INA's case, most of the legal resistance to enrolling adolescents without legal residency in Costa Rica arises from assumptions ostensibly based on juridical considerations but also grounded in prejudice, which is never explicit. Inferential racism plays a key role in motivating resistance in everyday life but also in injecting it into institutional procedures and policies.

WHAT SHOULD BE RESEARCHED?

This chapter has analyzed policies regarding Nicaraguan immigration to Costa Rica and described two cases of advocacy over the politics of immigration. Analytically, a main conclusion is that Costa Rican society finds it hard to recognize that Nicaraguan immigrants are arriving in a society that is experiencing a decrease in the fertility rate and an increase in life expectancy, both of which have long-term implications for citizens and migrants. The difficulties of locating Nicaraguan immigration within this demographic transition run parallel to the resistance to recognition of the interdependence between the migrant community and the rest of the Costa Rican society.

The opening toward new narratives of belonging becomes more difficult as Costa Rican society finds it hard to recognize how much it depends on Nicaraguans. For example, a good number of documentaries, novels, and academic research on Nicaraguan migrants have been produced during the last 20 years, but these accounts are rarely shared beyond those audiences who are concerned with violations of human rights toward migrants. Up to now, the most applauded fictional piece dealing with Nicaraguan migrants in Costa Rica is the theatre play, *El Nica* [The Nicaraguan], which consists of a monologue performed by Meléndez, a Nicaraguan who has lived in Costa Rica for a number of decades. Throughout El Nica, the main character, José Mejía-Espinoza, talks with an image of Jesus Christ, asking him to explain the discrimination against the Nicaraguan community in Costa Rica.[47]

These subjective and discursive approaches coincide with political difficulties associated with the paucity of trade unions in the private sector in Costa Rica, where most Nicaraguans work. Only about 5% of workers in the private sector belong to trade unions. Labor organizations are, thus, not a visible option for Nicaraguan workers, even though Nicaraguans have played important roles in strikes organized, for example, on banana plantations, throughout the years.

Nicaraguans also have joined collective actions and demands for housing. The Costa Rican state has disinvested in housing projects for families whose earnings do not allow them to qualify for mortgages. Social benefits are structured in such a way that those who apply tend to be those who have more resources, which reproduces inequities and impedes poorer families' chances of buying houses. In the past, families built their own houses on lands whose ownership was not apparent or which belonged to the State. Their struggle to obtain titles of property was long and the outcome uncertain.

The prominent role sometimes played by NGOs, often supported by the international community, in certain circumstances overshadowed migrants' own agency. Although Costa Ricans scholars and activists are the most visible advocates for migrant rights, members of migrant communities themselves find it hard to gain public visibility. This is not a case of "ethnic absolutism,"[48] in which only migrants can speak on their own behalf, but it is clear that more migrant voices must be heard. The engagement of scholar-activists also raises questions regarding how academic researchers build links with migrant communities. It is not sufficient to disseminate findings. Advocates must also—and perhaps more important—listen to migrants to understand what should be researched.[49]

Until now, the issue of migrant rights by itself has not stimulated the building of formal advocacy organizations. The relative newness of the Nicaraguan migrant community, which lacks a second generation to voice its evolving narrative in public spaces, might explain this. A vital challenge in the years to come will be to explore ways in which members of migrant communities might forge capabilities that enable them to speak on their own behalf and assume leadership of their own demands. Doubtless, Nicaraguans could be key political actors, but they have yet to claim the public space in which to realize their potential.

NOTES

1. Nicaraguan indigenous groups such as the Miskito also have their own history and experience of migration to Costa Rica. For details on this, see Elizabeth M Larson, "Nicaraguan Refugees in Costa Rica from 1980–1993." In *Yearbook: Conference of Latin Americanist Geographers* (1993), 67–79; "Situation of Nicaraguan Immigrants in Costa Rica," Central American Human Rights Commission Report (San José, Costa Rica, 2002); "La Población Migrante Nicaragüense en Costa Rica: Realidades y Respuestas," Comunicación, Universidad de Costa Rica. Fundación Arias para la Paz y el Progreso Humano Apartado (San José, Costa Rica, 2000); "Perfil Migratorio de Nicaragua," Organización Internacional para las Migraciones, 2013.
2. Carlos Sandoval, *No más muros. Exclusión y migración forzada en Centroamérica* (San José: EUCR, 2015).
3. Roger Bonilla and Carlos Sandoval, "Aspectos sociodemográficos de la migración nicaragüense en Costa Rica, según el Censo 2011," in *Costa Rica a la Luz del Censo 2011* (San José: INEC, 2014).

4. Adolfo Herrera, *Juan Varela* (San José: Editorial Costa Rica, 1939); Joaquín Gutiérrez, *Puerto Limón* (San José: Editorial Costa Rica, reimpresión, 1950).

5. Carlos Enrique Alemán, "Nicas belicosos: Nicaragüenses en la Guerra Civil de Costa Rica, 1948," *Anuario de Estudios Centroamericanos* 39 (2013): 111–141.

6. Manuel Gamboa, "El anticomunismo en Costa Rica y su uso como herramienta política antes y después de la Guerra Civil de 1948," *Anuario de Estudios Centroamericanos* 39 (2013): 143–165.

7. A. Geske Dijkstra, "Technocracy Questioned: Assessing Economic Stabilisation in Nicaragua," *Bulletin of Latin American Research* 18, no. 3 (1999).

8. Anna Brown and Eileen Patten, *Hispanics of Nicaraguan Origin in the United States, 2011* (Washington, DC: Pew Hispanic Center, 2013).

9. Sarah Radclifee and Sallie Westwood, *Re-Making the Nation: Place, Politics and Identity in Latin America* (New York: Routledge, 1996).

10. Hugo Murillo, "La controversia de límites entre Costa Rica y Nicaragua. El Laudo Cleveland y los derechos canaleros," *Anuario de Estudios Centroamericanos* 12, no. 2 (1986): 45–58.

11. Carlos Sandoval, "De Calero a la Trocha. La nueva disputa limítrofe entre los gobiernos de Costa Rica y Nicaragua (2010–2012)," *Anuario de Estudios Centroamericanos* 38 (2012): 177–192.

12. Bonilla and Sandoval, "Aspectos sociodemográficos de la migración nicaragüense en Costa Rica, según el Censo 2011."

13. INEC [Instituto Nacional de Estadística y Censos], *Indicadores Demográficos 2013* (San José: INEC, 2014).

14. Sandoval, *No más muros. Exclusión y migración forzada en Centroamérica.*

15. Anyelick Campos and Larissa Tristán, *Nicaragüenses en las noticias: Textos, contextos y audiencias* (San José: Editorial de la Universidad de Costa Rica, 2009).

16. Marc Edelman, *Campesinos contra la globalización. Movimientos sociales rurales en Costa Rica* (San José: Editorial de la Universidad de Costa Rica, 2005).

17. Carlos Sandoval, "Costa Rica: Many Channels, Scarce Communication," in *The Media in Latin America*, ed. J. Lugo (Buckingham: Open University Press, 2008).

18. Carlos Sandoval, "Presentación," in *Criminalidad y discurso en Costa Rica. Reflexiones críticas sobre un problema social*, by Sebastian Huhn (San José: Fundación Rosa Luxemburgo-FLACSO, 2012).

19. INEC [Instituto Nacional de Estadística y Censos], *Encuesta Nacional de Hogares. Cifras básicas sobre fuerza de trabajo, pobreza e ingresos* (San José: INEC, 2011).

20. Bonilla and Sandoval, "Aspectos sociodemográficos de la migración nicaragüense en Costa Rica, según el Censo 2011."

21. Bonilla and Sandoval, "Aspectos sociodemográficos de la migración nicaragüense en Costa Rica, según el Censo 2011."

22. Sandoval, "Costa Rica: Many Channels, Scarce Communication," in J. Lugo (ed.), *The Media in Latin America* (Buckingham: Open University Press, 2008).

23. Carlos Sandoval, *Threatening Others. Nicaraguans and the Formation of National Identities in Costa Rica* (Athens: Ohio University Press, 2004).

24. Boaventura Sousa Sansa, *Epistemologías desde el Sur* (Buenos Aires: CLACSO, 2009).

25. Sandoval, "Contested Discourses on National Identity. Representing the Nicaraguan Immigration to Costa Rica"; Sandoval, "Narrating Lived Experience in a Binational Community in Costa Rica."

26. Asamblea Legislativa de la República de Costa Rica 2009, *Ley de migración y extranjería* 8764, San Jose.
27. Press Conference on March 28, 2012, "La Ley de Migración en Costa Rica: A dos años de su entrada en vigencia. Promesas, realidades y desafíos," San José.
28. Caitlin E. Fouratt, " 'Those who come to do harm': The Framings of Immigration Problems in Costa Rican Immigration Law," *International Migration Review* 48, no. 1 (2014): 144–180.
29. Gargi Bhattacharyya, *Dangerous Brown Men. Exploiting Sex, Violence and Feminism in the War of Terror* (London: Zed Books, 2008); Nicholas De Genova, "Migrant 'Illegality' and Deportability in Everyday Life," *Annual Review of Anthropology* (2002): 1419–1447.
30. Sandoval, "Public Social Science at Work: Contesting Hostility Towards Nicaraguan Migrants in Costa Rica."
31. Sala Constitucional, *Resolución 2012011760* (San José: Corte Suprema de Justicia, 2012).
32. Carlos Sandoval, "Narrating a Lived Experience in a Binational Community in Costa Rica," in Gargi Bhattacharyya, ed., *Ethnicities and Values in a Changing World* (New York: Routledge, 2009).
33. "Nicaraguan Migrants in Costa Rica Face Deportation," *Unbound*, https://www.unbound.org/Stories/2015/January/NicaraguanMigrantsInCostaRica, accessed June 1, 2016.
34. *La Nación*, "Me venía preparando para atender algo muy complicado," August 27, 2011.
35. Carlos Sandoval, "De Calero a la Trocha. La nueva disputa limítrofe entre los gobiernos de Costa Rica y Nicaragua (2010–2012)."
36. CCSS [Caja Costarricense de Seguro Social], *Asunto: Respuesta a oficio SAFC-ASG2-095-12* (San José: CCSS-ACE-206-10-2012, 2012).
37. DH, Asunto: Otorgamiento del control prenatal a mujeres embarazadas extranjeras (San José: DH-MU-09-2013, 2013).
38. CCSS [Caja Costarricense de Seguro Social], *Asunto: Sobre la atención a mujeres extranjeras embarazadas indocumentadas* (San José: DJ-959-2013, 2013; CCSS [Caja Costarricense de Seguro Social]), *Asunto: Aclaración de directriz institucional sobre atención de mujeres embarazadas no aseguradas y/o indocumentadas* (San José: CCSS-GM-9033-5, 2013).
39. Carlos Sandoval, Mónica Brenes, and Laura Paniagua, *La dignidad vale mucho. Mujeres nicaragüenses forjan derechos en Costa Rica* (San José: Editorial de la Universidad de Costa Rica, 2012).
40. Olman Segura, Meeting Request to Carlos Sandoval García, August 20, 2012.
41. INA, Respuesta a la nota del 20 de noviembre de 2012, respecto a su solicitud del ingreso de personas migrantes en condición migratoria irregular a los servicios del INA (San José: SGI-1041-2013, 2012).
42. INA, Respuesta a nota con fecha 19 de febrero de 2013 (San José: SGI-153-2013, 2013).
43. Personal communication with Raquel Zuñiga, June 3, 2013.
44. DH, Minuta de reunión (San José: DH-DNA-0018-2013, 2013).
45. *La Nación*, "INA tramitará matrícula de estudiantes sin papeles," August 4, 2013, available at http://www.nacion.com/nacional/INA-tramitara-matricula-estudiantes-papeles_0_1357864281.html

46. Stuart Hall, "The Whites in Their Eyes. Racist Ideologies and the Media," in *The Media Reader*, ed. M. Alvarado and J. Thompson (London: British Film Institute, 1981), 13.
47. Sandoval, "Contested Discourses on National Identity. Representing the Nicaraguan Immigration to Costa Rica."
48. Paul Gilroy, *The Black Atlantic: Modernity and Double Consciousness* (London: Verso, 1993).
49. Carlos Sandoval, "To Whom and To What Is Research on Migration a Contribution," *Ethnic and Racial Studies* 36, no. 9 (2013).

CHAPTER 5

Central American Transmigration Through Mexico

Beyond the Border Crisis

RODOLFO CASILLAS R.

In July of 2014, the general public in the United States was in the throes of a debate. In a public statement, President Obama had recently declared the situation of Central American child migrants who were arriving in the United States, the vast majority of whom traveled alone and without immigration documents, to be a "humanitarian crisis."[1] Furthermore, tens of thousands more children were predicted to arrive in coming months if the United States did not come up with appropriate containment methods. Suddenly, high-level officials from the US, Mexican, Guatemalan, Honduran, and Salvadorian governments began to convene emergency meetings to design and implement new programs, some multilateral, others bilateral, and others unilateral. From this ensemble of initiatives, they hoped to find solutions not only to the growing number of child migrants but also the cumulative flow of Central American transmigrants displaced across Mexico en route to the United States. *Transmigrants* are international migrants who cross two or more national borders in the course of arriving at their foreign destination in a process known as *transmigration*.

Achieving positive results from a combination of many different emerging initiatives to address the phenomenon of Central America transmigration represents a great regional challenge, and each of the implicated governments will be put to the test in terms of its capacity to generate an extraordinary amount of economic resources, personnel, and infrastructure. The desirable outcome is good coordination among the many government agencies within the United States, Mexico, El Salvador, Honduras, and Guatemala. However, the current situation brings to light the underlying issues of why the situation of unaccompanied child migrants was not addressed sooner, before it reached the extreme of a "humanitarian crisis." In addition to providing the background for understanding the phenomenon of Central American transmigration through Mexico, this chapter will argue that given the absence of a regional vision and, moreover, a regional plan of action, this migratory flow will continue, with high human, social, and institutional costs in the countries of origin, transit, and destination.

Transmigration is a complex process in which different social actors interact within distinct countries simultaneously. It is not solely an issue of legality to be dealt with by the implicated governments. Historically and at the present, the societies of origin, transit, and destination have also been deeply involved in shaping this migratory phenomenon through their acceptance or rejection of undocumented migrants. In this particular case, the social reaction of Mexican society in favor of or against Central American migrants during their journey through the Mexican territory has featured practices along both extremes— acceptance and abuse. These abuses occur in the streets and in business interactions (both formal and informal), and they are the concrete expressions of the willingness to take advantage of migrants' vulnerability.

Since 2000, Mexico's southern border has undergone a transition from transborder flexibility, which favored social permeability, to a process that emerged out of an interest in strengthening economic and commercial ties with the United States, which favors control of the border and Central American migration flows. Transborder flexibility is the lax enforcement of immigration laws that permit foreigners to enter a neighboring country under the assumption that the foreigner has no intention of residing, or prolonging, his or her stay. Social permeability refers to conditions of coexistence and reciprocity between populations located in the border regions of two neighboring countries, which, in this context, provides favorable circumstances for the lax enforcement of immigration laws.

The changing conditions along the border have influenced migration in all its forms, from regional to extra-continental flows. Historically speaking, the regional migration flow has been composed overwhelmingly of Guatemalans whose final destination was southern Mexico. These regional flows tend to make use of established family ties and social networks along both sides of the border. Mexico has also experienced large entry flows of transmigrants who are simply passing through the country, with the United States as their final destination. Some of these migrants are from other continents, such as Asia and Africa, but since the beginning of the twenty-first century, the number of Central American migrants has been steadily growing. According to Mexico's National Institute of Migration, in the 1990s, an estimated 95% of migrants who transited through Mexico were Central Americans, as can be seen in Table 5.1.

A greater shift toward increased border control in Mexico can be traced back to the North American Free Trade Agreement of 1994 and, later, the September 11, 2001, attacks in the United States. As Mexico moved toward executing greater control over its southern border through militarization and the construction of immigration checkpoints along major migration routes, smuggling networks

TABLE 5.1   Deportations and Visa Denials by Nationality by the Instituto Nacional de Migración, 1990–2000.

YEAR	GUATEMALA	EL SALVADOR	HONDURAS	NICARAGUA	OTHER	TOTAL
1990	58,845	45,598	14,954	3,039	4,004	136,440
1991	69,991	40,441	18,419	1,265	3,226	133,342
1992	65,304	26,643	25,546	1,632	3,871	123,046
1993	58,910	28,646	26,734	3,438	4,277	122,005
1994	42,961	22,794	32,414	12,330	2,616	113,115
1995	52,051	19,526	27,236	2,521	4,686	105,040
1996	50,497	20,904	31,055	1,878	2,784	107,110
1997	37,837	18,857	24,890	1,172	2,832	85,588
1998	46,088	25,783	35,161	1,854	2,636	111,572
1999	50,924	26,176	44,818	1,394	3,106	126,498
2000	79,431	37,481	45,802	1,960	8,261	172,935
Total	612,839	312,849	327,029	32,533	42,349	1,327,599

The statistics discuss the total number of detention events, as opposed to the number of people detained, because the same person can be detained by immigration authorities two or more times within the same year. "Deportation" refers to those who are detained while already inside Mexico. "Visa denial" refers to those who are detained at the border when entering Mexico. These are the two primary actions applied by Mexican immigration authorities to detained migrants.

Source: http://www.inm.gob.mx

began to emerge, as transmigrants needed guides to cross the country without being detained by Mexican immigration authorities. These transnational smuggling networks now operate in collaboration with organized crime networks, as well as corrupt government officials. As we will see later in the chapter, migrants have become a very profitable market niche for organized crime groups, who, in the twenty-first century, began to form new criminal suborganizations dedicated exclusively to the exploitation and abuse of migrants for profit. Since the start of the Felipe Calderón administration (2006–2012) and the rise of the notoriously brutal Mexican cartel "Los Zetas," the human costs have reached catastrophic levels. In addition to highly publicized massacres of migrants, such as the seventy-one migrants who were murdered in San Fernando, Tamaulipas, in 2010, migrants are habitually subject to mass kidnappings and are frequently victims of human and sex trafficking rings. Their undocumented status makes them reluctant to report the crimes they suffer to Mexican authorities, who they fear will deport them. The situation is further complicated by the fact that Mexican authorities are often the perpetrators of crimes against migrants, either directly or in collaboration with criminal organizations. The habitual exploitation and abuse of migrants are exacerbated by Mexican immigration laws, which historically and currently have constructed migrants as "the Other." In the context of Mexico, the concept of "the Other" has not only been historically used to classify Mexico's indigenous population; it has also been used to classify undocumented foreigners and social minorities who are outside the State's control, as well as social dissidents. The construction of the social identity of minority groups as "the Other" is a marker of difference prescribed by the Mexican ruling class. This mentality has manifested in the wider society, fomenting a nationalistic fervor that serves as a pretext for taking advantage of migrants, who are widely seen as inferior and, furthermore, unwelcomed within the national territory. This chapter will provide the context for understanding how the historical, local, geographical, and nation-state context has created a breeding ground that perpetuates and normalizes the daily practices of abuse against migrants in border towns and along migratory routes.

REGIONAL MIGRATION FLOWS: NOT ALL CENTRAL AMERICANS MIGRATE NORTH

Regional migration is a phenomenon limited to populations located in the outskirts of a border that divides two countries, in this case, Mexico and Guatemala. On the other hand, transmigration, by definition, involves two or more national borders. The international flow of undocumented migrants who arrive and commute through Mexico comes principally from Central America (Guatemala, Honduras, El Salvador, and, to a lesser extent, Nicaragua). Before the phenomenon of transmigration, there was regional migration into southern Mexico, largely by Guatemalans. To a lesser degree, there have been constant migration flows surging from the Caribbean (primarily Cuba), the Andean region (principally Ecuadorans, who, since the beginning of the twenty-first century, have surpassed the number of Nicaraguan migrants), and extra-continental migration, for example, Chinese and Indian migrants, who can pay up to $60,000 (US) to smugglers. However, from the 1990s to the present, over 95% of the total number of undocumented migrants who pass through Mexico have been Central Americans.[2]

The overarching statement can be made that there are two flows of Central Americans—those whose destination is southeastern Mexico (regional migrants) and those who are simply passing through (transmigrants).[3] At times, both of these flows might share parts of the same migratory route and social network. In the twenty-first century, as will be discussed shortly, others have found or generated new networks along the way that help facilitate their journey.[4]

These regional migration flows follow their own migratory routes in southern Mexico, namely through Chiapas and Tabasco, the states that border Guatemala. As a result of long-standing relationships dating back to the beginning of the twentieth century, many of these migrants have been inserted into social and labor environments that generally operate with minimal participation from government agencies.[5] Since their final destination is southern Mexico, the routes utilized by these regional flows do not extend farther north. However, some regional migrants do manage to establish, in southern Mexico, a social articulation that also serves migrants whose final destination lies farther north. Although these transmigrants are just "passing through," they come from the same countries of origin as regional migrants and, therefore, are able to utilize parts of these regional routes and social networks. This, in turn, generates a common zone between regional and transmigration flows of migrants who strive to cross as rapidly and discreetly as possible, and who depend on preexisting networks to pass unseen through the shadows, with the least possible risk. It is important to highlight that these transmigrant flows are also the most vulnerable, and transmigrants suffer the most in terms of the quantity and frequency of aggression, the diversity of aggressors, and the span of territory in which they are targeted. Proof lies in the wide coverage of horrific aggression against migrants, in particular the mass kidnappings and murders that have been documented by the national and international press since 2010.[6]

This does not imply that regional migrant flows are safe from danger; they are frequently exposed to other types of assaults, abuses, and exploitation, often committed by those who contract with them for their labor, as well as those whose goods and services they purchase, who frequently charge them extralegal costs.[7] These regional migrants have been exposed to processes that, without ceasing to be exploitative and often illegal, are seen and accepted as "natural" by the local Mexican population. Because these tensions are seen as intrinsic to human interaction, regional migrants' vulnerability is downplayed and not examined to the full extent to which it should be.[8] Moreover, although regional migrants are exposed to a "normalized" exploitation, these regional flows have not been significantly touched by organized crime, namely Mexican drug cartels. Given their long-term presence and history of social relations constructed over time, they have, to a large extent, already been incorporated into the local society. Their social permeability serves as a layer of protection that is not extended to transmigrants, who lack the social networks enjoyed by regional migrants and, thus, are more subject to exploitation by organized crime groups.

TRANSMIGRATION FLOWS

On the other end of the spectrum, the extra-continental transmigrants, unlike regional migrants, do not have preexisting routes and social networks; they can only follow their trajectory through Mexico with the assistance of international human smuggling organizations. Because they must rely completely on smuggling and organized crime networks, transmigrants are exposed to another set of vulnerabilities and crimes that are mainly committed by smugglers, the corrupt public officials who facilitate their journey, and Mexican organized crime (cartels), who charge smugglers steep amounts to pass groups through the country.

As can be observed in Tables 5.1 and 5.2, there have not been significant changes in the composition of the national origins of Central American migratory flows that pass through Mexico. In other words, for the past 25 years, these undocumented migration flows have been composed almost entirely of Guatemalans, Hondurans, Salvadorians, and Nicaraguans, with the more recent incorporation of Ecuadorians, among other surfacing nationalities. However, there have been compelling shifts in terms of the origins within the interior of these countries, the social diversity of the flows, the age groups (more children and adolescents are migrating, which is feeding the present "humanitarian crisis"), and the fact that, today, there are many more women migrants than there were 10 years ago. These shifts have been provoked by the spike in gang violence in Honduras and El Salvador, which are arguably two of the most violent countries in the world. It is not startling that, according to border patrol apprehension data, over three-quarters of the child migrants detained at the US border are from poor and violent towns in El Salvador, Honduras, and Guatemala. Nor is it surprising that more minors arrived from San Pedro Sula, Honduras, than any other city, considering that it had the world's highest homicide rate in 2013.[9] It is also fitting to mention that the volume of Central American migrants has been steadily growing over the long term, despite the fact that, in the short term, there has been a diminution observed in the number of those detained and deported by migration authorities, a decrease which is due to several factors.[10] When considering the total number of migrants, it must be understood that a significant volume of this population is not detained; nor does there exist the capacity to detain them.

TABLE 5.2   Deportations and Visa Denials by Nationality by the Instituto Nacional de Migración, 2001–2010

YEAR	GUATEMALA	HONDURAS	EL SALVADOR	NICARAGUA	PARTIAL TOTAL	OTHERS	TOTAL
2001	67,522	40,105	35,007	1,712	144,346	6,184	150,530
2002	67,336	41,801	20,800	1,609	131,546	6,515	138,061
2003	86,023	61,900	29,301	2,150	179,374	8,240	187,614
2004	94,404	72,684	34,572	2,453	204,113	11,582	215,695
2005	100,948	78,326	42,674	3,980	225,928	14,341	240,269
2006	84,523	58,001	27,287	3,590	173,401	9,304	182,705
2007	14,939	22,980	5,777	855	44,551	7,149	51,700
2008	11,656	16,624	4,233	626	33,139	6,297	39,436
2009	29,604	24,040	10,355	53	64,052	4,981	69,033
2010	28,933	23,811	10,567	839	64,150	5,753	69,903
Total	585,888	440,272	220,573	17,867	1,264,600	80,346	1,344,946

The statistics discuss the total number of detention events, as opposed to the number of people detained, because the same person can be detained by immigration authorities two or more times within the same year. "Deportation" refers to those who are detained while already inside Mexico. "Visa denial" refers to those who are detained at the border when entering Mexico. These are the two primary actions applied by Mexican immigration authorities to detained migrants.

Source: http://www.inm.gob.mx

Although they share certain characteristics, further differences can be highlighted between regional flows and the flow of Central American transmigrants. In the case of regional flows, some migrants have established family and social networks over time. These networks provide them with a social fabric that facilitates employment, as well as the development of social and religious relationships, as in the case of neighboring communities in Guatemala and Mexico that have forged a long-lasting transborder social community.[11] Historically, Guatemalans have the deepest ties with Mexico, followed by Hondurans and Salvadorians, whose presence is relatively recent in comparison with Guatemalans. These flows, above all the Guatemalan refugees who arrived during the Guatemalan Civil War in the 1980s,[12] form part of a social schematic that is of great importance for contextualizing the daily interactions along the southern border of Mexico. Without first understanding this context, it is difficult to process the rapid development of Central American transmigration and, subsequently, the social networks that facilitate it.

MEXICAN GOVERNMENT EFFORTS TO REGULATE MIGRATION FLOWS

For many years, Mexican immigration authorities opted to facilitate the entry and residency of undocumented Central American regional migrants. They practiced a flexibility that favored transborder social permeability, which provided stability along the border, in addition to a cheap labor force, particularly within the service industry, domestic labor, and the agricultural sector (namely coffee, cocoa, mango, and sugar farms). One prime example would be the Guatemalan farm laborers who work in Mexican-owned coffee plantations in southern Chiapas. These Central American workers are easy to exploit. Beyond the fact that they lack documents to work legally, they are often too fragmented to form unions, and many Guatemalan migrants from indigenous communities, for example, may be illiterate or not speak Spanish. This border flexibility favored a labor culture outside the legal framework and simultaneously permitted authorities to do little to nothing to counteract the abuses and exploitation committed by contractors of undocumented migrants, as well as the local populations who, in one way or another, thrived on regional migration and still do. These abuses and exploitation prevail to this day, although now they occur in other places and related social spheres.[13]

Toward the end of the 1980s, Mexico encountered a significant spike in transmigrants largely due to ongoing civil wars in El Salvador, Guatemala, and Nicaragua. The Mexican government began to move toward a process that favored control of these Central American migration flows, which was seen as beneficial for strengthening its economic and commercial ties with the United States.[14] As a consequence of this shift, the government of Mexico gradually started to advance toward a better registry of the regional flows,[15] a process that, to date, has led to the generation of a new regional migratory document that must be presented at the border. In theory, this regulation seeks to achieve better social and labor conditions through government intervention. However, the new migratory document, which permits Central Americans multiple entries and prolonged stays in the border region of Mexico, faces the cultural legacy of migrants who are accustomed to crossing without any sort of legal authorization, as well as Mexican locals who are used to taking advantage of undocumented migrants. It is also important to note that the new immigration document is unattainable for most transmigrants, who would be unable to meet its strict requirements.

This shift toward controlling the migration flows also resulted in the Mexican government establishing the first containment measures to deter transmigration flows, which were followed by further measures at the close of the twentieth century, and even more in the twenty-first century. "Plan Sur" (the Southern Plan), which was implemented between 2001 and 2002, sought to establish two containment belts, as can be seen in Figure 5.1,[16] as well as new detection and detention schemes. These containment belts were implemented across the Isthmus of Tehuantepec, which is composed of four states: Oaxaca, Veracruz, Chiapas, and Tabasco. In the twenty-first century, the Isthmus has been a strategic region for constricting transmigration flows, as it is the narrowest stretch of Mexico and, furthermore, a region that all transmigrants must cross as they make their way north. In addition to improvements in the registration system and in the number and conditions of the detention centers, there was also a significant increase in the number of events of detention and deportation, which reached a climax in 2005, when there were nearly a quarter of a million apprehensions.

THE RISE OF INTERNATIONAL SMUGGLING NETWORKS

With greater governmental control of the border, one unanticipated side effect was the appearance of human smugglers, who emerged out of the need for transmigrants to have guides to pass through Mexico. Once the door to legal entry was closed, new clandestine paths began to materialize. It is important to emphasize that not all human smugglers operated independently. After the institution of stricter legal measures to control transmigration, many smugglers began to operate in collaboration with corrupt government officials. There were also corrupt officials who operated alone or as part of wider networks. This was the origin of smuggling networks that were unseen and least attacked. Gradually, a criminal market began to form that viewed migrants as a market niche where smugglers essentially had total impunity.[17] In the twenty-first century, new criminal entities emerged, some already associated with organized crime and human trafficking. Criminals evolved, innovated, and formed new kinds of macro organizations. Traditional forms of smuggling had to evolve, or they ran the risk of being incorporated into new criminal organizations, some of which (the minority) were strictly dedicated to criminal activities involving the abuse of migrants, and

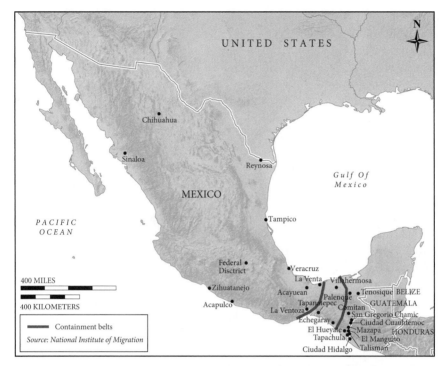

Figure 5.1 Location of contention belts in southeastern Mexico: *Plan Sur*. Through the execution of *Plan Sur*, Mexican immigration authorities created additional checkpoints and multiplied the number of immigration detention centers along key points on the migrations routes. These containment belts were established across the narrowest expanse of Mexico, the Isthmus of Tehuantepec, which stretches across Oaxaca, Veracruz, Chiapas, and Tabasco, as can be seen here. Source: Rodolfo Casillas R.

others that came from or were linked to other criminal activities, such as drug trafficking, the latter being the more dangerous. A practice has emerged where these criminal organizations incorporate the traditional smuggling organizations and transmigrants, and charge them for the right to pass through the territory. The participants within smuggling networks are by no means limited to the smugglers themselves. There is an extensive roster of players who are implicated and serve as "freelance" participants and who contract out their services when needed or when the opportunity arises. These players include food and clothing vendors, hotel personnel, and other community members who offer their goods and services. Thus, traditional smugglers continue to prey on migrants while simultaneously being victims of second-level criminal structures, in the sense that these smugglers are being exploited by Mexican criminal organizations, most often cartels. Undocumented migrants and their families pay both directly and indirectly, as they are being exploited both by the smugglers and Mexican criminal organizations.

Are we sure we want to delete the statement explaining the map? Through the years, undocumented migrants have been forced to adapt to the dangers that face them along the journey and, with the passage of time, some have developed a body of knowledge about how to migrate that has been transmitted from generation to generation. This knowledge includes the securest routes (which constantly fluctuate), how to avoid authorities, how to dress if one does not want to be easily detected as a migrant, and other helpful tips. Migrants have also developed their own social networks and adjusted their organizational culture to the fluctuations of the journey, as well as their integration into the places of destination. They have generated techniques for interacting with humanitarian organizations and human smuggling networks, as well as institutions in the places of transit and destination, whether to receive some type of assistance or to avoid interactions when possible or necessary. This knowledge constitutes a specific form of social power for those who have no institutional power.

Nevertheless, there remain other undocumented migrants who are less prepared economically, socially, and personally for the journey. Recently, these migrants have tended to surge from Honduras, a country that does not have as extensive a legacy of migration as El Salvador or Guatemala, which both have histories of civil wars and mass exoduses of refugees dating back to the 1970s. Those migrants who lack the organizational culture and social resources to tap into the existing collective knowledge to help them facilitate their journey are often the ones who pay the steepest costs, sometimes even with their lives. Working against them are their relatively meager collective experience migrating, a lack of accumulated knowledge, and, therefore, less transmission of this knowledge to future generations, which ultimately contributes to a greater deterioration of their sociocultural fabric. Even their physical phenotype (mestizo, indigenous, etc.) and mode of dress make them more identifiable: they embody Otherness, to be blunt. To one degree or another, parties from organized crime to government authorities consistently have taken advantage of these migrants.

TRANSNATIONAL CRIMINAL NETWORKS

Whatever their economic situation might be, undocumented migrants do not have the full guarantee of transit and arrival without being robbed or exposing their physical integrity to a distinct range of risks. To migrate in an undocumented manner is an experience that leaves an unforgettable mark. Beyond looting and constant exploitation, undocumented migration is a matter of life and death. Kidnapping and murder constitute the newest threats from criminal networks dedicated to the exploitation of migrants. Mass kidnappings became more frequent beginning in 2007, but they came more into the spotlight after a report from Mexico's National Commission for Human Rights (CNDH) in 2009.[18]

Criminal networks have added new transborder links. Today, migrants coming from the south are subject to a range of aggressions in Honduras, El Salvador, and, above all, Guatemala even before they arrive in Mexico. At this point in the journey, the cost is out of pocket, often accompanied by physical assault. And that does not even include the sexual violence, loss of body parts, torture, and kidnapping that await migrants as they head farther north. It is only a matter of time before they are assaulted.[19] The routes from the south make their way to the north, including into southern counties of the United States, where, under different terms and conditions, people also take advantage of the vulnerability of undocumented persons, as migrants deported along the northern border of Mexico attest.

At play are transnational criminal processes whose sole objective is the targeting of undocumented migrants and their family members. These processes incorporate a wide range of means, collaborators, and subordinate actors. In this way, criminal networks merge individual and local networks with other regional, national, or international networks. The systematization of violence is part of their modus operandi; casual contact is part of their natural daily affairs. The daily monitoring of territory is part of their geographic presence, and the trains and migrant shelters in their network are ideal places for mass kidnappings. The widely used public transit and commercial networks serve as more efficient and discrete means for the transportation of goods and persons, in comparison to the striking presence of the "Train of Death" or "the Beast," which travels loaded with hundreds of migrants atop the roofs and on the ladders of the cars.

The criminal chains also benefit from technological innovations, in particular the extension of financial networks that send and receive remittances, such as Western Union, which is most widely used by Central Americans during their transit through Mexico. At first used for sending small amounts of money for expenses during the journey, these financial networks have transformed into mechanisms utilized during hostage situations to send and collect payments for kidnapped undocumented migrants.

If there is no hope of extracting money from a kidnapped migrant or his or her family members, a migrant has two options: (1) paying for his or her own release by helping to kidnap others, carrying out supporting activities to help "take care" of those kidnapped during their stay, or joining the ranks of the kidnappers; or (2) become meat for the butchers who are in charge of killing, dismembering, and disappearing the bodies of those who lacked the means or disposition to pay in one form or another.[20]

The train yards serve as key spaces for the mass concentration of undocumented migrants as they await the train to take them north. Today, these spaces are strategic sites for kidnappers who dispatch agents to detect, classify, and even distribute the migrants in train cars according to their circumstances: those who arrive at some sort of agreement about being transported; those who will be subject to kidnapping; and those migrants of "little value" who can be subject to assault by low-ranking criminals. The migrant shelters also provide spaces of impunity where kidnappers find, identify, and classify those they intend to kidnap. This is done using simple and practical means: infiltrating migrant shelters with criminal agents who wait for them to leave the shelter, at which point they can kidnap the migrants and bring them to safe houses. Thus begins the most painful part of the nightmare.

Organized crime also has its own rationality, and these networks dedicate time and energy to improve the administration of resources and thus achieve the maximum possible profit. Another strategy employed by these criminal networks is not attracting public attention. They are careful not to disturb the public peace of the local communities or involve the locals, which becomes a manner of achieving complicity and social silence. That is precisely why undocumented migrants are the perfect prey. They are not from the area. The prejudices, ignorance, lack of awareness, individualism, and local and national identities all culminate into an attitude of opposition and distrust toward transmigrants, making them the quintessential victims for abuse and exploitation.

These pervasive abusive practices face criticism and opposition even from within the very society which perpetuates them. Even humanitarian shelters, which serve as daily expressions of solidarity and ultimately help protect migrants, have become subject to constant infiltration by organized crime. Previously, the infiltrators were human smugglers who had come to seek out potential clients, or *coyotes* making a stop so that their group could recuperate strength. Other infiltrators included security agents who entered covertly for any variety of motives. These criminal activities also take a toll on the social fabric of the local community and, on a larger scale, the country as a whole.

Although the growing violence perpetrated against undocumented migrants may seem to be affecting only those persons living in remote communities, it is also necessary to "zoom out" and frame these localities as part of a whole, not simply fragmented, isolated communities. The crimes committed against migrants hurt the collective good of communities, as locals, consciously or unconsciously, begin to form part of this system of exploitation by taking advantage of migrants, often overcharging them or simply being complicit in their exploitation. Migrants are being robbed of their money, dignity, and sometimes their lives; meanwhile, the very integrity of Mexico's social fabric is being destroyed.

The social environments through which migrants pass are not always places of solidarity and understanding. There are people who lend them a hand but also people who lend them a hand with the underlying intention to abuse them. The criminal context of today cannot be understood without reference to the crimes of the past, which, to varying scales, have been and are currently carried out by locals. These local communities are both breeding grounds and crop fields. A single kidnapping operation, in which, on average, thirty migrants are abducted, requires logistical personnel and vehicles, strategic access to the predetermined public roads, and coordinated transfers to sites where those abducted are to be housed, as well as the sites themselves where the kidnappers can punish, beat, torture, and sometimes amputate the body parts of their victims, or even kill them. In so-called safe houses, victims are sporadically given food and water.

According to testimonies, between the persons kidnapped, the watchmen, the criminals who charge the ransom, and those who do the "dirty work," dozens and dozens of people are involved.[21] How can it be, then, that no one sees them; that no one knows what is happening; that nobody sells them anything; that no one receives a particular benefit in exchange for a particular activity? The social silence is akin to criminal complicity, which has profound systemic effects, impacting the entire community and nation. How do we disentangle these processes in order to determine the driving forces? What inspires, or entitles, criminals and local communities alike to carry out this form of violence against transmigrants? To answer these questions, it is necessary to go through a conceptual process, a somewhat abstract narrative that requires a different language altogether.

THE CONSTRUCTION OF SOCIAL OTHERNESS THROUGH POLICY

The construction of citizenship is neither a quick nor easy social process. The complex articulation of nationhood and transnational processes that play out on a local level produce tensions, collisions, and social conflicts. These tensions and conflicts are amplified when the disagreements are reproduced on a larger scale, and, often, their intensity goes beyond the margins of social tolerance. The following section briefly explores how the national model of citizenship has interacted with legal processes regarding immigration and legality. This section will also address how state policies and discourses have influenced the subjectivity of noncitizens, especially in the case of Central American migrants, and, furthermore, how the ideology of nationalism has been used as an oppressive tool to devalue immigrants and justify abuses. In the context of Mexico, it is fundamental to underscore how the nation-state's adoption of exclusionary policies has helped to perpetuate the notion of foreign Otherness. Institutional approaches to immigration have shaped the subjectivity of migrants, making them vulnerable to a series of exploitations and abuses.

In the construction of nationalism, the social conception of citizenship produces its counterpart, which is the foreign Other, a being who is constantly constructed in terms of "us" and "them." This creates a pretext for the notion that "we" are superior to "them," and ultimately produces an ideology of supremacy that seeps deep into the social consciousness. In this context, the nation-state produces a legal fiction that justifies imposing a state-sanctioned conceptual framework for understanding and constructing identity. Nationalism, in its pursuit of strengthened national identity, glorifies certain local virtues while devaluing the national identities of neighboring countries. This ideology fosters the mistreatment of the foreign Other. Abuses are justified by a nationalistic logic that gives citizens the grounds to behave abusively toward undocumented migrants, who are seen as being of lesser value.

Beyond the institutional production of subjectivities (such as illegal and foreign, among others), state policies historically have outright criminalized foreigners. Unless, of course, the foreigner in question fits in the category of white

Anglo-Saxon immigrant who can aid in the Mexican government's project to "whiten" the Mexican mestizo and indigenous population, the foreigner was not welcome in the country. When examining the legal framework of current Mexican immigration law and the social construction of identity, the following historical precursors must be taken into account.[22]

The Immigration Act of 1909 first established the Mexican government's policy of selective immigration, which has favored immigration from more developed countries and discouraged immigration from less-developed countries, such as those of Central America. Restrictions were often established on the grounds of "public health and contagious diseases." Criteria were established to permit the entry of minors, the elderly, and women under the age of 25, but these were later altered to be more restrictive because they constituted "an obstacle to the adequate regulation of the entry of *pernicious*[23] foreigners within the national territory," in other words, those immigrants who might be considered dependents and who could become an economic drain on state resources. The Statement of Purpose of the Immigration Act of 1926 dictates that "it is considered that for women above the age of 25, a woman has enough judgment, as well as physical and mental maturity, to be able to sustain herself alone, and *poses less risk of becoming a detriment to society.*"[24] Foreigners were obligated to submit themselves to inspection by Mexican authorities in order to prove their good conduct and honest lifestyle, and the act enumerated cases in which foreign immigration was restricted.

The Immigration Act of 1926 was responsible for creating the first National Alien Registry, as well as establishing a distinction between immigrant and non-immigrant. However, it was the Immigration Act of 1930 that first formalized the Alien Registry and established a conceptual and legal difference between "immigrant" and "nonimmigrant." In 1932, the first immigration laws were put in place. Article 6, Section X states: "It is regarded as beneficial to the general well-being, the individual or collective immigration of healthy, well-behaved foreigners who are trained for the workforce, and who pertain to races that can be easily *assimilated*[25] into our midst, for the benefit of our species and the economic conditions of our country." The particular type of assimilation, also known as "*mestizaje*," which these immigration laws were intended to encourage was aimed at "whitening" the indigenous and mestizo Mexican population through mixing with white Anglo-Saxon immigrants. Although these immigration laws were designed to be selective, they were equally discriminatory.

The laws demonstrated an undeniable preference for whiter, more "civilized" immigrants as part of the mission to "*mestizar*" the Mexican indigenous population, and they thus established an enduring legal framework that was exclusionary by nature. The 1936 General Law of Population went on to prohibit "for an indefinite period of time the entry of immigrant workers into the country" and fined the contractors of *illegal*[26] immigrants. Meanwhile, Article. 1, Sect. II highlighted, "the ethnic fusion of national groups," and Section III remarked on "the enhancement of the national mestizo population through the *assimilation* of foreigners."[27]

Despite a legal framework designed to stimulate the assimilation of select immigrants, the Statement of Purpose of the 1947 General Law of Population, in reference to previous legal provisions, notes that "a high percentage of attempts to *assimilate*[28] preexisting immigrants have failed." In other words, Mexico was unable to attract and assimilate the envisioned pool of Anglo-Saxon immigrants. The 1947 law was the direct antecedent to current immigration law in Mexico, instituting the need to be selective with migratory flows by means of limiting entry to professionals, such as investors, experts, and other specialized personnel. It also established the right to asylum for political refugees from Latin American countries, a right that the 1974 General Law of Population later extended to all foreigners.

On October 19, 1993, the National Institute of Migration (INM) was created, although it was not until May 18, 2006, that the INM was recognized as an agency of Mexico's Homeland Security Department. This recognition meant that "[the INM's] databases and information systems that could be considered relevant should henceforth be integrated into the National Network of Information" (Art. I). However for national security reasons, the information provided by the INM would remain confidential (Art. IV).

The Migration Act of May 25, 2011, was the first act in Mexico created specifically to address the issue of immigration.[29] Previously, as articulated earlier, there existed a group of migration regulations within the legal framework of the General Law of Population. In comparison to previous laws, the 2011 Migration Act represented an undeniable advance. However, it is limited in the sense that it does not fully take into account the cumulative international migration flows that occur within the country. Furthermore, it contains constitutionally controversial aspects, for example, the existence and practices of "migration stations," which are essentially prisons for migrants and contrary to the Mexican Constitution. In regard to the future of migration, the law reveals a number of biases and inadequacies, and it does not properly address the high level of operation and complex development of smuggling networks. It also lacks specific application of the immigration policies, and there is a grave disconnect between the law and practice. In other words, the law is essentially nothing more than a document for the executive branch to execute at its convenience.

Through the aforementioned sets of laws, the Mexican state was eventually able to institute a distinction between a "national" and "foreigner." As shown earlier, the state also established conceptual and legal elements that, in the long term, helped to foster the devaluation of aliens, especially if they are associated with sociocultural and historical elements that signal different types of national Otherness. These laws instituted limitations based on anything from an immigrant or migrant's state of health, age, or gender, to questions of national security, all of which are defined in legal documents with restricted circulation, in other words, not public.[30] The statistical results of the extensive legal framework can be observed in Table 5.3.

Table 5.3 reveals that the policies intended to encourage selective immigration have only been successful in attracting a small number of foreigners to

TABLE 5.3   Percentage of Foreign-Born Residents in Mexico
from Population and Housing Censuses, 1930–2010

YEAR	PERCENTAGE
1930	0.97
1940	0.90
1950	0.71
1960	0.64
1970	0.40
1980	0.40
1990	0.42
2000	0.51
2010	0.85

Source: Population and Housing Censuses, Mexico, INEGI.

formally reside in the country. The percentage of foreign-born immigrants residing in Mexico has yet to reach a mere 1% of the total population. However, since
around 1970, Mexico has encountered large inflows of mainly undocumented
Central Americans. Although their total number is unknown, it could easily
equal a large proportion of the entirety of documented foreigners.

Mexican immigration authorities estimate that around 2 million people
cross the southern border of Mexico each year.[31] This quantity may seem minus-
cule when taking into account the estimated 300 million crossings that are estimated to happen yearly along the northern border. But considering that the
entirety of Central America is composed of roughly 45 million people, including
2 million undocumented Central American migrants in Mexico, the vast majority of whom come from Guatemala, Honduras, and El Salvador, the number
begins to carry more weight. Furthermore, from the perspective of regional and
transnational migration, it is noteworthy that a significant number of these undocumented migrants are transborder workers who also invigorate the economy
and commerce of southeastern Mexico.[32] From this vantage point, the current
immigration law and social perceptions of foreign Otherness will have significant influences on the daily interactions among the distinct implicated social
sectors. Beyond harming migrants, these preconceptions and prejudices can
damage the terms of the established social relations and, consequently, have negative effects on the social fabric of local transborder communities.

When taking into account the historical legacy and legal framework of immigration in Mexico, anti-immigrant sentiments among Mexican citizens seem only
logical, perhaps even understandable, although not justifiable. Even high-ranking
government officials, such as Bernardo Espino de Castillo, the general coordinator of
the Central Zone of the Attorney General's Office, have ventured to publicly express
their strong anti-immigrant views regarding undocumented migrants. Reminiscent

of the first Immigration Act of 1909, which restricted immigration for "motives of public health and contagious diseases," he advised that the health and hygiene of undocumented persons represent a "public health threat" in the places of transit and destination. He went on to claim that the very culture and social condition of undocumented migrants resemble a contagious disease, stating, "When it comes to illegal immigrants who have escaped from their country of origin for political or ideological motives, they come to represent a serious cultural infiltration that is impossible for authorities to control in both the countries of destination and transit." He continued, stating that illegal immigrants have "lost their sense of belonging and national identity, which is reflected and manifested through their conduct, and even spread among their neighbors during their stay, in their place of transit or residence. . . . The customs or habits of undocumented persons and their culture, in general, are often reproduced in the country where they are living either temporarily or permanently. This situation simultaneously provokes family disintegration and even permeates the loss of an authentic nationalistic sentiment among citizens."[33] The rhetoric of this high-ranking official constructs illegal migrants as though they were nothing more than carriers of a degenerative disease, transmittable through social contact. However, he dared to say what many Mexicans (government officials and civilians alike) were thinking at that moment, and what many continue to think up to this day, although they may choose not to state these opinions publicly.

The role the nation-state plays in defining Otherness is largely determined by its integration policies and the level of inclusiveness of citizenship. Fear of the "alien"—that which is "foreign"—can be understood as a reaction provoked by a perceived danger. In the case of Mexico, the social impulse to fear the foreign "Other" has been readily incorporated into political programs. The reaction of fear and distrust toward Otherness is especially reasonable considering that the Mexican State has historically perceived the foreign "Other" as a public health and security threat. Due to a lack of integration policies and a strong notion of exclusive citizenship, Mexico, on both an administrative and societal level, has not been able to integrate the preexisting immigrant populations; nor have they been able to attract the type of highly skilled foreigners from more developed countries, as desired. The Mexican State has tended to adopt legal and administrative forms that, in concrete terms, have produced practices of separation, segregation, and ostracism. Through framing the foreigner as existing outside of the law (from which the connotation of "undocumented" is derived), the Mexican State has declared them as *vulnerably different*. In essence, the foreign "Other" is made vulnerable by the simple fact of being foreign.

DIVERSE FORMS OF VIOLENCE

Although it is impossible to quantify or verify the exact number of undocumented migrants who have been assaulted or injured, there is an abundance of evidence that suggests the existence of a criminal element that has incorporated migrants, specifically undocumented migrants, into the nucleus of its business practices.[34] In any commercial pursuit, the entrepreneur must develop a diversity of techniques in order to maximize profits. In the "business" of exploiting undocumented migrants, there are different techniques in terms of the means, collaborators, objectives, and scope. As mentioned at the beginning of the chapter, different undocumented migrants are vulnerable to different kinds of exploitation at the hands of the criminal organizations, government authorities, and general public. The most common forms of aggression and violence are (1) assault and robbery, (2) physical violence, (3) sexual violence, (4) kidnapping, (5) torture and amputations, (6) blackmail, (7) labor exploitation (trafficking), (8) sexual exploitation (trafficking), (9) imprisonment, and (10) murder. It is common knowledge that an uncountable number of migrants are victims of multiple aggressions throughout their journey. Even legal immigrants are exposed to abuses, corrupt acts, and administrative torments that are not limited to this list. Documented immigrants are frequently victims of extortion or other abuses committed by those who process their paperwork. Their offenders may be acting independently or in collusion with corrupt officials—another murky issue of abuse that is little known, documented, or punished.

Generalized corruption in Mexico is an institutional disease that thrives throughout the country. This situation, when combined with a legal framework that persecutes migrants simply for being foreigners, has created a fertile breeding ground for the habitual abuse of migrants. These abusive practices occur across all contexts but especially in border towns and along the migratory routes. From casual exchanges in the street to formal business interactions, they are concrete expressions of a process of normalization that promotes and perpetuates a societal willingness to take advantage of migrants' vulnerabilities.

When discussing the larger social matrix of violence suffered by Central Americans in Mexico, it does not suffice to vaguely mention the fact that migrants are subject to abuses. To comprehend the full extent of these abusive processes, it is necessary to provide a panorama of the diversity of abuses and forms of exploitation suffered by the Central American migrants who venture into Mexican territory.

Beginning at the southern border, Guatemalan domestic workers in the state of Chiapas suffer exaggerated abuses at the hands of their employers. Farm laborers are habitually denied legal, let alone humane, wages—if their employers even bother to pay them at all. Central American children and adolescents commonly suffer exploitation at the hands of business owners who employ them to sell candy, cigarettes, household goods, and other "pirated" products, and force them to work incredibly long days for miserable wages without receiving any sort of social, educational, or health benefits whatsoever. These abuses may seem tame in comparison to the conditions of forced labor suffered by those transmigrants who fall into the hands of human trafficking organizations, including Mexican drug traffickers, who kidnap and enslave migrants to work as drug mules or to cultivate drug crops such as marijuana or opium. Transmigrants can expect to be taken advantage of along every step of the journey, from the brakemen and private guards who torment and exploit them from the moment they mount the train, "the Beast," to the bus drivers who notoriously quadruple the fare for Central American passengers. When taking into account the variety and diversity of agents who are implicated in the market of exploiting undocumented migrants, it is unsurprising that one of the most common pieces of advice that circulates in the transmigrant community is "Trust no one."

Narco-traffickers are highly skilled at luring migrants into their clutches by offering them protection and other benefits. However, once they fall into their grasp, the migrants become nothing more than pawns in their scheme for the mass distribution of narcotics, running the risk of being blackmailed, kidnapped, or worse. Even receiving a money order is an opportunity for exploitation because, in Mexico, undocumented migrants cannot collect money orders without a passport, which means that they must rely on the goodwill of others. Seemingly well-intentioned people who offer to collect money orders from companies such as Western Union pose as do-gooders, advertising their services as free, then ultimately charging migrants a steep commission, or sometimes stealing the money altogether.

These abusive practices seem mild in comparison to the more severe forms of assault committed by criminal networks and government authorities. From the criminal network of delinquents dedicated to assaulting and robbing migrants to the vast underworld of sex trafficking of women and child migrants, we see a multiplicity of underworlds that individually poses current or potential public safety problems and, when combined, constitutes one enormous public security problem for all.[35] Even humanitarian organizations, such as migrant shelters, are not exempt. Shelters are targeted by criminal groups who come to scout out their next victims. Those who have just received a money order are ripe victims for robbery, whereas those who have family members in the United States can be potential kidnapping victims, as they likely have someone who will pay their ransom. Young women and girls are ideal victims for sex trafficking. Government agents are also constantly infiltrating migrant shelters under the pretext that they are hubs of criminal activity. This situation generates a sense of insecurity for those who work at the shelters, as well as for the migrants who pass through them.

Given the diversity of ways to think and act in order to extract some benefit from the vulnerability of the undocumented migrant, it is relevant to distinguish between aggression and violence. Aggression implies an isolated event, restricted to a limited number of actors, whereas violence is more diffused across time and space. Furthermore, violence undergoes a process of internalization within individuals or groups, and thus becomes a fixed part of the social landscape. The internalization of violence within individuals or groups through "experienced-based learning" serves as a way to analyze situational violence and, furthermore, determine at what point these situational causes of violence become internal motivations within a society as groups, institutions, and individuals emerge who increasingly display these violent behaviors in situational events.

The dynamics within Mexican communities along principal migration routes have created hostile and violent contexts for the transmigrant communities that pass through them. In many cities where the train, "La Bestia" (the Beast) arrives (such as Arriaga, Ixtepec, Tenosique, Lecheria, and Saltillo, among others), members of the local community complain that Central American migrants attract crime to their communities. As a reaction to the inconvenience of having a constant flow of undocumented migrants passing through the community, locals find ways to take advantage of the limitations, shortcomings, or any element of vulnerability posed by the Otherness of migrants. These hostilities manifest in a multiplicity of activities, from vendors who charge migrants highly inflated prices for food and beverages, to the local police who extort them by threatening to turn them into immigration authorities or imprison them.

It is necessary to examine how migration policies that promote Otherness precipitate hostile social relations and everyday interactions, especially in the communities through which migrants most frequently transit. As previously stated, in Mexico there is a social tendency that establishes vertical and unequal relationships with the foreign "Other," thus perpetuating discriminatory practices based on a form of nationalism that, in order to lift itself up, disqualifies the "Other." This manifestation of nationalism promotes relationships of "domestic versus foreign" in terms of "dominant versus dominated." In other words, it establishes who is entitled to take versus who is obligated to give, or who has impunity versus who is vulnerable and defenseless. However, in the development of national/foreign domination, this dynamic is determined by the relative weight of the countries of origin, as well as the protection policies provided by their consulates, in comparison to the political weight of the country of destination or transit, such as Mexico. We can note the prevalence of disparaging adjectives, such as "gringo," for those who are from the north. Those who originate from the country to the south of the Mexican border are from "Guatemala" or "Guatepeor" (mala meaning "bad," peor meaning "worse"). Thus, although the derogatory adjective "gringo" persists, citizens from the United States do not need a visa to enter Mexican territory, and, until very recently, US citizens did not even need a passport. In contrast, Mexicans are required to have both a passport and visa to enter the United States. In other words, there is a lack of reciprocity, which, in this case, is detrimental to Mexicans. We see a reproduction of this relationship between Mexico and Central America. Mexicans traveling to Central America do not need visas, whereas Central Americans do require visas if they wish to enter Mexico legally, and these visas are categorized according to the type of labor activity in order to screen out those whose intention is to reach the United States via Mexico.[36] Again, we encounter a lack of reciprocity between neighboring states.

Foreigners are subject to differential treatment from authorities, as well as the society or those who see them as an opportunity for profit. Once the distinction is made between a Mexican and a foreigner, the variety and graveness of criminal acts against the person relate directly to the national identity of the foreign Other, without taking into account the person's migratory status. In this ensemble of differences, the Central American undocumented migrant becomes the most vulnerable of them all, although more subtleties can be identified even within this category. Those who will be the most susceptible to being identified and treated as the "exploitable Other" are migrants who have a limited collective knowledge regarding the transmigratory experience, less developed social networks of assistance, and less established organizational culture, and who possess the physical characteristics that make them easier to distinguish from Mexicans. The migrants who tend to meet all of these conditions are Hondurans.

Furthermore, age and sex differences in adult-centric and patriarchal cultures like those of Mexico and Central America worsen the situation. Girls, adolescents, and women are particularly susceptible in any given environment to sexual violence in the form of sex trafficking. Central American women and girls face a severe reality in Mexico, where they are viewed as sexual objects, as well as extremely vulnerable. Each and every migrant embodies an expression of vulnerability that is amplified by the dynamic of domestic/foreign as well as the hierarchical system of power among the competing social and institutional sectors.

CONCLUSION

Within their respective territories, Mexico and the United States have enacted strict legal regulations for the granting of visas, entry, and residency for foreigners. However, with respect to Central America, there are divergences between the two countries.[37] Furthermore, there are profound gaps in the immigration debates in Mexico, the United States, and Central America at a governmental, as well as social, level. In the United States, migration is perceived as a domestic policy issue. In Mexico, migration is a foreign policy issue with the United States, and in Central America, it is a matter of old political loyalty to the United States and a humanitarian issue with Mexico. The principal concern of the government of the United States is security, and, for Mexico, it is the economic and social aspects, as well as human rights issues. Central America governments are concerned with solidarity and understanding with the United States and Mexico. Although there is a deep division in US society regarding how to open or close itself to immigration flows, in Mexico, there is a social consensus in favor of the free mobility of the labor force and an open border with the north. However, within Mexican society, there exists indifference, ambiguity, even denial regarding Central American immigration and transmigration. Meanwhile, the Central American societies perceive emigration as a legitimate solution to domestic problems that deserve international support and solidarity, although these countries still do not promote, or even accept, intraregional migration within Central America, for instance, the regional flows of Nicaraguans to Costa Rica, Hondurans to El Salvador, or Salvadorians and Hondurans to Guatemala. Taking into account the lengthy list of disagreements and opposing positions held by the various countries involved, what actions can be taken, especially in the face of the undeniable fact that undocumented international migration is in full force and growing? How do we mediate the disagreements and avoid confrontation in order to create the conditions needed to arrive at a common ground? Today, the unceasing flow of transmigrants, as well as the "humanitarian crisis" they are suffering, indicates that the current legal formulation is antiquated and inefficient, especially if the governments are supposed to be taking into account the human rights of migrants. Perhaps from the physical and social space of southern borders, officials can start to reorient paths, attitudes, perceptions, and public interventions.

NOTES

1. *The New York Times*, public statement made by President Obama, June 2, 2014.
2. Between 2001 and 2010, the Instituto Nacional de Migración recorded 6,671 detentions of persons from the continent of Asia, 4,369 detentions of persons from the continent of Africa, and 1,264,600 detentions of Central Americans from Guatemala, Honduras, El Salvador, and Nicaragua (http://www.inm.gob.mx). Beyond the sheer numbers, also noteworthy is that the natures of these international smuggling networks are very different. To migrate from Asia or Africa requires a much larger and more complicated international network than those for migration from Central America.
3. Instituto Nacional de Migración, *Dossier flujo de entradas de extranjeros por la frontera sur terrestre de México registradas por el Instituto Nacional de Migración* (Mexico: Instituto Nacional de Migración, 2005).
4. Rodolfo Casillas, "La labor humanitaria y los organismos civiles: la experiencia de los albergues y casas de migrantes, realidades y desafíos," in *Las políticas públicas sobre migraciones y la sociedad civil en América Latina. Los casos de Argentina, Brasil, Colombia y México*, ed. Leonir M. Chiarello (New York: Scalabrini International Migration Network, 2011), 524–559.
5. María del Carmen García A. and Daniel Villafuerte, *Migración, derechos humanos y desarrollo* (Mexico: Universidad de Ciencias y Artes de Chiapas, 2014).
6. Oscar Martínez, *Los migrantes que no importan* (Mexico: elfaro.net, 2010).
7. See, for example, Jéssica Natalia Nájera Aguirre, "Trabajo extradoméstico de las migrantes guatemaltecas en Chiapas," in *Flujos migratorios en la Frontera Guatemala-México*, ed. Ma. Eugenia Anguiano Téllez and Rodolfo Corona Vázquez (Mexico City: COLEF-INM/Centro de Estudios Migratorios-DGE/Editions, 2009).
8. Daniella Spenser, "Trabajo forzado en Guatemala, bracerismo guatemalteco en Chiapas," *Cuicuilco* 4, no. 12 (1984): 5–10.
9. *The New York Times*, "Questions about the Border Kids," accessed on July 15, 2014. http://www.nytimes.com/interactive/2014/07/15/us/questions-about-the-border-kids.html?_r=0
10. Rodolfo Casillas, "La construcción del dato oficial y la realidad institucional: La disminución del flujo indocumentado en los registros del INM," *Migración y Desarrollo* 10, no. 19 (2012): 33–60.
11. Germán Martínez Velasco, *Plantaciones, trabajo guatemalteco y política migratoria en la frontera sur de México* (Chiapas: Government of the State of Chiapas-Instituto Chiapaneco de Cultura, 1994), 197.
12. Guadalupe Rodríguez De Ita, "Una mirada urgente al sur: los refugiados guatemaltecos en Chiapas," in *Chiapas: Rupturas y continuidades de una sociedad fragmentada*, ed. Diana Guillén (México: Instituto Mora, 2003), 223–270.
13. See Carolina Rivera, "El trabajo de niñas, niños y adolescentes guatemaltecos en el Soconusco, Chiapas," in *Migración, seguridad, violencia y derechos humanos en el sur de México y Centroamérica*, Mexico, ed. Daniel Villafuerte and María del Carmen

García (Mexico City: Miguel Ángel Porrúa, 2011); Rodolfo Corona and Miguel Ángel Reyes, "Identificación, caracterización y cuantificación," in *Flujos migratorios en la Frontera Guatemala-México*, ed. Ma. Eugenia Anguiano and Rodolfo Corona (México: INM, Colegio de la Frontera Norte, 2009), 371–401; Jaime Rivas, "Los que se quedan en el camino. Inmigrantes salvadoreños en Puerto Madero, Chiapas" (Ph.D. diss., CIESAS Occidente, 2013).

14. The North Atlantic Free Trade Agreement, in January 1994, which also included Canada, is a prime example of the creation of a regional market in the northern hemisphere.

15. See, for example, the National Institute of Migration. *Apuntes sobre migración*. Ministry of the Interior, Mexican National Institute of Migration, Center for Migration Studies, 2011; National Institute of Migration. *Flujo de entradas de extranjeros por la frontera sur terrestre de México registradas por el Instituto Nacional de Migración*. Center for Migration Studies, 2005.

16. "Plan Sur" was a program enacted by the National Institute for Migration (INM) in July 2001 that sought to increase the ability to control the migratory flows coming through southern Mexico. Its objective was to enhance security and control of migratory flows en route to the United States from the southern border to the Isthmus of Tehauntepec, Oaxaca. "Plan Sur," as such, did not last very long due to strong criticism from the civil society and even from the Mexican federal government. However, it managed to establish the operational bases of the National Institute of Migration for contention programs of transmigration flows.

17. Olivia Ruiz, "Los riesgos de migrar: La migración centroamericana en la frontera México-Guatemala," in *Nuevas tendencias y nuevos desafíos de la migración internacional; memorias del seminario permanente sobre migración internacional*, ed. M. Á. Castillo and J. Santibáñez (Tijuana: Colegio de la Frontera Norte, 2004), 333–364.

18. National Commission of Human Rights (CNDH), *Special Report of the National Commission for Human Rights on the Case of Kidnapping against Migrants* (Mexico: CNDH, 2009).

19. To provide context for understanding the deep and extensive roots of violence within Central American society that this chapter touches upon, see Sala Negra de el Faro, ed., *Crónicas negras desde una región que no cuenta* (México: Aguilar, 2014).

20. Rodolfo Casillas, "Masacre de transmigrantes," *Foreign Affairs Latinoamérica* 10, no. 4 (2010): 52–59.

21. National Commission of Human Rights (CNDH), *Bienvenidos al infierno del secuestro. Testimonios de migrantes* (Mexico: CNDH, 2009).

22. See National Institute of Migration, *Compilación histórica de la legislación migratoria en México 1909–1996* (México: Talleres Gráficos de México, 1996). The laws cited here and annotations in quotes all come from the same source, with the exception of the Migration Act of 2012, whose corresponding source will be cited when appropriate.

23. Author's emphasis.

24. Author's emphasis.

25. Author's emphasis. The assimilation will be the purpose for including the distinct ethnic groups in the country, as recorded in other laws and the law of 1936. In other words, the assimilation of foreign and indigenous people according to a model "mestizaje" of citizenship, based on the logic of the modern Mexican state.

26. Author's emphasis.

27. Author's emphasis.

28. Author's emphasis.

29. *Diario Oficial de la Federación* (Mexico: Ministry of the Interior, 2011).

30. These elements do not deny the legal, social, political, and cultural expressions that exist in favor of foreigners in particular circumstances, for example, Spanish refugees, or asylum granted to South American politicians and intellectuals, or Central American refugees. However, each of these aforementioned restrictions needs to be placed in its historical context to be analyzed and appraised. The argument is that, over time, these restrictions linger in the society as differentiating elements that are applied to the foreigner in an undifferentiated manner, in other words, out of context. When they become incorporated into the social imagination, they lose their historical context and begin to be used indiscriminately as the basis for prejudice.

31. See Instituto Nacional de Migración, *Dossier Flujo de entradas de extranjeros por la frontera sur terrestre de México registradas por el Instituto Nacional de Migración* (México: INM, Centro de Estudios Migratorios, 2005).

32. The transmigrant, as previously stated, is a foreigner who passes through two or more national borders in the course of arriving at a foreign destination. A transborder worker, on the other hand, lives in one country and works in another. In the case of Mexico's southern border, there are transborder Guatemalan workers who reside in a region geographically close to the border with Mexico, and who habitually cross the national border to work in Mexico, while continuing to reside in Guatemala. A regional migrant is one who travels between the country of origin and a neighboring country to carry out a task or activity, and whose motive for crossing the national border need not be limited to work-related activities.

33. Bernardo Espino Del Castillo, "Combate al tráfico de indocumentados," in *Asuntos migratorios en México, Opiniones de la sociedad* (Mexico: National Institute of Migration, Ministry of the Interior, 1996): 151–152. Espino speaks from his position as general coordinator of the Central Zone, in the Attorney General's Office.

34. See, for example, the publication by the Jesuit Service for Migrants: *Narrativas de la transmigración centroamericana en su paso por México: Resumen ejecutivo* (Mexico: Jesuit Service for Migrants, 2013).

35. See National Commission for Human Rights (CNDH) and the International Organization for Migration (IOM), ed., *Una vida discreta, fugaz y anónima: Los centroamericanos transmigrantes en México* (Mexico City: Centro Nacional de Derechos Humanos, 2007), 59 and 60.

36. In 2006, there existed a "Local Pass" that was issued by Guatemala and stamped by Mexico (valid for Guatemalans, but not for Belizeans). The Immigration Form 3 (FM3), Immigration Form 2 (FM2), and the immigration form for tourists, transmigrants, visitors, business people, and ministers all required a passport. Recently, they introduced an administrative simplification that expands the breadth of activities, span of time, among other changes; however, the differentiating scheme essentially remains intact.

37. For more information on this topic, see Guadalupe González, J. A. Schiavon, D. Crow, and G. Maldonado, *México, las Américas y el mundo, 2010. Política exterior: opinión pública y líderes* (Mexico: Center for Economic Research and Teaching, 2011); and Guadalupe González, "Percepciones sociales sobre la migración en México y Estados Unidos: ¿Hay espacios para cooperar?" in *México, país de migración*, ed. Luis Herrera-Lasso M. (Mexico: D.F.: Center for Economic Research and Teaching, 2009), 107–153.

CHAPTER 6

Between "Here" and "There"

Transnational Latino/a Youth in Madrid

ANDREA DYRNESS AND ENRIQUE SEPÚLVEDA

In the 2000s, Spain became the second most important destination country for immigrants from Latin America after the United States, and the first-ever European Union country whose immigration is predominantly Latino. By 2012, immigrants made up 14% of Spain's population. As a new receiving context for the Latino diaspora, Spain offers a stark contrast to the United States. Latino immigration began only in the late 1980s, with the most rapid growth occurring between 2000 and 2008, bringing a significant Latin American presence to Spanish society almost overnight. Spain offers a much more favorable legal and political framework for Latin American immigrants than the United States, privileging Latin American nationals over other groups in its immigration and citizenship laws. However, expectations of smooth integration, based on friendly citizenship laws and official rhetoric of cultural, linguistic, and historical similarity between Spaniards and Latin Americans, belie complicated and conflicting realities for Latino immigrants in Spain. Do Latin Americans in Spain really *feel* culturally similar to Spaniards? Are they accepted as such by ordinary Spaniards? What are the implications of a discourse of integration predicated on cultural sameness—or the erasure of cultural difference over time—for immigrant youth who are growing up between cultures? These are the questions we take up in this chapter.

In this chapter, we explore the citizenship formation processes of first- and second-generation immigrant youth of Latin American origin at three community associations in Madrid. The bulk of the data come from ethnographically informed participatory research conducted with adolescent youth at a neighborhood-based family service agency in Malasaña, a central city neighborhood with a large concentration of Latino immigrants, in 2013–2014.[1] Data were also collected from a second neighborhood association in Malasaña, and from Latin American women involved in an activist women's association founded by first-generation immigrants from Guatemala. These two groups—second-generation immigrant adolescents and first-generation immigrant women—offer contrasting experiences with migration and integration in Madrid characteristic of the two principal groups of Latin Americans in Spain: those who come to work (and their children) and those who come to study. As we will see, Latin Americans in both groups—whether they were brought to Spain as young children or arrived in their 20s on student visas—navigate complex relationships of belonging with Spain and their countries of origin and form diasporic identities that do not conform to the dominant discourse of integration. The expectation of integration based on cultural similarity or assimilation both denies Latino immigrants' lived experiences with racism in Spain and their attachments to transnational communities. Here we explore the implications of this integration discourse along with their participation in diasporic communities for their developing identities and civic engagement.

FROM BOOM TO CRISIS: THE CONTEXT OF LATIN AMERICAN IMMIGRATION IN SPAIN

In the boom years of 2000–2007, Latin American immigrants to Spain encountered a growing economy with a seemingly endless capacity to absorb new workers, along with comparatively friendly immigration policies, especially after the election of the Socialist party in 2004.[2] In 2005 the new Socialist government under President Zapatero initiated the largest legalization campaign ever in Europe, legalizing nearly 600,000 unauthorized immigrants, and designated a large fund for integration programs, emphasizing education.[3] Integration policy was of central importance for the Socialist government, which cooperated closely with the civil society and migrants' associations to develop the Strategic Plan for Citizenship and Integration, 2006–2009, aimed at promoting social cohesion. "Interculturality," the idea of mutual exchange and enrichment between cultures, was an explicit principle guiding integration and education policy in the 2000s, in line with broader discourses circulating in the European Union.[4] However, there was also a recognition from leaders in both parties that immigration challenged democratic life together (*convivencia*), and that some cultures were more easily integrated than others.[5]

Latin Americans, as stated previously, have been favored in Spain's immigration laws, due to the historical relationship between the regions and presumed cultural and linguistic similarities that facilitate integration.[6] Latin Americans are eligible to apply for citizenship after only 2 years of legal stay in the country, compared to 10 years for other immigrant groups. Spanish political discourse about migration and foreign policy reflects a commitment to Latin America and a sense of cultural kinship with the region, stemming from Spain's colonial past on the continent. For example, in a speech given in January 2005 to the Spanish community in Argentina, President Zapatero defined Spain as being both European and Ibero-American, and held that Spain had an obligation "to look at Ibero-America, to fight for Ibero-America, and feel its successes, because its progresses are Spanish progresses, too."[7] Conservative Popular Party politicians also referenced Latin Americans' cultural proximity to Spain as reasons why they were more easily integrated, compared to other immigrant groups like Moroccans.[8] One member of Congress predicted in 2005 that "within one generation . . . they [Latin Americans] will be indistinguishable [from Spaniards]."[9]

Later we will explore how these predictions bear out in the experiences of the second-generation immigrant youth we worked with. However, the era of government spending on immigrant integration ended abruptly with the advent of the economic crisis in 2008, which brought Spain one of the highest unemployment rates in the Eurozone. Immigrants were the hardest hit by the crisis, being concentrated in the most vulnerable positions in the economy: domestic service, hotel and restaurant service, and construction. By 2013 the unemployment rate was 24.8% for native Spaniards and 36.4% for immigrants.[10] In 16% of immigrant households, all breadwinners (economically active people) were unemployed. In 2010, 43.5% of foreign-born adults in Spain were living in poverty.[11]

The crisis ushered in an era of austerity and government cutbacks, eliminating many public services just when they were most needed. The integration fund for immigrants that had been lavishly funded from 2005 to 2008 was steadily cut until its final disappearance in 2012.[12] The staff in the agencies we worked with directly felt the impact of these cuts, finding themselves with more work and fewer resources. ASI, the family service agency that was our primary research site, depended heavily on public funds from the municipal government of Madrid which had been channeled from the government's integration fund. Since the advent of the crisis, its annual budget had been reduced by sevenfold. In 2012, one of the first moves of the new Popular Party government was to eliminate health care for unauthorized immigrants, a social right they had enjoyed since 2000. The move reflected a growing public hostility toward immigrants. In fact, the crisis accelerated what had already been a steady trend since 2000 of deteriorating public attitudes toward immigrants.[13]

After the intense immigration growth in the early 2000s, the years after the crisis saw a leveling off, and by 2013, the talk in Madrid was of return migration: Latin American families returning to their countries of origin after failing to find (or regain) work. However, data from the municipal registers in 2013 showed that there was not a generalized or massive exodus, and that not all groups were leaving.[14] For example, Dominicans, Peruvians, and Venezuelans maintained their numbers, while Ecuadorians, Argentineans, and Bolivians saw significant drops from 2008 to 2013. In a further twist, as the crisis deepened, many native Spaniards began emigrating to Latin America. In 2012, the number of people who left Spain for Latin America exceeded the number of Latin Americans who migrated to the European Union, according to the International Organization for Migration, and this trend continued through 2014.[15] It remains to be seen how renewed Spanish emigration to Latin America will affect views of Latin American immigrants in Spain or the experience of the Spanish Latino diaspora.

LATINO STUDENTS IN SPANISH SCHOOLS

In the wake of the crisis, growing concern has focused on the second generation—children of immigrants born in Spain or brought there as young children—who are coming of age in a time of poor economic prospects. Education, and how the children of immigrants fare in schools, has been a chief preoccupation of policy-makers and researchers, as it is seen as an indicator of the state's ability to integrate them. Much like in the United States, researchers in Spain have documented a significant educational achievement gap between immigrant and nonimmigrant students.[16] The children of Latin American immigrants are among the lowest performing.[17] Recent qualitative research has pointed to the institutional contexts that produce these patterns of failure, highlighting such factors as tracking and segregation of immigrant students, unchallenging classes, poorly trained teachers, and enduring ethnic stereotypes.[18] Latino students in Spain are overrepresented in compensatory and vocational education programs and underrepresented in academic tracks that lead to the university,[19] and they are far more likely to drop out of school.[20] Such research challenges the supposedly integrative role of educational policies and programs.[21]

The poor school performance of Latin American students also challenges assumptions of smooth integration based on their shared linguistic and cultural heritage with Spain. A growing body of ethnographic research on Latino students in Spain points to the role of educators' discourses about Latin Americans, and deficit views of Latin American cultures, in shaping Latino students' poor school trajectories.[22] According to a multiyear ethnographic study of a majority-Latino high school in Madrid, teachers held a series of beliefs about Latin American students in which their "cultural origin" played a central explanatory role in their school performance. Latin American students were described as culturally and cognitively deprived. Educational placement decisions were rationalized based on perceptions of linguistic deficiencies (due to the different forms of Spanish they spoke), assumptions about inferior schooling in Latin American countries, and speculations about students' family backgrounds and values as not supporting educational achievement.[23] Another ethnographic study in Madrid showed that stereotypes circulating in schools portrayed Latino immigrants as poor and uneducated; culturally inferior and socially backward; illegal; dangerous; and a threat to social cohesion in the country.[24] An ethnographic study at a Barcelona institute similarly found that educators used "culture-based" explanations for the underachievement of South American students, feared that Latin American students would join gangs, and associated Latin American students' self-segregation in the school with "ghettoes."[25] In these studies, expressions of Latin American solidarity or ethnic identity were perceived by educators as threats to both school achievement and social cohesion.

Latino students are thus given the message that their "cultures" and ethnic identities are obstacles to their school success and integration, even as they are exposed to official discourses that portray Spain as an open and tolerant society, welcoming of immigrants. As Ríos-Rojas writes, the lives of immigrant youth in

Spain are shaped by "this fundamental tension between the welcoming of difference and a more tacit nationalist impulse to discipline difference in the interest of preserving the nation."[26] Concerns for national integration based on cultural assimilation cast immigrant youth as either victims or problems for Spanish society.[27] In our view, research and policymaking driven by nationalist concerns obscures the barriers to national belonging for immigrant youth and the formative role of transnational and diasporic communities on young immigrants' developing identities. The national integration bias both conceals the complexity of immigrant youths' lives and reveals and reflects broader social anxieties about immigrant integration and cultural diversity.

A prominent example here is the work of sociologist Alejandro Portes and his Spanish colleagues,[28] who conducted the first longitudinal study of immigrant self-identity in Spain, focusing on the second generation.[29] Their bias in favor of the nation-state is immediately apparent: "This second generation poses a series of challenges for receiving societies and governments that must seek to integrate and educate its members to become law-abiding and productive citizens."[30] To determine the Spanish state's success at meeting this challenge, their quantitative study, based on a survey of roughly 7,000 immigrant teens, inquired whether these youth self-identified as Spanish or not. The study poses a rigid binary between "resilient foreign identities," which they associate with resistance, protest mobilizations, and revolts, and "identification with the host society," which represents, for them, a "definite sign of integration and establishes the psychological basis for pursuing upward mobility within it."[31] Throughout their writing, youth who did not self-identify as Spanish are described with negative words such as *alienated, confrontational, reactive, militant, oppositional.* In their first survey in 2008, only a third of the youth self-identified as Spanish. A follow-up survey reinterviewed 73% of the youth 3–4 years later (2011–2012), plus a new sample in the same schools. In this follow-up survey, 50% of the youth self-identified as Spanish and 50% did not. This made headlines in Spain as evidence of integration.[32] The authors write in 2013: "the data lead us to conclude that the children of immigrants have integrated into Spanish youth and the differences between them and the children of natives are diminishing over time."[33]

This research, although seemingly aimed at quelling alarmist rhetoric about failed integration, inadvertently supports the conceptual scheme on which such alarmist discourse rests. The absence of threat is predicated upon ethnocultural national identification and the "diminishing" of differences between the children of immigrants and the children of natives over time. Immigrants who reject Spanish identification and embrace their cultural and ethnic identities are therefore to be viewed with suspicion, since there is no alternative to the *either* Spanish *or* oppositional binary. The immigrant youth we worked with in Madrid, who were brought to Spain as young children or born in Spain to immigrant parents, rejected such binaries for their own identities and defied the categories of assimilated Spaniard or dangerous other. But only through the lens of diasporic citizenship do their complex and nuanced experiences of citizenship become visible.

DIASPORIC CITIZENSHIP

In seeking to examine the citizenship formation of immigrant youth, we draw on anthropological understandings of citizenship that encompass cultural processes of subject formation, not simply the legal-juridical aspects of citizenship.[34] In particular, we look to studies of diasporic citizenship to help us understand the identity formations of youth who are coming of age between nations. Lok Siu defines diasporic citizenship as "the processes by which diasporic subjects experience and practice cultural and social belonging amid shifting geopolitical circumstances and webs of transnational relations."[35] The focus on practices of belonging highlights the agency of migrants—who may lack legal citizenship—and the transnational communities that give them meaning.

A growing number of scholars have called for a greater focus on transnational processes to better understand the citizenship formation of immigrant youth.[36] Sánchez writes, "To understand the lives of immigrants, it is critical to not only consider the traditional ways that newcomers incorporate or assimilate but also the ways in which they maintain ties to their homelands and how this shapes their understanding of belonging to two places simultaneously."[37] While some scholars, including Portes, highlight the benefits of transnational ties for host-country incorporation,[38] others argue for an expansive redefinition of citizenship that transcends the nation-state.[39] Anna Ríos-Rojas, in her study of immigrant youth in Barcelona, Spain, argues that their visions of citizenship do not fit the molds of more formal definitions of citizenship.[40] "For many of the youth," she writes, "their identities were being forged in the in-between spaces of here and there, origin and destination, as they negotiated and straddled multiple worlds—the state, family, peers, school, and popular culture. Therefore, these youth of immigration asserted more expanded notions of belonging as they enacted more hybrid, "flexible," and "polycultural" citizenships."[41]

Although such flexible citizenships are usually not recognized by nation-state institutions, they provide resources for immigrant youths' civic engagement.[42] As Sánchez writes, "the transnational 'funds of knowledge'" accumulated by immigrant youth in both home and host countries, along with the "cultural flexibility" they develop, form the basis of their enactment and understanding of global citizenship.[43] U.S.-based Latino scholars have been at the forefront of highlighting the benefits of transnationalism for Latino immigrant students. As Henry Trueba describes, transnationalism "consists of a unique capacity to handle different cultures and lifestyles, different social status, different roles and relationships, and to function effectively in different social, political, and economic systems."[44]

Integral to our conceptual lens is a methodological approach open to diasporic subjects' complex experiences of belonging. Participatory research is a methodology well suited to studying diasporic citizenship, because it engages research participants in examining and reflecting on their own realities. Participatory action research with youth (YPAR) typically involves young people as coinvestigators, giving them the tools to investigate and address social problems that affect their lives.[45] Although the types of research activities participants engage in might vary, a key feature of all participatory research is dialogue, based on Paulo Freire's notion of praxis: collective reflection and action on the world in order to change it.[46]

In this research, we adapted the tools of PAR to examine diasporic citizenship with immigrant youth at two neighborhood associations in Malasaña, Madrid. Both associations, funded by the Municipality of Madrid, aimed to integrate low-income, "at-risk" youth, almost all of whom were children of Latin American immigrants. In the first association and our primary research site, *Asociación de Servicios Integrales* (ASI),[47] we conducted a citizenship workshop, consisting of twelve weekly sessions with structured activities designed to provoke reflection and dialogue on issues of identity and citizenship. We introduced poetry written by other migrant students, identity reflection exercises, dramatic role play, and videos to stimulate discussion on complex issues of race, culture, and identity. At the end of the workshop, we conducted individual interviews with each of the participating youth (twelve of whom were children of immigrants), and collectively planned and delivered a presentation on our research with five of the youth at the Autonomous University of Madrid. In the second association, we held a series of three focus group sessions, incorporating some of the activities we used in the workshop. All sessions were recorded and transcribed. Finally, Andrea also conducted participant-observation, focus groups, and interviews with young women involved in the *Asociación de Mujeres de Guatemala* (AMG, Association of Women of Guatemala). In these three locations, through poetry, identity reflection exercises, photography, interviews, and group discussions, we engaged in a process of collective inquiry that shed light on how migrants' participation in transnational social fields shapes their identities, their civic awareness, and their motivation to engage in social change.

DEMOCRATIC INTEGRATION AS CULTURAL ASSIMILATION

The slogan of ASI, printed on its organizational materials, is "*Construyendo la democracia más pequeña en el corazón de la sociedad*" (building the smallest democracy in the heart of society). Staff at the nongovernmental organization (NGO) considered their organization and other NGOs to be playing a vital role in preparing immigrants for citizenship and for a healthy democratic life together. In their view, made clear in interviews and informal conversations, a healthy democratic life together meant the absence of ethnic conflicts and the absence of "ghettoes." They expressed that Madrid, and the neighborhood of Malasaña in particular, had made progress in this regard, because there was not the level of conflicts in 2013 that there had been in the late 1990s and early 2000s. Their view echoed those we heard from a variety of stakeholders in Madrid— social workers, city officials, university scholars, and students—that immigrants were assimilating and racism was diminishing, and that Madrid was exceptional in this regard from other European cities because of the absence of ghettoes.

In 2005, the Socialist Minister of Labor and Social Affairs had discussed the challenge of immigrant integration saying, "The Spanish society can be proud of the way it has responded to this challenge. There have been a few outbursts of rejection, but fortunately they have been overcome."[48] This point of view reflects a dominant optimistic narrative we heard in Madrid, that the problems around immigrants had largely been resolved, and that the worst period of conflict and xenophobia was safely in the past. The advent of the economic recession in 2008 and mounting public anxiety about immigration brought a new urgency to the public discourse around integration and new pressure to show that Spanish society was not at risk of major conflicts. However, the centrality of conflict prevention in the integration discourse communicated the idea that immigrants *could* pose a threat if they remained visible as immigrants: if they associated only with other immigrants and made visible displays of their ethnic identities.[49] This idea was exemplified in a 2-day conference we attended in Madrid entitled, "The Challenge of Big Cities in the Context of Crisis: Present and Future of the Children of Immigration." The conference, sponsored by the Madrid municipal government's Department of Public Safety and attended primarily by police and other public safety workers, aimed to provide information on the children of immigrants that would facilitate the goals of *convivencia* (living together) and *seguridad* (safety) in Madrid. Invited speakers presented various perspectives on immigrant conflict and revolt and ways to avoid it. A recurring theme was that Madrid had so far managed to avoid the major conflicts around immigrants that had afflicted other European cities because it did not have immigrant barrios, or "ghettoes."

Spanish educators and social workers we interviewed shared the view that ethnic association was equivalent to "ghettoes" and a threat to integration. Even as they lamented cuts to the budget for their services, they expressed criticism for previous government initiatives that had fomented immigrant associations. During the heyday of Socialist government-financed integration, the Madrid municipal government had sponsored ethnic associations for immigrants known as CEPIs, *Centros de Encuentro y Participación para Inmigrantes*, focused on national-origin groups, for example, Centro Hispano-Colombiano and Centro Hispano-Peruano. By 2013 these were being eliminated due to budget cuts, but in the view of ASI's director, they had "generated their own ghettoes." A social worker at a major Madrid agency even told us they did not use the word "immigrant" when referring to immigrant youth because to do so would be "a way of stigmatizing them." Such sentiments revealed a vision of integration that erased cultural differences and ethnic distinctions in the name of equality, similar to the colorblind discourse among educators in the United States.[50]

Echoing the findings of ethnographies of Latino education cited previously, educators in our study expressed the belief that healthy integration for immigrant youth was based on identification with Spanish culture and dissociation from Latino culture, which was seen as backward and inferior. The adolescent educator at ASI insisted that the youth in our group identified as Spanish, since they had lived in Spain since they were small: "they have lived in a more European culture; they feel like they're from here." She added that they might still identify with their cultures in their homes, but not outside: "*Quizás en sus casas, los papás pueden ser más machistas, pero saben que la sociedad española no es así.*" (Maybe in their homes, their fathers might be *machista*, but they know that Spanish society is not like that.) This educator's only references to Latino culture(s) were about machismo and sexism, which she found difficult to transform in her young Latino/a charges: "*Lo llevan muy dentro, aunque lo que te decía que han crecido aquí y tal, eso de la cultura latina.*" (They carry that [sexism] deep inside, even though like I told you they've grown up here and everything, that from the Latino culture.) This echoed a very common view that Latino students' home cultures were an obstacle to their integration.[51]

When the Congressman predicted in 2005 that Latino immigrants would be "indistinguishable" from Spaniards within a generation, he was also making a normative statement that they *should* become indistinguishable: successful integration required the erasure of difference. As we will see, this expectation put immigrant youth, who were at the margins of national belonging, in an impossible bind.

ON (UN)BELONGING: NAVIGATING THIRD SPACE IDENTITIES

The adolescent youth in our study, if asked whether they considered themselves Spanish, would not have been able to answer a simple "yes" or "no," nor did their identities fit neatly into either category of "Spanish" or immigrant other. Our exploration illuminated a more complex reality: immigrant youth navigate multiple forms of belonging in Spain and their countries of origin, and multiple forms of exclusion. Their efforts to belong in both national and transnational communities are marked by contradiction and must be understood in the context of the policing of their identities by the state, the media, peer groups, and their own transnational family networks.

In the following section we highlight the voices and lived realities of immigrant youth in Madrid to illuminate (a) complex forms of attachment and belonging; (b) hybrid identities; and (c) challenging, even oppressive, paths to transnational belonging. Latino immigrant youths' transnational experiences and complicated processes of belonging to the Spanish nation help us understand how this complexity isn't simply about transgression of territorial borders on their part, but rather points to the paradoxical social production of Spanish subjects of immigrant background who are both familiar and strange, far and near (in a cultural sense), and included and integrated into the social fabric that serves to render their "intrusive" and "visible" migrant identities into palatable, less intrusive, and thus invisible (read erased) subjectivities.[52]

Complex Transnational Belongings and Hybrid Identities

For Rolando, a 15-year-old born in Madrid to an Ecuadorian mother and Domini-can father, adjusting to life in Madrid initially was very difficult. He had been taken back to Ecuador at age 1 and spent the next 4 years there with his maternal grandmother and the rest of their vast clan of uncles and aunts, in what he says was "a whole country village of cousins and relatives." Because Rolando hadn't known his mother for the first years of his conscious life, he didn't have any emo-tional connections to her (or to his country of birth). When Rolando was 5 years old, his mom returned to Ecuador to take him back to Spain with her. He recalled that period of transition as one full of endless tears and deep loss. He described going from a known and secure environment to feeling disoriented in unknown surroundings; from a small village to a big metropolis; from nature to concrete; from being surrounded by a big family (where everyone seemed to be related) to living with only his mom, a woman he didn't know, and no one to play with. At his Spanish school, Rolando eventually befriended two other students who were also marked as different from the rest of the kids: an autistic Spanish boy and a Colom-bian immigrant girl. He shared: "they loved me and I loved them."

Returning to Ecuador has always been a real possibility for Rolando, espe-cially in times of economic precarity. So when asked if he would like to return to Ecuador, he responded quickly, with a seemingly contradictory answer. He said he wasn't sure because he was plagued by divided sentiments. He says, *cuando estoy allí quiero quedarme, pero cuando estoy aquí no quiero irme. Es así, un poco* . . . ("When I'm there I want to stay, but when I'm here I don't want to leave. It's like that, a little . . . "). His voice trailed, but it was clear that his desires for either place were contextual and depended on those he was with at the time. He added, "Truthfully, I couldn't tell you because here I have my friends and my mom."

When asked about how he viewed himself, whether a Spanish or Ecuadoran identity fitted him, he said that he didn't see himself as Spanish, despite having been born in Madrid and having lived there most of his life. "Perhaps because I have a stronger, more vivid memory of where I lived my early childhood as op-posed to where I live now that I don't consider myself so Spanish . . . knowing that I was raised in a certain place in a particular way, and here, I live another way." When asked if he thought he could ever become a Spaniard, he said he wasn't sure. And yet, he also said that while he identified with each of his cultural back-grounds (Ecuadorian, Dominican, and Spanish) at different moments and con-texts, he didn't "side" with any particular one: "*no me decanto por ningún lado. O sea, ni por español, ni por ecuatoriano, ni nada.*" For Rolando, becoming Span-ish was a question mark. Many of his answers highlighted uncertainty, nuanced thinking, and a yet-to-be-determined quality. They defied easy categorization because his experiences and belongings are transnational, different from his Spanish contemporaries, with different histories that fall outside of the norma-tive national narrative.

These complexities and hybridities were not unique to Rolando. They sur-faced consistently when the immigrant youth in our study were interviewed, or when they shared their stories of migration and cultural perspectives of their lives here and there. In our discussions it was common for the youth to talk about "*mi país*" (my country), referring to their parent's country of origin, even if they had been born and raised in Spain. The students referenced strong ties to family back home, and cultural differences between themselves and Spanish youth, as reasons why they could not belong fully in Spain. In individual interviews and group discussions, almost all of the youth expressed that they (Latinos) were different from Spanish youth: in the way they spoke, dressed, danced, and in their family values and expectations. Such differences were usually expressed proudly, as when Marilyn, from Ecuador, shared, "To be Latino is to be a little bit warmer, we're closer. I see a Latino as more affectionate." Having family in their countries of origin was a key feature separating them from national belonging in Spain. Raquel, from the Dominican Republic, shared that she did not feel at home in Spain. When asked why, she explained, "*Aquí no estoy ni con la mitad de mi familia.*" (Here [in Spain] I'm not even with half of my family.) Several of the youth had siblings still living in their country of origin; all of them had cousins, aunts, and uncles there. Students often spoke longingly of their countries and the good times they had there with cousins and extended family.

And yet they were also clear that they would not go back to live there. When asked if she would ever want to live in the Dominican Republic, Luisa's answer was illustrative: "Me, for vacation, perfect, but to live, I wouldn't last." She went on to explain the poverty, scarcity, and poor-quality education that made life there difficult. Her sister Mariela put it this way: "If I were living in the Dominican Republic, I would surely be barefoot and pregnant, with no schooling." Their awareness of the material advantages, opportunities, and safety of life in Spain made it impossible for them to "belong" in their home countries. Ana Silvia explained how back home in Brazil, if you're out on the streets after dark, "you could get raped, robbed, or killed. . . . I wouldn't like to live there because there is no security." The youth were also aware that they were different from their family members who had not migrated, a difference they were made to feel each time they returned or visited with family members: different in their clothing style, their way of speaking Spanish, their values. For all of these reasons, in spite of strong attachments to their home countries, most said they could not go back to live there: that it was no longer home.

That left these youth in an in-between space, what diaspora scholars have called a "third space," in the words of Ritty Lukose, "a difference situated between the 'here' of the host country and the 'there' of origin, between the 'us' of a dominant community and the 'them' of multiple forms of racialized identification."[53] Many of the youth in our study were poignantly reflective about their in-between identities.

Claude, a 15-year-old Brazilian youth who came to Spain at age 7, expressed complex forms of attachment and belonging to his native country and his current country, Spain. When asked in an interview if he felt he belonged to Spain, his response was straight forward, *yo no* (not me). This response seemed to contradict his preference for living in Spain over Brazil. When asked where he would prefer to be, he said, "*España . . . claro, porque aquí hay mejor modo de vida, pero . . . yo siempre voy a recordar de donde he venido.*" (Spain . . . of course, because there is a better quality of life here . . . but, I will always remember where I have come from.) He says that at home his family still maintains Brazilian traditions and that some of his classmates are also Brazilian and they gather to converse in Portuguese. He adds that there *is* a connection to Spain because he has lived here/there for the past 8 years. But for Claude this connection isn't the same as belonging. When talking about Spain and Spanish citizens, he shares that he and his family know the language well, and "We know how they live, their customs . . . we are accustomed to them . . . but deep inside we continue to belong to our country."

Being different from the Spanish cultural and linguistic norm was enough to create social distances between Latino immigrants and their Spanish peers. For Latinos, cultural difference meant having transnational relations and experiences that were rooted both outside of the nation-state as well as within. Isabela, a 14-year-old from Venezuela, expressed the following when asked whether she considered herself Spanish: "*Yo pues no del todo porque, o sea, cuando llegué yo era latina, o sea no sabía el idioma no sé qué, hablaba con acento, ahora no, y que he estado toda mi vida aquí, pero no sé cómo que hay un huequito en mi cuerpo de que soy latina y eso sabes, y que pues que aunque quiera renunciar no puedo.*" (Me, not entirely because, well, when I got here I was Latina, I mean I didn't speak the language, and I don't know what, I spoke with an accent, and now, no, I've been here my whole life, but I don't know, there's like a little hole in my body that I'm Latina and that you know, I can't renounce even if I wanted to.) Here, Isabela describes going from not speaking the language (which she clarified meant speaking with an accent) to speaking like a Spaniard, and yet still feeling different because a part of her was Latina. In other words, having a deep belonging to another country or culture (Venezuela, Ecuador, Perú, etc.) meant having a different set of cultural and relational experiences that transcended national lines but also being positioned differently by Spaniards here within. Being Latina, for Isabela, meant "*tener mis raíces en otro sitio, o sea ser diferente a los demás*" (having my roots in another place, [and] being different from everyone else).

Teresa, a young adult activist and teacher in Madrid, self-identified as Guatemalan, even though she had acquired Spanish nationality, because "*no me siento española para nada.*" (I don't feel Spanish at all.) "No matter how long I live here, people will always ask me where I'm from," she said. "I will never be Spanish." She described the challenge of making herself understood in Madrid, because of language and cultural barriers, as one of the greatest challenges in her life as an immigrant. She said, "I've lost my sense of humor." She pointed out that if nobody understands it, you stop using it. "*Voy a cumplir ocho años aquí en cuatro días, y sigo sin entenderme!*" (In 4 days it will be 8 years being here and I continue to be misunderstood! People still don't understand my Spanish!) Such testimony, from a native Spanish speaker, defies the assumption of linguistic coherence between

Latin America and Spain and underscores the intimate connection between language varieties and cultural identity: for Teresa, not being able to use her Guatemalan Spanish meant losing a part of herself.

Melinda, a 35-year-old Guatemalan activist and founder of the Guatemalan women's association, also expressed the weight of exclusion in Spain. She explained, "*a pesar de que yo me muevo generalmente dentro de ese mundo [el mundo del activismo], es un mundo en el que por ejemplo el origen nacional pesa mucho! Y pesa generalmente para todo lo negativo, tú eres otra, no conoces a España, siempre te están hablando de España como que tú no lo conocieras, cuando con diez años yo creo que algo habré conocido ya!*" (In spite of the fact that I generally move within this world [the world of activism], it's a world in which national origin weighs a lot. And weighs generally in all the negative ways—"you are other, you don't know Spain," they are always talking to you about Spain as if you don't know it, when after 10 years I think I should know something!)

The participants in our study, both first-generation immigrants and second-generation "Spanish Latinos," demonstrated that an accumulation of many years lived in Spain, a well-developed understanding of Spanish society, and the acquisition of Spanish nationality did not translate automatically into a sense of belonging to the nation-state. Their stories and perspectives challenge the conventional wisdom and assumptions about how cultural and linguistic similarities and affinities between Latinos and Spaniards would ease the path of belonging to the Spanish nation.

The following poem by Razena, a 16-year-old immigrant from the Dominican Republic who participated in our study, illuminates the difficulties that young migrants face as they negotiate transnational realities. It captures the ruptures with an established, seemingly cohesive past, where the presence of family relations are both here and there, and where the emotional toll of migrations are to be confronted and found in the most quotidian of daily life: fitting in, ways of speaking, and the search for new friends. Razena writes,

> *Intentar encajar*
> *conseguir nuevos amigos*
> *cambiar tu forma de hablar*
> *Esos días que pasabas con toda la familia*
> *ya no pasarán*
> *Unos aquí, otros allá*
> *Pasar días llorando, sola en tu habitación . . .*[54]

Transnational Latino youth in our study exemplify lived experiences and identity formations forged at the interstices and margins of nation-states and cultures, where multiple layers of isolating discontinuities abound, and where geographic dislocation is accompanied by intense and severe racism and other micro forms of othering. The following section highlights the voices and perspectives of Latinas/os in negotiating belonging to the nation in the context of racialized experiences.

Negotiating Racism on the Path to Belonging

The activist women affiliated with *Asociación de Mujeres de Guatemala*, most of whom had migrated to Spain on their own in their 20s, were distinct from the adolescent youth in many ways that gave them privileges, including middle-class family backgrounds, higher education, and legal status. Despite these distinctions, they expressed similar sentiments of not belonging in Spain and shared many of the same experiences of discrimination. Often they had a more sophisticated critique of racism against Latinos as stemming from Spain's colonial past. Sara, a highly educated immigrant woman from Peru, who arrived in Spain armed with a master's degree, expressed in her interview that *"Hay un tema de racismo clarísimo. . . un tema colonial de superioridad, una serie de prejuicios."* (There is an obvious theme of racism . . . a theme of colonial superiority . . . a series of prejudices.) Sara shared that her abilities and talents were constantly in question simply because of her Peruvian background. In every single work experience and environment in Madrid, Sara had to prove her worth. There was never a moment of being accepted. She was often told by her superiors, "We don't know if you're capable, even though you've completed a master's degree or you've done that or have worked here."

Maria was a 26-year-old Guatemalan-American who had been in Spain for 4 years. She had originally come to work as an English teaching assistant in a public school, and to accompany her Guatemalan boyfriend, who had found a job in Madrid after failing to get his papers in Los Angeles. Maria was now enrolled in a master's program in a university in Madrid, and struggled to belong in a place where American Latina was not a recognized social identity. "In the U.S., I was Latina," she said. She explained that in the United States there was a large Latino community that helped her to belong, but not here. In Spain, she said, people expected Americans to be blonde and blue-eyed and she didn't fit this image. Although her English skills brought her social capital and her first job, her right to this capital was questioned because she was not white. She explained that in the school where she first worked in Madrid, she had tried to educate them about the category of "Latina" in the United States, but they didn't want to hear it. *"Aquí no pertenezco porque no soy lo que los españoles esperan."* (Here I don't belong because I'm not what the Spaniards expect.)

Maria's story is interesting because it shows how the social privileges of a bachelor's degree, a job as an English teacher, and US identity and citizenship were not enough to insulate her from racism: she could not belong in Spain because her phenotype did not match what Spaniards expected from someone with her skills and status. Her story also challenges the prevalent Spanish belief, described earlier, that ethnic communities or barrios were a barrier to integration. The Latino community in Los Angeles, where Maria had lived since she was 2, had helped her belong and had given her a recognized social identity in the United States. In Madrid, without this community, she found herself having to explain and justify her identity. Like Teresa's sense of humor—lost in Spain because Spaniards didn't get it—Maria lost her sense of belonging.

Elena, a Venezuelan immigrant woman who had come to Madrid on a student visa at the age of 25, spoke about the racism, the exclusion, and the rejection of immigrants by members of Spanish society. She shared, "You see how the police show no mercy with immigrants . . . I've experienced that myself. I felt horrible, like a non-human." Many of the participants in our study, both first and second generation, described witnessing or being a victim of police harassment and racial and cultural profiling, including the detention of immigrants with little or no reasonable cause.[55] In the words of 17-year-old Maritza, "*Los policías paran a la gente que no es española y eso a mí me fastidia un montón.*" (The police stop people who aren't Spanish, and that bothers me a lot.)

In one of our group discussions, Marilyn, a 17-year-old Ecuadorian who had lived in Spain since the age of 5, shared the story of her brother going out to the store to buy rice for their mother. While on his way home with the bag of rice in his arms, the police stopped him and insisted on checking to see if there were drugs in the bag. Her mother saw the altercation through the window and leaned out to shout at the police to leave her son alone, that he was doing nothing wrong. Following this story of Marilyn's, two other girls in the group each shared similar stories of police confrontations.

The youth participants in our study were well aware of discrimination against Latinos. Luisa, a 16-year-old born in Madrid to a Dominican immigrant mother, felt that Spaniards lumped all Latinos together: "*Da igual de que país, de la Republica Dominicana, Venezuela de todos los sitios, los españoles tienen la mentalidad de que los latinos vienen aquí a robarle el trabajo.*" (It doesn't matter what country they're from, the Dominican Republic, Venezuela, anywhere, Spaniards have the mentality that Latinos come here to steal their jobs.) She shared how these tensions flare up in the most quotidian of moments. She recalled one incident at a movie theatre when a Latino and a Spanish youth became embroiled in a heated exchange. Whatever the initial issue was, it quickly turned into an anti-Latino immigrant rant on the part of the Spaniard when he said: "*Es que los latinos habéis venido y le habéis quitado el trabajo a nuestros padres . . . que los españoles son mejores y los latinos solo venís a coger el dinero de nuestros padres.*" (It's because Latinos have come and have taken the jobs away from our parents . . . that Spaniards are superior and Latinos you only come to grab our parents' money.) This very sentiment could be found in the newspapers and TV news as well as in the discourse and policy acts of the conservative party then in power, Partido Popular.

When Claude, the Brazilian youth, was asked in an interview what worried him most about the plight of immigrants in Spain, he responded that he was worried about them being expelled from the country. He said, "*Porque ahora el presidente del gobierno ha dado orden de echar a todos los que no tengan la nacionalidad.*" ("Because now the president of the government has given the order to expel everyone who doesn't have nationality-citizenship.") When Rolando was asked the same question, he responded, "*Pues . . . el desprecio.*" ("Well . . . the contempt.") He said he felt bad inside, and livid and impotent to do anything about it.

Claude also shared how he couldn't speak his native tongue, Portuguese, in school. Teachers wouldn't allow it. He explained: *"Los profesores nos echan la bronca. Ellos quieren que hablemos todos en español, no les gusta . . .* (The teachers get mad at us. They want all of us to speak in Spanish, they don't like it . . .). When discussing racism, Claude said it happens all of the time in his classes. He said that when there is a problem between a white person and a black person, it inevitably became a racial incident because the first thing Spaniards would do is insult you by calling you "negro" or "go back to your country!"

In our group discussions and individual interviews, students described teachers who "look at us with disgust" (*nos miran con cara de asco*), or, worse, who refused to intervene when other students made racially insulting remarks. Although immigrant youth were not always quick to identify this as racism, they remarked that this behavior was only directed at immigrant students. Two students shared of approaching school staff or administration about discriminatory treatment and receiving no support. Isabela had transferred schools because of this. Racism on the street was also a common theme. In one group discussion, all of the students claimed to have received "dirty looks" from passersby on the street: usually older Spanish women. Such looks, whether they originated from racist intent or not, contributed to the youths' sense of not belonging, their "daily sense of surveillance" in Spain.[56]

THE PRECARIOUS CITIZENSHIP
OF LATINA/O YOUTH IN SPAIN

The youth in our study were engaged in tremendous work to form their identities from the third space, navigating a contradictory terrain of conflicting allegiances and messages of inclusion and exclusion. It is clear that they experienced significant racism and discrimination as immigrants in Spain, but little or no support for addressing this from the educators or adults in their lives. They told us that they did not discuss issues of diversity, migration, race, or racism in their schools or neighborhood associations and, until our workshop, had never had the opportunity to discuss their experiences as immigrant youth. Without this opportunity, without the space to build community around their shared experiences, they had no support for developing a critical consciousness of inequality or taking action to challenge it.[57] Furthermore, the national discourse of integration—which imagined Latino immigrants to be integrating smoothly, and expected national identification and cultural assimilation as the basis for integration—erased immigrant youths' experiences of exclusion and the complexity of their transnational belonging. The persistent discourse that immigrants were assimilating and racism was diminishing both denied immigrant youths' lived experiences of racism and complicated their efforts to understand it, rendering their very identities precarious. The violence experienced by immigrants daily in the form of racial harassment and discrimination was rendered invisible, absorbed by the immigrants themselves, while the sustaining role of their attachments to culture and community was also lost to the public view.

Our participatory research process, even with many limitations, provided the means to engage in a sustained dialogue that allowed the youth to express their complex identities and critique the ways they were positioned by the dominant society. This dialogue made visible aspects of their lives and identities that were invisible in the public sphere. Their expression came out in the individual interviews, in poetry written by the youth, and in the public presentation of our research with some of the youth at the Autonomous University of Madrid. The presentation at the university assumed symbolic importance for the youth as an effort to engage in the public sphere and recast their identities on their own terms. It also illustrated the struggle immigrant youth have to be heard.

During the presentation, the youth shared their findings on the challenges facing immigrants, their connections to Spain and their home countries, and their struggle to belong. Marilyn shared the challenges of growing up as a black Ecuadorian in Spain and said that she used to be ashamed of being black ("*me daba verguenza*"). Ana Silvia, from Brazil, shared that since she had arrived in Spain, she had felt lonely ("*me he sentido sola*"), and that she would like to hang out with more Spanish youth, but they did not seem to want her. Despite these personal testimonies of exclusion, some members of the audience challenged the existence of racism. One young woman in the audience suggested that immigrants may be inviting the treatment they receive because of their attitude toward Spaniards: that they assume Spaniards will be hostile and they close themselves off. Raquel, a 14-year-old presenter from the Dominican Republic, responded thoughtfully that perhaps she was right: immigrants do share some of the blame for their isolation. Later, a man in the audience asked, "Isn't it true that racism seems to be diminishing in Spain? A few years ago it was very strong, and the media was full of hostile reports about immigrants, but now that seems to have gone away."

Such comments illustrate the strength of the discourse of integration in Spain, where even to speak of difference is to challenge the fragile peace, to threaten the social fabric. And yet our findings reveal the cost of not speaking of difference: it is the precarious citizenship of immigrant youth, who are not equipped with the tools to understand their experiences of marginalization, their rights, or their ability to work for change. Spanish society is a contradictory place for Latino immigrants. There is an active civil society and several social movements promoting citizen participation and social change: a strong class-based, anti-austerity movement that began with *los indignados* in 2011 and is now called 15M,[58] a strong feminist movement, and an active public education movement, among others. Many of the Latina activists in our interviews were connected to these movements and found solidarity with Spanish activists. But these movements have not yet been able to connect to the concerns of immigrant youth or provide support for cultural rights and identity-based inclusion. The second-generation immigrant youth in our study were profoundly disconnected from

these social movements. Instead of inquiring whether immigrant youth feel identified with the Spanish nation-state, researchers and policymakers should ask
whether they are connected to spaces of civic participation where they can address their own experiences and connect with others working for social change
within and beyond the nation.

Our research highlights the need for more spaces that allow immigrant youth
to reflect on their identities and collectively process their experiences in a way that
allows them to understand the multiple forces shaping their lives. This is a coming
to consciousness, in Paulo Freire's terms,[59] where consciousness combines the
naming of one's personal experience of oppression with a critical understanding
of the structural conditions—especially structures of domination—that shape
that experience. It may be that without strong ethnic communities or ethnic organizations, Latino youth in Madrid lack a key source of support for this process.

From the perspective of democratic citizenship formation, examining
third-space identities allows us to identify those aspects of immigrants' multiple
affiliations that could promote engaged democratic citizenship, and those aspects
of their experiences that discourage democratic citizenship. From our findings,
students' strong emotional connection to their parents' countries of origin, and
their awareness of disparities between Spain and their countries, suggest the potential for active civic identities. Their multiple experiences with hardship and
privilege, from both sides, lend them a unique vantage point from which to analyze structures of inequality and engage in social change. But these experiences
must be tapped by culturally aware educators in order to harness their potential
for democratic citizenship. Immigrant students' experiences of racial inequality
in Spain, and their lack of support for addressing this, suppress their democratic
citizenship formation and their ability to engage in efforts for democratic change.
Furthermore, the silencing of their cultural identities from the public sphere and
the negative stigma on their enduring ethnic ties erode an important resource for
citizenship and virtually ensure their continued exclusion.

Analyzing immigrant identities from the third space, through the lens of
diasporic citizenship, reveals the richness and complexity of immigrant experiences and the limits of the nation-state optic with its either/or binaries. Whereas
perceiving Latino transnational youth through a national lens finds them lacking
at best and dangerous at worst, viewing them through the lens of diasporic, hybrid
identities allows us to begin to value them for "their unique cross-cultural perspectives and their potential for bringing cultures together for mutual critique
and enrichment."[60] Chicana feminist Gloria Anzaldúa allows us to see how third
spaces offer immigrants new ways of thinking and forms of consciousness—
pensamiento fronterizo.[61] This border thinking, for Anzaldúa, "is a site of criss-
crossed experience, language and identity . . . caught between various hegemonic
colonial and postcolonial languages, and subaltern dialects, and vernacular expressions."[62] As border thinkers, the youth in our study demonstrate a different
transnational border mapping of the world, one that contains multiple visions and perspectives, a mixing of languages and cultures, a back-and-forth

epistemological movement, and the in-between thinking that emerges from this. It is a *pensamiento fronterizo* that is both within nation-state boundaries and at the same time outside of them, thus beyond their purview and understanding.

ACKNOWLEDGMENTS

The authors are grateful for financial support from the Spencer Foundation, New Civics Initiative, which made this research possible. We would also like to thank David Poveda at the Universidad Autónoma de Madrid for his collaboration, and the staff at the three organizations in Madrid who welcomed our research and facilitated our connection to the young Latina/o immigrants in this study.

NOTES

1. "Latino" is a term used by the youth in our study of Central and South American origin, to self-identify and distinguish themselves from Spanish youth. Caribbean-origin youth, who are also included in our study as Latin Americans, did not always identify as Latino but were more likely to identify as "Caribeño/a".

2. Between 1994 and 2007 the employed population grew by 67%, with 8.2 million new jobs. W. Actis, "Impactos de la crisis sobre la población inmigrada. Entre la invisibilidad y el rechazo latente," paper presented at the "El desafío de las grandes ciudades en un contexto de crisis: presente y futuro de los hijos de la inmigración," Madrid, October 8–9, 2013.

3. D. Kleiner-Liebau, *Migration and the Construction of National Identity in Spain* (Madrid: Iberoamericana, 2009).

4. Kleiner-Liebau, *Migration and the Construction of National Identity in Spain*; Teresa Aguado, "The Education of Ethnic, Racial and Cultural Minority Groups in Spain," in *The Routledge International Companion to Multicultural Education*, James Banks, ed. (New York: Routledge, 2009); A. Ríos-Rojas, "Managing and Disciplining Diversity: The Politics of Conditional Belonging in a Catalonian Institut," *Anthropology & Education Quarterly* 45, no. 1 (2014): 2–21.

5. Kleiner-Liebau, *Migration and the Construction of National Identity in Spain*.

6. María Hierro, "Latin American Migration to Spain: Main Reasons and Future Perspectives," *International Migration* (2013).

7. Kleiner-Liebau, *Migration and the Construction of National Identity in Spain*, 151.

8. Kleiner-Liebau, *Migration and the Construction of National Identity in Spain*, 176.

9. Kleiner-Liebau, *Migration and the Construction of National Identity in Spain*, 176.

10. Actis, "Impactos de la crisis sobre la población inmigrada. Entre la invisibilidad y el rechazo latente."

11. Actis, "Impactos de la crisis sobre la población inmigrada. Entre la invisibilidad y el rechazo latente."

12. C. González-Enríquez, "Spain," in *European Immigration: A Sourcebook*, A. Triandafyllidou and R. Gropas, eds., 339–350 (Farnham: Ashgate, 2014).

13. Actis, "Impactos de la crisis sobre la población inmigrada. Entre la invisibilidad y el rechazo latente."; González-Enríquez, "Spain."

14. Actis, "Impactos de la crisis sobre la población inmigrada. Entre la invisibilidad y el rechazo latente."

15. Belén Domínguez Cebrián, "La Unión Europea pierde brillo para los inmigrantes de Latinoamérica," *El País*, June 5, 2015. The authors of a report on this trend for the International Organization for Migration decided not to disaggregate data or to differentiate between Latin Americans who were returning and Spaniards who were leaving.

16. Aguado, "The Education of Ethnic, Racial and Cultural Minority Groups in Spain"; M. A. Gibson and S. Carrasco, "The Education of Immigrant Youth: Some Lessons from the U.S. and Spain," *Theory into Practice* 48 (2009): 249–257; J. Lucko, "Tracking Identity: Academic Performance and Ethnic Identity among Ecuadorian Immigrant Teenagers in Madrid," *Anthropology & Education Quarterly* 42, no. 3 (2011): 213–229.

17. Most studies report disparities in rates of completion of compulsory secondary education (ESO), enrollment in *bachillerato* (pre-university), and university enrollment. However, at least one study analyzed results from the Programme for International Student Assessment (PISA) and found that "non-Spanish-speaking immigrant students have better educational results than those whose mother tongue is Spanish," irrespective of parents' cultural backgrounds (F. J. García Castaño, M. Rubio Gómez, and O. Bouachra, "Immigrant Students at School in Spain: Constructing a Subject of Study," *Dve Domovini: Two Homelands* 41 [2015]: 42). Spanish-speaking Latino immigrant students thus enjoy no advantages in the Spanish educational system.

18. Gibson and Carrasco, "The Education of Immigrant Youth: Some Lessons from the U.S. and Spain"; Aguado, "The Education of Ethnic, Racial and Cultural Minority Groups in Spain"; Margarita Del Olmo, *Reshaping Kids Through Public Policy on Diversity: Lessons from Madrid* (Madrid: Navreme Publications, 2010); Adela Franzé, "Diversidad cultural en la escuela: algunas contribuciones antropológicas," *Revista de Educación* 345 (2008): 111–132; D. Poveda, M. Jociles, A. Franzé, M. Moscoso, and A. Calvo, "The Role of Institutional, Family and Peer-Based Discourses and Practices in the Construction of Students' Socioacademic Trajectories," *Ethnography and Education* 7, no. 1 (2012): 39–57; Lucko, "Tracking Identity: Academic Performance and Ethnic Identity among Ecuadorian Immigrant Teenagers in Madrid."

19. Poveda, Jociles, and Franzé, "La Diversidad Cultural en la Educación Secundaria en Madrid: Experiencias y prácticas institucionales con alumnado inmigrante latinoamericano," Papeles de Trabajo Sobre Cultura, Educación y Desarollo Humano, Año 2009, Volumen 5, Número 3 (Diciembre); Poveda, Jociles, and Franzé, "Immigrant Students and the Ecology of Externalization in a Secondary School in Spain," Anthropology & Education Quarterly, Vol. 45, Issue 2, pp. 185–202, 2014; and Franzé, Moscoso & Calvo Sánchez, "Donde Nunca Hemos Llegado: Alumnado de origen Latinoamericano entre la escuela y el mundo laboral", in A.A. Garrido, F. Checa y Olmos, and T. Belmonte García (eds.), Biculturalismo y Segundas Generaciones: Integración Social, Escuela y Bilingüismo. Barcelona: Icaria + Antrazyt, 2011.

20. Poveda, Jociles, and Franzé, "La Diversidad Cultural en la Educación Secundaria en Madrid: Experiencias y prácticas institucionales con alumnado inmigrante latinoamericano"; Poveda, Jociles, and Franzé, "Immigrant Students and the Ecology of Externalization in a Secondary School in Spain"; and Franzé, Moscoso & Calvo Sánchez, "Donde Nunca Hemos Llegado: Alumnado de origen Latinoamericano entre la escuela y el mundo laboral"; and Gibson and Carrasco, "The Education of Immigrant Youth: Some Lessons from the U.S. and Spain."

21. Franzé, Moscoso & Calvo Sánchez, "Donde Nunca Hemos Llegado: Alumnado de origen Latinoamericano entre la escuela y el mundo laboral"; Ríos-Rojas, "Managing

and Disciplining Diversity: The Politics of Conditional Belonging in a Catalonian Institut."

22. Poveda, Jociles, and Franzé, "La Diversidad Cultural en la Educación Secundaria en Madrid: Experiencias y prácticas institucionales con alumnado inmigrante latino-americano"; Poveda, Jociles, and Franzé, "Immigrant Students and the Ecology of Externalization in a Secondary School in Spain"; and Franzé, Moscoso & Calvo Sánchez, "Donde Nunca Hemos Llegado: Alumnado de origen Latinoamericano entre la escuela y el mundo laboral"; Lucko, "Tracking Identity: Academic Performance and Ethnic Identity among Ecuadorian Immigrant Teenagers in Madrid"; Ríos-Rojas, "Managing and Disciplining Diversity: The Politics of Conditional Belonging in a Catalonian Institut."

23. Poveda, Jociles, and Franzé, "La Diversidad Cultural en la Educación Secundaria en Madrid: Experiencias y prácticas institucionales con alumnado inmigrante latino-americano"; Poveda, Jociles, and Franzé, "Immigrant Students and the Ecology of Externalization in a Secondary School in Spain"; and Franzé, Moscoso & Calvo Sánchez, "Donde Nunca Hemos Llegado: Alumnado de origen Latinoamericano entre la escuela y el mundo laboral."

24. Lucko, "Tracking Identity: Academic Performance and Ethnic Identity among Ecuadorian Immigrant Teenagers in Madrid."

25. Ríos-Rojas, "Managing and Disciplining Diversity: The Politics of Conditional Belonging in a Catalonian Institut."

26. Ríos-Rojas, "Managing and Disciplining Diversity: The Politics of Conditional Belonging in a Catalonian Institut," 3.

27. A. Ríos-Rojas, "Beyond Delinquent Citizenships: Immigrant Youth's (Re)visions of Citizenship and Belonging in a Globalized World," *Harvard Educational Review* 81 (2011).

28. A. Portes, E. Vickstrom, and R. Aparicio, "Coming of Age in Spain: The Self-Identification, Beliefs, and Self-Esteem of the Second Generation," *The British Journal of Sociology* 62, no. 3 (2011): 387–417; A. Portes and R. Aparicio, "Investigación longitudinal sobre la segunda generación en España: avance de resultados" (Madrid: Fundación Ortega-Marañón, 2013).

29. The second generation was defined in their study as children of immigrants born in Spain or brought to the country before age 12.

30. Portes, Vickstrom, and Aparicio, "Coming of Age in Spain: The Self-Identification, Beliefs, and Self-Esteem of the Second Generation," 409.

31. Portes, Vickstrom, and Aparicio, "Coming of Age in Spain: The Self-Identification, Beliefs, and Self-Esteem of the Second Generation," 409.

32. Alejandro Agudo, "El 50% de inmigrantes de segunda generación se siente español," *El País*, May 13, 2013.

33. Portes and Aparicio. "Investigación longitudinal sobre la segunda generación en España: avance de resultados," 13. European Commission, accessed on February 26, 2015. http://ec.europa.eu/ewsi/UDRW/images/items/docl_35105_974253369.pdf. Our translation is from the Spanish.

34. K. Hall, *Lives in Translation: Sikh Youth as British Citizens* (Philadelphia: University of Pennsylvania Press, 2002); Lok Siu, *Memories of a Future Home: Diasporic Citizenship of Chinese in Panama* (Stanford, CA: Stanford University Press, 2005); A. Ong, "Cultural Citizenship as Subject-Making: Immigrants Negotiate Racial and Cultural Boundaries in the United States," *Current Anthropology* 37, no. 5 (1996): 737–751.

35. Siu, *Memories of a Future Home: Diasporic Citizenship of Chinese in Panama*, 5.
36. Hall, *Lives in Translation: Sikh Youth as British Citizens;* P. Sanchez, "Urban Immigrant Students: How Transnationalism Shapes Their World Learning," *The Urban Review* 39, no. 5 (2007): 489–517; Thea R. Abu El-Haj, "Becoming Citizens in an Era of Globalization and Transnational Migration: Re-Imagining Citizenship as Critical Practice," *Theory into Practice* 4, no. 8 (2009): 274–282; Ríos-Rojas, "Managing and Disciplining Diversity: The Politics of Conditional Belonging in a Catalonian Institut."
37. Sanchez, "Urban Immigrant Students: How Transnationalism Shapes Their World Learning." 494.
38. A. Portes, L. E. Guarnizo, and P. Landolt. "The Study of Transnationalism: Pitfalls and Promise of an Emergent Research Field," *Ethnic and Racial Studies* 22, no. 2 (1999): 217–237; Arpi Miller, "'Doing' Transnationalism: The Integrative Impact of Salvadoran Cross-Border Activism," *Journal of Ethnic and Migration Studies* 37, no. 1 (2011); Sanchez, "Urban Immigrant Students: How Transnationalism Shapes Their World Learning"; P. Sanchez and G. S. Kasun. "Connecting Transnationalism to the Classroom and to Theories of Immigrant Student Adaptation," *Berkeley Review of Education* 3, no. 1 (2012): 71–93; D. Reed-Danahay and C. B. Brettell, *Citizenship, Political Engagement, and Belonging: Immigrants in Europe and the United States* (New Brunswick, NJ: Rutgers University Press, 2008).
39. Ríos-Rojas, "Beyond Delinquent Citizenships: Immigrant Youth's (Re)visions of Citizenship and Belonging in a Globalized World"; Abu El-Haj, "Becoming Citizens in an Era of Globalization and Transnational Migration: Re-Imagining Citizenship as Critical Practice"; Thea R. Abu El-Haj, "'I Was Born Here, but My Home, It's Not Here': Educating for Democratic Citizenship in an Era of Transnational Migration and Global Conflict." *Harvard Educational Review* 77, no. 3 (2007): 285–316.
40. Ríos-Rojas, "Beyond Delinquent Citizenships: Immigrant Youth's (Re)visions of Citizenship and Belonging in a Globalized World."
41. Ríos-Rojas, "Beyond Delinquent Citizenships: Immigrant Youth's (Re)visions of Citizenship and Belonging in a Globalized World," 84.
42. Abu El-Haj, "Becoming Citizens in an Era of Globalization and Transnational Migration: Re-Imagining Citizenship as Critical Practice."
43. Sánchez, "Urban Immigrant Students: How Transnationalism Shapes their World Learning," 492; Sánchez cites N. González, L. C. Moll, and C. Amanti, "Funds of Knowledge: Theorizing Practices in Households, Communities, and Classrooms," within her text.
44. H. T. Trueba, "Immigration and the Transnational Experience," in *The New Americans: Immigrants and Transnationals at Work*, H. Trueba, Pedro Reyes, and Yali Zou, eds. (Lanham, MD: Rowman & Littlefield Publishers, Inc., 2004).
45. Julio Cammarota, and Michelle Fine, *Revolutionizing Education: Youth Participatory Action Research in Motion* (New York: Routledge, 2008); Jason Irizzary, *The Latinization of U.S. Schools: Successful Teaching and Learning in Shifting Cultural Contexts* (Boulder, CO: Paradigm Publishers, 2011).
46. Paulo Freire, *Pedagogy of the Oppressed* (New York: The Continuum Publishing Company, 1970).
47. A pseudonym. All personal names here are also pseudonyms to protect the identities of the participants.
48. Kleiner-Liebau, *Migration and the Construction of National Identity in Spain*, 174.

49. This idea was also found in Anna Ríos-Rojas' research with immigrant youth in Barcelona. Ríos-Rojas, "Managing and Disciplining Diversity: The Politics of Conditional Belonging in a Catalonian Institut."

50. M. Pollock, *Colormute: Race Talk Dilemmas in an American School* (Princeton, NJ: Princeton University Press, 2004).

51. Despite such deficit views of their cultures, it must be noted that Latino students enjoyed affectionate relationships with the staff at ASI and several said ASI was one of the places they felt most at home in Madrid. The youths' relationship to ASI was complex and marked by contradictions.

52. M. Yegenoglu, "From Guest Worker to Hybrid Immigrant: Changing Themes of German-Turkish Literature," in *Migrant Cartographies: New Cultural and Literary Spaces in Post-Colonial Europe*, S. Ponzanesi and D. Merolla, eds., 137–149 (Lanham. MD: Lexington Books, 2005).

53. Ritty Lukose, "The Difference That Diaspora Makes: Thinking Through the Anthropology of Immigrant Education in the United States," *Anthropology & Education Quarterly* 38, no. 4 (2007): 410.

54. Trying to fit in
    Making new friends
    Changing your way of speaking
    Those days of being with the entire family
    will no longer happen.
    Some here, others over there.
    Spending days crying, alone in your bedroom. . . (authors' translation).

55. See Enrique Sepúlveda, "Viviendo en Madrid: Observaciones de una ciudadanía diversa y desigual," *Diagonal,* April 7, 2014. https://www.diagonalperiodico.net/blogs/fuera-clase/viviendo-madrid-observaciones-ciudadania-diversa-y-desigual.html

56. Ríos-Rojas, "Beyond Delinquent Citizenships: Immigrant Youth's (Re)visions of Citizenship and Belonging in a Globalized World," 79.

57. Andrea Dyrness, "'Contra Viento y Marea (Against Wind and Tide)': Building Civic Identity among Children of Emigration in El Salvador," *Anthropology & Education Quarterly* 43, no. 1 (2012); Abu El-Haj, "Becoming Citizens in an Era of Globalization and Transnational Migration: Re-Imagining Citizenship as Critical Practice"; Beth Rubin, "There's Still Not Justice: Youth Civic Identity Development Amid Distinct School and Community Contexts," *Teachers College Record* 109, no. 2 (2007): 449–481.

58. Joana García Grenzner, "Indignant Feminisms in Spain: Placing the Body before Patriarchal and Capitalist Austerity," *Signs* 40, no. 1 (2014): 59–69.

59. Freire, *Pedagogy of the Oppressed*.

60. W. S. E. Lam, "Border Discourses and Identities in Transnational Youth Culture," in *What They Don't Learn in School: Literacy in the Lives of Urban Youth*, J. Mahiri, ed., 79–97 (New York: Peter Lang Publishers, 2004), 95.

61. José David Saldivar, "Border Thinking: The Coloniality of Power from Gloria Anzaldúa to Arundhati Roy," in *Identity Politics Reconsidered*, Linda Martin Alcoff, Michael Hames-García, Satya P. Mohanty, and Paula M. L. Moya, eds. (London: Palgrave-Macmillan, 2006).

62. Saldivar, "Border Thinking: The Coloniality of Power from Gloria Anzaldúa to Arundhati Roy," 161–162.

CHAPTER 7

"They Look Like Us, But They Don't Act Like Us"

The Transnational Experience of Japanese Brazilians in Japan

MAXINE L. MARGOLIS

Every day a Tam Airlines flight leaves from São Paulo for Tokyo's Narita airport. Beginning in the early 1990s, each 28-hour flight brought a new contingent of *dekasseguis*, Brazilians of Japanese descent, to Japan to seek economic opportunities in the land of their ancestors. The term *dekassegui* refers to Brazilian immigrants of Japanese descent living in Japan. It is a combination of the Japanese verbs "to leave" and "to earn." In Japan, the term *dekasseguis* once referred to rural workers who went to Tokyo in the winter to look for odd jobs to make ends meet. It now has the more general meaning of leaving one's hometown to seek work elsewhere.

This chapter outlines the early twentieth-century history of Japanese immigration to Brazil and then, nearly a century later, documents the reverse flow in the early 1990s of Japanese Brazilians to Japan. It goes on to provide data on just who the *dekasseguis* are, why they were drawn to Japan, and the conditions they encountered once they arrived. This is followed by an account of the various cultural "misunderstandings" between the Japanese and the Japanese Brazilians and their impact on the latter's sense of their own ethnicity. The chapter concludes with an analysis of the transnational behavior of many *dekasseguis* as they return to Brazil from Japan and then, once again, travel back to the land of their ancestors.

THE JAPANESE ARRIVE IN BRAZIL

When and how did the Japanese first arrive in Brazil and subsequently depart the country for their ancestral homeland? It all dates back to the start of the twentieth century. Labor shortages plagued Brazil's coffee industry after the abolition of slavery in 1888. European immigrants were encouraged to emigrate to work on the nation's coffee plantations, and, as a result, millions of Europeans, particularly Italians, migrated to Brazil. Once there, however, conditions on the plantations were so poor that by 1902 Italy prohibited migration to Brazil. With a new shortage of labor plaguing Brazil's coffee industry—coffee was Brazil's major export from the late nineteenth to the mid-twentieth centuries—the Japanese and Brazilian governments signed a treaty in 1907 permitting Japanese migration to Brazil. The trip from Japan to Brazil was subsidized by the Brazilian government. Moreover, another law passed that same year allowing each Brazilian state to establish its own immigration guidelines, and the state of São Paulo, the heart of Brazil's coffee industry, passed legislation permitting 3,000 Japanese to immigrate there over a 3-year period.[1]

Campaigns advertising economic opportunities in Brazil aimed at rural Japanese promised success to anyone willing to work on the nation's coffee estates. The first wave of some 800 Japanese migrants consisted mostly of poor farmers forced to look abroad for work. Heavy land taxes and other changes following the demise of the centuries-long feudal system in Japan caused economic hardship, especially in rural areas of the country. Lured by the promise of employment, an additional 15,000 Japanese traveled to Brazil between 1908 and 1914, most settling in the state of São Paulo. Japan's entry into World War I was the impetus for subsequent waves of migration that, between 1917 and 1940, saw more than 164,000 Japanese migrate to Brazil, and by the late 1970s that figure had risen to approximately 260,000.[2]

While the Japanese in Brazil were initially subject to discrimination and were considered "inassimilable" by some, a majority have since prospered in their adopted land. After years working in the countryside many Japanese immigrants moved to urban areas, particularly the city of São Paulo, seeking greater economic opportunities. Few places better illustrate the impact of Japanese migration on Brazil than São Paulo's Liberdade neighborhood. Its shops, restaurants, food markets, and street festivals make Liberdade seem more like a neighborhood in Tokyo than like a city in Latin America. Today Brazil's population of over 1.5 million people of Japanese descent is the largest such population outside Japan.[3]

How do these figures compare to Japanese emigration to other parts of the Americas? Japanese immigration to the United States began with immigration to Hawaii in 1868. Then between 1886 and 1911, more than 400,000 Japanese left for the United States, where a majority settled on the West Coast. Although the Immigration Act of 1924 banned the immigration of nearly all Japanese, by 2010 some 1.3 million Japanese were living in the United States, a figure that includes those of mixed ethnicity.[4]

The Japanese also traveled to Peru in the late 1800s. Several factors motivated them to immigrate there. Difficult economic conditions in Japan created a surplus of skilled farmers and, as was the case in Brazil, Peru provided a new job market that appeared to meet their needs. Then, too, by the end of the nineteenth century rumors spread in Japan that a distant country called Peru was "full of gold." Moreover, this country, according to advertisements placed by Japanese emigration companies, was said to have a mild climate and rich soil for farming. By the 1980s the Japanese-descended population in Peru was estimated to number some 50,000, the second-largest Japanese community in South America.[5]

THE REVERSE FLOW

By the late 1980s the migration flow began to reverse its direction. A deep and prolonged economic crisis in Brazil combined with an economic boom in Japan—the so-called Japanese miracle—combined with an innovative government policy drew many Japanese Brazilians to Japan, the vast majority of whom belonged to the second and third generation. This migration, in turn, was part of a larger phenomenon in which, because of the economic crisis in Brazil, several hundred thousand middle- and lower-middle-class Brazilians left their homeland for the United States, Canada, Great Britain, and several countries in Europe in search of improved economic opportunities.[6]

The legal framework that allowed the flow of Japanese Brazilians back to Japan should be explained. In 1990 the Japanese government passed a law that was an attempt to ameliorate the labor shortage in those industrial jobs that the Japanese themselves shunned. These were the so-called three K jobs, the disagreeable *kitui* (arduous), *kitanai* (dirty), and *kiken* (dangerous) jobs. This legal reform permitted Brazilians (and Peruvians) of Japanese descent, that is, *nikkejin*—Japanese people who emigrated from Japan and their descendants—to work legally in Japan. The law created the category "long-term resident" for *nikkejin*. It applied to both *nisei* (children of people born in Japan) and *sansei* (grandchildren of people born in Japan), allowing them to live and work legally in Japan for up to 3 years with the possibility of renewal. After the legislation was passed, a majority of Brazilians going to Japan were young *nisei* and *sansei* in their 20s and 30s. The reform also strengthened the prohibition on hiring illegal workers; now it could mean a 2-year prison sentence or a fine of up to 2 million yen—about $20,000 at the time.[7]

The value of the *nikkejin* was two-fold: as a large pool of relatively cheap, docile labor, they would help solve Japan's labor shortage and at the same time they would not disturb what was perceived as the nation's racial and social homogeneity. Because most Japanese pride themselves on belonging to a single, cohesive ethnic group, *nikkejin* were preferred over other foreign workers because it was thought that their "race," regardless of nationality, would allow them to absorb Japanese customs with ease. As a result of this legislation, company owners were not only worried about fines incurred for hiring undocumented workers but many also felt that hiring foreign labor—labor that looked foreign—might hurt their company's image.[8]

In 1989, 29,000 Brazilians entered Japan, many of whom were older and also held Japanese citizenship. The following year after the new legislation was passed some 67,000 were admitted and in 1991, the high point of Brazilian emigration to Japan, around 96,000 *nikkejin* entered Japan. By the mid-1990s as unemployment in Japan grew, this immigrant flow gradually declined so that between 1993 and 1994 the number of Japanese Brazilians living in Japan appears to have stabilized. Nevertheless, by then, the size of the *nikkejin* population was considerable with some 160,000 living in Japan, which represented over 10% of Brazil's residents of Japanese ancestry. Moreover, for a time their number continued to grow. According to Japanese government data, there were some 176,000 *nikkejin* living in Japan by the late 1990s. In other words, in less than a decade this immigration stream almost equaled the nearly 190,000 Japanese who had emigrated to Brazil in the 42-year period that ended right before World War II. Even more remarkable is that by the mid-2000s close to 20% of the population of Japanese Brazilians in Brazil were now living in Japan.[9]

Like Brazilian immigrants in the United States and elsewhere, most *nikkejin* had traveled to Japan envisioning immigration as a temporary journey to take advantage of an opportunity that would improve their lives in Brazil. For most, at least initially, there was no doubt that Brazil was their homeland, where their real lives were lived. Japan was no more than a way station, a temporary workplace to acquire the means to better their lives upon their return home. As such, most *nikkejin* went to Japan planning to stay from about 1 to 3 years and return to Brazil to build a house, start a business, pay for their education, buy a car, or have a comfortable retirement. Although many did return to Brazil within the time frame planned, others extended their stay. The cost of living in Japan was higher than expected, and in the mid-1990s the recession reduced wages and overtime pay so that many had to stay longer to meet their savings goals or pay off the debt incurred for travel to Japan. Whereas most still expressed the desire to return to Brazil eventually, others began to consider staying in Japan longer than originally anticipated.[10]

Nikkejin who did put off the return home were less willing to work overtime and traded night shifts for more regular working hours. Some began traveling as tourists in Japan and elsewhere in Asia and spending more money on leisure in bars and restaurants. The growing rootedness of some *nikkejin* in Japan is highlighted by how they spend their money. Where they once bought bicycles to get around, several were now buying expensive Japanese cars. Other signs of permanence included investing resources locally and purchasing major consumer items in Japan that are not easily transported back to Brazil. In short, every yen was no longer being saved for the return home.[11]

Over time somewhat enhanced job opportunities also tied some *nikkejin* more closely to Japan. In the last few years several Japanese Brazilians found themselves no longer limited to unskilled jobs in factories. They moved into a variety of jobs catering to the ethnic market, a result of the local growth of the Brazilian community. Such new opportunities also changed the outlook of some. Rather than saving money for the return home, many began investing in Japan. Nevertheless, there was and still is a definite limit to their social mobility as immigrants, to wit: "[B]ecoming upwardly mobile in Japanese society seems almost impossible," noted Angelo Ishi, a *nikkejin* journalist who has lived in Japan for over a decade. "They lack the language fluency and Japanese companies seem reluctant to accept foreigners into skilled jobs: lawyers, doctors, or engineers in Brazil have little chance of working in their own profession in Japan," he concluded. This is one of the reasons they are anxious to earn as much money as possible for the return to Brazil. "Our life in Japan is *not* our *real* life."[12]

WHO ARE THE *NIKKEJIN?*

Just who were the *nikkejin* migrating to Japan under this new legislation? The first wave of immigrants were mostly young Japanese Brazilians who, with access to the new guest worker program, chose to work in Japan for a few years after finishing high school. For some this was viewed as an alternative to trying to pass the difficult college entrance exam (*vestibular*) in Brazil and then attempting to get a "top job" there. Most such immigrants were low-wage white-collar workers or students. As such, they viewed temporary migration to Japan as a chance to improve their economic situation back home. They arrived intending merely to sojourn in Japan, staying for perhaps 2 or 3 years, to earn some money, and then return to Brazil with their savings.

A majority of *nikkejin* work in the manufacturing sector of the Japanese economy. There, as we know, they do the difficult blue-collar jobs that are shunned by the Japanese themselves. Over half of Japanese Brazilian immigrants in Japan, both men and women, are employed on assembly lines in factories that manufacture car parts, electronics, and foodstuffs. Others work in cleaning firms, hotels, as security guards and home care attendants, in construction, and some *nikkejin* women are employed as caddies on golf courses.[13]

Wages earned by Brazilians in Japan compare favorably to those in the United States and Europe. Trading their "third-class Brazilian currency" for the "first-class yen," they eagerly took jobs which, they believed, could mean saving in 1 year what it took 10 years to earn in Brazil. In the early 1990s when *nikkejin* first arrived in Japan, the average male immigrant factory worker earned $3,000 a month. Wages fell with the recession during the decade that followed, and by 2001 income had declined on average by about one-third with reduced opportunities for overtime pay. Nevertheless, *nikkejin* still earned five to ten times what they had been earning in Brazil. The typical middle-class monthly income in Brazil is equal to the earnings of about 5 days' work in Japanese factories. The wages of Brazilians in Japan range from $1,500 to $2,500 a month, the latter figure higher than the income of many doctors, lawyers, and university professors in Brazil.[14]

Nikkejin women are regularly paid 20%–30% less than men for the same jobs. For example, during the period of top pay in the 1990s women in manufacturing averaged $2,000 a month compared to an average of $3,000 earned by men. These pay differentials even appear in want ads published in Portuguese language newspapers in Japan. Still, despite such gender discrimination, the income of *nikkejin* women was far more than what they had earned in Brazil as white-collar and professional workers.[15]

Some older women who emigrated from Brazil to Japan were actually born in Japan, having arrived in Brazil as children after World War II. Because they speak Japanese, they returned to Japan to work as home care attendants. These jobs paid an average of $140 a day in the 1990s, again far more than these women or their families had ever earned in Brazil. In effect, because of their knowledge of Japanese, older *nikkejin* women created an economic niche for themselves as health care aides in hospitals and private homes. These large wage differentials were and still are the primary catalyst for the exodus from Brazil to Japan.[16]

HOW THEY ARRIVE

How did Japanese Brazilians come to travel to Japan? Some were recruited by Brazilian travel agencies, but most were contracted by labor brokers (*empreiteiros*) who not only found jobs but housing for the *nikkejin* they contracted; some also loaned them money to cover the cost of passports, airfare, and other travel expenses. Earlier many of these Brazilian labor brokers had themselves been immigrants in Japan. They signed up would-be immigrants wherever they found them in southern Brazil—home to most Brazilians of Japanese descent—and sent them to wherever there was a demand for workers in Japan. As such, it was labor recruiters who determined where to seek out would-be immigrants in Brazil and where to send them in Japan. Recruiters, who received fees from Japanese companies for each immigrant contracted, welcomed all comers regardless of where they lived in Brazil. Even immigrants contracted by the same recruiter might be dispersed in Japan since they were sent where their labor was needed. As a result, Japanese Brazilians from the same town in Brazil do not necessarily settle in the same city in Japan. This pattern suggests that *nikkejin* in Japan of necessity are less dependent on family and friends to cushion the immigrant experience than Brazilian immigrants in the United States and elsewhere.[17]

Because *nikkejin* were legally foreigners, most were hired through labor brokers, which meant that their terms of employment were less favorable than those of Japanese workers. Although they often received negligible benefits and lower salaries than Japanese holding the same positions, because of their legal status, *nikkejin* were usually paid more than undocumented workers from Asia. Employment under labor contracts meant that they had no paid vacations or holidays and had no access to the Japanese social security system. Doubtless the greatest disadvantage of being contracted by an employment broker was the lack of health insurance and the denial of compensation for being injured on the job. Although *nikkejin* were originally employed because of labor scarcity during the economic boom of the early 1990s, even after the boom ended they could still find jobs because, as foreigners, they were hired as a highly flexible labor force that could be easily laid off.[18]

One interesting—although perhaps not unexpected—outcome of Japan's new labor law is what I call "Green Card marriage, Japanese-style."[19] As we know, to work legally in Japan, one must be of Japanese ancestry. As a result, after the law passed there was a surge in the number of marriages between *nikkejin* and non-*nikkejin* Brazilians since upon marriage the non-*nikkejin* gained the same right to work in Japan as his or her Japanese-descended spouse. After arriving in Japan some of these couples separated. Another tactic involved counterfeit identification papers purporting to show Japanese ancestry. In at least one case the same document "proving" Japanese descent—a grandparent born in Japan—was reproduced and presented to the Japanese Consulate in São Paulo by dozens of would-be immigrants seeking work in Japan.[20]

Just who are these *nikkejin* traveling to an unknown land, albeit one of their forbearers? We already know that at the start of the emigration surge in 1990, most emigrants were young, second- and third-generation Japanese descendants. Moreover, most had a middle- or lower middle-class background with fairly high levels of education by Brazilian standards; over half had at least a high school education. They contrasted with earlier Japanese immigrants from Brazil who were mainly *issei*, first-generation *nikkejin* who retained their native language and culture. The newer arrivals were born and raised as Brazilians, and they spoke little or no Japanese.[21]

About equal numbers of men and women traveled to Japan. Like their male counterparts, most *nikkejin* women were young, from the middle strata of Brazilian society, and quite well educated. The experience of Brazilian women in Japan differs primarily by generation and language ability. Older *nikkejin* women with few skills other than fluency in Japanese usually work as home health aides and attendants to the elderly. While certainly earning a good deal of money, many also traveled to Japan to experience what life was like there. Younger *nikkejin* women, both *nisei* and *sansei*, while often well educated, do not speak fluent Japanese and usually hold factory jobs. These women traveled to Japan largely for economic reasons—to save money to establish a business back home or to pay for their own education or that of a family member.[22]

Then, too, the initiation of the labor program in 1990 provided an opportunity for whole families to pick up and leave the economic chaos then raging in Brazil. As long as parents could prove they were *nissei*, they could bring their *sansei* children with them to Japan. In time more and more *nikkejin* children traveled to Japan with their parents and by 2008 an estimated 33,000 children of school age were living there, while 17% of the Brazilian population in Japan were children age 14 and under. Brazilian children are not subject to compulsory education laws in Japan, although about one-third of them do attend Japanese schools. The rest go to one of the many Portuguese language schools in Japan or do not attend school at all. For some families the tuition at Portuguese language schools, which are private, is simply too expensive to enroll their children. And according to one Brazilian official, "The Brazilian schools prepare people for their past in Brazil, not their future in Japan."[23]

A diplomat in Brazil's Ministry of Foreign Affairs whom I interviewed told me that both her own government and the Japanese government were very concerned about the children and adolescents of Japanese Brazilians in Japan. Those who have lived in Japan for several years are "neither Brazilian nor Japanese," she said. "The major problem is schooling. Children need to know 8,000 Japanese characters to be minimally literate in Japan, to be able to read a newspaper and eventually get a job." Many Brazilian youth do not have this skill, and a few are not literate in either Portuguese or Japanese. Those who do not attend Japanese language schools may feel alienated from Japanese society because of their inability to communicate with facility in Japanese. Culture shock for Brazilian immigrants in Japan is greater than in other countries, the diplomat told me, because of the stark contrast between Brazilian and Japanese culture and the isolation of Brazilian immigrants in Japan. Many adolescents suffer an identity crisis in Japan that can lead to emotional problems. As a result, some get involved with drugs and gangs, she noted ruefully.[24]

ORIGINS IN BRAZIL AND SETTLEMENT IN JAPAN

Whether seeking individuals or families, labor recruiters set their sights on southern Brazil, which, as we know, is home to most Japanese descendants in the country. Some 65% of Brazilians in Japan are from São Paulo, and just under 20% are from the neighboring state of Paraná. One city in particular, Maringá, in the northern part of that state has a large number of its Japanese-descended residents living in Japan. Labor recruiters representing large Japanese companies came to Maringá to recruit would-be *dekasseguis*. One company, a Japanese food manufacturer, hired some two hundred townspeople.[25] One such émigré explains Japan's attraction by recounting his own story:

> I went [to Japan] when I was 50. I was a peddler and was at the age when things were not going to change. I took my wife. We both went to work in a plant that manufactured Ford parts. One year and eight months later I bought two farms in Maringá. But it wasn't enough. We went back again for another year and a half. Then I bought an apartment in a good condominium . . . and 47 *alquieres* of land (about 280 acres). My father, who came from Japan at age 13, is now 82 and working all these years in farming was never able to amass so much land."[26]

We know that most Japanese Brazilians headed to Japan come from southern Brazil, but where do they settle in that country? About half of the *nikkejin* population lives in five prefectures in central Japan that have high concentrations of labor-intensive industries such as manufacturers of automobile parts and electrical appliances. These include cities like Toyota, Nagoya, and Hamamatsu. Take the latter, for example. About 20,000 Brazilians live in Hamamatsu, most of whom work for subcontractors that supply parts to larger manufacturers. In some smaller cities like Ota and Oizumi, *nikkejin* compose up to 10% of the local population.[27]

CULTURAL MISUNDERSTANDINGS

Before 1990 when Brazilians began arriving, these cities had very few foreign residents and the arrival of *nikkejin* set the stage for many well-documented examples of cultural misunderstanding and cultural conflict. Although the *nisei* and *sansei* look Japanese, most do not speak the language well, if at all. Estimates are that some 20%–30% of *nikkejin* can communicate in Japanese at least to some extent, but only about 5% actually study the language. But it is not just their lack of language proficiency that leads to friction between *nikkejin* and their Japanese hosts. Cultural clashes with Japanese—the fact that Brazilians often play loud music, barbecue on their balconies, do not keep appointments on time or recycle properly—have abated in some locations as Japanese disturbed by such behavior have moved away from large housing complexes like those in Toyota City where Japanese Brazilians make up half of all residents.[28]

Yet these conflicts are ongoing and miscommunication and misunderstanding are rife. Another public housing complex in Toyota City, home to thousands of workers at Toyota, its subsidiaries and suppliers, with 11,000 residents, including 3,000 *nikkejin*, has signs posted in Japanese and Portuguese that read: "Don't turn up your television or radio early in the morning or late at night" and "Don't barbecue on the balcony." There are reportedly daily disputes over noise, garbage, and parking. A report in a 1999 online issue of *Time Magazine* summarizes the sources of many of these squabbles:

> To Japanese in one densely populated public housing complex, it feels as if the foreigners are closing in on them, the smoke from the barbecues suffocating them, the Latin music drowning out an imagined tranquility. Ten years ago there were 200 Brazilians in the complex. Today there are 3500. "There's no room for us anymore," said one Japanese woman.
>
> After a dispute with a street vendor got out of hand, about 100 supporters of a right-wing nationalist group paraded around the housing complex where many Brazilians live. They shouted through a loudspeaker, "Foreigners, go home," and taunted the Brazilians to come out and fight. "I was really scared to leave my flat to even go to the store to buy food," recalls one Brazilian. "I was afraid that I would be beaten up."
>
> "A lot of the Brazilians work very hard," says Toyota City's deputy police chief, adding that this is because "they are of Japanese descent." But as the Brazilian population grew the cherished peace was disrupted. "They thought they would be getting people like them who would fit in," says one Brazilian who has lived in Japan for nine years. "They found out we are more Brazilian than Japanese."
>
> The Toyota City government has formed a committee to work on improving relations between the two nationalities. The committee does not include any Brazilians.[29]

One source of discord is the *nikkejin* custom of hanging out on the street and congregating outside grocery stores, train stations, and other public spaces. Japanese cities do not have the usual meeting places where casual contact is made—the *praça* (public square) and the *botequim* (neighborhood bar)—that are omnipresent in Brazilian towns and cities. There is no easy neighborhood conviviality that is so much a part of daily life in Brazil, no similar public space where people run into each other and chat. As a consequence, it is a mystery to many Japanese why these immigrants spend so much time socializing on the street. But from the Brazilians' perspective, while they welcome the safety of Japanese cities—so different from those in Brazil—they dislike their reserve, their lack of novelty and spontaneity.[30]

Another common Brazilian behavior, couples being affectionate toward one another in public, holding hands and kissing on the street (*namorando na rua*), is something rarely or never seen in Japan. What *nikkejin* see as Japanese aloofness, a lack of human warmth, the Japanese view as good manners. In short, the Japanese take on all of this can be best summarized as follows: "They look like us, but they certainly don't act like us!"

Some of these misunderstandings and conflicts are also linked to the *nikkejin*'s broad segregation from Japanese workers in the companies where they are employed, reinforcing their position as outsiders. The system of labor brokers, with the tacit agreement of manufacturers and the Japanese government, serves to segment and differentiate *nikkejin* and Japanese workers from one another. And this too leads to friction. Japanese often criticize Brazilians as not being "hard workers" and for "goofing off." They are accused of being disloyal to the companies that employ them when they change jobs for higher pay, a marked contrast to the traditional lifetime employment of Japanese in a single company.[31]

The isolation of Brazilians in Japan is not just based on their segregated work sites. Brazilians are also isolated because they are excluded both culturally and linguistically from Japanese mass media, from all forms of entertainment in Japan, and from Japanese life in general. Sixty percent of *nikkejin*, in fact, report little or no contact with Japanese citizens. Their marginalization is both ethnic—as culturally deficient Japanese—and economic since they are largely confined to the reviled "3 K job" sector of the labor market. One could say, then, that Brazilians in Japan live *among* the Japanese but not *with* the Japanese; that is, there is very little interaction between the two populations either at work or at play.[32]

NIKKEJIN ETHNICITY IN JAPAN

To some degree this isolation is tied to the relative invisibility of the *nikkejin*. Even in cities with large concentrations of Japanese Brazilians—Hamamatsu, Nagoya, and Toyota City—their presence is not obvious. There are no "Brazil Towns" of "Brazil Streets" with distinct ethnic community centers, businesses, schools, or churches. Other than the occasional Brazilian flag poking out of a window, the Brazilian presence is largely unnoticed, especially during the week when everyone is at work. It is only on weekends when *nikkejin* gather at places like train stations and shopping malls that they are conspicuous—groups of Japanese-looking individuals animatedly conversing in Portuguese.[33]

Some *nikkejin* try to overcome this invisibility by stressing their ethnic roots through dress and behavior. Distinctive clothes in Brazil's national colors—green and yellow—are worn along with t-shirts displaying the Brazilian flag and Brazilian icons like Sugar Loaf Mountain and Corcovado, its Christ's outstretched arms looming over Rio de Janeiro. Collective traditions like samba parades are unambiguous signs of Brazilian ethnicity. Some claim that the *nikkejin* present culturally flawed performances because they rarely or never participate in samba schools or carnival parades in Brazil. But while both their dancing and makeshift costumes would be considered deficient by Brazilian standards, they have become popular spectacles in Japan because the Japanese know even less about samba parades and such than the *nikkejin* do.[34]

The Japanese media pay a disproportionate amount of attention to Japanese Brazilians who are exoticized as "amusing anomalies." At the outset *nikkejin* were usually portrayed in a favorable light when, because of their physical appearance, they were expected to absorb Japanese culture easily. But when they failed to do so, they were derided as "inadequate Japanese." As such, the Japanese media can be considered a conservative force that upholds rather than challenges cultural assumptions. It stresses the potential for cultural disorder caused by foreigners—even those that look like "real" Japanese.[35]

In contrast, North Americans and Europeans are generally treated with more respect as *gaijin* (foreigners) than are Japanese Brazilians. The former are praised even when they speak broken Japanese because Europeans and Americans are expected to be incompetent in Japanese ways. Nevertheless, they are still admired because they come from "modern" first-world nations. But when expectations of Japanese Brazilian's "Japaneseness" are contradicted by their behavior, they may be verbally abused and called "stupid, uncivilized people from a backward country." Says one researcher about the Japanese view of the *nikkejin* "their Brazilianess is at best a mystery, at worst a sad third-world affliction."[36]

THEY LOOK LIKE US, BUT THEY CERTAINLY DON'T ACT LIKE US!

Our hardware is Japanese, but our software is Brazilian.
—Angelo Ishi, Japanese Brazilian journalist living in Japan[37]

Just how does the reception *nikkejin* receive in Japan impact their own awareness of ethnicity? We have a good deal of research as to the ways in which *nikkejins'* sense of themselves plays out in Japan. In fact, one of the most discussed facets of Japanese Brazilians in Japan is their shifting ethnic identity. In Brazil they are perceived—and in many instances see themselves—as Japanese rather than as Brazilians, but in Japan they are viewed as Brazilians. Having grown up as "*Japones*" in Brazil, the unexpectedly cool reception they receive in their ancestral homeland undermines the sense of their own cultural identity. When they emigrate to Japan, their ethnic pride plummets as they realize they are regarded and are treated as inferior to "real" Japanese. To escape this stigmatized image, they eventually come to define themselves as foreigners—as Brazilians rather than as *nikkejin*.[38]

Many *nikkejin* feel a strong empathy for Brazil as a multicultural and multiracial society where a majority has prospered at least to some degree. At the same time they hold a sentimental regard for Japan since most *nikkejin* were raised in families that highlighted their distinctive Japanese ancestry and valued things Japanese. Although most had never visited Japan before emigrating there, they still maintained a Japanese sense of themselves through the food they ate, the traditional festivals they celebrated, and, for some, the Japanese language classes they attended.[39]

In spite of these cultural and ancestral roots, after the move to Japan the Japanese identity that most *nikkejin* enjoyed while living in Brazil gradually begins to fade. Instead of becoming *more* Japanese, they become *more* Brazilian; that is, they have a far stronger sense of their own Brazilian pedigree in Japan than they had in Brazil. The longer *nikkejin* reside in Japan, the more they come to think of themselves as a distinct Brazilian minority living there. Because they have few social relationships with Japanese and remain isolated from many spheres of Japanese life, they begin to emphasize and celebrate markers of Brazilian identity such as the samba to which most were indifferent in Brazil. One researcher found that over 90% of the *nikkejin* she interviewed who had identified as Japanese in Brazil shifted their identity in Japan, either becoming Nikkei-Brazilian or, more commonly, simply, Brazilian.[40]

This turn of events was perhaps as surprising to the Japanese as it was to the *nikkejin* themselves. After all, the latter are of Japanese descent and share physical features and ethnic names with native-born Japanese so that few Japanese doubted that these *nisei* and *sansei* would readily adopt Japanese ways. When they did not, the Japanese began vilifying the *nikkejin* because of their legacy of ancestral emigration from Japan—only "failures" left the homeland—as well as the belief that their status as recent immigrants meant they also had been failures in Brazil. Then, too, Brazilians commanded little respect from the Japanese because not only do few speak Japanese but they suffer from their low social status as unskilled factory workers. In sum, they are treated as "second-class or defective Japanese."[41]

Feeling unwelcome and not fitting into Japanese society, as noted earlier, many *nikkeijin* adopt an overtly Brazilian bearing. Or, as one observer put it, they "perform a Brazilian counter identity" by wearing colorful Brazilian clothes, dancing in carnival parades, and speaking Portuguese loudly in public. Indeed, Angelo Ishi, the Japanese Brazilian journalist quoted earlier, notes that the sting of downward mobility and the disparagement of their ethnicity impels *nikkejin* to reassert their middle-class status through intense consumption and by hanging out exclusively in Brazilian spaces, including bars, dance halls, shops, and restaurants. Given life's difficulties for *nikkejin* in Japan, Brazilian restaurants and similar ethnic meeting places serve as a "green and yellow beacon of welcome" with their casual relaxed style that Japanese Brazilians contrast with the strained formality of Japanese venues. In such places *nikkejin* can feel comfortable acting like Brazilians. This is why such locales provide a "paradoxical message—that *one is not in Brazil*, for Brazil itself is never so overtly, intensely Brazilian."[42]

In short, many *nikkejin* are deeply distressed by the irony of being regarded as Japanese in Brazil, and then once in Japan discovering the profound differences between themselves and native-born Japanese. But their anguish also stems from other shifts in status: from being regarded positively in Brazil because of their Japanese heritage, they become unwelcome in Japan because of their Brazilian roots; from being middle class and white collar in Brazil, they turn into a derided underclass holding low-level, blue-collar jobs in Japan.[43]

LEGAL TRANSNATIONALISM

The unease enveloping *nikkejin* ethnic identity and the negative stereotypes attached to it are perhaps more pronounced in Japan than is Brazilian identity in other destinations where Brazilians settle outside Brazil. Yet *nikkejin* do enjoy one distinct advantage over their compatriots in other countries. Until the last few years they could easily travel between Brazil and Japan and back again because of the legal basis for such travel. Moreover, there is a lot of evidence that they did just that. At one point in the mid-1990s for every ten Japanese Brazilians applying for a Japanese work visa, nine were applying for re-entry to Japan. Other *nikkejin* returned to Japan two or three times after they could not find suitable employment in Brazil. Their salaries in Japan in unskilled jobs—even during the recession—were many times those in Brazil even for more highly skilled positions. This stark contrast in earning power likely contributed to a sense of rootlessness, the back-and-forth travel between Japan and Brazil and the disquieting sense of not being quite satisfied or feeling truly at home in either place.[44]

Evidence suggests that many *nikkejin* engage in what I have previously termed "yo-yo migration" in reference to the behavior of Brazilian immigrants in the United States. Yo-yo migration is the remigration of immigrants who, in their own words, had purportedly returned home "for good." Economic insecurity led a number of *nikkejin*, who had previously declared that they were returning home permanently, to remigrate to Japan after their new businesses in Brazil failed, projects started with savings from their prior work in Japan. Others returned to Brazil with the intention of remaining there, lived on the money they had saved in Japan until it ran out, and found poor prospects for new employment in Brazil. As one Japanese Brazilian told anthropologist Daniel T. Linger, "Many people here say they're going [back to Brazil] once and for all, never to return. And in three, four months . . . they're back again."[45]

This is an example of transnationalism, a phenomenon in which immigrants move from home country to host country and back again, a pattern which was enhanced for the *nikkejin* because of the ease with which they were able to travel legally between Brazil and Japan. Some *nikkejin* traveled back and forth between Japan and Brazil, unsure as to where they should settle. In a sense, they found themselves suspended between two nations. Others have returned to Brazil permanently, while still others have begun settling in Japan while maintaining their identification with all things Brazilian. By the mid-1990s, the figures on those leaving Brazil for Japan and those in Japan returning home suggest that the wave of sojourning, that is, staying abroad for a defined period of time, had begun to wane and circular migration and its concomitant transnationalism was on the rise.[46]

Transnationalism rests, in part, on modern transportation and communication technologies that allow immigrants not only to travel great distances across international borders but to follow what is taking place back home via the Internet, e-mail, Skype, homeland TV channels beamed into host countries, phone, and fax. Since 1996 satellite TV from Brazil has been available in Japan and videos of Brazilian *telenovelas* are widely available for rent. At least four Portuguese language newspapers with news of home are published weekly in Japan, and the *nikkejin* are said to be international telephone companies' "best customers."[47]

COMING AND GOING

During the first several years of the current millennium, an additional 10,000 Brazilians annually established permanent residence in Japan, apparently altering their initial migratory project by settling in the land of their ancestors. What are the actual numbers involved in terms of the decision to return to Brazil or to remain in Japan? According to the 2010 Brazilian census, in the 5 years between 2005 and 2010 almost 175,000 Brazilians who were living abroad returned to Brazil, twice as many as returned in the previous 5-year period. Of these returnees, 41,000 had been living in Japan. There are also what I would characterize as "guesstimates" of the size of the returnee population provided by Brazil's Ministry of Foreign Affairs. The Ministry estimates that since the economic recession began in 2008, 25% of Brazilians in Japan have returned home.[48]

The return of some of these immigrants was financed by the Japanese government. As the effects of the financial crisis and unemployment took hold in 2008, Japan as well as some countries in Europe with resident Brazilian populations adopted "pay-to-go" policies, which offered cash payments to immigrants willing to return home voluntarily. Japan's pay-to-go program appears to have been more successful than similar programs in other countries. Perhaps one reason is that the situation of unemployed *nikkejin* is different from that of immigrants elsewhere. In Japan if a Japanese Brazilian loses a job, especially a factory job, there is very little chance of finding other work and the only alternative is to return to Brazil.[49]

As such, after thousands of Brazilians of Japanese ancestry lost their jobs, Japan's pay-to-go scheme was instituted. It applies only to those *nikkejin* who received the special visas first issued in 1990 to enter the country to work in manufacturing plants. The government offered 300,000 yen (about $3,000) to an unemployed foreigner and 200,000 yen (about $2,000) to each family member. However, the catch was that in accepting the money the immigrant would not be allowed to return to Japan for at least 10 years. Some 60,000 *nikkejin* did, in fact, go back to Brazil since the recession took hold, about one-third through the government's program.[50]

The flights from Japan to Brazil are said to be full with a large increase in the sale of one-way tickets home. As a consequence, many Brazilian schools in Japan have closed either because the students returned to Brazil with their parents or their unemployed parents could no longer afford tuition. One school which opened in 2007 and had as many as eighty-five students before the economic crisis hit finally closed its doors at the end of 2009 with only thirty-one students enrolled. To be sure, not all *nikkejin* were heading home; an estimated 110,000 Brazilians in Japan have established permanent residence there, and by 2013 Brazilian residents in Japan numbered over 181,000, making them the second largest foreign population in the country.[51]

Still, are *nikkejin* actually limited to only two options in terms of their futures? To stay in Japan for the long term, try to assimilate to Japanese culture, and make the best of being confined to low-prestige jobs as most still are? Or to leave for home and resume their lives as Brazilians? It is perhaps too soon to tell which path most Japanese Brazilians will take, but one researcher, Joshua Hotaka Roth (2002), suggests a third alternative: that *nikkejin* may remain in Japan for the long term but retain a strong sense of themselves as Brazilians.[52] Indeed, recent statistics suggest the greater permanence of many *nikkejin* in Japan, especially the young. Nonetheless, it is impossible to say what this will mean for maintaining Brazilian national identity over the long run. Only time will tell.

NOTES

1. Elisa Massae Sasaki, "Ser ou Não Ser Japonês?: A Construção da Identidade dos Brasileiros Descendentes de Japoneses no Contexto das Migrações Internacionais do Japão Contemporâneo," PhD diss., Department of Social Sciences, UNICAMP, Campinas, São Paulo, 2009.
2. Sasaki, "Ser ou Não Ser Japonês?: A Construção da Identidade dos Brasileiros Descendentes de Japoneses no Contexto das Migrações Internacionais do Japão Contemporâneo."
3. Jeffrey Lesser, *Immigration, Ethnicity, and National Identity in Brazil, 1808 to the Present* (New York: Cambridge University Press, 2013).
4. Stanley E. Easton and Lucien Ellington, "Japanese-Americans," in *Countries and Their Cultures* (Farmington Hills, MI: Gale Reference, 2005). http://www.everyculture.com/multi/Ha-La/Japanese-Americans.html

5. Ayumi Takenaka, "The Japanese in Peru: History of Immigration, Settlement, and Racialization," *Latin American Perspectives* 31, no. 3 (2004): 77–98.

6. Maxine L. Margolis, "Brazilians in the United States, Canada, Europe, Japan and Paraguay," in *Encyclopedia of Diasporas*, Melvin Ember, Carol R. Ember, and Ian Skoggard, eds., 602–615 (New York: Kluwer Academic/Plenum, 2004); Maxine L. Margolis, *Goodbye Brazil: Emigrés from the Land of Soccer and Samba* (Madison: University of Wisconsin Press, 2013).

7. Elisa Massae Sasaki, "Depois de duas décadas de movimento migratório entre o Brasil e o Japão," paper presented at the Seminário "20 anos dos Brasileiros no Japão" at the Universidade das Nações Unidas, Tokyo, 2010; Keiko Yamanaka, "New Immigration Policy and Unskilled Foreign Workers in Japan," *Pacific Affairs* 66 (1993): 72–90; Keiko Yamanaka, "Factory Workers and Convalescent Attendants: Japanese-Brazilian Migrant Women and Their Families in Japan," in *International Female Migration and Japan: Networking, Settlement and Human Rights,* 87–116 (Tokyo: International Peace Research Institute, 1996).

8. Yamanaka, "New Immigration Policy and Unskilled Foreign Workers in Japan"; Jason Fox, "Little Burajiru: Brazilians of Non-Japanese Descent in Japan," research proposal, Department of Anthropology, University of Florida, 1997.

9. Victor Hugo Klagsbrunn, "Globalização da Economia Mundial e Mercado de Trabalho: A Emigração de Brasileiros Para os Estados Unidos e Japão," in *Migrações Internacionais: Herança XX, Agenda XXI*, Neide Lopes Patarra, ed., 33–48 (Campinas: Program Interinstitucional de Avaliação e Acompanhamento das Migrações Internacionais no Brasil, 1996); Keiko Yamanaka, "Factory Workers and Convalescent Attendants: Japanese-Brazilian Migrant Women and Their Families in Japan," in *International Female Migration and Japan: Networking, Settlement and Human Rights*, 87–116 (Tokyo: International Peace Research Institute, 1996); Chieko Koyama, "Japanese-Brazilians: The Transformation of Ethnic Identity in the Country of Their Ancestors," M.A. thesis, Department of Anthropology, University of Florida, 1998; Marcos Sá Corrêa, "O Brasil Se Expande," *Veja,* September 7, 1994; Takeyuki Tsuda, "No Place to Call Home," *Natural History* (2004): 50–55.

10. Yamanaka, "Factory Workers and Convalescent Attendants: Japanese-Brazilian Migrant Women and Their Families in Japan"; Yamanaka, "Return Migration of Japanese Brazilian Women: Household Strategies and the Search for the 'Homeland.'"

11. Joshua Hotaka Roth, *Brokered Homeland: Japanese Brazilian Migrants in Japan* (Ithaca, NY: Cornell University Press, 2002); Sasaki, "Ser ou Não Ser Japonês? A Construção da Identidade dos Brasileiros Descendentes de Japoneses no Contexto das Migrações Internacionais do Japão Contemporâneo."

12. Angelo Ishi, "Searching for Home, Pride, and 'Class': Japanese Brazilians in the Land of the Yen," in *Searching for Home Abroad: Japanese Brazilians and Transnationalism*, Jeffrey Lesser, ed., 75–102 (Durham, NC: Duke University Press, 2003), 81; Angelo Ishi, "Social and Cultural Aspects of Brazilians in Japan," *IDB Migration Seminar: Migration and Remittances in the Context of Globalization: The Case of Japan and Latin America*, 2004. idbdocs.iadb.org/wsdocs/getdocument.aspx?docnum=556433

13. Joshua Hotaka Roth, *Brokered Homeland: Japanese Brazilian Migrants in Japan* (Ithaca, NY: Cornell University Press, 2002); Takeyuki Tsuda, *Strangers in the Ethnic Homeland* (New York: Columbia University Press, 2003); Rosa Ester Rossini, "O Retorno as Origens ou o Sonho de Encontro com o Eldorado Japonês: O Exemplo dos Dekassequis do Brasil em Direção ao Japão," in *Emigração e Imigração no Brasil Contemporânea*, Neide

Lopes Patarra, ed., 104–110 (Campinas: Programa Interinstitucional de Avaliação e Acompanhamento das Migrações Internacionais no Brasil, 1995).

14. Ishi, "Searching for Home, Pride, and 'Class': Japanese Brazilians in the Land of the Yen"; Yamanaka, "Return Migration of Japanese-Brazilians to Japan: The Nikkejin as Ethnic Minority and Political Construct"; Yamanaka, "Factory Workers and Convalescent Attendants: Japanese-Brazilian Migrant Women and Their Families in Japan"; Salgado, "Eles Fogem da Bagunça"; Takeyuki Tsuda, "Crossing Ethnic Boundaries: Nikkejin Return Migrants and the Ethnic Challenge of Japan's Newest Immigrant Minority," paper presented at the meetings of the American Anthropological Association, New Orleans, 2002.

15. Yamanaka, "Return Migration of Japanese Brazilian Women: Household Strategies and the Search for the 'Homeland.'"

16. Yamanaka, "Return Migration of Japanese Brazilian Women: Household Strategies and the Search for the 'Homeland.'"

17. Naoto Higuchi, "Migration Process of Nikkei Brazilians," paper presented at the International Symposium on Latin American Emigration at the National Museum of Ethnology, Osaka, 2001; Roth, *Brokered Homeland: Japanese Brazilian Migrants in Japan*; Elisa Massae Sasaki, "A Imigração para o Japão," *Estudos Avançados. Dossiê Migrações* 20, no. 57 (2007).

18. Fox, "Little Burajiru: Brazilians of Non-Japanese Descent in Japan"; Sasaki, "Depois de duas décadas de movimento migratório entre o Brasil e o Japão." Naoto Higuchi, "Migration Process of Nikkei Brazilians," paper presented at the International Symposium on Latin American Emigration at the National Museum of Ethnology, Osaka, 2001.

19. Margolis, Maxine L. *Goodbye Brazil: Emigrés from the Land of Soccer and Samba.*

20. Rossini, "O Retorno as Origens ou o Sonho de Encontro com o Eldorado Japonês: O Exemplo dos Dekassequis do Brasil em Direção ao Japão."

21. Sasaki, Elisa Massae. "Dekasseguis: Trabalhadores Nipo-Brasileiros no Japão" *Travessia: Revista do Migrante* (1995): 20–22; Koyama, "Japanese-Brazilians: The Transformation of Ethnic Identity in the Country of Their Ancestors."

22. Yamanaka, "Factory Workers and Convalescent Attendants: Japanese-Brazilian Migrant Women and Their Families in Japan"; Yamanaka, "Return Migration of Japanese Brazilian Women: Household Strategies and the Search for the 'Homeland.'"

23. Sasaki, "Depois de duas décadas de movimento migratório entre o Brasil e o Japão"; James Brooke, "Sons and Daughters of Japan: Back from Brazil," *New York Times*, November 27, 2001.

24. Personal communication with Vera Machado.

25. Rubem Guimarães Amaral, "Perfil da Comunidade Brasileira no Exterior," Brasília Departamento das Comunidades Brasileiras no Exterior, Ministério das Relações Exteriores, 2005; Sasaki, "Ser ou Não Ser Japonês?: A Construção da Identidade dos Brasileiros Descendentes de Japoneses no Contexto das Migrações Internacionais do Japão Contemporâneo."

26. Marcos Sá Corrêa, "O Brasil Se Expande," *Veja,* September 7, 1994, 74.

27. Yamanaka, "Factory Workers and Convalescent Attendants: Japanese-Brazilian Migrant Women and Their Families in Japan"; Roth, *Brokered Homeland: Japanese Brazilian Migrants in Japan*; Sasaki, "A Imigração para o Japão."

28. Takeyuki Tsuda, "Reality Versus Representations: Ethnic Essentialization and Tradition in Japanese Media Images of Japanese Brazilian Return Migrants," paper presented at the meetings of the American Anthropological Association, Washington,

DC, 2001; Norimitsu Onishi, "Enclave of Brazilians Tests Insular Japan," *New York Times*, November 2, 2008.

29. Adapted from Tim Larimer and Hiroko Tashiro, "Battling the Bloodlines," *Time*, August 9, 1999. http://www.time.com /time/world/article/0,8599,2054423,00.html

30. Daniel T. Linger, *No One Home: Brazilian Selves Remade in Japan* (Durham, NC: Duke University Press, 2001).

31. Joshua Hotaka Roth, *Brokered Homeland: Japanese Brazilian Migrants in Japan*. Ithaca, NY: Cornell University Press, 2002.

32. Daniel T. Linger, "The Identity Path of Eduardo Mori," in *History in Person*, Dorothy Holland and Jean Lave, eds., 217–244 (Santa Fe: School of American Research Press, 2001); Shigehiro Ikegami, "Brazilians and Local Industrailization in Hamamatsu: A Case of an Industrial City in Japan," paper presented at the International Symposium on Latin American Emigration at the National Museum of Ethnology, Osaka, 2001; Tsuda, "Crossing Ethnic Boundaries: Nikkejin Return Migrants and the Ethnic Challenge of Japan's Newest Immigrant Minority."

33. Koyama, "Japanese-Brazilians: The Transformation of Ethnic Identity in the Country of Their Ancestors."

34. Tsuda, "Crossing Ethnic Boundaries: Nikkejin Return Migrants and the Ethnic Challenge of Japan's Newest Immigrant Minority."

35. Tsuda, "Reality Versus Representations: Ethnic Essentialization and Tradition in Japanese Media Images of Japanese Brazilian Return Migrants."

36. Yamanaka, "Return Migration of Japanese Brazilian Women: Household Strategies and the Search for the 'Homeland'"; Linger, "The Identity Path of Eduardo Mori," 6.

37. George Wehrfritz and Takayama Hideko, "A New Open Door Policy?" *Newsweek*, June 5, 2000, 29.

38. Angelo Ishi, "Searching for Home, Pride, and 'Class': Japanese Brazilians in the Land of the Yen"; Tsuda, *Strangers in the Ethnic Homeland*; Yamanaka, "Return Migration of Japanese Brazilian Women: Household Strategies and the Search for the 'Homeland.'"

39. Linger, *No One Home: Brazilian Selves Remade in Japan*.

40. Roth, *Brokered Homeland: Japanese Brazilian Migrants in Japan*; Koyama, "Japanese-Brazilians: The Transformation of Ethnic Identity in the Country of Their Ancestors."

41. Koyama, "Japanese-Brazilians: The Transformation of Ethnic Identity in the Country of Their Ancestors"; Tsuda, *Strangers in the Ethnic Homeland*; Linger, "Brazil Displaced: Restaurante 51 in Nagoya, Japan," 16.

42. Tsuda, *Strangers in the Ethnic Homeland*, 262, 82; Linger, "Brazil Displaced: Restaurante 51 in Nagoya, Japan," 15.

43. Rocha, Cristina. "Triangular Transnationalism: Japanese Brazilians on the Move Between Japan, Australia and Brazil." Mimeo, 2009.

44. Jaime Klintowitz, "Nossa Gente Lá Fora," *Veja*, April 3, 1996; Koyama, "Japanese-Brazilians: The Transformation of Ethnic Identity in the Country of Their Ancestors"; Sasaki, "Ser ou Não Ser Japonês?: A Construção da Identidade dos Brasileiros Descendentes de Japoneses no Contexto das Migrações Internacionais do Japão Contemporâneo"; Sasaki, "A Imigração para o Japão."

45. Maxine L. Margolis, *Little Brazil: An Ethnography of Brazilian Immigrants in New York City* (Princeton, NJ: Princeton University Press, 1994), 263; Yamanaka, "Return Migration of Japanese Brazilian Women: Household Strategies and the Search for the 'Homeland'"; Linger, "The Identity Path of Eduardo Mori."

46. Linda Basch, Nina Glick Schiller, and Cristina Szanton Blanc, *Nations Unbound: Transnational Projects, Postcolonial Predicaments, and Deterritorialized Nation-States* (Langhorne, PA: Gordon and Breach, 1994); Margolis, "Notes on Transnational Migration: The Case of Brazilian Immigrants"; Linger, *No One Home: Brazilian Selves Remade in Japan*; Roth, *Brokered Homeland: Japanese Brazilian Migrants in Japan*; Yamanaka, "Return Migration of Japanese-Brazilians to Japan: The Nikkejin as Ethnic Minority and Political Construct."

47. Maxine L. Margolis, "Transnationalism and Popular Culture: The Case of Brazilian Immigrants in the United States," *Journal of Popular Culture* 29, no. 1 (1995): 29–41; Brooke, "Sons and Daughters of Japan: Back from Brazil"; Koyama, "Japanese-Brazilians: The Transformation of Ethnic Identity in the Country of Their Ancestors."

48. Instituto Brasileiro de Geografia e Estatística (IBGE), "Para IBGE, crise internacional atraiu mais imigrantes ao Brasil," April 27, 2012. noticias.uol.com.br/cotidiano/ultimasnoticias/2012/04/27/para-ibge-crise-internacional-atraiu-mais-imigrantes-ao-brasil.htm; Globo, "A volta dos brasileiros que moravam no exterior," April 17, 2012. http://globotv.globo.com /rede-globo/profissao-reporter/v/a-volta-dos-brasileiros-que-moravam-no-exterior-parte-1/1908007/

49. Valéria Ribeiro, "Crise reduziu envio de recursos de imigrantes brasileiros para suas famílias," *Comunidade News*, June 25, 2009. http://www.comunidadenews.com/brasil/crise-reduziu-envio-de-recursos-de-imigrantes-brasileiros-para-suas-familias-5073

50. Hiroko Tabuchi, "Goodbye, Honored Guests," *New York Times*, April 23, 2009; Luciano Máximo and Gustavo Faleiros, "Crise traz de volta ao país 400 mil 'expatriados,'" *EU& Valor Econômico*, May 24, 2010. http://www.vermelho.org.br/noticia.php?id_noticia =130037&id_secao=2

51. Sasaki, "Depois de duas décadas de movimento migratório entre o Brasil e o Japão."

52. Roth, *Brokered Homeland: Japanese Brazilian Migrants in Japan*.

CHAPTER 8

The Making and Unmaking of a Community of Latino Labor Migrants in Israel

ADRIANA KEMP AND REBECA RAIJMAN

This chapter examines the emergence and demise of the community of un-documented non-Jewish Latino labor migrants in Israel. According to the Ministry of Interior, by the mid-1990s about 15,000 Latin American labor migrants resided in Israel without a legal permit, comprising 15% of the estimated population of the country's undocumented migrants.[1] By the end of the 2000s, their numbers had fallen drastically as a consequence of a harsh policy of detention and deportation deliberately implemented by the state. Deportation led not only to the numerical decline in Israel of *Latinos*,[2] as they were commonly identified, but also to the dismantling of a diverse and vibrant community that in the course of a decade seemed to have become an integral part of Tel Aviv's metropolitan ethnoscape.

Drawing on the case of undocumented Latino migrant workers in Israel, the chapter has a twofold focus. First, we examine the social, economic, and political constellations that encouraged the mobility of Latin American migrants to new destinations and produced the type of networks that sustained the ongoing inflows of migrants throughout the 1990s. We pay particular attention to the socioeconomic factors that channeled Latino migrant workers to Israel at the "push" and "pull" ends of the migration flow, and we document the main patterns of informal recruitment and labor market incorporation that mediate them. Second, we portray the key social settings in which Latino labor migrants developed a sense of community and negotiated different forms of social belonging within constraining circumstances. We show how despite the positive reception that Latinos experienced on the level of society, political interventions eventually contributed to the effective unmaking of the Latino community and its forced dispersal.

The case of Latinos in Israel raises valuable insights into the dynamics of recent migrations from Latin America and more generally into undocumented migrations worldwide. Our case contributes to extant scholarship in at least two senses. First, whereas much of the literature highlights the significance of previous links between the countries of origin and destination in mediating migratory flows, less attention has been paid to religious factors influencing the choice of destination. Underscoring the multiple forms in which religion—as practice, institution, and identity marker—intersects with migration-related phenomena, we examine the Latino experience in less traditional "immigration" contexts than the North American and Western European. Additionally, we aim to contribute to research on undocumented migrant communities and associations in a situated context. Whereas much literature has dealt with processes leading to the establishment of communities, including those positioned at the margins of legality, and their survival strategies in an adversarial context,[3] we extend our analysis to the political interventions and social conditions that bring about the dismantling of existing communities and the unmaking of migratory flows. We contend that control policies targeting communities form an inextricable part of contemporary dynamics of mobility containment and boundary remaking.[4]

THE ISRAELI SETTING

Israel is a country of many contradictions. Observers have presented the Israeli case as a "typological" challenge in regard to migration and citizenship regimes.[5] On the one hand, Israel exemplifies the characteristics of a "classic" immigration state and society where settler immigration, or *aliyah* (Hebrew: literally "ascent"), performs as a major mechanism for the making of the nation or "ingathering of exiles." At the beginning of the twenty-first century, two out of three members of the Jewish majority are foreign-born (40%) or of the second generation (30%).[6] In 2012, 32% of all foreign-born had arrived from countries in the Middle East and North Africa and 68% from countries in Europe (including the former Soviet Union) and the United States.

On the other hand, though self-defined as a Westernized society based on the adoption of liberal norms and civic principles in many realms, Israel also stands out as a resilient ethnonational regime that grants institutional and ideological priority to ethnic origin.[7] The Israeli Law of Nationality, which came into force on 1952, complemented the Law of Return of 1950. The latter law, based on the *jus sanguinis* principle, confers onto Jews and their relatives up to the third generation the right of immigration, while the former gives them Israeli citizenship virtually automatically.[8]

Strains between civic and ethnoreligious principles, and age-old debates over "Jewish" and "democratic" constitutional values, intensify in regard to relations between the Jewish majority and the large Arab indigenous minority, and more recently in the realm of nonethnic migration.[9] While Israel is committed to the successful absorption of Jewish immigrants and actively encourages their immigration, it is also highly exclusionary toward nonethnic immigration, and official policies actively discourage it.

The recent history of Latin American immigration to Israel is underlined by ethnonational divisions as well as by different migratory dynamics. Jews of Latin American origin comprise 2% of the total Jewish population, and upon immigration through the Law of Return they become incorporated in the social, economic, and political life of the nation as full citizens.[10] Conversely, as we show later, Latin American migrant workers arrived through informal channels, into a context of reception devoid of institutional mechanisms for their incorporation, and upon arrival they were channeled into social positions that set them clearly apart from the Jewish Latin American immigrants.

Distinctions between the two groups are, of course, legal, as the non-Jews are undocumented and have few if any channels for regularization; but they are also symbolic, social, and economic. Labor migrants have generally distinguished themselves from "South Americans," as Jewish immigrants from Latin America are usually called in Israel, by identifying themselves through the label "Latinos."[11] Despite their sharing a common language and culturally resonant codes, social contacts between these two groups of Latin American immigrants were mainly at the workplace as many Latino labor migrants worked as cleaners in households of Latino Israeli citizens. Difference in ethnoreligious definitions of nationality, legal status, and class positions intersected in the Israeli context, to create distinctions and structured relations between immigrants from the same countries of origin. Moreover, while the immigration of Jews is perceived as part of the ongoing nation-building project, labor migrations from the Global South are perceived as a challenge to national sovereignty and identity.

LABOR MIGRATION TO ISRAEL

Overseas labor migration to Israel is relatively new. It started in the early 1990s, when the government authorized recruitment of a large number of labor migrants to replace Palestinian workers from the occupied territories after the first intifada.[12] Official recruitment is through manpower agencies and employers, to whom the permits are allocated. Legally recruited workers come alone without families. They live and work in the workplace: construction workers on construction sites, agricultural workers at agricultural sites, and long-term caregiving workers in the patients' homes. The workplace conditions resemble a kind of "total institution," which leaves little or no margin for migrant associational initiatives.

According to estimates of the Central Bureau of Statistics, by 2002 (during our fieldwork) there were some 238,000 labor migrants in Israel, about 40% of whom had work permits. As in other countries, the official recruitment of labor migration brought about an influx of undocumented migrants. According to Interior Ministry data, undocumented foreign workers arrived in Israel from almost every corner of the world—though mainly from East Europe, South Asia, Africa, and South America—and are employed primarily in the services sector.

In contrast to their documented counterparts, undocumented migrant workers arrived haphazardly. During the 1990s they entered the country on tourist visas valid for up to 90 days, which forbade them to work, and became undocumented by overstaying it. An undocumented status makes a migrant not only vulnerable to the authorities' pursuit but also "invisible" in the eyes of state apparatuses in regard to social, political, and many civil rights. The lack of legal status and work permits has been a powerful catalyst for the development of informal patterns of organization and the emergence of new ethnic communities, concentrated in Tel Aviv-Jaffa;[13] they have rewoven the ethnic fabric of Israel's major metropolitan area. Paradoxically, the lack of state regulation of working and living conditions for undocumented migrant workers leaves room for the emergence of new ethnic communities as a strategy for survival in a new society. In the 1990s three new ethnic communities developed in Israel among migrant workers: Black African, Latin American, and Filipino. The great majority of African and Latino migrants were undocumented, and the Filipino community displays a mixed pattern.[14] By 1996, undocumented Latino migrants made up about 15% of the total undocumented labor migrant population.[15] By 2002 the total number of Latinos in Israel was estimated at 13,000 people, arriving from a wide variety of countries but mainly Ecuador and Colombia (see Table 8.1).

TABLE 8.1   Estimated Number of Latino Migrants in Israel, 2002.

COUNTRY OF ORIGIN	NO. OF MIGRANTS	RELATIVE PROPORTION
Ecuador	5,000	38
Colombia	4,500	35
Chile	1,200	9
Peru	1,200	9
Bolivia	500	4
Venezuela	250	2
Brazil	250	2
Other	100	1
N	13,000	100%

Source: Kalir, 2010, Table 2, 47.

UNDOCUMENTED LABOR MIGRATION
AND DEPORTATION POLICY

The primary method of the Israeli state for dealing with undocumented labor migrants has been to make their deportation a systematic policy. After years of turning a blind eye to them, between 1995 and 2008 over 76,000 migrant workers were deported, the figure peaking in 2003 and 2004.[16] The most significant organizational and institutional expression of the deportation policy was the establishment of the new Immigration Administration in 2002.[17] Since then, the immigration police have not refrained from expounding to the public in detail the supposed threats latent in the situation: an economic threat ("the illegal foreign workers make a significant impact on natives' unemployment"; "there is a financial drain from Israel to their countries of origin"; "they hardly pay taxes, which creates a heavy burden on infrastructure without promoting its maintenance"); a demographic and national threat ("demographically speaking, a 'state' within a 'state' is taking shape"; "the Jewish character of the state is being damaged by intermarriage"); and even a security threat ("because of their lack of affinity to Israel, the illegal residents are liable to be a platform for security crimes and hostile destructive activity."[18]

The formation of the immigration police was an important turning point in the scope of the deportation of undocumented labor migrants: according to its own reports, since its establishment in September 2002, 118,105 people have left Israel, 40,000 of them as deportees. Mass deportations were implemented after the arrest of migrants in raids on houses, workplaces, buses, and shopping centers, and even after street pursuits. Such arrests, many of them accompanied by callous violence on the part of the police and the trampling of rights, became an everyday spectacle.[19] Not only did the sheer volume of deportations change but also the targeted groups. Recognizing the central role played by community networks and organizations in the lives of undocumented migrants, the police directed their activity at individuals but also at dismantling entire communities. Extensive policing and intelligence work was dedicated to locating and deporting community leaders, and raiding places where labor migrants held community gatherings and spent their leisure time.[20] This context is important for comprehending the dwindling and demise of the Latino community of migrant workers in Israel.

METHODOLOGY

The findings and analysis in this chapter are based on a multiyear qualitative study with key ethnographic components. Data were collected by three main methods. First, we held in-depth interviews with labor migrants, as well as informal conversations on visits to households and other sites of social gatherings in 1997 and in 2005. Gathering data on migrant workers in general and on undocumented foreigners in particular is difficult, so representative samples could not be assembled. Therefore, we used the so-called snowball technique to detect and construct a sample of Latino labor migrants in Israel. Because the target was to assemble a group diverse in national origin and gender, we applied multiple-entry snowballing to avoid the danger of interviewing limited personal social networks, which was inherent to the traditional snowball approach. We conducted eighty individual in-depth, semistructured interviews. All were conducted in Spanish and were recorded with the consent of the participants.

Second, we conducted fieldwork in various social and institutional settings such as soccer games, salsa clubs, churches and religious congregations, organized tours, fairs, kindergartens, schools, and private homes in order to document the ways the Latino community was emerging in the city of Tel Aviv.

Third, we conducted documentary analysis of government decisions, parliamentary protocols, and special committees' reports to track the formulation of labor migration policies in general and on undocumented migrations in particular. We also relied on nongovernmental organizations' reports, public campaigns, and legal advocacy among migrants and on their behalf.

LATINOS IN ISRAEL: BETWEEN THE PUSH OF LATIN AMERICA AND THE PULL OF THE HOLY LAND

What factors drove thousands of non-Jewish migrants from Latin American countries—mainly Ecuador and Colombia—to move through unofficial venues to the Jewish state from the mid-1990s and establish their own communities?

Undocumented Latino labor migration to Israel can be explained in terms of three intersecting dynamics: (1) unstable socioeconomic and political conditions that pushed Latinos out of their homelands; (2) factors in Israel that pulled them to that country (employment opportunities, higher wages, easier entry than to North America and Western Europe, at least until 1997); (3) the emergence of social networks and institutional frameworks (ethnic associations) that link the two foregoing factors for informal recruitment and consolidation of a distinct ethnic community.

The structural constraints affecting most Latin American countries provide the general context for understanding Latin American migrants' motivation to migrate. Since the early 1980s most Latin American countries entered a transition period, where authoritarian and repressive regimes gave way to the democratization of national politics. That said, such processes of democratization should be understood more as formal reforms whereby political mechanisms were re-established (such as the reinstallment of the political party system, press freedom, and human rights discourses), but not necessarily accompanied by deep socioeconomic reforms. The increasing foreign debt, austerity plans dictated by the International Monetary Fund, high inflation, and consequent internal recession and economic stagnation widened social gaps and poverty rates.[21] The combination of falling incomes, frustrated ambitions, and restructuring of many Latin American economies generated powerful pressures for emigration in skilled blue-collar workers as well as the educated urban middle classes. Hence, political and socioeconomic conditions alike should be considered important push factors for emigration from different countries in South America.[22]

The impact of structural push factors resurfaces in our empirical data on premigration characteristics of labor migrants, including reasons for migration and sociodemographic and human capital attributes.

REASONS FOR MIGRATION

The reasons migrants themselves gave for their move reflect the grim economic situation in their home countries. The major motivating factors were lack of opportunities for upward social and economic mobility in the sending societies. The majority gave economic reasons for leaving their countries of origin. These subsume five main themes: (1) the opportunity to save large amounts of money in a short time; (2) a strong desire for economic independence and a preference for self-employment/ business ownership by the time they return to their home countries (this is the main reason for saving large amounts of money); (3) buying a house or a plot of land; (4) securing a better future for their children (high education); and (5) guaranteeing adequate financial support in old age (after retirement).

Second to economic reasons, the existence of social networks abroad (in Israel or elsewhere) was also singled out as one of the determinant reasons for migration. Many of our respondents told us that they thought of Europe and Australia as the original destination but finally decided on Israel because they had someone there to help them upon arrival. Social networks established in Israel prior to migration were quite common among immigrants in our study. Before their departure almost half our interviewees had family members or friends residing in Israel, and almost two-thirds had at least one family member living there during their stay in Israel. For example, Rosita, 24 years old, a woman from Armenia, Colombia, presents an interesting pattern of family drafting and network migration to Israel. At the time of the interview, thirty-three members of her family lived in Israel. For Rosita, family ties were a fundamental component in taking the decision to "have a try" in Israel. The extended family functioned as a source of support, helping her both financially and emotionally to overcome the difficulties of migration. Rosita's case illustrates how relatives initiate other people in the migration process by providing them support, thus reducing its costs and risks. In this way, migration as a *virus* "spreads from person to person and from family to family," increasing the probabilities of other people migrating to Israel. As social networks mature, they acquire a momentum that feeds labor migration, and this seems to be the major mechanism that perpetuated Latino labor migration to Israel in the 1990s.

Similarities to other countries notwithstanding, labor migration to Israel has a singular feature: as the Holy Land, Israel has a unique attraction for Chistians worldwide who aspire to visit the country as pilgrims. Moreover, with the coming of the new millennium, many of them wanted to assuage their yearning for the coming of the Messiah. The religious motivation is significant for two main reasons: first, one fifth of our respondents adduced religious reasons for choosing Israel as the preferred destination; second, and most important, religious motivations were translated into action through the creation of religious organizations which mushroomed within the Latino community. Later in this chapter we shall show that religious life is one of the most important aspects of Latino community organization and development.

SOCIODEMOGRAPHIC CHARACTERISTICS
OF THE LATINO LABOR MIGRANTS

The demographic and social characteristics of Latino migrant workers classified by gender are presented in Table 8.2. Half the respondents in our sample came from Colombia, whence arrived the largest group of Latino migrants. Approximately a quarter migrated from Ecuador, the rest from Bolivia, Peru, Chile, and Venezuela.

Migrants, whether men or women, were young (34 years on average), which confirms what other studies have shown: migrants were concentrated in the central labor-force ages. There were substantial differences among gender groups regarding marital status. Migrant men were more likely than women to be single or married, whereas migrant women were more likely to be divorced and widowed. The high proportion of married men and women and separated/widowed women migrants suggests that the role of income provider impels men and women alike to look for migration as an alternative to local employment.

The bulk of Latino migrants arrived in Israel between 1993 and 1995, the period of high legal and organized recruitment (which did not include Latin American countries). At the time of the interview, respondents' length of stay in Israel averaged 4 years. The data suggest several patterns of migration according to family situation:[23] (1) family migration (spouses and children migrate together); (2) family migration in stages (one spouse migrates before the other spouse and children); (3) single-parent family in stages (single parent migrates before the children); (4) independent migration (men or women migrate independently); (5) spouses migrate together, leaving the children behind; (6) single parent leaves children in country of origin; and (7) one spouse migrates to Israel, leaving spouse and children in country of origin. As expected, men and women displayed significant differences in pattern of migration by family situation. Over half the migrant men were single, coming independently to Israel, compared with only 30% of the migrant women in this category. Particularly interesting is that a high percentage of women migrated alone (25% compared to only 3% among males), leaving their children in the home country in the care of ex-husbands, parents, or other family members. Likewise, many of the male workers left wives and children behind (15% and 9% of male and female migrants, respectively); or both parents migrated to Israel and left the children with

TABLE 8.2 Socio-Demographic Characteristics of Latino Migrant Workers.

	MALES	FEMALES
Age	32.7 (7.9)	34.3 (8.2)
Marital Status		
Single	48.4	34.1
Married-Living together	36.4	29.5
Divorced-Separated	15.2	29.6
Widowed	-	6.8
Year of Arrival		
% 1989-1992	21.1	11.4
% 1993-1995	42.5	36.4
% 1996-1998	36.4	52.2
Patterns of Migration		
Family migration	21.3	15.9
Family migration (single parent)	3.0	9.1
Both spouses-leaving children	6.1	11.4
Single parent-leaving children	3.0	25.0
One spouse-leaving spouse + children	15.3	9.1
Independent migration	51.3	29.5
Occupation in Country of Origin		
Professional and Technical	18.8	11.4
Clerks and Sales	31.2	36.3
Services-Craft	50.0	52.3
Education		
Years of formal education	12.9 (3.6)	11.0 (3.1)
% holding academic degree	22.6	14.3
Income in country of origin ($)	415.0 (240.1)	256.3 (195.5)
Occupation in Israel		
Domestic Work	41.0	100.0
Construction	19.0	-
Light Industry	22	-
Services	18.0	-
N	**33**	**44**

relatives in their countries of origin. Both male and female migrants sent money to their kin who cared for their children.

Over a quarter of female and male respondents reported having children residing with them in Israel. Fifty percent of these children were between the ages of 6 and 12 and attended primary schools at the time of the interview. Approximately one-fifth were younger than 6 and attended private kindergartens run by other Latino migrant women. Another 20% were children aged 12 to 18 who attended secondary schools. At the time of the interview most of our respondents in the sample lived in south Tel Aviv, near the bus central station area, which in time became an enclave of labor migrants.

HUMAN CAPITAL AND SOCIOECONOMIC ATTAINMENT PRIOR TO ARRIVAL

Table 8.2 also displays the levels of human capital acquired by Latino migrants in their countries of origin. Men on average had higher levels of formal education than their female counterparts (13 and 12 years of schooling, respectively) and were more likely to hold academic degrees (22.6% and 14.3%, respectively).[24] On average, half the Latino migrants had worked in white-collar occupations in their country of origin before migrating to Israel. One-third of female migrants had worked in pink-collar occupations (clerks and sales). Half of migrant males had worked at blue-collar jobs (e.g., taxi and truck drivers, mechanics, welders, electricians), and many of them were self-employed.

The bottom panel of Table 8.2 provides information on the migrants' monthly income prior to migration. On average, respondents reported they earned $378 (from all type of sources) with significant differences between men and women (women earned 50% of men's income). These low-income levels contrast with wages migrants expected to earn in Israel, namely $1,000 to $1,500 per month on average. Hence, the wage gap (especially for women) might have operated as a powerful magnet pulling people to Israel.[25] Also, all labor migrants in our sample lived and worked in Israel without legal authorization.

PULL FACTORS

Whatever the migrants' motivation, immigrants would not have gone to Israel in the absence of a propitious political economic opportunity structure for their reception. The segmented and dual structure of the Israeli labor market is crucial for understanding the demand for their labor mainly in the domestic and services sectors. As Portes and Rumbaut have pointed out, "the match between the goals and aspirations of foreign workers and the interests of firms [or employers] that hire them is the key factor sustaining the movement from year to year."[26] Demand for foreign labor in host societies is caused by the inability or the unwillingness of local employers to recruit workers to the secondary sector of the economy because native workers are not "willing" to work under hard conditions, low salaries, instability, and lack of future prospects.[27] In Israel demand for a low-skilled labor force was met in the past by Jewish immigrants from Arab countries in the Middle East and North Africa,[28] and later by Palestinian cross-border workers from the occupied territories in West Bank and Gaza.[29] However, following the deterioration of the security situation in 1991 and the signing of the Oslo agreements, Israel enacted closure policies that prevented the entry of Palestinian workers, opening the gates to the official and nonofficial recruitment of labor migrants from overseas.[30]

LABOR MARKET INSERTION IN ISRAEL

Latino migrants have a limited range of economic alternatives available in the Israeli labor market (see bottom panel of Table 8.2). Because of their undocumented status, they are excluded from most jobs regardless of their actual skills, and they cannot enter the occupations for which they are qualified. The great majority of Latino women were employed as domestic workers in Israel but only 10% of them had worked in domestic service in their countries of origin. Likewise, 41% of Latino migrant men were employed as domestic workers in Israel; they were called *nikyoneros* or *cleaning guys*—a hybrid of Spanish and Hebrew. Other Latino men worked in construction (19%), light industry (22%), and other services (restaurants, moving services, religious services: 18%).

Although the majority of the Latin American migrants were salaried workers, some entrepreneurial activities within the community took place. Examples are private kindergartens organized by Latino women (who took care of Latin American children living with their parents, many of them born in Israel), hair salons operated at home, tour organizers (especially to the Holy Places), cookery, photography, removals services, and electric appliance repairs (especially among men).

Although it has been argued that the source of pride for temporary migrant workers is the achievement of their goals as economic providers for their families back home,[31] for some of our respondents their downward occupational mobility in Israel was traumatic, even though they saw their stay as a transitional experience.[32] Female migrants experienced their entry into the domestic service niche as extremely traumatic, especially those taking live-in jobs (*internas*) in private households, because of the limitations on their freedom and their isolation from Latino social ties. With the passage of time in the country, women managed to move away from the live-in situation, rented an apartment with friends or family members, and worked as freelancers in private houses.[33]

As undocumented residents and workers in the informal sector of the economy, they received no employment benefits, even though they were supposed to be protected by local labor laws.[34] There were a number of ways in which employers could exploit this asymmetrical situation to their own advantage. For example, prearranged rates of payment could be lowered, earnings could be paid much later than previously agreed—or not at all. Although undocumented workers had the right to claim their share, they rarely took this option even when nongovernment organizations could act on their behalf. As a rule, they preferred to lose their money and change jobs rather than take legal action, which could risk capture by the police and deportation.

MEDIATING NETWORKS: PATTERNS OF RECRUITMENT OF LATINO MIGRANTS

Although push factors at origin and pull factors at destination create the conditions for international migration flows, with time new and independent factors such as social networks and institutional frameworks develop in consequence of migration. Once in place, social networks (based on kin and friendship) expand, connecting present and prospective migrants (in countries of origin). Migrant networks tend to become self-sustaining over time because they constitute social capital available to prospective and new migrants. Among people considering migration, ties to an earlier immigrant present in the host country are likely to increase the probability of selecting that place of destination. Moreover, knowing or being related to migrants gives access to sources of information and connections, reducing the uncertainty related to migration, especially among undocumented migrants.[35]

Patterns of recruitment of Latin American migrants, especially in the domestic sector where most women and 40% of the men worked, were informal and assumed two main forms: (1) direct recruitment through Israelis (from a Latin American background) and (2) recruitment conducted by coethnic social networks. Direct recruitment of domestic workers was effected through Latin American Jewish families living in Israel. Family members or friends residing in the sending country acted as recruiters on their behalf while the recruiting Israeli family sent money for ticket and other expenses of the prospective migrant. The migrants went to Israel as tourists, on a 3-month tourist visa, which did not entitle them to work. When their visa expired, they became undocumented residents in Israel and could be caught and deported. With the second form of recruitment, through coethnic social networks, people in countries of origin responded to "invitations" from friends and family already living and working in Israel; or they decided to try for a similar experience, stimulated by rumors that earning money was easy, which sparked hopes of an opportunity to "make it in Israel." These methods proved successful as long as the tourist loophole in Israel was relatively open, thereby minimizing the costs and risks of transatlantic migration.[36]

Parallel to these two forms of recruitment, we identify other private "entrepreneurs" in countries of origin that promoted Latino migration to Israel. These were travel agencies in the home countries that spread the image of a "golden Israel," a land of opportunity with high salaries and excellent labor conditions; they sold packages (including flights and hotels) for a trip to Israel. Religious practices and networks also functioned as informal channels of recruitment. For example, many interviewees mentioned organized religious pilgrimages to the Holy Places as the first venue for gaining acquaintance with Israeli society and as an easy way to enter the country.

Next we shall see that religious and other social types of associations generated social capital for prospective migrants. They also served as a social space for interaction, mutual aid, and the formation of community life.

THE MAKING OF A LATINO COMMUNITY

Scholars have consistently called attention to immigrants' disposition to form their own communities and voluntary associations.[37] Although there is considerable debate over the factors driving the formation of immigrant associations—whether they relate to the civic and political culture of the immigrants or their hosts—most scholarship concurs that migrants organize and associate where neither traditional institutions (e.g., kinship) nor newer ones in the host countries (e.g., a welfare state(can satisfy their social, cultural, and economic needs.[38]

In this sense, there is nothing exceptional in the dynamic driving the formation of community organizations among Latino migrants in Israel or in the needs they went to fulfill. Deprived of social status, prestige, and power in the occupational and social spheres, and also of more traditional support structures, many migrants search for alternative spaces to meet their needs, maintaining ties with the communities back "home," as well as articulating their own sense of community in the new country.

Throughout the 1990s Latino migrants in Israel created a wide array of social arenas that included religious and lay activities, as well as educational and political forms of organizing.[39] These formed the backbone of an emergent and distinct community. We begin by describing the first two types of social arenas: recreational, mainly sport and dancing clubs, and religious congregations. Both were often presented by our interviewees as a measure for classifying different types of Latinos according to their "moral" virtues and codes of behavior.

RECREATIONAL ACTIVITIES: SOCCER AND SALSA

Soccer games and clubs were a salient axis around which Latino migrants organized their leisure activities, mainly on weekends. Soccer games were played in public places, within and beyond the limits of south Tel Aviv, where most undocumented migrants resided; they served as a meeting point for men, women, and children of the whole community. Matches were taken seriously to the point of organizing nationwide championships such as *Copa America* (at Dolphinarium Park in one of the Tel Aviv beaches) and the *Mundial* (at Hayarkon Park in Tel Aviv). The latter included teams representing different countries, so it also created an opportunity to interact with labor migrants then in Israel from elsewhere in the world (Rumania, Turkey, Ghana, etc.).

Sports events provided a suitable base for pursuing other community activities as well. During the gatherings, improvised stalls sold traditional food; this was not only an intrinsic part of the happening but also a way to make extra cash. Money for mutual aid was raised mainly through the occasional holding of fairs (*kermesse*), raffles, and other creative arrangements. Funds were collected to help members of the community facing difficulties in finding employment, health problems, or deportation but also to aid communities back home struck by disasters, as was the case with the 1999 earthquake that affected the city of Armenia, in Colombia's "*eje cafetero*," whence most Colombian migrants originated.

Gatherings for dancing and listening to Latino music were another common leisure activity that brought Latinos together. Like other organizational initiatives, salsa dancing also fulfilled several functions, from overcoming homesickness to consolidating a pan-Latin identity that superseded differences in national identity. However, as Morad points out,[40] as they brought together Latinos and Israelis, salsa gatherings created opportunities not only to reaffirm identity boundaries but also to cross boundaries and transform social hierarchies.

Places for salsa and other types of Latino dancing sprang up in Tel Aviv with the arrival of migrant workers, but Israelis' attraction to salsa is part of a broader "enchantment" with all "Latino things." This is manifest, inter alia, in the highly positive attitude toward Spanish language and culture in general that Israelis display[41]; the popularity of Latin American telenovelas; and the "traditional" treks to South America on which young Israelis embark as *mochileros* upon their demobilization. [42] In this context, salsa clubs became not only a magnet of attraction but also a setting where Latinos can interact on an equal basis with Israelis, thus bolstering their self-esteem as well as usually outstripping the local dancers.[43]

RELIGIOUS SPACES: THE CATHOLIC CHURCH AND EVANGELIST CHURCHES

A well-known fact is that migrants move with their religious beliefs, practices, and institutions.[44] These often provide spiritual solace within the experiential context of displacement,[45] as well as a social space for the constitution of new identities in the face of discrimination and exclusion.

Latino migrants attended two kinds of religious organizations: the Catholic Church in Jaffa, which congregated once a week for Latino gatherings around the Mass offered in Spanish; and independent religious organizations, mostly evangelist, established by and for migrant workers. Regarding the latter, Latino migrants became spiritual entrepreneurs, both as "importers" of religious practices and institutions from their home countries, and as founders of new churches, which until their arrival did not have a strong hold in Israel. Our fieldwork showed that nearly ten Latino evangelical churches operated in south Tel Aviv by the early 2000s. They varied in size, activity, and denomination—Pentecostal, Baptist, Assembly of God, Adventists, or groups organized by Messianic Jews, but all were evangelical. As is usually the case,[46] boundaries between different types of popular Protestant denominations were very fluid, with members moving between congregations or churches changing their affiliations. According to our data, evangelical communities comprised more than a thousand congregants, about half of them regular attendees, the rest occasional passersby. Arguably then, about 7% of the Latino migrant workers were active to one degree or another in evangelical churches.[47]

Many of the churches were supported by the central headquarters outside Israel, whereas others had established connections with the network of Protestant Arab churches in Israel. Migrants attended the churches regularly to pray and receive moral support or for special occasions such as weddings, festivals, and baptizing their Israeli-born children. Besides the religious and social aspect, churches organized group lessons in the local language, Hebrew, and in the country's "unofficial" second language, English. There were also "capacitation and training" classes in sewing and hairdressing for adult members, and after-school activities for youngsters. All in all, churches served simultaneously as spiritual center, bank, school, employment bureau, and community center.[48]

Undocumented migrants saw in churches a "shelter" from the vicissitudes of everyday life. Anita from Colombia and a regular worshipper at the CC church[49] explained to us that she was drawn there as "compensation" for the threatening and alienating surroundings of the area where she lived, near Tel Aviv's old central bus station: "There are a lot of drunk migrants from Poland, Romania, Portugal, and Russia. It's frightening," she says, adding, "The CC is like my family in Israel." For Maria, who like many of her friends left her children in her home country to be raised by her mother, the church constituted "a form of self-help. It gives me the strength to go on." For others, churches provided an alternative structure of opportunity wherein participation afforded status and power in the community hierarchy.[50] This was especially so regarding the church leaders and those who held key positions in the community's religious life, such as becoming a deacon, participating in the choir, or organizing the weekly canasta round robin among community members to raise funds.

The churches' existence was hardly a secret. Some were registered as autonomous associations or as the "subsidiary" of a recognized church in Israel. Although the churches did not go out of their way to declare their presence, especially the newly founded, they were far from underground organizations. Anyone who happened to walk by during a service could hear the soulful chant emanating from their open windows. The churches' public nature stood in contrast to the desperate attempts by undocumented migrants to disguise their presence in public arenas in times of deportation campaigns and thus avoid attracting the authorities' attention. Much of the churches' attraction for the migrant workers, and part of their sociotherapeutic function, was that they could offer not only spiritual but also physical sanctuary. This was related to the fact that religious places were protected from police intervention and surveillance, becoming a "free space" for undocumented migrants, if only for a short time.[51]

A less obvious way in which religion was linked to migration was migrants' making religious claims not only to express their beliefs but also to support their inclusion in the host society. Such was the case with Evangelist churches, in which both leaders and lay members usually translated their interpretation of Christian theology into a claim of belonging, in line with hegemonic definitions of belonging and membership in Israel.[52]

For example, in our conversations with pastors and congregants, they often emphasized their Christian beliefs in the Return to Zion as a prologue to the advent of the Messiah and their concomitant identification with the Jewish people's right to the Land of Israel. Asked to define the main goal of his church, the pastor of the ER church declared ardently, "Its purpose is to encourage Christians in the world to pray for the people of Israel, to connect with the tradition of Israel, and to become acquainted with the reality in the Land of Israel."[53] The desire to "work for Israel" as Christians was a recurrent motif in personal conversations with church leaders and in the collective prayers and petitions of the church members. However, "working for Israel" acquired a double meanings in the context of migrants, who during the day worked at domestic chores for Israelis and feared deportation, and in the church articulated their desire to support the Jewish state and help solve the Israeli-Palestinian conflict (perceived in religious terms) as their raison d'être in the Holy Land. An example is Gloria, wife of a Baptist pastor, who also worked at cleaning houses, or as she called it "*limpia el polvo y reza.*"[54] As she explained to us:

> Zionism was and remains a national movement with the goal of establishing the State of Israel. We are Zionists. We love everything about the Jewish people. Our powerful desire for a visa stems precisely from the desire to help the Jews. Otherwise, why should we be here? We are here to serve the Jewish people.[55]

Thus, theology blurred differences between Evangelical Christianity and Jewish Zionism as articulated in religious practice and in the believers' narratives of identity. It also framed congregants' precarious legal situation as undocumented migrants seeking legitimacy.

THE UNMAKING OF THE LATINO COMMUNITY

Usually theories that describe the emergence of new ethnic communities do not deal with the mechanisms that may dismantle the formal and informal associations created through the migrants' own initiatives. In this section we analyze the impact of policies of control and deportation on the institutional setup of the Latino community in Israel and how they eventually contributed to stemming the inflow of Latino migration to that country. We focus on two main types of organization—political and educational—and show how they were reshaped by political interventions.

POLITICAL ORGANIZATION: THE OTL

The formation of community patterns and institutions just described was not only the result of migrants' resourcefulness.[56] To some extent it also made evident the fissures between a stringent regime of "nonimmigration" that officially sought to prevent the settlement of nonethnic migrants and the positive reception that Latinos enjoyed on the level of society. The latter enabled the de facto social incorporation of undocumented Latinos as participants in an array of social networks and daily interactions with nongovernmental organizations advocating for migrants, municipal welfare agencies, schools, youth movements, activists, and more.[57]

According to Roer-Strier and Olshtain-Mann, this positive reception derives from the broader positive stereotype of South American Jewish immigrants in Israel[58]; others relate it to perceived similarities between the Latino and Israeli "outgoing nature"[59] or to the presence of a "sympathetic" South American Jewish community already established in Israel.[60] Another and perhaps more tangible factor here was Latino migrants' ability to "go unnoticed." Unlike migrant workers from black Africa or Southeast Asia, Latin Americans could pass as Israelis because of their physical similarity. This reduced the chances of their being sought or jailed by the immigration police, and likewise helped them in their interaction with the host society.[61]

All these enabling factors led Latino migrants to engage in what Kalir calls a strategy of "practical accumulation of belonging,"[62] namely a form of cumulative symbolic capital that defies the "either-or" logic of formal citizenship and is recognized as legitimate and legitimating by the dominant national community.[63] This pragmatic form of belonging worked at the individual and collective levels, and drew on the Latinos' ability to manipulate their public (in)visibility as a resource in what we may call a "politics of visibility," namely to be "seen" or "unseen" according to context.

In 1998 this politics was evident in a brief attempt to organize the community to mobilize collective claims.[64] Following the experience of undocumented African migrants who established the African Workers Union (AWU), Latinos attempted to create their own union, the Organización de Trabajadores Latinoamericanos (OTL), which would function as a channel for interaction with Israeli authorities and organizations dealing with labor migrants. The initiative followed previous unsuccessful attempts by activists in the community to gather Latinos from different parts of the continent under one common organization. However, the significant catalyst for organizing was the government's declaration about its intention to implement tougher arrest and deportation measures against undocumented migrants.

The first assembly of the OTL was convened by a local journalist and was followed by a series of meetings and consultations of OTL members with AWU (African Workers Union) leaders, Knesset members, and nongovernmental organizations. Participants discussed the steps required to address successfully both Israeli public opinion and members of the community reluctant to participate in political activities. The OTL's short-lived political activity reached its peak at a meeting between Latino and black African representatives and the chair of the Knesset Committee on Migrant Workers (May 17, 1998), at which an alternative policy to deportation was discussed. The meeting resulted in the submission of a joint proposal by both migrant communities' representatives and members of the Knesset committee, which recommended the grant of 1-year work permits for undocumented migrants already residing in Israel and a $5,000 deposit meant to ensure that migrants would leave the country when the permit expired. The government rejected this proposal.

The Latino political organization was nipped in the bud when police raided the homes of some community leaders. From interviews with Latino leaders, we learned that members of the community believed that the escalation in the arrest and deportation policy was a direct reaction to the community's organizational activities. Conversely, the OTL leaders related the failure at organizing politically to the lack of an integrated and coordinated organizational infrastructure, and of a participatory political culture among Latinos in general. According to Kalir, who conducted ethnographic work mainly in the Ecuadorian community, this explanation is shortsighted as it fails to consider that the achievements of the Latino community until then greatly depended on its ability to keep out of the authorities' spotlight while accumulating social belonging in Israeli society.[65]

In either case, as we will show next, whether choosing "quiet" accumulation of practical belonging or "noisy" mobilization of collective claims, the politics of (in)visibility of the Latino community was disabled by governmental interventions that eventually caused its unmaking.

LA ESCUELITA AND THE GREAT DEPORTATION

As stated before, Israeli state policy on undocumented migration took a dramatic turn in 2002 with the creation of the immigration police. This organization launched a multipronged attack to deliver a severe blow to labor migrants' networks and organizations. Its officers arrested and deported many of the immigrant activists with the clear objective of deterring undocumented migrants from attempts at organizing and settling.[66]

From the establishment of the immigration police, Latino migrants felt under siege. Being "undocumented" became a permanent burden affecting migrants' everyday lives, and it constituted a recurrent theme in community gatherings. Viviana, from Bolivia, shared with us her consternation regarding her status.

> I live with tension. We never have a moment of peace. We are not free to act and interact as normal people. People take advantage of this situation. Take for instance the questions of renting an apartment. You know that they charge you more just because you are illegal and you cannot say a word. I already left two apartments and my money guarantee was not returned. Again, I couldn't complain. If you need a medicine, you cannot get it because illegal workers don't have medical insurance. Most employers do not want to pay for that.

Suddenly home and street turned into dangerous places. Fearing arrest and deportation, migrants avoid gathering in public places.[67]

Police raids targeting the old and new central bus station area in Tel Aviv led many migrants to move out to the surrounding areas with a lower concentration of foreign workers, hoping to reduce the chances of being caught. A case in point is Irene, from Venezuela, who moved to a northern suburb of Tel Aviv:

> Although living in the suburbs makes me feel a little more secure, I know that the police can catch me in any bus at any time. To be on the safe side, I always have an amount of money reserved for the ticket in case of deportation. You know, when I leave my house I never know if I'll be back.

In other cases, many women working as live-out domestics considered the possibility of taking a live-in position as a strategy to avoid being arrested on their way to work.

As rising numbers were detained and deported, many decided to leave the country of their "own accord." Deportation campaigns were particularly hard on families. Until the establishment of the immigration police, the authorities had refrained from deporting families with children or deported the father with the expectation that the wife and children would follow suit. As many families realized that they were not immune to deportation and that integration into Israeli society was not a viable option for non-Jewish migrants, parents began thinking about the moment of returning home to their countries of origin.

In 1999 preparing children for return led to the creation of *La Escuelita*, a Sunday school–like framework operated by migrants and Israeli volunteers. Whereas arrest and deportation policies resulted in the dismantling of most of the other community institutions, *La Escuelita* exemplifies how migrants' associations and initiatives change and adapt to new political constellations.

In the relatively short history of *La Escuelita*, two distinct periods can be identified: the first from its foundation until the wave of deportations in 2005, the second from 2005 to the present. *La Escuelita* was the initiative of a Colombian migrant worker who operated an "underground" kindergarten for undocumented Latino children, and of Mesila.[68] Its main objective was to provide an educational framework where Latinos' children could preserve their linguistic and cultural heritage for the time span until they returned to their (parents') countries; the chief objective was to facilitate the children's return to those countries. It was operated by volunteers from the Latino and the South American Jewish community on Friday afternoons.[69]

In 2005, *La Escuelita* changed its principal objective from a primary focus on nurturing the Latin American cultural and linguistic heritage of the children to a larger focus on the assimilation of children and adults in Israeli culture and society. As mentioned, deportation campaigns targeted families but in fact deported mainly men and women who had resolved to remain in Israel with their children. Many of those who stayed were eventually naturalized as a result of two government decisions in 2005 and 2010 that granted legal status to children and their families.[70] The determination to stay and the legalization campaigns re-shaped the focus of *La Escuelita*'s activities: it would not only be a place for children's activities in Spanish but would have to adapt itself to the new reality meeting the needs of the whole community by becoming a learning center for children, and offering language courses in Hebrew and English and lectures for adults.

Today the target groups of educational activities are mainly female migrant workers, aged 25 to 50−, originating from five countries: Colombia, Ecuador, Peru, Bolivia, and Puerto Rico.[71] With respect to children, the emphasis is not on Spanish language but on offering tutoring as a compliment to the regular school's educational agenda.

Unlike their parents, who define themselves by country of origin and take pride in it, the children, many of them Israeli-born, define themselves as Latinos and are less interested in their parents' culture of origin, which their families would like.[72] The staff composition has also changed: presently the majority of volunteers and staff are Israeli-born Jews of Latin American descent; there is no representative of the migrant workers' community. All have command of the Spanish language. Indeed, while staff and children mix and switch between Spanish and Hebrew, which highlights the children's dual identity as "Latino and Israeli," their parents speak mainly Spanish since their Hebrew level is very low, regardless of the number of years they have lived in Israel.[73]

LATINO MIGRANTS AND THEIR FAMILIES: "LEGAL LIMINALITY" IN A JEWISH STATE

The experience of Latino migrants who had children born and raised in Israel could be best described as one of "legal liminality."[74] Coined by Menjivar,[75] the concept refers to the social position and forms of belonging of individuals and social groups who lack legal personhood but gain nonetheless different types of recognition and social presence. The Israeli migration regime is based on explicit no-family policies aiming to prevent the creation and settlement of families of nonethnic migrants, with or without documents.[76] Nevertheless, Latinos with children in Israel usually found themselves caught in between contradictory pol-icies and logics of inclusion. Thus, for example, pregnant migrants were entitled to reproductive health services such as labor and delivery at public hospitals cov-ered by the National Insurance Institute if registered by an Israeli employer, sub-sidized prenatal care at municipality centers, and full preventive medical services for babies until the age of 1–1.5 years, regardless of their parents' legal status. Migrant workers' children were undocumented by virtue of their presence in Israel, yet they were entitled to medical coverage partly subsidized by the state and to compulsory free public education.[77] Thus, whether driven by public health logics protective of citizens or by residence-based definitions of entitlement, these regulations include migrants lacking legal status in the Israeli social protec-tion system in ways that acknowledge their reproductive life.

Latinos also experienced the tensions between official policies that rendered their families invisible and everyday social interactions that reaffirmed their social ways of belonging and presence. Thus, while raising children under the constant shadow of deportability took a great toll from Latino families, having children also enlarged the circles of association and interaction of Latino migrants with Israelis beyond the worksite to teachers, volunteers, and parents in schools such as Bialik-Rogozin, where half of the students are migrant workers' children, or in youth movements such as the Zionist Scouts movement (Tzofim), which created the Eitan troop for migrant children. Albeit partial and segmented, these forms of social integration accorded Latino families a social personhood anchored on everyday cooperation and interpersonal networks of solidarity which proved crucial during the antideportation campaigns that led to the naturalization of children and their families in 2005 and 2010.[78]

CONCLUSION

The present chapter has focused on the making and unmaking of the Latino community of undocumented migrant workers in Israel. Our contribution is twofold. First, whereas much of the literature on migrant communities has dealt with the processes leading to its emergence and reproduction in host countries, less has been written on the political interventions and social conditions that bring about their dismantling and the stemming of migratory flows. Here we aimed to fill this gap by extending our analysis to the control and enforcement policies that have brought down the Latino community in Israel and put a stop to the migratory flows into the country.

Second, by focusing on the specific case of Israel, we wanted to contribute to the existing literature on undocumented Latino immigrants in non-English-speaking countries. To date, most research on Latino migrants has been conducted in the United States, where Latinos constitute 17% of the total population and 73% of unauthorized migration.[79] The migration experiences of undocumented Latinos to other destinations have largely been neglected; therefore, the Israeli case provides a broader comparative perspective for the study of modes of incorporation of Latino immigrants into host societies.

Throughout the chapter we examined the social, economic, and political constellations that encouraged the mobility of Latin Americans to a new destination in the Middle East. We highlighted the type of formal and informal networks that sustained the ongoing flows of Latino migrants to Israel throughout the 1990s, and the emergence of a wide variety of community networks and informal associations. Furthermore, we have underscored the significance of religious factors for choice of destination but also regarding the ways religious activities led to the establishment of immigrant churches providing protected spaces against the backdrop of the constant threat of arrest and deportation.[80]

The emergence of migrant workers' communities in Israel is of special interest since it challenges the basic definition of Israeli society as an ethnonational polity which encourages permanent settlement of Jewish immigrants and discourages settlement of non-Jewish migrants.[81] Like other labor-importing societies, Israel was forced to confront new dilemmas posed by the presence of the new undocumented migrant populations, the Latino community included, and their reproduction costs. The migrants' rights to basic education, health, and welfare evolved into a new conflictive arena where the limits of membership in the traditional ethnonational state were being questioned. Claims were advanced by the migrants themselves as well as a diverse array of nongovernmental organizations, trying to work out a tolerable modus vivendi for what seems to have become a de facto multiethnic society far exceeding the limits of the ethnonational Jewish Israel.[82]

Since 1996, the Israeli state has resorted to the detection, detention, and deportation of undocumented migrants as a multipronged approach to control, deter, and halt undocumented migratory flows to Israel. Non-Jewish migration was seen as a threat to the Jewish character of the state, internal security, and the socioeconomic well-being of the native population. Detention and deportation strategies implemented in Israel since the mid-1990s, and most harshly in the 2000s, made a forcible impact on the precarious organization of the Latino community. Deportations and the mass exodus of Latino labor migrants exerted a devastating effect on the social organizations that during the 1990s promoted a Latino sense of community. The social spaces that were run by and for Latinos that provided the basis for the community were crushed, and friendship and kin networks formed around these informal social organizations were decisively truncated. When community leaders, pastor churches, and Latino migrants were pursued, detained, and deported by the state, social and religious activities ceased and the community finally collapsed.

Detention and deportation are some of the more visible forms of internal enforcement prevalent not only in Israel but in other host countries such as the United States and countries in the European Union. The practice of deportation is another way for states to reaffirm the contours and importance of national citizenship and sovereignty in the global context.[83] They constitute the normative boundary lines between citizens and noncitizens, and within different groups of noncitizens (documented and undocumented). As our case study has shown, policing of immigrants and enforcement controls through detention and deportation shape the everyday lives of immigrants, their families, and communities in major receiving countries, and intensify their socioeconomic vulnerabilities.

NOTES

1. Data of the Central Bureau of Statistics (CBS) show that between November 1995 and December 1996 the number of migrants from Latin America in Israel without a permit increased by 43%—a highly significant rise by any standards (CBS, Press Release 159 on July 30, 1998).

2. Herein, we use the emic concept of Latino interchangeably with the etic Latin American; the former relates to the categorical designations used by the research subjects (from the insiders' perspective) and the latter to the categories we used as observers.

3. For a summary of this literature, see Jose C. Moya, "Immigrants and Associations: A Global and Historical Perspective," *Journal of Ethnic and Migration Studies* 31, no. 5 (2005): 833–864.

4. Bridget Anderson, Matthew J. Gibney, and Emanuela Paoletti, "Citizenship, Deportation and the Boundaries of Belonging," *Citizenship Studies* 15, no. 5 (2011): 547–563.

5. Arisitide Zolberg, Introduction to *From Immigrants to Citizens: Membership in a Changing World,* T. Alexander Aleinikoff and Douglas Klusmeyer, eds. (Washington, DC: Carnegie Endowment for International Peace, 2000), 383–385.

6. Yinon Cohen, "From Haven to Heaven: Changing Patterns of Immigration to Israel," in *Citizenship and Identity: Germany and Israel in Comparative Perspective*, Daniel Levy and Yfat Weiss, eds. (New York: Berghahn Books, 2002), 36–56; Rebeca Raijman and Adriana Kemp, "The New Immigration to Israel: Becoming a De-Facto Immigration State in the 1990s," in *Immigration Worldwide*, Uma Segal, Doreen Elliott, and Nazneen S. Mayadas, eds., 227–243 (Oxford: Oxford University Press, 2010).

7. Christian Joppke, *Selecting by Origin* (Cambridge, MA: Harvard University Press, 2007).

8. For a detailed explanation of the definition of a Jew for the purpose of return, and the complex ways in which religious and ethnonational components articulate in the question "Who Is a Jew," see Ayelet Shachar, "Whose Republic? Citizenship and Membership in the Israeli Polity," *Georgetown Immigration Law Journal* 13, no. 2 (1999): 233–272.

9. Israeli society is divided across ethnonational lines of approximately 80% Jews and 20% Arabs. The latter, although legally considered equal citizens, in fact form a subordinate social, political, and national minority (S. Smooha, *Arabs and Jews in Israel. Vol.1. Conflicting and Shared Attitudes in a Divided Society* [Boulder, CO: Westview Press, 1992]). Ethnicity divides not only Jews from non-Jews but also Jewish ethnic groups (see Cohen, "From Haven to Heaven: Changing Patterns of Immigration to Israel"); Schlomo Avinery, Liav Orgad, and Amnon Rubinstein, "Managing Global Migration: A Strategy for Immigration Policy in Israel," position paper, Jerusalem, Metzilah Center for Zionist, Jewish, Liberal and Humanist Thought, 2010.

10. Luis Roniger and Deby Babis, "Latin American Israelis: The Collective Identity of an Invisible Community," in *Identities in an Era of Globalization and Multiculturalism: Latin America in the Jewish World*, Judit Bokser de Liwerant, eds. (Leiden, Netherlands: Brill, 2008), 297–320; Rebeca Raijman and Ariane Ophir, "The Economic Integration of Latin Americans in Israel," *Canadian Ethnic Studies* 46, no. 2 (2014): 77–102.

11. See Alejandro Paz, "Discursive Transformation: The Emergence of Ethnolinguistic Identity among Latin American Labor Migrants and Their Children in Israel," PhD diss. (Chicago: The University of Chicago, 2010).

12. David Bartram, "Foreign Workers in Israel: History and Theory," *International Migration Review* 32 (1998): 303–325; Rebeca Raijman and Adriana Kemp, "Labor Migration, Managing the Ethno-national Conflict, and Client Politics in Israel," in *Transnational Migration to Israel in Global Comparative Context*, Sarah Willen, ed. (Lanham, MD: Lexington Books, 2007), 31–50.

13. The majority of the undocumented population of migrant workers resides in Tel Aviv, where there is high demand for cheap and flexible low-skilled labor. In addition, as we shall see, the municipality of Tel Aviv developed a relatively inclusionary local

policy that took care of migrants' needs (Adriana Kemp and Rebecca Raijman, "Tel Aviv Is Not Foreign to You: Urban Incorporation Policy on Labor Migrants in Israel," *International Migration Review* 38, no. 1 [2004]: 26–51).

14. This is because Filipino immigrants are legally recruited to work in the caregiving sector. Many migrants become documented when they leave their employers or over-stay their visa.

15. Adriana Kemp and Rebeca Raijman, *"Workers" and "Foreigners": The Political Economy of Labor Migration in Israel* (Jerusalem: Van-Leer Institute and Kibbutz Hamehuhad, 2008).

16. Roni Bar-Tzuri, *Foreign Workers Without Permits That Were Deported in 2008* (Jerusalem: Research and Economy Department, MoITaL, 2009).

17. A. Gill and Yossi Dahan, "Between Neo-Liberalism and Ethno-Nationalism: Theory, Policy, and Law in the Deportation of Migrant Workers in Israel," *Law and Government in Israel* 10, no. 1 (2006): 347–386.

18. Gill and Dahan, "Between Neo-Liberalism and Ethno-Nationalism: Theory, Policy, and Law in the Deportation of Migrant Workers in Israel."

19. Gill and Dahan, "Between Neo-Liberalism and Ethno-Nationalism: Theory, Policy, and Law in the Deportation of Migrant Workers in Israel."

20. Wurgaft, "Shalom, and Thanks for the Humiliating Treatment," Ha'aretz, April 5, 2004, B-9; Galia Sabar, "The Rise and Fall of African Independent Christianity in Israel, 1990–2004," in *Transnational Migration to Israel in Global Comparative Context*, Sarah Willen, ed. (Lanham, MD: Lexington Books, 2007), 31–50.

21. Arend Lijphart and Carlos H. Waisman, *Institutional Design in New Democracies in Eastern Europe and Latin America* (Boulder, CO: Westview, 1996); Mario Sznajder, "Legitimidad y Poder Politicos frente a las Herencias Autoritarias: Transicion y Consolidacion Democratica en America Latina," *Estudios Interdisciplinarios de America Latina y el Caribe* 4, no. 1 (1993): 27–55.

22. Douglas Massey, Rafael Alarcon, Jorge Durand, and Hunmberto Gonzalez, *Return to Aztlan: The Social Process of International Migration from Western Mexico* (Berkeley: University of California Press, 1990).

23. In our analysis of patterns of migration, we partly rely on the classification of Pierrette Hondagneu-Sotelo, *Gendered Transitions: Mexican Experiences of Immigration* (Berkeley: University of California Press, 1994).

24. At the time of the study the educational achievements of populations across Latin-American countries showed great variation. For example, approximately 11% of the adult population (aged 25+) in Bolivia, Chile, and Ecuador had attained post-secondary education. In Peru this figure was 19% (UNESCO, *Statistical Yearbook* [Paris: Unesco Publishing & Bernan Press, 1997]; Table 1.3). In any event, the average educational attainment of populations in Latin America is lower than that of Latino migrants arriving in Israel.

25. Women working in domestic service 10 hours a day 6 days a week reported an average income of $1,200– $1,500 per month.

26. Alejandro Portes and Ruben Rumbaut, *Immigrant America: A Portrait* (Berkeley: University of California Press, 1996), 17.

27. John R. Harris and Michael P. Todaro, "Migration, Unemployment, and Development: A Two Sector Analysis," *American Economic Review* 60 (1970): 126–142; Michael Piore, *Birds of Passage: Migrant Labor in Industrial Societies* (Cambridge: Cambridge University Press, 1979).

28. Deborah Bernstein and Shlomo Swirsky, "The Rapid Economic Development of Israel and the Emergence of the Ethnic Division of Labour," *The British Journal of Sociology* 33, no. 1 (1982): 64–85.

29. Moshe Semyonov and Noah Lewin-Epstein, *Hewers of Wood and Drawers of Water. Noncitizen Arabs in the Israeli Labor Market* (New York: ILR Press, 1987).

30. Raijman and Kemp, "Labor Migration, Managing the Ethno-national Conflict, and Client Politics in Israel."

31. Piore, *Birds of Passage: Migrant Labor in Industrial Societies.*

32. Being at the crossroads, many are planning to migrate to a European country (primarily Spain). This step is seen as an alternative strategy—as the opportunity to become a legal resident in Israel is almost nonexistent, and the hope of finding a more suitable job, if not for them at least for their children, is doomed to failure (Rebeca Raijman, Silvina Schammah, and Adriana Kemp, "International Migration, Domestic and Care Work: Undocumented Latina Migrant Women in Israel," *Gender & Society* 17, no. 5 (2003): 727–749.

33. Raijman, Schammah, and Kemp, "International Migration, Domestic and Care Work: Undocumented Latina Migrant Women in Israel."

34. Rebeca Raijman and Adriana Kemp, "State and Non-State Actors: A Multi-Layered Analysis of Labor Migration Policy in Israel," in *Perspectives and Practices of Public Policy: The Case of Israel,* D. Korn, ed., 155–173 (Lanham, MD: Lexington Books, 2002).

35. Massey, Alarcon, Durand, and Gonzalez, *Return to Aztlan: The Social Process of International Migration from Western Mexico*; Douglas Massey and Kristine Espinosa, "What's Driving Mexico-U.S. Migration? A Theoretical, Empirical, and Policy Analysis," *American Journal of Sociology* 102 (1997): 939–999.

36. Since 2000, border control has become much tighter in general, and also for Latin American tourists perceived as "prospective" illegal migrants (Moshe Morad, "Salsa and Falafel—Music and Identity among Illegal Latino Immigrants in Tel Aviv," 2005, accessed July 2014, http://www.soas.ac.uk/research/rsa/journalofgraduateresearch/editon1/file58316.pdf, 3)

37. Jose C. Moya, "Immigrants and Associations: A Global and Historical Perspective," *Journal of Ethnic and Migration Studies* 31, no. 5 (2005): 833–864.

38. Moya, "Immigrants and Associations: A Global and Historical Perspective," 836–840.

39. Silvina Schammah, Rebeca Raijman, Adriana Kemp, and Julia Reznik, "'Making It' in Israel?: Non-Jewish Latino Undocumented Migrant Workers in the Holy Land," *Estudios Interdisciplinarios de America Latina y el Caribe* 11, no. 2 (2000): 113–136; Adriana Kemp and Rebeca Raijman, "Christian Zionists in the Holy Land Evangelical Churches, Labor Migrants and the Jewish State," *Identities: Global Studies in Culture and Power* 10 (2003): 295–318.

40. Morad, "Salsa and Falafel—Music and Identity among Illegal Latino Immigrants in Tel Aviv," 6.

41. Ivonne Lerner and Beatriz Katz, "Spanish Teaching in Israel: An Overview," in *El español en el mundo* (Madrid: Plaza y Janés, 2003), 205–252. http://cvc.cervantes.es/obref/anuario/anuario_03/lerner_katz/

42. Except for Palestinian citizens and orthodox religious Jews, military conscription in Israel is mandatory for all citizens who reach the age of 18 and is perceived as the cornerstone of civic duty in Israeli national discourse. The lengthy period of military service (2 and 3 years for women and men, respectively) is mostly perceived as a liminal stage before entrance to "adulthood." Since the early 1980s, leaving the country

to treks in far-away and "exotic" places like South America, Asia, and Australia has become a common "rite of passage" for Israeli youngsters once they finish their military service and before they start their adult life.

43. Morad, "Salsa and Falafel—Music and Identity among Illegal Latino Immigrants in Tel Aviv."

44. R. Stephen Warner, "Immigration and Religious Communities in the United States," in *Gatherings in Diaspora: Religious Communities and the New Immigration*, R. Stephen Warner and Judith G. Wittner, eds. (Philadelphia: Temple University Press, 1998), 3–34; Peggy Levitt, "Redefining the Boundaries of Belonging: The Institutional Character of Transnational Religious Life," *Sociology of Religion* 65, no. 1 (2004): 1–18. For a detailed analysis of the religious life of Latinos in Israel, see Kemp and Raijman, "Christian Zionists in the Holy Land Evangelical Churches, Labor Migrants and the Jewish State."

45. Rijk A. Van Dijk, "From Camp to Encompassment: Discourses of Transsubjectivity in the Ghanaian Pentecostal Diaspora," *Journal of Religion in Africa* 27, no. 2 (1997): 135–159.

46. Paul Freston, "Pentecostalism in Latin America: Characteristics and Controversies," *Social Compass* 45, no. 3 (1998): 335–358; Bernice Martin, "New Mutations of the Protestant Ethic among Latin American Pentecostals," *Religion* 25, no. 2 (1995): 101–117.

47. This figure is comparable to the membership of evangelical churches in Latin America itself, where a "genuine Protestant revolution" has been under way since the 1960s. Paul Freston, "Pentecostalism in Latin America: Characteristics and Controversies"; Martin, "New Mutations of the Protestant Ethic among Latin American Pentecostals"; Kemp and Raijman, "Christian Zionists in the Holy Land Evangelical Churches, Labor Migrants and the Jewish State."

48. Mary Patillo-McCoy, "Church Culture as a Strategy of Action in the Black Community," *American Sociological Review* 63, no. 6 (1998): 767–784.

49. The churches are referred to by their initials only.

50. Warner, "Immigration and Religious Communities in the United States," 25.

51. Kemp and Raijman, "Christian Zionists in the Holy Land Evangelical Churches, Labor Migrants and the Jewish State."

52. Kemp and Raijman, "Christian Zionists in the Holy Land Evangelical Churches, Labor Migrants and the Jewish State."

53. Kemp and Raijman, "Christian Zionists in the Holy Land Evangelical Churches, Labor Migrants and the Jewish State," 307.

54. "Clean the dust and pray."

55. Gloria, the pastor's wife, ER Baptist church, Tel Aviv, Israel, February 8, 2001.

56. For a detailed analysis of the political organization of Latinos in Israel, see Adriana Kemp, Rebeca Raijman, Julia Resnik, and Silvina Schammah-Gesser, "Contesting the Limits of Political Participation: Latinos and Black African Migrant Workers in Israel," *Ethnic and Racial Studies* 23, no. 1 (2000): 94–119.

57. Municipal policies and advocacy NGOs mediated the needs and claims of undocumented communities in general, especially those in which families were formed. See Kemp and Raijman, "Tel Aviv Is Not Foreign to You: Urban Incorporation Policy on Labor Migrants in Israel."

58. Dorit Roer-Strier and Orly Olshtain-Mann, "To See and Not Be Seen: Latin American Illegal Foreign Workers in Jerusalem," *International Migration* 37, no. 2 (1999): 413–434.

59. Yitzhak Schnell, *Foreign Workers in Southern Tel Aviv-Yafo* (Jerusalem: The Floers-haimer Institute for Policy Studies, 1999).

60. Morad, "Salsa and Falafel—Music and Identity among Illegal Latino Immigrants in Tel Aviv," 14.

61. Roer-Strier and Olshtain-Mann, "To See and Not Be Seen: Latin American Illegal Foreign Workers in Jerusalem."

62. Barak Kalir, *Latino Migrants in the Jewish State. Undocumented Lives in Israel* (Bloomington: Indiana University Press, 2010).

63. Kalir, *Latino Migrants in the Jewish State. Undocumented Lives in Israel*, 13.

64. Silvina Schammah, Rebeca Raijman, Adriana Kemp, and Julia Reznik. "'Making it' in Israel? Non-Jewish Latino Undocumented Migrant Workers in the Holy Land." *Estudios Interdisciplinarios de America Latina y el Caribe* 11, no. 2 (2000).

65. Barak Kalir, *Latino Migrants in the Jewish State. Undocumented Lives in Israel*. Bloomington: Indiana University Press, 2010.

66. See Yosef Algazy, "Targeting the Leaders: Civil Rights Organizations Are Delighted at the Activities of Local Leaders of Foreign Workers," Ha'aretz, August 6, 2001; Ruth Sinai, "Leader of Local Filipino Workers Faces Deportation," Ha'aretz, October 10, 2001; Wurgaft, "The Term of the Leaders of Foreign Workers Is Very Short. Then Came the Deportation," Ha'aretz, May, 6 2003. B-4; Wurgaft, "Shalom, and Thanks for the Humiliating Treatment," Ha'aretz, April 5, 2004, B-9.

67. Raijman, Schammah and Kemp, "International Migration, Domestic and Care Work: Undocumented Latina Migrant Women in Israel."

68. The Tel Aviv-Yafo municipality founded Mesila in 1999 to grant social, educational, and health assistance to undocumented migrants who concentrated in and around the city.

69. Adriana Kemp and Rebeca Raijman, *"Workers" and "Foreigners": The Political Economy of Labor Migration in Israel.*

70. Adriana Kemp, "Managing Migration, reprioritizing National Citizenship: Undocumented Labor Migrants' Children and Policy Reforms in Israel," *Theoretical Inquiries in Law* 8, no. 2 (2007): 663–691. In 2005, 562 of the 862 applications were accepted. In 2010, 221 of the 700 children's applications were accepted. See Prime Minister's Office. *Decision no. 2183.* 2010, accessed on December 31, 2013. http://www.pmo.gov .il/Secretary/GovDecisions/2010/Pages/des2183.aspx Prime Minister's Office. *Decision no. 3807.* 2005, accessed on December 31, 2013. http://www.pmo.gov.il/Secretary/ GovDecisions/2005/Pages/des3807.aspx

71. Ivonne Lerner, "Two Latino NGOs in Israel: Languages and Identities," unpublished manuscript, Tel Aviv University, 2014.

72. Lerner, "Two Latino NGOs in Israel: Languages and Identities," 4–5.

73. Lerner, "Two Latino NGOs in Israel: Languages and Identities."

74. Cecilia Menjívar, "Liminal Legality: Salvadoran and Guatemalan Immigrants' Lives in the United States," *American Journal of Sociology* 111, no. 4 (2006): 999–1037.

75. Menjívar, "Liminal Legality: Salvadoran and Guatemalan Immigrants' Lives in the United States."

76. Nelly Kfir and Adriana Kemp, "Struggling Between Routine and Emergency: Migrants' Legalization and Human Rights Activism in Israel," *Critical Sociology* (2015).

77. Kemp and Raijman, "Tel Aviv Is Not Foreign to You: Urban Incorporation Policy on Labor Migrants in Israel," 41.

78. Kemp, "Managing Migration, Reprioritizing National Citizenship: Undocumented Labor Migrants' Children and Policy Reforms in Israel"; Adriana Kemp and Nelly Kfir, "Between State Biopower and Social Politics of Life: Documented and Undocumented Care Workers in Israel," *Social Problems* (2015).

79. Michael Hoefer, Nancy Rytina, and Bryan Baker, "Estimates of the Unauthorized Immigrant Population Residing in the United States: 1990 to 2000," U.S. Department of Homeland Security, 2012. http://www.dhs.gov/xlibrary/assets/statistics/publications/ois_ill_pe_2011.pdf

80. Kemp and Raijman, "Christian Zionists in the Holy Land Evangelical Churches, Labor Migrants and the Jewish State."

81. Kemp, Raijman, Resnik, and Schammah-Gesser, "Contesting the Limits of Political Participation: Latinos and Black African Migrant Workers in Israel."

82. Kemp and Raijman, "Tel Aviv Is Not Foreign to You: Urban Incorporation Policy on Labor Migrants in Israel."

83. Menjívar, "Liminal Legality: Salvadoran and Guatemalan Immigrants' Lives in the United States."

CHAPTER 9

Latino Canadians

A Distinct and Diverse North American Diaspora

VICTOR ARMONY

The case of Latin American Canadians offers an exceptional opportunity to examine and compare how minorities are constructed and transformed in different host societies. Minorities are shaped differently by their societal context, and Canada is especially relevant in that regard because of the existence of two main dominant cultural environments—grounded on political and territorial configurations—within the same country: an English-language Canadian majority at the national level and a French-language Québécois majority in its second most-populated province. Indeed, Canada's Latin Americans can provide unique insights into diasporic citizenship, as this rapidly growing population settles and grows as part and parcel of a highly multiethnic immigrant society, one with a greatly decentralized state and a constitutionally enshrined bilingual character, one marked by the presence of a large number of Aboriginal communities whose self-determination claims are recognized on the basis of their own "distinctive culture."[1] Not surprisingly, compared to most other countries, Canada possesses a weaker national identity and its collective life is framed, to a large extent, by "nations within a nation" phenomena. Furthermore, given the increased linkages across the Americas, Canada holds a very particular and often overlooked position as a major country that is not contained in the United States–Latin America oppositional system that underlies how the hemispheric reality is commonly understood. That is why Canadian Latin Americans can help us think about the Latino diaspora formation in ways that are not necessarily tied to a strong, single nation-state or subject to a sole hegemonic cultural framework.

But even after pointing out Canada's very particular characteristics, it is difficult to ignore the potential parallels and convergences with the United States. Also, this country, demographically equal to ten Canadas, exerts a huge influence on its northern neighbor. The vast impact of the US Hispanic reality, as well as the deepening interconnectedness between Latin America and North

America, are bound to emphasize the significance of the Latino presence in Canada, regardless of its relative size or political weight. Should we then compare Canada's Latino population with that of the United States, or at least try to grasp their commonalities? Let us look at some figures: Canada is home to a little over half a million people "with Latin, Central or South American origins," or 1.6% of its total population[2]; in the United States, there were over 50 million people "with Hispanic origins" in 2010, accounting for 16.3% of all inhabitants. In other words, the Latino community in Canada is a hundred times smaller in absolute terms, and ten times smaller in relative terms (i.e., proportional to its demographic size) than the Latino community in the United States. Even within the Canadian context, people of Latin American background do not particularly stand out among other minorities: while in the United States Latinos constitute the largest ethnic (non-white) group, Canadians with East and Southeast Asian origins form a group five times larger than Canada's Latino population.[3] Given such disparity, one might certainly wonder about the relevance of focusing on the Latin American community in Canada!

Yet, let us also consider some trends that give a sense of an emergent phenomenon to be reckoned with. If we take the narrowest definition possible and consider a "Latin American" any person born in a Latin American country (that is, first-generation immigrants), we realize that this group represents just about 6% of all immigrants in Canada. However, its growth rate is roughly three times higher than that of the overall immigrant population (32% vs. 10% between 1996 and 2001; 47% vs. 12.7% between 2001 and 2006; 49% vs. 12.9% between 2006 and 2011), due to the increasing share of Latin American newcomers, most of them having arrived from Colombia, Mexico, Peru, and El Salvador during the last decade and a half. Interestingly, Latin Americans represent almost 11% of all immigrants in Québec, proportionally twice the size of this community at the national level. Given such inflow, the Latino population in Canada with respect to national origins reflects a much wider diversity than what we see in the United States, where 63% of Hispanics declare a Mexican origin, 9.3% a Puerto Rican origin, and 3.5% a Cuban origin. In Canada, the three main nationalities—Mexican, Colombian, and Salvadorian—only represent, respectively, 17.8%, 14.2%, and 11.9% of the total Latino population. Let us also consider that seven out of ten Colombians (the predominant origin among first-generation Latino Canadians) immigrated after 2001, making it a markedly "young" community. In a larger timeframe, the growth rate of the Latino population in Canada is even more striking: for example, between 1971 and 2011, the number of individuals with Spanish as their mother tongue swelled more than ten times both in Toronto (7,155 and 75,305 respectively) and in Montreal (8,210 and 82,935). In brief, Latino Canadians are a relatively newly settled, still coalescing group, very diverse in terms of national origins, and rapidly growing, even more so in the French-speaking province of Québec.

Now, if being "Latino" is not simply a remnant of cultural baggage brought from abroad, but a complex, often contested, and ever-evolving outcome in a specific sociopolitical and cultural context, then the "Latino question," when raised in Canada, must certainly be examined in the light of the heritage of immigrants, as well as in terms of the influence of the US Latino reality, while also taking into account the twofold cultural nature of Canada. In brief, a "Latino" individual or group in Canada is to be seen as shaped by his or her culture of origin (as a nationality and as a pan-ethnic Latin American identification), their English Canadian or French Québécois society of adoption, and the wider North American environment in which US Latinos—themselves quite different from non-US Latin Americans—play an increasingly pivotal role. This chapter, even if based on reliable quantitative and qualitative data, only offers a glimpse into the relevance of investigating an aspect that should be obvious to any researcher and, still, does not attract sufficient attention from scholars in the field of immigration and integration studies: how a minority develops is influenced by the larger societal context, which means that US Latinos, English Canadian Latinos, and French Québécois Latinos share common traits—some probably stemming from their Latin American background and others being a North American disaporic construct—but they may also diverge in their values, attitudes, and sense of belonging.

CANADA, THE UNITED STATES, AND LATIN AMERICA

"Canada is an American country." This simple and straightforward statement of fact may actually be met with some confusion. The ambiguity not only stems from the United States' appropriation of the term "America" but also from the equivocal place the northern country occupies—in terms of history, identity, and representation—in the Americas. The plural form of the continent's name generally evokes either a geographical diversity (North, Central, South America; the Caribbean) or a cultural and geopolitical divide. That opposition is what José Enrique Rodó had in mind when he censured the rise of "Nordomanía" among the youth in Latin America at the onset of the twentieth century, and also what José Martí evoked as he famously celebrated "Our America" in his well-known essay.[4] It was the fundamental idea that the hemisphere was split into two essentially diverging worldviews. "Norteamérica"—meaning the United States—was one of them. Still today, in usual parlance (including the media and, often, even diplomatic discourse), Latin Americans call US citizens and residents "Norteamericanos." But what about Canada? Where does it fit? Is it just a blander version of the United States, as the US popular culture usually depicts it, or all but an appendage of the United States, as many Latin Americans perceive it?

In fact, contrary to common belief, Canada is a very particular case, and an extremely complex reality too, especially when we focus on the management of diversity, the dynamics of nation building, and the integration of minorities. On the one hand, despite having kept the Queen of England as formal head of state and maintaining strong links to its British institutional heritage, Canada is a truly American country: like almost all nations in the hemisphere (as opposed to practically all others in the world), *jus solis* (the acquisition of citizenship by virtue of being born in the homeland) has long been a deeply entrenched core of national membership, a juridical expression of the "New World" revolutionary principle that people's destiny is not determined by their parents' station in life. Canada is a so-called settler or frontier society, a "country of immigration," and one that has fully embraced—albeit much later than the rest—a typically American myth of racial harmonious coexistence: Canada's multiculturalism[5]; the US melting pot[6]; Mexico's "cosmic race"[7]; Brazil's "racial democracy"[8]; Argentina's "race crucible."[9]

On the other hand, Canada is very different from the United States and the Latin American countries in some important regards. Let's start with the fact that Canada is a highly decentralized federation with constitutionally enshrined bilingualism and multiculturalism. The link that bonds together the ten provinces is much more tenuous than the one that connects the US states. In recent years, Canada has displayed the second highest per capita immigration rate in the developed world (after Australia). In 2011, Ottawa delivered 280,000 immigration visas, and it has admitted a quarter of a million newcomers each year for the past two decades (proportionally, twice the number of immigrants admitted by the US government). Today, more than 20% of the Canadian population is foreign-born, and it will reach 25% by 2030, compared to 12.5% currently in the United States. Not surprisingly, one of the key features of Canadian society is the colossal challenge that it faces in order to simply hold together such an "improbable country," as the cliché goes.[10]

Furthermore, the province of Québec, with almost one-quarter of Canada's population, has acquired a quasi-state status over the past four decades, becoming a sort of "nation within the nation," formally recognized as such by the federal parliament. The government of that province, supported by a majority of the French Québécois people, imposes restrictions on the choice of language of business and education, openly rejects Canadian-style multiculturalism, and enforces different selection and integration criteria for economic immigrants, based on Québec's particular interests rather than Canada's. In order to grasp the challenge to national unity that this unique situation represents, let's imagine that the two most populous states in the United States (California and Texas) adopted Spanish as the sole official language and banned the use of English in most public signs; that public and subsidized private schools were required to teach only in Spanish (with only a weekly period for English as a second language) unless the students possessed demonstrable inherited rights to an English-language education; and that the state governments picked most of its own immigrants abroad—without any substantial federal interference—deliberately giving priority to Spanish-speaking foreigners! It is actually surprising that internal diversity has not generated any serious social or political rifts in Canada. How such a disjointed, fragmented country can even exist, never mind be an example of interethnic cohabitation where "compared to other countries there appears to be a relatively smooth integration of immigrants into the mainstream," who themselves "have become an integral part of the Canadian community, and their social and cultural contributions are frequently celebrated"?[11]

A historical fact, seemingly removed from current affairs, might prove relevant to today's issues of immigration and integration: aside from a small number of anticolonial (failed) rebellions in the 1830s, Canada did not fight an independence war, or a civil war for that matter. Among all the major countries in the Americas, Canada is alone in lacking a collective memory of founding armed acts of emancipation, revolution, nation building, or territorial conquest. There is no "Canadian Revolution" to speak of, as there is an American Revolution or a Mexican Revolution. It can be argued that is one of the reasons why Canadians do not possess a powerful narrative on the basis of which strong expressions of patriotism could have been built, or even a robust sense of national destiny (as opposed to the overwhelming sense of "manifest destiny" in the United States, or the imaginary of *grandeza nacional* in the larger Latin American countries). This has a clearly beneficial effect: politics as a game of compromise is built-in throughout Canada's institutional design and civic culture. Although some view this as a phenomenal achievement (i.e., a centrist politics of moderation as civic religion), others blame this soft, somewhat relativistic approach for Canada's less assertive, less aspiring national character. This has a direct bearing on the issue of diversity: "culture wars" and social polarization on values are much less prevalent in Canada (than, say, in its southern neighbor), because of its weaker national core, thus opening up space for diversity itself. But it can be argued that it also congeals the widely held idea of Canada as a work in progress, as something to be assembled in the future rather than an essence to be searched in its past. In brief: a collective mindset that naturally encourages the rise of "multiculturalism" and may epitomize what some describe as a very particular sort of "exceptionalism"—one of deep intergroup tolerance.[12]

If we endeavor to understand Canada's place in the Americas, especially in the light of the emblematic North-South, "Anglo-Latino" divide and the current trends toward mutual interpenetration, but also in the context of what could be described as the increasing "Latinization" of the United States, we need to establish what the Pan-American common denominators are—unless we conclude that Canada embodies a fundamentally distinct "Americanity" vis-à-vis the rest of the hemisphere. This is an interesting challenge, as it compels us to reflect on shared values and experiences among different societies, and the fact that inter-American migration and diaspora formation processes may entail certain peculiarities. Many have argued that the construction of racial categories and the dynamic of intergroup relations in Latin America follow very different social and political rules when compared to those prevailing in the United States. US Latinos, and particularly Latin Americans settling in that country, are confronted with the need to negotiate their conception of race and ethnicity.[13] Does Canada's own brand of multiculturalism—much more open to linguistic diversity and sometimes equated with the image of a "cultural mosaic" of coexisting groups—stand even further from Latin America's ethnic order or, conversely, is it closer to the ideal of "racial harmony" that most Latin Americans have embraced through the myths of *mestizaje*?

Or is it Canada's French component that offers Latin Americans a more familiar cultural environment in the "Other America"? Québec is not only distinct from Anglophone North America because of the language spoken by the vast majority of its inhabitants (about 80%) but also on the basis of its politics and public institutions. Unlike the United States and the other Canadian provinces, which all adhere to the British Common Law tradition, Québec's civil law is inspired by the French Napoleonic Code, the same model that most Latin American countries have adopted since their independence. Québec's approach to policy is also closer to Latin America's more state-centered patterns, both in economic matters (with higher levels of government intervention in the markets and in economic development) and social issues (e.g., in the name of the common good, the government may favor collectivist goals over individual choices). Although few people would argue that Québec is part of Latin America, many have stressed the affinities of this former French colony's economic, political, and cultural characteristics with those found in the former Spanish and Portuguese ones. If the Québécois and Latin Americans share some identity traits—and both groups tend to see "Anglos" as "the Other"—could we expect to observe a different sort of "Latino-ness" arise in that North American corner as the result of an encounter between the French and Latino worldviews and heritages?

IMMIGRATION AND DIVERSITY IN CANADA

Canada's immigration policy and multicultural model are often hailed as successful examples to follow. This stands in stark contrast with the idea of a "broken immigration system" in the United States, a trope that highlights the gap between the enduring self-image of a "country of immigration" and present-day policies mostly geared toward law enforcement and border control. But, in spite of its reputation as a very open country, Canada has a dark side to its history with respect to immigration and minorities, and that past helps understand the present. Some events have become symbols of past injustices, and they are commonly addressed in history school textbooks: the shameful "Chinese head tax" established in 1885 with the aim of discouraging immigration from China, the "None is too many" infamous comment by an immigration agent at the end of World War II referring to the government's systematic rejection of Jewish refugees between 1933 and 1948, and the forced relocation of all people of Japanese descent living in Canada to internment camps "as enemy aliens" between 1941 and 1948. While these (and other) well-known examples reveal deep streaks of intolerance among Canadian political leaders at least up to the mid-twentieth century, prejudiced attitudes toward certain minorities pervaded as well the general population, both of British and French origin. Many Canadians still remember the "Jewish quotas" at Montreal's English-language McGill University from the 1920s to the 1960s (similar to those at Harvard and other Ivy League schools in the United States during that period). Although this reflected a more elitist practice of discrimination in British Canadian society (not only against Jews, but to most other groups too, including the Irish and the French Canadians), some forms of populist, street-level prejudice took grasp in Québec; for example, in 1938, an astounding 128,000 citizens in that province signed a petition demanding a stop to "all immigration and specially Jewish immigration."

Religious and language tensions obviously played a role in shaping people's attitudes and government's policy measures (i.e., French Canadians perceived foreigners and non-Catholics as a threat to their cultural survival), as well as the fact that Canada was still a "Dominion" in the British Empire (i.e., subject to London's geopolitical goals and needs, and dominated by a defensive mindset vis-à-vis the United States). These are all rather well-known historical facts. What is less known (even by many Canadians), however, is that the legislative framework itself was, for many years, clearly and effectively discriminatory, even explicitly racist. In other words, Canada's intolerant approach to diversity for almost the entire first century of its existence was not limited to the behavior of an anxious populace, certain high-class institutions, and some narrow-minded officials, but was rather a sanctioned and deliberate state policy, implemented and upheld by the judiciary and the public service. Of course, we cannot ignore, in such context, the colonial nature of Canada, and the continued mistreatment and dispossession of the native population. The Indian Act of 1876 was the main legal instrument of segregation and exploitation until the 1960s—a law in which "race and gender were two powerful ideologies that legitimized government policy" toward the indigenous people, making them "non-citizens, wards of the state."[14]

Canada's first immigration law, adopted only two years after the Confederation (the birth of the country in 1867), established—at least formally—a very accessible immigration policy, something that was usual practice among other settler or "frontier" societies (such as Argentina and Australia) eager to have their vast territories occupied and developed. But this initial unrestrictive approach to immigration was indeed deceptive, in that not all groups were equally welcome. Argentina, very akin to Canada at that time, is a quite telling case (and typically duplicitous) in this respect: its very liberal nineteenth-century Constitution invited "all men in the world who wish to reside on Argentinean soil" in its lofty Preamble, but then specified in the First Part that "the federal government will foment European immigration." Canada's similar preference for certain ethnic groups would be rendered explicit when, in 1919, the Immigration Act was amended. Until then, the capacity to pronounce an "absolute prohibition of any class of immigrants" whenever the government "considers it necessary or expedient" (Article 30, 1906) granted the executive branch discretionary powers for precluding specific groups—though not named in the law—from coming to Canada (due notice was to be given to the transportation companies, a proviso that implies a practice of profiling and rejecting banned categories at the port of embarkation). No judiciary overview could interfere with the Ministry of

Immigration's decision and, in 1910, a further restriction was included in the law, stating that immigrants deemed to be "unsuited to the climate requirements" (which can be interpreted as a coded reference to non-Nordic peoples) could be denied entry or be deported. In 1919, the racialized approach to immigration became entirely evident through an amendment that gave the government the authority to "prohibit or limit the number . . . of immigrants belonging to any nationality or race . . . or because such immigrants are deemed undesirable owing to their peculiar customs, habits, modes of life, and methods of holding property." Under this provision, ethnic origin and cultural traits (e.g., religion) could be invoked as reasons for "undesirability." But the same article (13, paragraph c) went even further: immigrants could be banned from Canada "because of their probable inability to become readily assimilated." In other words, any group could be preemptively declared "inassimilable." In 1952, the Immigration Act was overhauled and all mentions of race and ethnicity were removed (while political restrictions were added, particularly concerning "subversive activities"). However, the new law conferred even more discretionary and procedural powers to the Ministry, while doing nothing to remove the restrictions already embedded in the immigration system and its administrative practices. For another decade, race and ethnicity would remain a cornerstone for immigrant selection in Canada.

Finally, new regulations adopted in 1962 eliminated all forms of racial discrimination in the selection process (in line with a Bill of Rights adopted by the federal government in 1960), and the entire policy approach to immigration was now to be geared toward meeting the needs of Canada's economic development (and, at the same time, in line with such a "modernizing" view, the federal government proposed the assimilation of Aboriginals into mainstream society). In 1967, the notorious "point system" (still in use) was established: any person in the world, regardless of race, ethnicity, or nationality, could apply. A score is calculated by adding points gained on the basis of education, training, employment opportunities, languages skills, and so on, and if the total tally is high enough, admission as a permanent resident is granted. It goes without saying that this was a momentous shift, and immigration rates soared, with a marked reversal in the origins of newcomers, now mostly coming from Asia, Africa, and Latin America. Since then, the Canadian immigration system has been lauded as one of the most generous and fair-minded in the world, and many have proposed that it should be adopted in other countries.[15] But, even if Australia and New Zealand have followed a similar path (albeit not identical, as important differences remain), Canada still stands out as a particular case. It may argued that some structural factors—many of them the result of chance rather than will—play a major role in Canada's exceptional approach to immigration: notably, geography, demography, and political history.

Of course, each country is unique in its institutional and sociological makeup, evolution, and public culture. Although similar in many respects, Canada is very different from the United States on several crucial aspects.

I referred to history in the previous section. Let's now consider geography: Canada is a vast territory with a relatively scarce population, most of it concentrated in the south, stretched from ocean to ocean within a hundred kilometers from its only international border. The United States, while attracting millions of Latin American immigrants, shields Canada from any mass population movement, a reality that allows Canada to exert maximum control on who enters the country. This location advantage translates into the ability to develop a rational, highly selective, planned immigration policy, particularly for a country where the legacy of slavery (or colonial rule) has not left insurmountable racial injustices, as is the case in the United States (and, to a certain extent, in former European imperial powers). Ironically, the dark past of restrictive—and often racially motivated—immigration laws that prevailed in Canada until the 1960s contributed to weaken racial tensions within the country (ensuring the European-descent population kept an unchallenged demographic majority), a context that allowed Canadians to react favorably to a groundbreaking immigration policy that was framed as a vital lever of economic development. Almost 50 years later, Canada remains an outlier, as a country "where one in five persons is an immigrant, and several of the largest cities can claim that half of the population was born abroad, [and] public opinion about immigration is largely positive."[16]

In such context, where Latin American immigrants only started to arrive in significant numbers mostly as designated workers or as political refugees (under special programs; e.g., Chileans in the 1970s and Salvadorians in the 1980s), it is not surprising that three out of four Canadians (74%) hold today a positive perception of Latinos in their country (while, interestingly, Canadians appear to be less sympathetic toward Aboriginals and Muslims: 61% and 43% respectively), and Anglophones and Francophones evenly share this favorable opinion of Latinos.[17] It is also worth reminding that, unlike the United States, Canada does not have a conflictive past with Latin America, and this is reflected in the relative indifference of Canadians toward that region, as shown by an opinion poll[18]: for example, Mexico, a NAFTA partner, was considered "vitally important" to Canada's national interests by only 16% of Canadians, while 78% viewed Great Britain and 63% viewed France as "vitally important" to Canada. In brief, Latin Americans seem to represent the emblematic "distant cousin": vaguely familiar, nonthreatening, but not actively engaged. It could be argued that this situation gives Latinos in Canada, compared to those in the United States (and to a certain degree to, say, Spain), more freedom to define themselves as a group—no collective labels are immediately assigned to them, no historically rooted boundaries force them to assume a given racial identity. This is not to say, of course, that the Canadian context is ideal or that no prejudices exist. Nevertheless, it is reasonable to expect that a different type of "Latino-ness" will eventually materialize in Canada, not isolated from the rest of the continent, but probably with a few distinctive traits— and all the more so in Québec.

Canada's kind of diversity—that is, defined, as we have seen, by a complex set of factors such as a weaker national core and significant provincial autonomy, a bicultural and bilingual character grounded on political and territorial configurations, a substantially recent (in historical terms) and increasingly heterogeneous population with no deep-seated racial or ethnic categories—naturally tends to foster both intracommunity and intercommunity ties. Yet it also may generate some tensions between the societal push toward integration into mainstream culture and the pull from ancestral identities and heritages. In such context, Latino Canadians, who generally lack a strong sense of collective self (as a distinct minority among other groups) and are internally fragmented (by national origins, socioeconomic background, ethnicity), as well as spatially dispersed, tend to reject homogenizing labels while, at the same time, face the challenge of constructing a community through a "process of negotiating intra-group differences and building a common voice in the struggle for equal participation".[19] That is why, when they describe Toronto's Latin American "organizational landscape," Landolt, Goldring, and Bernhard observe "a layered character," where "different political, cultural, social, and economic agendas and modes of organizing coexist and at times compete for public recognition and resources."[20] Though clearly underrepresented in political spheres (less so at the municipal level) and less "visible" in the media and public arena than other groups in Canada, there exists "relatively consolidated Latin American grass-roots networks."[21]

Québec's government is, by far, the main provider and source of funding in settlement services to immigrants in that province. This reality creates many opportunities for grassroots networks and organizations, but access to resources may require the acceptance of specific views regarding ethnicity and language. In Montreal, among several of its kind, CAFLA (Help Center for Latin American Families), a mostly volunteer-based organization that receives funding from government agencies, offers free support to immigrants' integration needs, particularly in high school settings, as well as psychological and law counseling services. Other community organizations also cater mainly to the Latin American population, but during the last decade, they have diversified their clientele (and sometimes even changed their name), in part because of Québec's "intercultural" turn, which strongly encourages multiethnic endeavors instead of single-community initiatives. For example, the Latin American and Multi-Ethnic Association of Côte-des-Neiges focuses on settlement programs (including help with job-seeking) for recent immigrants, and it also receives subsidies from the provincial government, which is conditional on the association's embracing of Québec's intercultural approach and, of course, on their fostering of the adoption of French among newcomers. Even many minority-based undertakings in the private sector not directly related to immigration issues (e.g., business, art, education) turn to the provincial government for support through its numerous programs (run from various ministries and agencies), a situation that can only foster competition and fragmentation within a given community.

In Toronto, the nongovernmental organization sector is quite larger and much more independent from government funding, and a single-community approach is more prevalent, as opposed to what happens in Québec, given English Canada's multicultural framework. This also affects how minorities organize and represent themselves. While describing the Latin American case, Landolt and Goldrin argue that "the ethnicizing imperative of the state frames out-group and in-group negotiations around political identities and organizational agendas."[22] Thus, many conventional (pan-ethnic or nationality-based) groups emerged over the past two decades, mostly geared toward immigrants' needs and issues. Still, alternative organizations were also created, such as the Latin American Women Collective, which "developed a multi-layered feminist critique of male-dominated country-of origin organizations."[23] However, such networks, even if quite established in Toronto (and Montreal), do not converge in any large-scale communal structure, despite some efforts that have been made in that direction in both cities. Given the language divide, no truly pan-Canadian umbrella organization has ever been founded or even given serious consideration (the Canadian Hispanic Congress purports "to represent Hispanic Canadians" but, in practice, it has no reach or recognition outside Ontario). Ironically, the fact that Latin Americans are not, as a population, a significant target of discriminatory or stigmatizing practices and discourse in Canada—combined with the relative absence of collective memories as an excluded or dispossessed minority—may contribute to a lesser sense of urgency to mobilize themselves as a unified group.

LATINO CANADIANS

Latin Americans in Canada—undeniably a "younger," much smaller and, on all accounts, a far less salient group than the US Latinos—are anything but homogeneous. They have settled over several decades, not gradually but rather through so-called waves.[24] Between the 1970s and the 1990s, most immigrants from Latin America came to Canada for political reasons (i.e., fleeing military dictatorships in South America and civil wars in Central America). However, since the 1990s, and even more clearly during the following decades, most Latin Americans in Canada have been admitted under the "economic category": 70% in 2012.[25] This means, in general (in terms of *majority* and *average*, but certainly not as a constant reality for the whole group), that they have been granted permanent residency on account of their prospective "employability" as "skilled workers" in Canada, a condition evaluated on the basis of their level of education, demonstrable work experience in "eligible occupations," and sufficient knowledge of official languages, among other factors. Although no information exists about these immigrants' socioeconomic status in their country of origin, it is safe to assume, given the class structure and ethnic stratification present, with varying degrees, in all Latin American countries, that they tend to be of middle class, urban extraction, and possibly of nonindigenous or non-African descent (as opposed to a rural, mestizo, indigenous, or black background).[26] This fact unquestionably marks a key contrast with the situation of many Latinos in the United States.

However, Latino Canadians' more middle-class origin does not necessarily translate into a higher socioeconomic status in the host society: Latin Americans show a higher prevalence of low income than other immigrant groups (except black and Arab Canadians) and, interestingly, this gap is much wider in Québec. As a minority group, Canadian Latinos show one of the lowest average employment incomes: $26,241 (Canadian dollars, 2006), compared to $28,231 among black Canadians, $29,441 among Arab Canadians, and $31,102 among South Asian Canadians. However, unemployment rates are lower among Latin Americans (9%) than among blacks (10.6%) and Arabs (13%), a fact that seems to confirm qualitative evidence suggesting that Latin Americans in Canada may be more prone to accept lower wage (and sometimes undeclared) jobs.[27] This pattern also appears among highly educated Latin Americans (with university diploma): their average income is $42,636 ($32,836 in Québec), while the average income for all minority workers with university diploma is $47,113 ($39,582 in Québec).

But does this statistical picture accurately depict the experience of Latinos in Canada? Indeed, Latino Canadians' understanding of their own condition will be affected not only by their nationality but also by their socioeconomic and ethnic background (including their self-perception within the class system in their country of origin), their legal and symbolic standing in the new country (as permanent residents, chosen through a point-system meritocratic scale), and, last not least, by the model of integration in place in the host society. A survey on identification and sense of belonging showed that Latin Americans in Canada tend to define themselves less by their religion and more by their province and city of residence, and by their ethnic origin and language than other immigrants (for example, 12% of Latin Americans said that their province of residence was "most important to how they define themselves," compared to only 6% among other immigrants; language was "most important" to 15.5% of Latin Americans, compared to 7.6% of other immigrants).[28] Also, results revealed that Latin American immigrants are prone to define themselves less by their Canadian identity and more by their country of origin than other immigrants. Interestingly, immigrants born in Latin America express lower feelings of attachment to Canada, with even lower scores when they reside in Québec (where attachment to Canada among the native-born population is already significantly lower). Overall, the survey suggests that Latin Americans in Canada give priority to their origins (nationality, language) and to more localized identities in the host country (cities, provinces) and display less fervor toward their new homeland. One possible explanation for this disposition is that, having settled in Canada as sought-after, individually prescreened skilled workers, many Latinos understand their integration in terms of a pragmatic arrangement—and their economic situation often does not match their skills and aspirations, leading to disappointment with the "Canadian dream."

But, as we already asked, should we even talk about "Latinos" in Canada, if they do not (yet) constitute a community, a fully formed minority with a shared history and identity? And aren't we comparing "apples and oranges," as Blomenraad puts it regarding the seemingly hopeless project of linking the Latino populations on both sides of the border?[29] Given the hotly debated issue of how to count Hispanics/Latinos in the United States and, more controversially yet, how to define their ethnic or racial status and distinctiveness, we need to examine the definitions and methods that are available in the Canadian context. Statistics Canada uses two different questions to establish ethnic or racial background: the first is "What were the ethnic or cultural origins of this person's ancestors?" and allows the respondent to write one or several answers (with no proposed categories, but only some quoted examples such as "Canadian," "English," "French," "Chinese," "Italian"); the second aims at collecting information "to support programs that promote equal opportunity" and offers the following options (in this order): "White," "Chinese," "South Asian," "Black," "Filipino," "Latin American," "Southeast Asian," "West Asian," "Korean," "Japanese," and "Other." These groups (except the first, "White") are defined by the federal government as "visible minorities."[30] Both questions allow for multiple responses and are based on self-identification. The number of Latin Americans can thus be established through the declaration of ancestry, by aggregating all the answers that refer to Latin American nationalities (Mexican, etc.), ethnicities (Mayan), and pan-ethnic categories (Latin American, Hispanic, etc.), or through self-definition as "Latin American" in a question that focuses on vulnerability to discrimination (implicitly referring to race, although the word is not used). Unsurprisingly, as is the case in the United States with the ambiguity between ethnicity and "race," answers are not always consistent: more people declare Latin American ancestry than a Latin American identity in the sense of membership in a racialized minority. But the aggregation made by Statistics Canada is also problematic, as Central and South American origins are lumped together, while excluding the Caribbean. Therefore, Cubans and Dominican, while Spanish-speaking and culturally Latin American, are excluded from the Latin American ancestry definition, whereas people from Belize and Guyana are included. Two other approaches can also be used in order to count Latin Americans in Canada: place of birth and mother tongue.

Data from the 2006 census show that two-thirds of individuals who indicated a Latin American ethnic origin (in the question about ancestry) also identified themselves as members of the Latin American community (in the question about "visible minorities").[31] The other third was distributed as follows (under categories defined by Statistics Canada): 29% "not a visible minority," 2% "black," 1% "Aboriginal," and 2% "multiple visible minority." But these proportions vary quite widely when national origins are taken into account. Immigrants who declared a Central American national origin (Salvadorians, Nicaraguans, Guatemalans, Hondurans) are more prone to see themselves as members of the Latin American minority (80% or more), and those from the Southern Cone (Paraguayans, Brazilians, Argentinians, Uruguayans) generally do not identify themselves as such (43% or less). Venezuelans and Mexican are somewhat in the middle (51% to 53%). Another difference emerges from the comparison between first-generation Latin Americans (foreign-born) and their offspring (the so-called second generation): while 83% of Latin American immigrants declare themselves minority members, only 56% of second-generation Latin Americans identify as such. It goes without saying that these results are impossible to compare to data from the United States. The concepts and social representation (of "race," "Latino," etc.) are extremely different, as are the policy and methodological approaches to ethnic diversity deployed by government agencies in either country. But maybe that is precisely the point: one could argue that the two realities are so far apart that no parallels can be reasonably ascertained regarding the Latino population in Canada and the United States. In this sense, the contrast may still be useful as a way of exploring the diverging forms of "Latino-ness" developing in the North American context. However, it is also possible to speculate that the Latino reality in the United States is so massively important—and becoming more so in the near future—that Canadian Latinos will eventually gravitate towards the US model of pan-ethnicity. If Anglo-American multiculturalism and even the racial-relations perspective gains ground in English-speaking Canada, what will happen with Québec's Latinos? Will they follow the continental trend, will they assimilate into the *Québécois* society, or will they create a different mode of diasporic identity?

LATINOS IN FRENCH QUÉBEC

Despite globalization, and confronted by powerful trends toward economic integration and the "Americanization" of almost every aspect of their social life, Canadians appear to hold to some distinct values (although this may well change in the future). In contrast with their US neighbors, they have somewhat different attitudes toward violence, material possession, religious authority, and government services, among other things.[32] Obviously, any generalization about a national "ideology" must be met with a good dose of skepticism, but it is still possible to talk about tendencies, particularly when they reflect a worldview that informs the institutional organization of a given country. In this sense, fundamental views about the individual's rights and responsibilities, for example, are reflected in the judicial and political systems (as is the case when Canada and the United States are compared on issues such as mandatory sentencing or electoral funding). But Québec is, in turn, rather different from the rest of Canada and, in some ways, stands even further from the United States. Civic values held by the Québécois, and particularly among Francophones, are more in line with those that are prevalent in Northern European countries when individual moral choices are at stake (e.g., more tolerance about drug use, premarital or extramarital sex, prostitution, euthanasia), but they also display some intriguing similarities with Latin America: less conformity to formal rules, a more substantive conception of equality, a weaker belief in the market's fairness.[33] These positions are associated with a more left-of-center political perspective or, at the very least, with a more government-driven notion of social progress. Not surprisingly, many in Québec openly show sympathy toward Latin American revolutionary leaders and movements (Che Guevara's iconic image is often used in student demonstrations) and tend to embrace anti-US views in foreign affairs.

Could language proximity play a role in those cultural and political affinities? Survey data on Latin Americans in Canada show that the relative weight of those who declare Spanish as their mother tongue is affected by the place of residence: almost a third (32.1%) of Canadians who have Spanish as their "first language learned at home in childhood and still understood by the individual" (as defined by Statistics Canada) live in Québec, but the proportion of immigrants born in Latin America in that province is 28.5% (if we exclude Portuguese-speaking Brazilians). The 5-percentage point gap could be evidence of a higher rate of first language retention of Spanish among Latin Americans in Québec.[34] The French-speaking Québécois show, on their part, a predilection for Spanish when they chose to learn a second language.[35] On the other hand, an intriguing phenomenon transpires when we take into account the self-perception of Latin Americans in Québec as members of a "visible minority": immigrants who were born in a Latin American country and live in Québec represent 27.8% of the total Latin American immigrant population nationwide, but they account for 30.8% of all first-generation "ethnic" Latin Americans in the country, as measured by Statistics Canada. This 3-percentage point difference may point to a stronger sense of belonging to a "minority" within the French-language province. In other words, the sense of community is affected by the way in which the host society conceives in-group and out-group relations. Cultural and language proximity does not necessarily translate into an erasure of intergroup boundaries.

Data drawn from focus groups show that Latin American immigrants in Québec are generally aware of the idea of a "cultural affinity" between them and the Francophone society. Sometimes they see it as real (e.g., language proximity, Catholic background, etc.), and sometimes they discard it as a myth (the Québécois would be as "cold," "superficial," "materialistic," and "individualistic" as other North Americans, as opposed to Latin Americans). Ironically, when Québec is considered as culturally and politically close to Latin America, some Latin American immigrants express a preference for the "Anglo" world, because of its more dynamic economy, broader individual freedoms, and pragmatic outlook (while Québec would be more like Latin America: corrupt, bureaucracy laden, ideologically driven, etc.). In their view, "Anglos" would be more open to "Others" than "Francos" and would offer more opportunities to minorities and immigrants. Latin Americans are also keen on noticing that community "ghettos"— that is, too much "multiculturalism"—are not socially acceptable in Québec, and integration (including language learning) is considered a civic duty. The reality of trilingualism (Spanish as mother tongue, plus English and French as both necessary for employment) is sometimes seen as a burden, but many consider it an advantage, particularly for their children. But, even if they criticize Québec's shortcomings, Latin Americans still see value in their cultural affinity with the Québécois: the French-language population usually holds "positive stereotypes" about Latinos, whom they recognize as reliable, hard-working, law-abiding citizens (especially when compared to other groups, less favorably perceived).

Many studies on Latino values and identity in the United States implicitly convey the notion that a set of cultural orientations is "imported" by immigrants and their descendants, and that those orientations may persist or weaken from one generation to the next. Sometimes the representation of a cultural dichotomy or even a contradiction—along the lines of the two opposing Americas—surfaces indirectly in their appreciation of the integration process of Latino in the United States. This does not mean that their authors are oblivious to the fact that the very idea of a common, well-defined, and stable "Latin American culture" is highly debatable. Some of them take into consideration the contrasts between the various Latino communities (Mexican Americans, Cuban Americans, Porto Ricans, Chicanos, etc.), as their respective demographic and socioeconomic configuration, even their identity and history, is different.[36] Several scholars develop comparative studies between US Latinos and other minorities (particularly African Americans and Asians), and some examine the Latino population through the prism of the racial structure and dynamic that underlies their society. A few even explore the reciprocal effect of acculturation: the "Latinization" of US mainstream culture.[37] Thus, they will focus, for example, on differences between "White" and "non-White" Latinos, or even on the correlation of skin tone among Hispanics and the level of discrimination they experience.[38] Although it seems obviously futile to attempt to fully grasp the Latino cultural identity because of its extraordinary heterogeneity and its multilayered evolution as a component of a host society, the challenge of pinpointing its core value orientations may be worth the effort, as long as this pursuit is framed by the assumption that any element of a "Latino identity" is the negotiated or imposed result of an encounter between different cultural outlooks.

In conclusion, if a North American perspective needs to take into account a two-country reality, it can be argued that, in fact, there are not two, but three host societies to consider: Québec, a highly autonomous political jurisdiction that selects most of its immigrants and develops its own integration policies, offers newcomers and ethnic groups a very different cultural and institutional environment. Canada is bilingual at the federal level (English and French have a formally equal status), and eight out of ten provinces, as well as the three territories, are overwhelmingly English-speaking (New Brunswick is officially bilingual), while, in Québec, French is the only official language, and its public use is widely considered a core civic value and, in some circumstances, an enforced legal obligation (even to the extent of overriding certain constitutionally protected individual freedoms).[39] Canada has a national multicultural policy in effect since the 1970s, while Québec has established an official "intercultural" policy (closer to assimilationist/secularist European models), linked to a more collectivist, state-centered public culture. Canada has a federal immigration policy based on a points system open to all applicants with an emphasis on economic factors, while Québec handles the selection of its own "skilled workers"

(70% of all immigrants) with a similar system but with different weighing given to language skills (giving preference to the French language) and other priorities (such as the provincial labour market needs). Overall in Canada, the top country sources of immigration in 2012 were China, the Philippines, India, Pakistan, and the United States, while in Québec the top sources were China, France, Haiti, Algeria, and Morocco. Naturally, given these national origins, the largest minorities in English Canada are South Asian and Chinese, whereas in Québec the largest are black, Arab, and *Latin American*. The most spoken nonofficial languages in English Canada are Cantonese, Punjabi, and Mandarin, while in Québec the most spoken nonofficial languages are Arabic and *Spanish*. In short, on the basis of current immigration trends, even putting aside language and institutional differences, Québec's very social fabric sets this province apart from all others, and Latinos may well play a significant role in its future evolution.

BEYOND THE NORTH-SOUTH, ANGLO-LATINO DIVIDE

In this chapter, I argued that Canadians of Latin American heritage constitute a fascinating case of how ethnocultural minorities are shaped in interaction with particular national majorities. In Canada, given the dual character of the country, shared heritages among immigrants evolve differently in the context of dissimilar institutional and linguistic configurations. As a highly decentralized state with a "soft" patriotic core—effectively challenged by competing national narratives—and capable of sustaining mass immigration while upholding social cohesion, Canada stands out as constitutionally prone to multiculturalist ideas. This reality, which I described as a particularly fertile "space for diversity," offers Latin Americans the chance to reinvent themselves as a multilayered diaspora, and to escape—at least to some extent—preset labels and identities (including those imported from other countries). Indeed, this rather "young" population does not directly fit in any historically defined or institutionally assigned view of their "right" or "due" place within Canada, and its internal diversity, relative lack of a collective self, and comparatively low level of "visibility," as well as its small demographic size, create many opportunities as to the ways in which Canadian "Latino-ness" may arise. Because of the bilingual split, it is already clear that the Latin American heritage, lived either in English or in French, will take, not one, but two profoundly dissimilar cultural profiles in Canada. But many questions remain unanswered, particularly regarding the influence of the growing US Latino communities: Will diasporas in Canada veer toward them, eventually joining their organizational structures and adopting their modes of self-representation? Or, conversely, will they continue on their current integration path into the Canadian bilingual and multicultural fabric, that is, in ways that reflect a dynamic of diaspora formation that is not subject to a single hegemonic cultural framework? If so, will that lead to the emergence of a pan-ethnic Latin American sense of community in Canada, distinct from what exists in Latin America and in the United States, or will internal heterogeneity foster fragmentation and, in the end, assimilation?

NOTES

1. The Supreme Court of Canada interprets the constitutional provisions about Aboriginal self-determination with a focus on cultural rights; Martin Papillon, "Framing Self-Determination: The Politics of Indigenous Rights in Canada and the United States," in *Comparing Canada: Methods and Perspectives on Canadian Politics*, ed. Luc Turgeon, Martin Papillon, Jennifer Wallner, and Stephen White (Vancouver: UBC Press, 2014).

2. Unless otherwise noted, all figures about Canada are based on data drawn from the 2011 census.

3. It goes without saying that the politics of labeling, not to mention the sociological and methodological issues raised by any attempt to grasp a population's identity, complicates further the task of comparing the two realities. I will address this problem later in the chapter. In general, I will refer to "Latinos" for convenience purposes only (and I will sometimes use the term "Hispanics" for the US context, and the term "Latin Americans" for Canada, keeping with common practice in each country). In Canada's' English-language settings, the use of "Latino" by people of Latin American heritage appears in entities such as the Latino Canadian Chamber of Commerce (which hosts an annual "Latino Awards Gala") and in several local networks (for example, the Latino-Canadian Association of Northern BC, Latino-London, and the New Brunswick Latino Association). Some grassroots initiatives also include the label: Immediate Latino Care Centre (in Ottawa) and Latinos Positivos (a support group for HIV-positive people in Toronto). However, the term is not as predominant as in the United States. Also, in French-language contexts, the more usual designation is *Latino-américain* (as in *Chambre de commerce latino-américaine du Québec*).

4. José Enrique Rodó, *Ariel* (Valencia: Prometeo, 1900); José Martí, *Nuestra América* (Caracas: Fundación Biblioteca Ayacucho, 1977).

5. Neil Bissoondath, *Selling Illusions. The Cult of Multiculturalism in Canada* (Toronto: Penguin, 1994).

6. David Michael Smith, "The American Melting Pot: A National Myth in Public and Popular Discourse," *National Identities* 14, no. 4 (2012): 387–402.

7. José Vasconcelos, *The Cosmic Race / La Raza Cósmica* (Baltimore: JHU Press, 1979).

8. Petrônio Domingues, "O mito da democracia racial e a mestiçagem no Brasil (1889–1930)," *Diálogos Latinoamericanos* 10 (2005): 116–131.

9. Graciela Liliana Ferrás, "Ricardo Rojas: inmigración y nación en la Argentina del Centenario," *Memoria & Sociedad* 2, no. 22 (2007): 5–18.

10. For example, Thomas Walkom, a *Toronto Star* columnist, recently wrote: "It's been 141 years since this improbable country was created from a collection of disparate British colonies, with little linking them other than the fact they were not the United States. And yet we persist." (May 24, 2014).

11. Jeffery G. Reitz, "Multiculturalism Policies and Popular Multiculturalism in the Development of Canadian Immigration," in *The Multiculturalism Question. Debating Identity in 21st Century Canada*, ed. Jedwab, Jack (Montreal, McGill-Queen's University Press, 2014), 78.

12. Abdolmohammad Kazemipur, *The Muslim Question in Canada. A Story of Segmented Integration* (Vancouver: University of British Columbia Press, 2014).

13. T. E. Fuller-Rowell, A. D. Ong, and J. S. Phinney, "National Identity and Perceived Discrimination Predict Changes in Ethnic Identity Commitment: Evidence from a Longitudinal Study of Latino College Students," *Applied Psychology* 62 (2013): 406–426.

14. Carrie Bourassa, "Colonization, Racism and the Health of Indian People," *Prairie Forum* 29, no. 2 (2004): 207–224.
15. The Canadian-style point system was seriously considered by the US Congress in 2007, even if the whole immigration law reform was eventually rejected. The point system was mainly criticized (including by then Senator Obama) because it would seemingly favor higher skilled, better educated applicants, shifting the focus away from reuniting families, the main thrust of legal immigration in that country. This criticism is understandable, given the reality of millions of undocumented immigrants and the fact that many Latinos from underprivileged backgrounds would not attain the score required in order to be admitted into the United States.
16. Delancey Gustin and Astrid Ziebarth, "Transatlantic Opinion on Immigration: Greater Worries and Outlier Optimism," *International Migration Review* 44 (2010): 974–991.
17. These data are drawn from an online survey conducted by Léger Marketing in all regions of Canada with a representative sample of 2,345 Canadians, between September 20 and October 3, 2011.
18. Jack Jedwab and Victor Armony, "Hola Canadá. Spanish Is Third Most Spoken Language," *FOCAL Point* 8, no. 4 (2009).
19. Luisa Veronis, "Immigrant Participation in the Transnational Era: Latin Americans' Experiences with Collective Organising in Toronto." *International Migration and Integration* 11 (2010), 173.
20. Patricia Landolt, L. Goldring, and J. Bernhard, "Agenda Setting and Immigrant Politics: The Case of Latin Americans in Toronto," *American Behavioral Scientist* 55 (2011): 100.
21. Jorge Ginieniewicz, "Latin American Canadians Rethink Their Political Spaces: Grass-Roots or Electoral Participation?" *Political Studies* 58 (2010): 497–515.
22. Patricia Landolt and L. Goldring, "Immigrant Political Socialization as Bridging and Boundary Work: Mapping the Multi-Layered Incorporation of Latin American Immigrants in Toronto," *Ethnic and Racial Studies* 32 (2009): 1226–1247.
23. Landolt and Goldring, "Immigrant Political Socialization as Bridging and Boundary Work: Mapping the Multi-Layered Incorporation of Latin American Immigrants in Toronto."
24. Landolt and Goldring, "Immigrant Political Socialization as Bridging and Boundary Work: Mapping the Multi-Layered Incorporation of Latin American Immigrants in Toronto."
25. This does not mean that political asylum is no longer a relevant factor in current immigration trends from Latin America. Colombia stands out in that regard, with 4 in 10 immigrants from that country arriving under the "protected persons" category (2011).
26. Erin O'Connor, *Gender, Indian, Nation. The Contradictions of Making Ecuador, 1830–1925* (Tucson: University of Arizona Press, 2007).
27. That evidence was collected through several focus groups conducted in the context of a research project carried out by Sébastien Arcand, Victor Armony, and Pierre-Jean Darres in collaboration with Québec's Latin American Chamber of Commerce in 2013–2014.
28. This survey was carried out by Léger Marketing via web panel as part of a larger poll of 2,000 Canadians conducted in February–March 2013. It included an oversample (N = 193) of Latin American immigrants and allowed for comparisons between Latinos and non-Latinos, as well as between immigrants in Québec and in the rest of Canada.

29. Irene Bloemraad, "'Two Peas in a Pod', 'Apples and Oranges', and Other Food Meta-
    phors: Comparing Canada and the United States," *American Behavioral Scientist* 55
    (2011): 1131.

30. Question 17 (in the long-form questionnaire) asks: "What were the ethnic or cultural
    origins of this person's ancestors?" and includes a note stating that "an ancestor is
    usually more distant than a grandparent.." Question 19 (also in the long form) asks:
    "Is this person?" and explains that "This information is collected to support programs
    that promote equal opportunity for everyone to share in the social, cultural and eco-
    nomic life in Canada.." The categories are those of the recognized "visible minorities"
    ("persons who are non-Caucasian in race or non-white in color and who do not report
    being Aboriginal"), according to Canada's Employment Equity Act of 1986.

31. This cross-tabulation is not available for the 2011 census data. Statistics Canada uses
    the following criteria for "Latin American": "This category includes: persons who gave
    a mark-in response of 'Latin American' only; persons who gave a mark-in response of
    'Latin American' only with a non-European write-in that is not classified as visible
    minority, n.i.e. (e.g., Afghan, Cambodian, Nigerian); and persons with no mark-in
    response who gave a write-in response that is classified as Latin American. Some exam-
    ples of write-in responses classified as 'Latin American' include Chilean, Costa Rican,
    and Mexican." (http://www.statcan.gc.ca/concepts/definitions/minority01-minorite01a
    -eng.htm)

32. Michael Adams, *Fire and Ice: United States, Canada and the Myth of Converging
    Values* (Toronto: Penguin Canada, 2003).

33. Victor Armony, "Des Latins du Nord? L'identité culturelle québécoise dans le con-
    texte panaméricain," *Recherches sociographiques* 43, no. 1 (2002): 19–48.

34. This is consistent with findings in Jack Jedwab and Victor Armony, "Hola Canadá.
    Spanish is Third Most Spoken Language," *FOCAL Point* 8, no. 4 (2009): 10, regarding
    a higher rate of language retention among young Montrealers whose mother tongue
    is Spanish (and a higher prevalence of trilingualism) when compared to those living
    in Toronto.

35. Jack Jedwab and Victor Armony, "Hola Canadá. Spanish is Third Most Spoken Lan-
    guage," *FOCAL Point* 8, no. 4 (2009): 10.

36. Eileen Diaz McConnell and Edward A. Delgado-Romero, *Sociological Focus* 37, no. 4
    (2004): 297–312.

37. Frank Bonilla, Edwin Meléndez, Rebecca Morales, and María de los Angeles Torres,
    eds., *Borderless Borders. U.S. Latinos, Latin Americans, and the Paradox of Interde-
    pendence* (Philadelphia: Temple University Press, 2000).

38. "Research provides evidence of significant socioeconomic inequalities between light
    and dark Latinos within the same ethnic groups that cannot be explained by differ-
    ences in human capital or resources." Wendy D. Roth, "Racial Mismatch: The Diver-
    gence Between Form and Function in Data for Monitoring Racial Discrimination of
    Hispanics," *Social Science Quarterly* 91, no. 5 (2010): 1289–1311.

39. The most notorious example is Québec's Charter of the French language, adopted in
    1977. Some of its provisions regarding the ban on English and other languages in
    commercial signing were deemed unconstitutional by the Supreme Court of Canada,
    but they were maintained when the Québec government invoked the "notwithstand-
    ing clause" that allows provinces to override some fundamental rights (such as free-
    dom of expression).

CHAPTER 10

"Latinos" in Exile

Latin American Political Diasporas and Their National and Transnational Struggle

LUIS RONIGER

Exile has played a vital part in shaping the forms and styles of Latin American politics and in making Latino diasporas a global phenomenon. This chapter is part of a broader research program pointing out that the recurrent use of territorial banishment reflects on the exclusionary nature of the nation-states in the region, and that exiles have been a major transnational bridge re-creating time and again visions of collective identity while triggering institutional changes in the region.[1] Following developments in history, sociology, anthropology, and political science that highlight the centrality of diasporas and transnationalism, of mobility and multiple modernities, it suggests that the study of Latin American exile becomes a topic of central concern, closely related to basic theoretical problems and controversies in these disciplines. Its systematic study promises to lead to new readings of history and society in Latin America, away from the scripts of national histories and toward more regional, transnational, or even transcontinental dimensions.[2]

The chapter starts with a discussion of the historical roots and institutional logic of exile, followed by a detailed analysis of the Chilean political diaspora, a paradigmatic case energized by massive waves of exile in the Cold War era. It concludes with short comparative observations on other Latin American political diasporas, suggesting various institutional and contextual factors that shaped the differential role that political exiles played at the core of the various diasporas, throughout their configuration and development.

HISTORICAL ROOTS

Exile is a mechanism of exclusion and a practice that has been used by many societies and political systems since time immemorial and has persisted into modernity. In the Americas, the roots of this phenomenon go far beyond independence and deep into colonial times, when territorial displacement and expulsion were widely used against social offenders, outcasts, rebels, and criminals, at first from Europe to the Americas and soon replicated in Brazil and Hispanic America. As analysts of modern and contemporary processes, we should be aware of those deep roots of territorial banishment, used by many polities and historical empires, including the Iberian empires, and evolving into new forms under the impact of modern politics.

With the consolidation of Spanish rule and the establishment of new administrative jurisdictions, territorial displacement (*destierro*) was increasingly used to translocate individuals within, across, and beyond American lands, sending people who were perceived as endangering social peace into marginal or distant lands, where they were used as forced labor and for reinforcing the military defenses of the Spanish realm.[3] Within Brazil forced translocation—known as *degredo*—was used to push the frontier further away from the coast.[4] From Mexico individuals were mainly sentenced to forced labor in the Philippines and in other regions of Spanish America, particularly Puerto Rico, where they were drafted in the construction of fortresses and other public services. In late eighteenth century displaced individuals were also forcefully enrolled into the colonial army, which suffered from acute lack of manpower.[5] In parallel, the sentence of banishment was widely used against social transgressors, as in late colonial Mexico for those found guilty of lack of sexual restraint and of violation of the night curfew.[6] Authorities tended to recommend caution in the use of this practice, yet by late colonial times territorial displacement was widely known and used throughout the Americas.

In the transition to political independence, all Latin American states incorporated exile as a major political practice, along with other mechanisms of punishment. Territorial displacement and expulsion, instrumental in colonial times for dealing with social offenders and for reinforcing defenses on the margins of the empire, became used and abused in the realm of politics. In the collective imaginary and in the public spheres of the Latin American countries exile became a central mode of "doing politics."[7] Those who defied power could expect the fate of *encierro, destierro o entierro*, that is, prison, exile, or death, as put colorfully by historian Félix Luna for those opposing Juan Manuel de Rosas.[8] With the transition to state independence, exile developed the special political profile and role that, although transformed, persisted into the twentieth and early twenty-first centuries. Throughout the two centuries of independent statehood, political actors and rank-and-file citizens have been forced time and again to leave their country of residence in order to escape repression, as they suffered the loss of civil and political rights or as they feared persecution or even the loss of life.

INSTITUTIONAL LOGIC AND CONTESTED NATIONAL REPRESENTATIONS

What has been the institutional logic of the wide use of exile in Latin America? On the most basic level, exile resulted from the reluctance of power holders to open public spheres and the political realm to full participation. As dissent was seen as contestation, individuals found themselves on the run or expelled from their home countries, whether they were actually involved in politics or had an autonomous involvement in public arenas. As such, exile followed confrontations due to an active intervention in politics but resulted also from challenges to power identified in cultural, professional, academic, intellectual, student, peasant, or working-class circles.

In early statehood, under conditions of institutional weakness, fuzzy borders and fragmented competition for power, exile became instrumental for political elites involved in sharp political struggles. Political factionalism, while widespread, was perceived as extremely dangerous, as it could develop into a zero-sum struggle that could decimate the upper strata. Exile was especially suited to regulate the inner struggle of elites in the new polities. It reflected a trade-off between the will to rule in an authoritarian way, based on exclusion of political oppositions, and the unwillingness to conduct such struggle through executions, in a form that would lead to mounting violence in a zero-sum game of physical elimination. The very existence of the new polities could thus be endangered in the framework of escalating civil wars, repression, and dislocation. The social closeness of elites combined with the traditional forms of exclusion of wider strata to structure the forms of doing politics. Exile evolved then into a major mechanism of institutional exclusion, an alternative to incarceration and executions. By sending away those who led a defeated faction, the rulers could also claim to be moving in a lenient way toward organic unity, which they claimed to legitimately embody.[9]

The contestation over representation has been a major dimension of political exile in modern polities.[10] Exiles have often recovered their voice abroad, claiming that they and not the powers at home were the true representatives of the nation. In Yossi Shain's terms, their displacement from the homeland merely projected the frontier of loyalty abroad.[11] Unlike historical empires that did not build themselves on bottom-up legitimacy, modern states would be forced to lead such contestation with exiles over the national representation. Instead of silencing completely contesting elites and social and political forces, exile merely changed the spatial and temporal terms of the contestation, with international and transnational implications that became increasingly salient by the twentieth century.[12]

As the late political theorist Judith Shklar suggested, exile implies a rupture of state obligations that prompts reflexivity, a deep review of consciousness on what went wrong and decisions to be made about alternative loyalties and allegiances.[13] Such reflexivity also brings to the fore an ongoing tension between the principle of national membership and the principle of citizenship. Once a person is pushed into exile, she or he usually loses the entitlements—and obligations— attached to citizenship, but at the same time she or he may become even more attached than before to what is perceived as the "national soul." In modern nation-states there is a latent but distinct dimension of collective identity, often submerged in citizenship but necessarily recognized while in exile. Unsurprisingly, it is abroad that many displaced nationals discover, rediscover, or rather invent the "collective soul" of their countries in primordial or spiritual terms.[14]

Likewise, it has been abroad that exiles have rekindled the sense of attachment to "sister-nations" in the Americas. Exiles and expatriates even invented the term "Latin America" in mid-nineteenth-century France.[15,16] Since then, many exiles reinforced the recognition that the citizens of the various states shared common problems and interests. At certain times, exile led to the emergence of transnational political and cultural projects. Illustrations abound. José Martí and fellow Cubans befriending Ramón Emeterio Betances, a founding father of the Puerto Rican nationalism, and organized patriotic clubs, aimed at attaining the independence of both Cuba and Puerto Rico from Spain in the late nineteenth century. At one point, these patriots collaborated on a project of a future Confederation of the Antilles, partially thought of as a preemptive move aimed at precluding US political hegemony after the envisioned independence.[17] Likewise, in the 1910s–1920s thousands of Unionists tried to re-create the lost unity of Central America, wandering and preaching their vision in the Isthmus.[18] A generation later, Augusto César Sandino, Farabundo Martí, and others led a transnational armed struggle against international intervention and domestic dictatorships. For instance, starting in 1920, Sandino had experienced life in the economic enclaves of the Atlantic coast of Central America, first in Bluefields (Nicaragua), then in La Ceiba (Honduras), then briefly in Guiriguá (Guatemala), and finally in Tampico (Mexico). In these places, he got to know the diversity of the circum-Caribbean area populated by "British West Indian blacks," Garifunas, US plantation and farm managers, and a multinational labor force that included foreign radicals and adventurers, many of whom led economic struggles and fought US economic interests and imperialism.[19] Wandering through the Americas, Sandino developed a vision of resistance to international intervention and Bolivarian, transnational commitments. His key officers and part of the rank-and-file soldiers were drawn from all Central American territories, and some from even Mexico and the Dominican Republic. Imbued by such vision, he and his transnational cadre resisted the US military presence in Nicaragua from 1927 to his assassination in 1934.[20]

After periods of crisis, which produce a significant number of exiles, fascinating debates are generated between those who stayed in the home country and those who moved abroad over the definition of what are the components of national collective identity. Exiles, hoping to return some day to their home country, often attempt to define in novel ways the tenets of collective identity. In many instances, exile seems to have played an important role in defining or redefining both national and pan-Latin American identities. At the same time, though the exiles may claim they are the true representatives of the People while abroad, they interact in new environments, are exposed to exiles from other countries, and confront new models of social and political organization that transform them willing or not. This poses for every exile personal, familial, and collective dilemmas: how to relate to the host society and how willingly to become part of it, beyond the instrumental accommodation of everyday life, whether to develop hybrid identities and multiple commitments.

Their experience in exile also challenges them to reconsider their ideals and visions of both the host country and the homeland. A profound process of redefinition of cultural and political assumptions thus takes place in the diasporas of Latin Americans, which is crucial to trace as one analyzes later transformations in the countries of origin. The constellation of forces and the transnational dynamics described here were brought into full relief in the wave of Chilean political exile and diaspora formation in the last phases of the Cold War era.

THE CHILEAN DIASPORA

Traditionally, Chileans perceived their country as a rather insular state, at most a site of asylum for others. In the 1830s–1860s, the comparatively early institutional stability of the country attracted individuals fleeing from violence of the neighboring territories of the Rio de la Plata and the Andean region. Yet, while accepting exiles from other counties, in the nineteenth century Chile transferred part of its own elites into internal exile to remote parts of the country or expelled them, starting with the Carrera brothers and Bernardo O'Higgins. In the early twentieth century prominent members of society and politics were forced into external or internal exile. President Arturo Alessandri Palma went into exile in Italy in 1925 following a military coup. Emilio Bello Codecido spent the period between 1925 and 1936 in exile. Eliodoro Yáñez was exiled in Paris between 1927 and 1931, during Carlos Ibáñez del Campo's dictatorial rule. Ibáñez himself escaped to Argentina twice, the first time in 1931, when he lost power as a result of the demonstrations related to the economic crisis of that time and again in 1938 after the failed coup by the Nacional Socialist Movement of Chile that intended to place him in power, skipping the national elections. Later, in 1948–1958 the outlawing of the Communist Party forced many members of the Chilean Communist Party, among them Pablo Neruda, to move abroad.[21] Nonetheless, a massive Chilean political diaspora emerged only following the September 11, 1973, coup that brought General Pinochet to power. It was then that the Chilean phenomenon of exile acquired a distinctive character, both in terms of the global impact in the diaspora and the long-term political realignment of the country.

The military junta legalized administrative banishment from the national territory as a procedure to be used at the discretion of those in power.

> By decree 81 of November 1973, the military government required citizens who had left the country after the coup to obtain permission from the ministry of the interior to re-enter Chile. Thus no exile considered dangerous was allowed to return. When they renewed their passports at Chilean consulates, many exiles had the letter L stamped on them, indicating that the bearers were on the list of those prohibited from returning. Having portrayed exile as a humane

alternative to prison for "enemies of the nation," the regime had no intention of changing its policy on return. When foreign correspondents covering the plebiscite on the 1980 constitution asked Pinochet whether exiles would be allowed to return, he replied: "I have only one answer: No."[22]

Those regulations precluded the re-entrance of thousands of Chileans to the national territory and were enforced by the Ministry of Interior and the border police through the use of "black lists" of nationals and former residents who had left, were banished, or were not permitted to return to Chile. These lists of individuals considered "enemies of the nation" still included 4,942 names in 1984 and around 3,878 in 1985. The number dropped to several hundred by late 1987.[23]

Estimates of Chileans who left Chile between 1973 and 1990 vary immensely, ranging from a few hundred thousand to nearly 2 million. Shortly after the coup, international organizations in charge of assisting those in exile estimated that about 4,000 individuals had requested political asylum or had been expelled from the country. Some years later the estimate had increased to 10,000 (30,000 with family members). With democratization, the National Office of Return (ONR) in Chile estimated in 700,000 the number of Chileans abroad, of which 200,000 had left the country for political reasons.[24] Also in 1984 a study by the Centre for Research and Development in Education (CIDE) gave a total of 200,250.[25] That number was also mentioned by Jaime Esponda, the former director of the *Oficina Nacional del Retorno*, in an interview with Roniger and Sznajder.[26]

The number of people who move into exile has always been difficult to determine due to the multiple paths of displacement; the varied and often mixed motivations for emigration; and the balance between those who moved because of their involvement in politics. Expelling countries usually do not register those who escape abroad, but only those expelled formally; and in the host countries the newcomers find themselves under multiple statuses of asylum, refuge, or lack of registration. And then there are the relatives of those who fled or were expelled that find themselves under the dire alternative of living separated from their beloved or joining them abroad, in exile, becoming part of the larger Chilean diaspora.[27] The inner diversity of this conglomerate of people forced to leave the home country is not peculiar to the Chilean case. The following excerpt from Denise Rollemberg describing it for the Brazilian exiles can be easily applied to all other cases of Latin American exile:

> There were those affected by banishment. There were those who decided to leave, sometimes with legal documentation as they rejected the political climate in the country. There were those who, without being targeted by the political police, went into exile accompanying their spouse or parents. There were others persecuted by being involved in confrontation with the military regime. There were those who went to live abroad for non-political reasons, but [once there] through contacts with exiles, were integrated in the campaigns of denunciation of dictatorship and thus could not return easily to the country. . . . In this universe, there were all exiles. We could fall into a senseless abyss by pretending to establish who was or who was not an exile in the strict sense of the world.

Without doubt, the displacement of at least 200,000 and perhaps as much as 1,000,000 Chileans abroad was the greatest in Chilean history. Even deducting those clearly motivated by economic reasons, such as Chilean migrants flowing to Argentina, especially in periods of economic downturn in Chile, the figures are very high for a country with a population just above 10 million at the beginning of the Pinochet dictatorship and under 14 million at the end of it.[28] Adding the fact that Chile lived through two periods of prosperity under military rule—between 1978 and 1981 and between 1985 and 1990—the weight of political repression as an expelling factor becomes even more evident.

Political repression was directed against the left-wing parties, organizations, and anyone suspected of supporting them, with ca. 3,000 victims who lost their lives as a result of the coup and military rule. The closure of all forms of political expression, with the exception of military-sponsored ideas, placed a heavy burden on citizens and major parts of the political class in Chile, a country that had experienced a deep political polarization. The range of ideological visions allowed under Pinochet's rule included Catholic integralism, corporative nationalism, authoritarian neo-liberalism, and various versions of the Doctrine of National Security. Whoever resented these perspectives felt the rarified atmosphere of state repression. To some extent, this explains why not only activists of the *Unidad Popular* (UP), the coalition of forces supporting Allende,[29] and members of the *Movimiento de Izquierda Revolucionaria* (MIR) went into exile but also many of the leaders and activists of Chile's Christian Democratic Party, who actively opposed Allende's government before the coup, left for exile. Many of them moved to Italy, where they were well received by their political counterparts of the ruling Christian Democracy, and mobilized actively against the Chilean dictatorship. Among them were not only the haunted activists but also many former members of the state apparatus who were fired either because their loyalty to military rule was dubious and/or due to the downsizing of government agencies. Others were individuals freed from prison under the expressed purpose of expelling them abroad by decree in a legal mechanism known as "*pena de extrañamiento*," which included a non-return clause. In 1987, about 800 people were still affected by such a ban, precluding them from entering back into Chile. Many others had to leave Chile as they simply could not support themselves in a rapidly changing economic environment dominated by free market economics and a lack of political freedoms. Many of them would not return to Chile. The formation of a diaspora is a process that cannot be undone completely, even when the conditions in the home country change, especially where authoritarian rule lasts long, like in the cases of Brazil (1964–1985), Paraguay (1954–1989), and Chile (1973–1990).

DIASPORA ACTIVISM AND ORGANIZATION

Thousands of Chilean exiles spread across many countries formed a potent diaspora whose members disputed the legitimacy claimed by the military regime and struggled to energize the global campaign against Pinochet. Exiles formed "nuclei of *chilenidad*" aimed at reclaiming the true spirit of Chilean society and giving international projection to the plight of those persecuted. The parameters of their activity were shaped by the high level of politicization of Chilean society prior to military rule and by the length and forcefulness of the dictatorship. While abroad, many of those banished stressed the need for political activism, joined networks of solidarity and advocacy, and mobilized public opinion, providing alternative information about the situation in Chile and confronting the dictatorship on its claim of legitimacy.

Political activism abroad fed a sense of transience, of staying out of the fatherland for a short time while working to accelerate the fall of the dictatorship.[30] But the dictatorship lasted for nearly 17 years, and exiles faced all the challenges of living in exile and perhaps integrating into the host society. From the beginning, exile was marked by the constant tension between the need to accommodate to the host society and the tendency to remain attached to the homeland and committed to the political work that would enable their return and "dis-exile."

Until this wave of massive exile, Chile was perceived by its own citizens as a very far away country, located at Finis Terrae, at the End of the World, and as such, rather isolated from the international scene. Marxist Senator Salvador Allende's accession to power through democratic elections and his vision of moving toward Socialism within the constitutional and legal framework changed all that. It projected the experience of Chile into the awareness of the entire world, awarding a strongly universal meaning to the defense of the values of its democracy, soon to be crushed by the military. The Chilean experience was thus well known internationally and raised many questions on the possibility of reaching Socialism in a democratic framework in spite of the context of Cold War global confrontation. And yet it was only with the arrival of the Chilean exiles that networks of solidarity were created that energized the political arenas of the host countries while also breaking Chilean historical insularity.

Virtually the entire leadership of the Left that was not assassinated or imprisoned during the first stage of state terror was forced to flee into exile. Those in power intended their exile to be irreversible and prevented them from returning at least until 1984. Pinochet managed to consolidate his hold on Chile through this institutional exclusion of the opposition; and yet, in the long run, the creation of a Chilean diaspora proved dysfunctional for Pinochet's project. Immediately after the military coup, a Commission of Refugees (CONAR) was formed, led by the Lutheran Bishop Helmut Frenz. Its main role was to help persecuted Chileans reach and enter foreign embassies, where they would receive asylum. In 1974, an agreement was reached between the Inter-European Committee for Migration, the Red Cross International Committee, CONAR, and the Chilean government, to enable the exit of individuals placed under administrative detention but not scheduled to stand trial. In 1975, another agreement made possible for people who suffered from political persecution and were serving sentences also to leave Chile. Three thousand Chileans were freed from prisons and allowed to leave the country. In addition, since 1974, large numbers of detainees who under the provisions of the State of Siege Law were held without trials in concentration camps were expelled from Chile by decree. On April 30 1975, Decree Law 504 established that a sentence dictated by the military courts (prison, internal exile [*relegación*] or conditional sentences) could be exchanged into an *extrañamiento*, that is, the expulsion from the country without the right to return.

Soon a diaspora of Chileans emerged. In Latin America, the greater concentrations of Chilean exiles were in Argentina, Venezuela, Brazil, and Mexico. Argentina attracted Chileans as well as Uruguayans and other South American exiles due to its proximity and the vitality of its politics during the Democratic Spring that began with the presidential term of Héctor Cámpora and the return of Juan Domingo Perón from exile. With the increasing violence and repression of the Left after Perón died in July 1974 and the military coup of March 1976, Venezuela turned into a major site of asylum for Chileans.[31] Important, although more reduced, was the number of Chileans who moved to Cuba and later Nicaragua. Others went to Canada and the United States. In Europe, Chileans spread all across the continent but many went to the United Kingdom, Sweden (who helped especially in many urgent cases), Italy, Spain, France, and Denmark. In 1992, there were nearly 28,000 Chileans in Sweden, out of which 13,900 were political refugees in 1987.[32] Until August 1987, 800 Chileans had been received as refugees in Denmark.[33] A group, mainly of members of the Communist Party, received asylum in East Germany, and a few in the USSR.[34]

As any other group of exiles, the Chileans were a diverse group in terms of age and gender, occupational and class backgrounds, and regional or ethnic composition. In terms of class background, workers were a minority versus individuals of middle- and upper-class backgrounds. A relatively large group of Mapuches, 500-strong and particularly targeted by the military, found its way into Western Europe, where they founded their own organization, the *Comité Exterior Mapuche* that coordinated actions with other organizations and networks of Chilean exiles. The common denominator of the exiles was the banning of the political organizations back home, in which they had activated or sympathized, and the brutal state repression that drove them into exile. This commonality led to the re-establishment of the political parties abroad: the Socialist Party, the Communist Party, MAPU, MAPU-OC, the Radical Party, the Christian Left, MIR, all associated to the former coalition of Allende and reconstituted in exile, mainly in Europe.[35] The majority of exile organizations belonged to leftist parties, although there were also nonpartisans and a small group of Christian Democrats, who after their initial support of the coup opposed the ensuing policies of Pinochet and found themselves on the run.[36] Political action through parties, committees of solidarity, nongovernmental organizations, and local and international organizations took place almost immediately with the arrival of the Chilean exiles. Political activity was often hectic, with leaders participating in numerous meetings and intensely defining the methodologies of working in unison with the local waves of solidarity generated by the September 1973 events.

The Chilean case became a cause célèbre throughout the world and found strong echoes with administrators, parliamentarians, party activists, trade union activists, human rights associations, Catholic and Protestant churches, and student federations, primarily in Western democracies and in Communist countries. Massive marches of protest and popular demonstrations were organized in front of Chilean embassies. Stevedores' unions in Anvers, Liverpool, and Marseilles boycotted Chilean ships. In Israel and Spain, public protests managed to block the entry to port of the Esmeralda, the training ship of the Chilean Navy that in 1973 had served as a prison and torture center. Fearing for the safety and lives of those in Chilean prisons, exiles led hunger strikes that impacted public opinion in Europe. Folkloric *peñas* were organized to collect funds to support the families of political prisoners, widows and sons of the *desaparecidos* in Chile. Chilean music soon became a major medium for keeping spirits high. Exiled groups of performers such as the Quilapayún located in Paris and the Inti Illimanyi based in Rome traveled incessantly from community to community and energized with their songs of protest the struggle against the dictatorship, keeping the culture of resistance alive.[37] The concerts also served other purposes. Like the *empanadas*, the traditional meat and onion pies they made and sold, the concerts served to collect funds and continue with their campaigns to raise consciousness of the grim record of human rights violations by Pinochet's dictatorship.[38]

At first, all these activities were believed to articulate and support the consolidation of a strong and effective opposition that supposedly would lead to the demise of the dictatorship. Yet the margins for antimilitary political action in Chile were nearly closed by repression and persecution. Accordingly, as Pinochet's rule consolidated, a phase of questioning and reevaluation of the political methodology started. As time passed, the enthusiasm of the Chilean *cause célèbre* also waned and international solidarity shifted to other causes such as the cycle of civil wars and massive human rights violations in Central America. As distance and time took their toll in a long protracted process, Chilean political activism decreased and was replaced by social activism in the communities of exiles. Indeed, besides strict party political organizations, Chilean exiles had also reconstituted trade unions; they founded women organizations and created cultural centers and soccer teams. In many European cities, they established associations of family members of disappeared and prisoners, as well as institutions geared to the treatment of specific problems of exiles. Similar initiatives and frameworks sprung in France, Sweden, Italy, and other countries. In the mid-1970s the Chileans who had arrived with the first contingents of exiles had already established social organizations aimed at easing the landing and adaptation of new arrivals. In Brussels, COLAT (Latin American Collective of Psychosocial Work) was founded, later renamed as EXIL. In Copenhagen, a Committee of Assistance for Refugees and Migrants (CEPAR) was established. The University of Hamburg held a series of symposia on culture and psychosocial pressures in Latin America, with the participation of exiled academics and mental health professionals. In a third stage, committees pro-return were established, becoming part of a pan-European network.[39]

SITES OF EXILE AND TRANSNATIONAL NETWORKS

Chilean exiles faced similar challenges yet had multiple and even divergent experiences abroad. All exiles had problems of adaptation, but those settling in Latin American countries felt a sense of belonging that was mostly absent among those settling in Europe, Canada, Australia, Asia, or Africa, where they had to adjust to different cultures, foods, and lifestyles. In some cases, the difficulties led to self-closure in the exile community. Osvaldo Puccio, son of President Allende's secretary, was 20 years old when he arrived in Germany. Years after his arrival, in a testimony, he was highly critical of many Chileans who created cultural and social *ghettos*, surrendering to their music and their sadness. He noted that some lived in Germany for 10 and 15 years without learning the language and thus were secluded from communicating with the environment.[40]

Also in terms of their composition, the various communities of exiles differed. For instance, Mexico received a large group of exiles, close to 10,000. Four-fifths of them arrived after receiving asylum at the embassy in Santiago. Among them were professionals and technicians, in addition to individuals connected to the high echelons of the Allende's government and public administration. Among them were the widow of Salvador Allende and his two daughters, Clodomiro Almeida, Pedro Vuskovic, ministers and subsecretaries of state, senators and deputies, leaders of political parties, important academics, and core cultural figures, who found occupational opportunities and a strong welcome by the Mexican administration and the population, in a country that prided itself for having provided a refuge for the Spanish Republican exiles in the late 1930s. Chilean exiles established close relationships with Mexican peers and were active politically and socially as a community, influencing Mexico to adopt a strong position of condemnation of the Pinochet regime in the international arena. Due to their profile and professional background, some of them made major contributions to the host society. Notorious were Miguel Littín in cinematography, José de Rokha in the arts, Luis Enrique Delano in literature, Ángel Parra in music, Fernando Fajnzylber in economics, and Edgardo Enríquez in medicine. Contrastingly, the communities in Sweden, the United Kingdom, or Canada included larger percentages of individuals of popular background.[41]

The greater difficulties in adjusting to countries beyond Latin America were somehow compensated by state welfare programs of assistance in the developed countries. In Western Europe, Canada, and Australia, exiles were offered language classes, occupational training, scholarships, and even subsidized housing. The case of Sweden is paradigmatic. Most Chilean exiles were of middle-class extraction; 35–40 years old on average; students, professionals, individuals with technical background, artists and artisans, and labor leaders, with a substantial number of political activists. In Sweden the government belonging to the Social Democratic Party felt sympathy toward the cause of the Latin American political exiles. It is important to note that another factor that allowed an open reception policy was the national ethos of helping refugees and political exiles of the Third World.

Public opinion in Sweden identified itself with the Chilean political plight. Many young people had visited South America through nongovernmental organizations Some were imprisoned, others were killed, and still others were expelled, such as the ambassador Harald Edestam, who saved many lives and gave asylum to the persecuted. There were numerous committees of solidarity with Chile, and the main image of the Latin Americans was very positive. In the 1960s the Swedish were a source of inspiration for radical ideas, and they were also imbued by a missionary Lutheran spirit. Until the 1980s all Latin American immigrants were seen in Sweden as synonymous with political refugees, perceived as "heroes" or "martyrs." The combination of a receptive ethos and a supportive governmental action was maintained even as the Social Democratic government lost power in September 1976.[42]

Also the Soviet Union provided institutional assistance to the exiles. Wright and Oñate mention the case of the widow Viola Carrillo and the ten children of union leader Isidro Carrillo, executed 6 weeks after the coup, who moved to the Soviet Union and were provided housing, jobs, and educational opportunities through the university level.[43] Still many found themselves alienated from their new environments and in a process of mourning their defeat, feeling guilt for the dead, jailed, or disappeared left behind, which produced high rates of depression, divorce, alcoholism, and suicide. Most tried to adapt to their new environment by learning new occupational skills, engaging in higher education, keeping Chilean culture alive for their children, and retaining a spirit of resistance.

Pinochet used exile to suffocate political action, but once abroad, the exiles reconstructed a dense network replicating their former political organizations on the local, regional, national, and international plane. The crackdown of Pinochet on the leadership of the UP coalition and the failed attempts by some Socialists, Communists, and the MIR to launch armed and clandestine actions, which were crushed and decimated, transformed exiles into the most effective front for fighting the dictatorship, at least in the first decade of military rule.

Every leftist party of Chile was reconstructed abroad: the Socialists, Communists, MAPU, MAPU-OC, Radicales, Izquierda Cristiana, MIR, and in the first years—even the youth movements of each of these parties. Also established were the Movimiento Democrático Popular or MDP; the Convergencia Socialista; the Bloque Socialista; and later on, the MIDA and the PPD. The Socialists and the UP established their headquarters in Berlin. The Communists opted for Moscow and the MIR selected Havana and Paris. The exile community created several transnational networks, as they followed former ideological divisions and commitments.[44] Exiles worked with their parallel political parties and student, labor, church, and human rights associations in the host countries, and they formed numerous committees of solidarity with Chile. In Venezuela, Chilean political activists found easy interlocutors and supporters among the major political forces; namely, Acción Democrática (AD), a party affiliated to the Socialist International, and COPEI, a Christian Democratic Party. The committee of solidarity with Chile, led by the former Secretary General of the Chilean Socialist Party Aniceto

Rodríguez received full support of the AD. Moreover, the Venezuelan power-sharing model at that time brought Chilean Socialists and Christian Democrats to agree to the initiatives of the German Socialists and the Friedrich Ebert Foundation to start conversations in 1975 on how to join forces in their opposition to the Pinochet regime. In Mexico, President Echeverría and his wife provided the locale and support for the *Casa de Chile* in the Federal District, led by the exiled leadership of the Chilean Radical Party, a political force close in its secularism, anticlericalism and non-Marxist views to the *Partido Revolucionario Institucional* (PRI) ruling Mexico. The *Casa de Chile* served as a focus of coordination of anti-Pinochet activities of committees of solidarity in the Americas and a meeting ground for notorious Chilean exiles such as Allende's widow Hortensia Bussi, Anselmo Sule, Hugo Miranda, Pedro Vuskovic, and Luis Maira among others.[45]

In some sites of exile, as in the German Federal Republic, England, or Canada, there were a myriad of committees of solidarity with Chile. In the United Kingdom, committees of solidarity with Democratic Chile were established first at the initiative of the British leftist groups and the Labor Party, and the arrival of almost 3,000 exiles gave further impetus to the committees.[46] Exiles also activated in the framework of the union organizations (*Comité Sindical Chile* or CUT) and women's organizations linked to the UP, which they established in close to thirty-five countries, as well as cultural centers, soccer teams, and other associations. Moreover, the magnitude and brutality of the repression ignited the emergence of new associations such as the *Asociaciones de Familiares de Detenidos y Desaparecidos*, *Comité Exterior Mapuche*, *Pastoral Católica del Exilio*, youth centers, and children's ateliers. Chilean exiles created organizations that combined politics and cultural, sport, and other group activities. Among them were *Chile Democrático* in Rome, the *Instituto para el Nuevo Chile* and the *Centro Salvador Allende* in Rotterdam, *SEUL-Casa de América Latina* in Brussels, the *Comité Salvador Allende* in Laussane, the *Comité Salvador Allende* in Stockholm, the *Centro de Estudios Salvador Allende* in Madrid, the *Comité Chileno Anti-Fascista* and *Chile Democrático* in London, and *Chile Democrático* in Paris.[47]

Through these organizations, exiles lobbied host country governments and international organizations to condemn the Pinochet regime at the United Nations and other international forums, organized campaigns for the release of political prisoners, and banned Chilean imports. "These efforts were crucial to countering the influence of powerful business interests that supported the dictatorship for reopening Chile to international capital and, through the neo-liberal policies it imposed, creating an ideal investment climate."[48] Vis-à-vis those, exiles benefitted from the support of the Socialist International, the Communist International movement, the Social Democratic Organization, a wide spectrum of churches, trade union associations, the international Red Cross, the UN High Commissioner for Refugees and various nongovernmental organizations, and prominent figures of Western cultural, political, and social domains.[49]

Along with this impressive organizational impetus, while abroad the exiles replicated traditional political rivalries, although due to perhaps the pervasiveness and harshness of repression in Chile, they were able to combine efforts and collaborate for the sake of their common goal, which is the key to the exiles' effectiveness in keeping the plight of their homeland as a top-priority issue in the international agenda.

The exiled leaders of the UP, who lived on subsidies from host governments or political organizations or received well-paid jobs, traveled among exile populations and worked with world political and government leaders to gather support for their cause. Some of them turned into figures with international clout. Anselmo Sule, president of the Radical Party, was elected vice-president of the Socialist International in 1976, a reflection of the high priority the Chilean case had for this organization. The Socialist International lobbied governments and the UN supported think tanks and publishers active in the campaign for the 1988 plebiscite.[50] Similarly, the cross-party organization *Chile Democrático*, which received financial support from governments in Western Europe, lobbied at the highest levels, published a very influential periodical (*Chile América*) with information about Chile, and monitored the human rights situation there, while it also supported financially the movement of human rights anchored in the *Vicaría de la Solidaridad*, created by the Catholic Church in Chile at the initiative of Cardinal Raúl Silva Henríquez in 1976.

The socioeconomic profile of political exiles included rank-and-file activists of the parties, student and professional organizations, and labor unions. In exile, political solidarity and activism erased, to a some extent, class and rank differences that were salient in Chile. Activism and political solidarity went together, especially between members of the same political party in the home and the host countries. While the leading politicians worked at the supraorganizational level, it was the localized and social support of the myriad organizations of the exiles that kept the sense of confidence and direction alive and created domestic networks and committees of solidarity with Chile.

Even in countries with greater structural constrains for the Chileans, the political activism of the exiles kept the cause of Chile alive. On the basis of interviews with former exiles, Wright and Oñate reconstruct how the exiles worked under such conditions in Costa Rica and Brazil:

> [In] countries with fewer nongovernmental organizations, exiles used lower profile approaches to cultivate the support of their host countries. Frustrated by the divisions among the UP parties in Costa Rica, a group of exiles established a binational solidarity organization, *Por Chile*, to influence the media and the Costa Rican government in quiet but effective ways. In Brazil, the military government prohibited open political activity such as street demonstrations or leafleting but tolerated political events in private spaces such as churches.[51]

TRENDS OF TRANSFORMATION

The Chilean Left underwent a profound transformation in exile, albeit not in a unified direction. The experience in the Iron Curtain and other Socialist countries brought about early disenchantment and the will to go back to the West, leaving the ranks of the Communist Party. Such were the cases of high-ranking officials of the UP administration such as José Rodríguez Elizondo, a well-known Chilean intellectual and diplomat, who spent part of his exile in East Germany, and of Gustavo Silva, member of the PCCH, who visited Eastern Europe while in French exile.[52] While the Sandinista victory in Nicaragua in 1979 could still be interpreted within the framework of the Cold War, events in Europe—the transformation of Euro-Communism into a new kind of Social Democracy and the process of parallel rigidity, weakening, and disintegration of the Eastern Block and the USSR—went far beyond. The impact of reconfiguration of the European Left around its debates on Euro-communism, the struggle of solidarity in Poland, and the disillusion with the Soviet Union impacted the exile communities. These shifts contributed to the reconfiguration of the Chilean Left, reassessing the meaning of world events and politics by establishing a series of think tanks aimed at devising ways to modernize Chile. The think tanks and periodicals disseminated the renovated ideas. ASER in Paris, the *Instituto para el Nuevo Chile* in Rotterdam, and *Chile Democrático* in Rome were leading think tanks. *Plural* published in Rotterdam, *Convergencia Socialista* in Mexico City, and *Chile-América* in Rome were major media publications expressing and projecting this transformation.[53]

These trends of transformation were part of a process of redefinition of the political positions and horizons in the Chilean diaspora in a relatively short span of time. For instance, Chileans settling in Italy could reflect closely on the failed project of Enrico Berlinguer's "Historical Compromise" and yet follow it in Chile by establishing a broad coalition of seventeen parties, the *Concertación*, which revived ideas of citizenship built on individual active participation and reached out to other parties to find broader agreements in politics.[54] Yet, as indicated earlier, the changes took multiple forms as a result of the varied learning experiences and practices of the various communities of exiles in the Chilean diaspora. A retrospective reflection by President Ricardo Lagos stresses the impact of exile on the reformulation of his political ideas and attitudes toward democracy as well as recognizes such multiplicity of paths of transformation. Lagos, who was close to Allende and set to become the Chilean ambassador to Moscow at the time of the military takeover in 1973, remained an expatriate in the United States, where he served as visiting professor at the University of North Carolina, before taking a position as economist in the UN until 1984. In an interview with Mario Sznajder in May 2002, President Lagos indicated that

> Never in the history of Chile so many Chilean women and men with varied degrees of cultural exposure—social leaders, politicians, heads of local associations, and many more—move into the world (*se asoman al mundo*) and begin to see the world from the new reality they witness. This produces a change, especially in the Left-wing and most progressive thought of Chile. I recall my participation in a meeting of the Chilean PS in Bordeaux. . . . Someone would stand up and say: "We, the Socialists of Milan think. . ." Another would declare: "We, the Socialists of Stockholm, say . . ." You could perceive a Renaissance

cultural imprint in the way of thinking of the one of Milan and a Scandinavian worldview in the exile from Stockholm. I believe that exile left its imprint, leading us to recognize the value of democracy, the higher value of human-rights . . . abandoning the classic tools of the Left in the 1960s and '70s, to be replaced by the revalorization of democracy, of human-rights, of the place of the market, of the role of the means of production and service. In other words, there was a great *aggiornamento*, moving and preceding the move to globalization.[55]

The process of change was uneven and went through various phases. Chilean Communists, which had been a moderating force in the UP government, found themselves not supported in their idea of leading a broad antifascist front of the UP parties and the Christian Democracy. The Communists arriving in Cuba, for example, underwent strong pressures to change. Chileans arrived there in several waves and immediately encountered two facets of Cuban solidarity. On the one hand, a genuine will to facilitate their integration into the island, providing them with housing and employment. But at the same time, they faced explicit criticism and even contempt on the part of the leadership and citizens of the host country. Cubans attributed the Chilean developments to the cowardice of the leftist Chileans, who in their eyes did not put a fight to the military onslaught. As Javier Ortega indicated in the first of a series of investigative notes in *The Untold Story of the Olive Green Years*, published in 2001:

> First quietly, then openly, [Cuban] local authorities considered the Chilean Left, especially the Communists, responsible for the [1973] defeat. The opinion was that they did not "defend their conquests." Chileans suffered contempt by a ruling elite that many see as primarily "macho-Leninist" and whose greatest pride is to have reached power by force and be a thorn in the throat of the greatest military power in the world. The Cubans could not understand . . . that the military coup met little resistance and that the leaders of the UP fled without "firing a pea" (*sin "disparar un chícharo"*) as Cubans say. Fidel Castro . . . himself told his close circle that the Chilean defeat was not a "productive" one since, save for Allende, it did not leave martyrs, unlike the [Cuban] failed assault on the Moncada Barracks in 1953. It did not provide the sight of fallen heroes in combat to serve as guiding examples for the survivors.[56]

The leaders of the Chilean Left, particularly the Chilean Communist Party, which had previously refrained from armed struggle, finally changed strategy. The CCP then chose to accept the Cuban proposal of an armed struggle strategy against Pinochet, launching the idea of creating the Frente Patriótico Manuel Rodríguez (FPMR) as its armed wing in 1974. Months later, the young Communist militants started their training in Cuban military academies and other Central American frameworks. In September 1980, the Secretary General of the CCP, Luis Corvalán announced the new political strategy of mass popular rebellion on Radio Moscow, and by 1983 the FPMR began its actions in Chile, actions that included kidnapping, car bombs, and other urban guerrilla tactics. Failing to topple Pinochet by becoming a driver of insurrection, they formally separated from the CPC in 1987. The FPMR continued its violent actions even after the return of democracy and until the mid-1990s. Among other actions, in March 1991 they murdered Senator Jaime Guzmán, the legal mind behind the 1980 Constitution, an event that dwarfed the impact of the final report of the Truth and Reconciliation Commission by reviving the specter of left-wing revolutionary violence.[57]

Exile also prompted change among the Socialists, leading them progressively to embrace political democracy in a principled way. At first the Socialists split in 1979 into a radical and a more moderate wing. Whereas the latter became closer to the Christian Democracy, the hard-liners attempted to join the Communists and use the mass protests of 1982–1986 to topple the regime. With the return of exiles into Chile, the shifts also influenced the domestic front. After failing to defeat Pinochet through mass insurrection, the hard-liners joined the renovated wings of the Party in an alliance with the PDC to contest Pinochet in the 1988 plebiscite on the dictator's extended rule. Their success led to the *Concertación* coalition of seventeen parties that defeated Pinochet a year later in a referendum opening the way for the return to civilian rule by March 1990.

The experiences of exile in liberal democracies led to a better understanding of democratic practices, civil society, and the welfare state, institutions that in Europe and Venezuela were articulated differently than had been the case in Chile. The international public sphere, more aware and critical of the violations of human rights in Latin America, also allowed exiles to remain active politically. Exiles became aligned with national and transnational networks of advocacy that helped propel the democratic transition, in many cases providing material and discursive support to those fighting dictatorships in Chile as elsewhere in Latin America. Moreover, the process of transformation of the authoritarian regime in southern Europe, particularly in Spain but also in Italy and later on in Poland, produced a strong impression on exiles, who witnessed firsthand the accelerated processes of democratic opening.[58] In parallel, these experiences triggered a process of reassessment of the political processes that were conducive to the institutional crises at the basis of their own expatriation and exile. The combination of insight and firsthand knowledge of broader processes of political transformation was the basis for a new generation of activists that contributed to the renewal of political creeds, soon to be connected back with other forces of Chilean politics and public life.

COMPARATIVE OBSERVATIONS: CHILEAN AND OTHER LATIN AMERICAN POLITICAL DIASPORAS

Comparatively, all political diasporas formed in the 1960s–1970s faced challenges similar to those in the Chilean diaspora, derived from policies of disinformation carried out by the dictatorships, attempts to persecute and discredit them even abroad, the exiles' disconnection from the home country and society, the will to continue organizing and fighting while abroad, and of course the need to survive under the variable circumstances of the different sites of exile. They all participated to various degrees in the emerging human rights movement, establishing links with committees of solidarity and transnational networks of advocacy. Still, exiled nationals from other Latin American states under authoritarian rule had greater difficulties in impacting the international community, due to the distinct circumstances of their institutional background and environment. First was the lack of a clear-cut party system similar to that of the host countries, a hindrance that was evident particularly for Argentine exiles. The Argentinean case resembled the Chilean one in terms of dispersal of exile communities and the drive to create their own organizations, geared on the one hand to the political domain and on the other to support the exiles socially. Equally important, Argentine exiles seem to have been able to establish links with networks of solidarity in the host countries and the transnational arena. Yet it was hard for outsiders to position themselves vis-à-vis Argentina, a country where democracy broke down and massive repression started due to the in-fighting within Peronism, a multiclass Populist coalition of forces in which its Left and Right wings tried to kill one another already in the early 1970s, several years before the 1976 military coup. The propaganda of the Argentine military junta in the sense that exiles were individuals who had resorted to violence and remained committed to armed struggle could strike among the publics of other countries. It would take time and the emblematic case of the *Madres de Plaza de Mayo* and relatives of victims demanding justice and the return alive of their abducted beloved ones for the international community to become sensitive to their plight.

Likewise, as in the case of Paraguayan exiles, the fragmentation and personal rivalries in the exiled opposition and the existence of thousands of spies and collaborators among the Paraguayans abroad diminished the effectiveness of the exiled opposition. Adding to the equation was the strategy of the dictatorship of General Alfredo Stroessner of retaining the formalities of electoral democracy and relying on the backing of a major political force, the Colorado Party, that had a strong popular backing and enjoyed ancestral loyalties in that society.

Another major factor in the ability of exiles to become the voice and image of a diaspora stemmed from the relative mix of political and economic motivations projected by the community of co-nationals. In the paradigmatic case of Central Americans, despite the clear background of generalized violence and repression motivating the massive flow of individuals escaping Guatemala and El Salvador, primarily to Mexico, collective representations were tinted with the image of refugees on the move. Indeed, many of them hoped to move further north to the United States in search of better sources of livelihood. In the case of the Uruguayan diaspora, too, despite prominent exiles such as Senator Zelmar Michelini, speaker of the House Héctor Gutiérrez Ruiz (both abducted and murdered in Argentina in 1976), and of others who escaped such fate such as senators Wilson Ferreira Aldunate and Enrique Erro, their impact on global public opinion was not based, unlike the Chileans, on the massive mobilization of the Uruguayan diaspora. This contrasted, for instance, with the strategies carried out by the political organizations of the exiles in the Chilean diaspora. The crucial discriminating factors in this case seem to have been the different insertion of the Uruguayan exiles among their co-nationals, their limited organizational structure abroad, and their origins in a society with almost no tradition of political exile in the twentieth century.[59] Nonetheless, toward the end of the dictatorship exiles managed to regain centrality in the process of democratization, both by launching spectacular campaigns like the organized return of children of exiles to Uruguay, which sensitized all Uruguayans to their plight and demand of general amnesty, and by the principled position of Wilson Ferreira Aldunate, who disclosed and criticized harshly the terms of the Uruguayan transition. The transition was negotiated between the Colorado party leadership and the generals and predicated on the approval of a law that would prevent attaining wide accountability for the human rights abuses of the civilian-military dictatorship for over 25 years.[60]

Last and not least is the image an exile community assumes in the framework of foreign policy considerations of host countries, especially if the latter have a pivotal place in the international system. Paradigmatic perhaps is the case of Cubans playing such role since the late nineteenth century, at that time primarily from Paris and in the twentieth century from both Mexico in the 1950s and from the United States following the Cuban 1959 Revolution.[61] As Cuba adopted Communism, the representation of Cuban Americans became that of an exile community escaping authoritarian rule. This was in sharp contrast with the fate of thousands of Haitians who tried unsuccessfully to achieve a similar recognition while attempting to enter the United States and were still considered economic migrants whose entrance was to be strictly controlled and curtailed.

Against this comparative scenario, the case of Chile stood out for its international clout and the multiple ideological and institutional transformations that started with the process of massive exile and were brought into full circle in the late 1980s. The September 11 (1973) airstrikes on the Moneda presidential palace in Chile left a profound mark on global consciousness, similar to the September 11 (2001) attack on the Twin Towers a generation later. The Chileans who fled to exile or were expelled from Chile turned into the pivotal core of a vibrant diaspora that further projected into global awareness the plight of their society undergoing massive human rights violations. Chilean exiles came from a country with an articulated political system and political parties that found almost immediate resonance with sister-parties and intellectual circles both in the Western world and in Communist states, in Latin America, Europe, and many distant lands. They proactively projected themselves through networks of solidarity and advocacy and international organizations. The military takeover did constitute a breakdown of the Chilean constitutional tradition, and it ended the first experiment of a Marxist-Socialist administration reaching power through the ballots. The brutality and magnitude of repression following the military takeover made Chile into the cause célèbre both of the Left and of liberal democratic forces. The Chilean military rulers closed the political sphere, alienating many Christian Democrats and members of other nonrevolutionary and centrist parties, and creating a constellation of forces that transcended the East-West divide of the Cold War.

The Chilean diaspora involved a critical mass of politically proactive exiles who endowed the fight against the military dictatorship with a strong moral claim, in addition to the Byronic, heroic image many of them proudly projected in exile. The projection of the Chilean counterintelligence's activities to Latin America, the United States, and Europe, and the coordination of repression with other countries in the framework of Operation Condor led to the assassination of a few prominent exiles such as Orlando Letelier, but they were ineffective in silencing an opposition whose voice gained resonance through the multiplier factor of transnational networks and international organizations. Pinochet would soon have to face the political implications of a war that had become transnational and that, despite Pinochet's claim of being at the forefront of the struggle against Communism, eventually led to a loss of support in Western democracies. By becoming a voice for the entire diaspora, while being transformed by their global exposure, Chilean political exiles had a crucial impact on the internationalization of human rights and the struggle for the return of democracy in Chile.

NOTES

1. Mario Sznajder and Luis Roniger, *The Politics of Exile in Latin America* (Cambridge: Cambridge University Press, 2009); Luis Roniger, James N. Green, and Pablo Yankelevich, eds., *Exile and the Politics of Exclusion in the Americas* (Brighton and Portland, UK: Sussex Academic Press, 2012).
2. Barry Carr, "'Across Seas and Borders': Charting the Webs of Radical Internationalism in the Circum-Caribbean," in *Exile and the Politics of Exclusion in the Americas*, Luis Roniger, James N. Green, and Pablo Yankelevich, eds. (Brighton, UK: Sussex Academic Press, 2012); Luis Roniger, *Destierro y exilio en América Latina. Nuevos estudios y avances teóricos* (Buenos Aires: EUDEBA, 2014).
3. Ricardo Descalzi, *La Real Audiencia de Quito. Claustro en los Andes* (Barcelona: Seix Barral, 1978), 87. Tamar Herzog, *La administración como un fenómeno social. La justicia penal de la ciudad de Quito (1650–1750)* (Madrid: Centro de Estudios Constitucionales, 1995), 18; José María Mariluz Urquijo, *Ensayo sobre los juicios de residencia indianos* (Sevilla: Escuela de Estudios Hispanoamericanos, 1952), 208–209.
4. Geraldo Pieroni, *Vadios e ciganos, hereges e bruxos—os degradados no Brasil colonia* (Rio de Janeiro: Bertrand, 2000).
5. Gabriel Haslip, "Crime and the Administration of Justice in Colonial Mexico City 1696–1810" (Ann Arbor: University Microfilm International, 1982), 203–227.
6. Michael C. Scardaville, *Crime and the Urban Poor. Mexico City in the Late Colonial Period* (Ann Arbor: University Microfilms International, 1977), 304–350.
7. Luis Roniger and Mario Sznajder, *The Legacy of Human Rights Violations in the Southern Cone: Argentina, Chile and Uruguay* (Oxford: Oxford University Press, 1999).
8. Félix Luna, *Historia general de la Argentina* (Buenos Aires: Planeta, 1995), 202.
9. Rebecca Earl, ed., *Rumours of Wars: Civil Conflict in Nineteenth Century Latin America* (London: Institute of Latin American Studies, 2000).
10. Sylvie Aprile, *Le siècle des exilés. Bannis et proscrits de 1789 à la Commune* (Paris: CNRS Editions, 2010).

11. Yossi Shain, *The Frontier of Loyalty. Political Exiles in the Age of the Nation-State* (Middletown, PA: Wesleyan University Press, 1989).

12. Mario Sznajder and Luis Roniger. *The Politics of Exile in Latin America* (Cambridge: Cambridge University Press, 2009).

13. Judith N. Shklar, *Political Thought and Political Thinkers* (Chicago: University of Chicago Press, 1998), 57–58.

14. For a broader discussion, see S. N. Eisenstadt, "Collective Identities, Public Spheres, Civil Society and Citizenship in the Contemporary Era," *Marburger Forum: Beiträge zur geistigen Situation der Gegenwart* 7, no. 5 (2006): htpp://www.philosophia-online .de/mafo/heft2006-5/Ei_Col.html; and S. N. Eisenstadt, "Multiple Modernities: A Paradigm of Cultural and Social Evolution," *ProtoSociology* 24 (2007): 20.

15. Among them stands out José María Torres Caicedo (1830–1889), a writer and intellectual, born in Bogotá. A young political journalist harassed and wounded in his home country, he moved to Paris at the age of 20, with only short visits back home until his death. He served as representative of Colombia in London and Paris, was Venezuelan consul-general and *chargé d'affaires* in France and the Netherlands, and later *chargé d'affaires* of El Salvador in France and Belgium. From afar, he developed a continental perspective to the Hispanic, Portuguese, and French Americas and was among the first to coin the term "Latin America," no later than 1856. He participated actively in the International Literary Association led by Victor Hugo in France, and he supported the idea of a Latin American Union. On other exiles and expatriates contributing to a Latin American imagery in the nineteenth century, see Mario Sznajder and Luis Roniger, *The Politics of Exile in Latin America* (Cambridge: Cambridge University Press, 2009), 78–83.

16. By the mid-1970s, the security services of Argentina, Bolivia, Brazil, Chile, Paraguay, and Uruguay formalized their cooperation in Operation Condor, designed to co-ordinate the transnational repression against the opponents of the South American dictatorships and military governments. Patrice J. McSherry, *Predatory States* (Lanham, MD: Rowman and Littlefield, 2005); John Dinges, *The Condor Years* (New York: The New Press, 2005); Luis Roniger, "Represión y prácticas genocidas: El sustrato ideologico y discursivo de la violencia generalizada," in *La Guerra Fría y las Americas,* Avital Bloch and Rosario Rodríguez, ed. (Colima, Mexico: Universidad de Colima y la Universidad Michoacana de San Nicolás de Hidalgo, 2014).

17. Alfonso Rumazo González, *8 grandes biografías* (Caracas: Ediciones de la Presidencia de la República, 1993), 463–465.

18. Luis Roniger, *Transnational Politics in Central America* (Gainesville: University Press of Florida, 2011), xxx.

19. Volker Wünderich, *Sandino en la Costa* (Managua: Editorial Nueva Nicaragua, 1989); Barry Carr, "Across Seas and Borders': Charting the Webs of Radical Internationalism in the Circum-Caribbean," in *Exile and the Politics of Exclusion in the Americas,* Luis Roniger, James N Green y Pablo Yankelevich, eds. (Brighton, UK: Sussex Academic Press, 2012).

20. Luis Roniger, *Transnational Politics in Central America* (Gainesville: University Press of Florida, 2011).

21. Ana María Cobos and Ana Lya Sater, "Chilean Folk Music in Exile," in *Intellectual Migration: Transcultural Contributions of European and Latin American Émigrés,* Liliana Sontag, ed. (Madison: Wisconsin, 1986); Brian Loveman, *The Legacy of Hispanic Capitalism* (New York: Oxford University Press, 2001).

22. Thomas C. Wright and Rody Oñate Zúñiga, "Chilean Political Exile," *Latin American Perspectives* 34, no. 4 (2007), 31.

23. Chile, *Country Reports on Human Rights Practices for 1985 (and for 1987)* (Washington, DC: Department of State, 1986 and 1988), 452 and 412.

24. Fernando Montupil, ed., *Exilio, derechos humanos y democracia. El exilio chileno en Europa* (Santiago: Coordinación Europea de Comités Pro-Retorno, 1993), 10.

25. Alan Angell and Susan Carstairs, "The Exile Question in Chilean Politics," *Third World Quarterly* 9, no. 1 (1987) : 153.

26. There are even larger estimates, such as Jorge Arrate's, who places the number of exiles and migrants at 1,800,000 (Jorge Arrate, *Exilio textos de denuncia y esperanza* [Santiago: Ediciones Documentos, 1988], 90–91; Jorge Gilbert and Edgardo Enríquez Frödden, *Testimonio de un destierro* [Santiago: Mosquito Editores, 1992], 122.) As a rule, researchers of exile indicate that no accurate data are available to provide an objective follow-up on exiles and expatriates, a general problem stressed among others by Pablo Yankelevich, "Exilio y dictadura," in *Argentina 1976. Estudios en torno al golpe de Estado*, Clara E. Lida, Horacio Crespo, and Pablo Yankelevich, eds. (Mexico City: Fondo de Cultura Económica, 2007); interview with Rongier and Sznajder on July 11, 2013.

27. On the plight of family members and the tension between private and public lives, see, for example, Diana Kay, *Chileans in Exile. Private Struggles, Public Lives* (London: Macmillan, 1987); for an analysis of the Uruguayan case, see Gabriela Fried-Amivilia, "The Dynamics of Memory Transmission across Generations in Uruguay. The Experiences of families of the Disappeared, Political Prisoners, and Exiles, after the Era of State Repression, 1973–1984," (PhD diss., UCLA, 2004); and also Mario Sznajder and Luis Roniger, *The Politics of Exile in Latin America* (Cambridge: Cambridge University Press, 2009), 191–197.

28. Mónica Gatica, "Váyase donde Usted quiera, con tal que no se lo coman estos perros acá . . . ! Memorias de trabajadores chilenos en el Noreste de Chubut," *Testimonios* 3 (2013), 135.

29. The UP coalition included the following political forces: the Communist Party, the Socialist Party, the Radical Party, the MAPU (*Movimiento de Acción Popular Unitaria*), la Christian Left, the Social Democratic Party, and the *Acción Popular Independiente*.

30. Jorge Arrate, *Exilio textos de denuncia y esperanza*, 34.

31. Jaime Llambias-Wolff, "The Voluntary Repatriation Process of Chilean Exiles," *International Migration* 31, no. 4 (1993): 581.

32. Danièle Joly and Robin Cohen, eds., *Reluctant Hosts: Europe and its Refugees* (Avebury, UK: 1989), 198; Daniel Moore, "Latinoamericanos en Suecia," in *Suecia-Latinoamerica: Relaciones y cooperación,* eds., Weine Karlsson, Ake Magnusson, and Carlos Vidales (Stockholm: Latin American Institute of Stockholm University, 1993).

33. Danièle Joly and Robin Cohen, eds. *Reluctant Hosts: Europe and Its Refugees* (Avebury, UK: 1989), 43.

34. Jorge Arrate, *Exilio textos de denuncia y esperanza*, 95–96.

35. Fernando Montupil, ed., *Exilio, derechos humanos y democracia. El exilio chileno en Europa* (Santiago: Coordinación Europea de Comités Pro-Retorno, 1993), 14–15.

36. Thomas C. Wright, Rody Oñate and Irene Hodgson, *Flight from Chile: Voices of Exile* (University of New Mexico Press, 1998).

37. Ana María Cobos and Ana Lya Sater, "Chilean Folk Music in Exile," in *Intellectual Migration: Transcultural Contributions of European and Latin American Émigrés,* ed. Liliana Sontag (Madison: Wisconsin, 1986).

38. Thomas C. Wright and Rody Oñate Zúñiga, "Chilean Political Exile," *Latin American Perspectives* 34, no. 4 (2007): 8–9.

39. Fernando Montupil, ed., *Exilio, derechos humanos y democracia. El exilio chileno en Europa* (Santiago: Coordinación Europea de Comités Pro-Retorno, 1993), 13–16; Ana Vásquez and Angela Xavier de Brito, "La situation de l'exilé: Essai de généralisation fondé sur l'exemple de réfugiés latino-américains," *Intercultures* 21 (1993).

40. Mili Rodríguez Villouta, *Ya nunca me verás como me vieras* (Santiago: Las Ediciones del Ornitorrinco, 1990). See also the self-critical portrait of the exile community as depicted by *Diálogo de exiliados*. Directed by Raúl Ruiz. 1974; France.

41. Luís Mara, "Claroscuros de un exilio privilegiado," in *En México, entre exilios* by Pablo Yankelevich (Mexico City: ITAM, 1998), 129, 136–137.

42. Daniel Moore, "Latinoamericanos en Suecia," in *Suecia-Latinoamerica: Relaciones y cooperación,* Weine Karlsson, Ake Magnusson, and Carlos Vidales, eds. (Stockholm: Latin American Institute of Stockholm University, 1993), 161–183.

43. Thomas C. Wright and Rody Oñate Zúñiga, "Chilean Political Exile," *Latin American Perspectives* 34, no. 4 (2007): 6.

44. Ana Vásquez and Angela Xavier de Brito, "La situation de l'exilé: essai de généralisation fondé sur l'exemple de réfugiés latino-américainsm," *Intercultures* 21 (1993): 125–132; Jorge Arrate, *Exilio textos de denuncia y esperanza* (Santiago: Ediciones Documentos, 1987), 100–101.

45. Claudia Rojas Mira, "La Casa de Chile en México, 1973–1993," in *Exiliados, emigrados y retornados. Chilenos en América y Europa, 1973 a 2004,* ed. José Del Pozo (Santiago: RIL Editores, 2006); Claudia Rojas Mira and Alessandro Santoni, "Geografía política del exilio chileno: Los diferentes rostros de la solidaridad," *Perfiles Latinoamericanos* 41 (2013): 7, 9.

46. Fernando Montupil, ed., *Exilio, derechos humanos y democracia. El exilio chileno en Europa* (Santiago: Coordinación Europea de Comités Pro-Retorno, 1993), 59.

47. Fernando Montupil, ed., *Exilio, derechos humanos y democracia. El exilio chileno en Europa* (Santiago: Coordinación Europea de Comités Pro-Retorno, 1993), 17.

48. Thomas C. Wright and Rody Oñate Zúñiga, "Chilean Political Exile," *Latin American Perspectives* 34, no. 4 (2007).

49. See, for example, the work by Fernando Pedrosa, *La otra izquierda: La socialdemocracia en América Latina* (Buenos Aires: Capital Intelectual, 2012).

50. Fernando Pedrosa, *La otra izquierda: La socialdemocracia en América Latina* (Buenos Aires: Capital Intelectual, 2012).

51. Thomas C. Wright and Rody Oñate Zúñiga, "Chilean Political Exile," *Latin American Perspectives* 34, no. 4 (2007): 9.

52. Interview with Gustavo Silva by Mario Sznajder (Santiago: August 2001); interview with Rodríguez Elizondo (Jerusalem: March, 2000); see also José Rodríguez Elizondo, *La pasión de Iñaki* (Santiago: Editorial Andrés Bello, 1996).

53. "Revista a las revistas chilenas del exilio 1973–1990." 2006. http://www.abacq.net /imagineria/revistas.htm

54. Maria Rosaria Stabili, "Exiled Citizens: Chilean Political Leaders in Italy," in *Shifting Frontiers of Citizenship: The Latin American Experience,* eds. Mario Sznajder, Luis Roniger, and Carlos A. Forment (Leiden: Brill, 2012).

55. Interview with Mario Sznajder, May 2002.

56. Javier Ortega, "El test de los cojones, parte I," *La Tercera,* 2000, accessed November 28, 2001. http://www.tercera.cl/especiales/2001/verdeolivo/capitulo01/test01.htm

57. Luis Roniger and Mario Sznajder, *The Legacy of Human Rights Violations in the Southern Cone: Argentina, Chile and Uruguay* (Oxford: Oxford University Press, 1999), 103–107.

58. Alan Angell, "International Support for the Chilean Opposition, 1973–1989: Political Parties and the Role of Exiles," in *The International Dimensions of Democratization. Europe and the Americas*, ed. Laurence Whitehead (Oxford: Oxford University Press, 1996); Alexandra Barahona de Brito, *Human Rights and Democratization in Latin America. Uruguay and Chile* (Oxford: Oxford University Press, 1997); Luis Roniger and Mario Sznajder, *The Legacy of Human Rights Violations in the Southern Cone: Argentina, Chile and Uruguay* (Oxford: Oxford University Press, 1999).

59. Mario Sznajder and Luis Roniger, "Exile Communities and Their Differential Institutional Dynamics: A Comparative Analysis of the Chilean and Uruguayan Political Diasporas," *Revista de Ciencia Política* 27, no. 1 (2007): 43.

60. Luis Roniger, "La sacralización del consenso nacional y las pugnas por la memoria histórica y la justicia en el Uruguay post-dictatorial," *América Latina Hoy* 61 (2012): 51.

61. Paul Estrade, *La colonia cubana de París, 1895–1898* (La Habana: Editorial de Ciencias Sociales, 1984).

Global Latin(o) Americanos
Rethinking Diasporic Membership and Participation

MARK OVERMYER-VELÁZQUEZ AND ENRIQUE SEPÚLVEDA III

This chapter builds on the introductions by Massey and García to assess critical themes examined throughout the volume's case studies. We begin by exploring how different people have employed Global Latin(o) Americanos and related identity labels, and then define who the migrants are, how they represent themselves, and how government officials in the various nation-states through which they move categorize them. Next, we turn to the myriad ways these new migratory trends have led to a recasting of existing conceptions of membership, citizenship, and other forms of belonging. From there we consider the emergence of new ways of social and political participation among the Latin(o) Americano diaspora and examine how these empirical chapters challenge us to decenter the traditional subjects of study and locations of knowledge production in Latino and Latin American Studies. A conclusion considers some possible topics for future study.

DEFINING GLOBAL LATIN(O) AMERICANOS

Scholars, government elites, marketing professionals, and others historically have used the term "global" in relation to Latinos and Latin Americans in a variety of ways. "Global Latinos" and its cognates are most often used to describe the diversity of the Latin American and Caribbean population in the United States, particularly at the intersection of cultural production, capital accumulation, and mass marketing. For example, Nicole Guidotti-Hernández's study of the children's cartoon, Dora the Explorer, examines the "shifting terrain of a globalized juvenile Latino/a television market" and the construction of a "universal Latino/a subjectivity."[1] Events such as the International Latino Cultural Center of Chicago's "Global-Latino-Fest" celebrated pan-Latino art forms and "promoted the richness and great diversity found in more than 20 Latino nations in the United States."[2]

Latina/o Studies scholars increasingly have interrogated the experience of US Latinos beyond the context of the nation-state. The editors and authors of *Technofuturos: Critical Interventions in Latina/o Studies* examine the connection between globality and Latinidad, where Latinidad is both a production and sense of collective identity among people of Latin American descent.[3] The authors ask, "do definitions of Latina/o identity, Latina/o political formations, research and thinking change when we move past the nation-state to a more globalized framework?"[4] With a focus on how global forces and exchanges impact Latina/os in the United States, the contributors study topics such as transnational migration, mass media, and gang membership, which expand their "understanding of global Latinidades."[5]

Although Latin Americans only recently have been moving in greater numbers to non-US destinations, Latin American political and cultural influences have circulated globally since well before the national period.[6] Latin American government elites have long sought to gain global recognition for their nations. More recently, governments in places such as Peru have marketed their countries internationally, strategically branding and promoting them abroad to "attract tourists and investors, to increase the demand for their products and services, and to earn the respect of other nations." Peruvian officials launched the campaign *Marca Perú* to fashion a narrative about Peru's global relevance, demonstrating how some worldwide locations have historical connections to towns and populations in Peru.[7] As with the bilingual, binational lyrics of Dominican singer Juan Luis Guerra's 2010 hit song recognizing the singing and dancing of Latin music in Japan, "Bachata en Fukuoka," Latin American cultural forms have circulated and interacted widely with other cultures from around the world.[8] And certainly as the first Pope from the Americas and the global South, Pope Francis has further energized the discussion of Latin America's influence in the world. Similarly, Latin American *fútbol* has been globally exported with South American players leading European soccer teams and commanding top salaries in the world's most followed sport.

Scholars also have examined Latin America's role in contemporary international relations. The contributors to *The Handbook of Latin America in the World* explain how, in recent decades, countries in Latin American have both contributed and reacted to changing international dynamics. In her chapter for *The Handbook*, "Migration in the Americas," Alexandra Délano examines how migration influences the foreign policy of sending states and the how the relationship between sending countries and the diaspora is most often focused on protection of migrants and maximizing effect of remittances.[9] Increasingly, academics in the United States and their institutions are investing in the study of international financial and political exchanges between Latin America and regions such as the Middle East and Asia.[10]

While acknowledging these and other important contributions to understanding the many dimensions of Latin America in the world, *Global Latin(o) Americanos* focuses on the displacement, movement, and settlement of Latin

American migrants in regional and global locations. The chapters in this volume clearly have demonstrated the diversity and range of identities and experiences of Latin America's diaspora. Together, they allow us to understand some of the many common and contrasting characteristics of this migratory community. Disaggregating the many terms of identity and movement used by the authors and migrants themselves sheds light on the historical forces that shaped those identities and movements in the first place.

Although most members of the Latin American diaspora in the region identify themselves by their national affiliation (e.g., Peruvian, Haitian, Guatemalan), Latin Americans living outside Latin America utilize additional identifiers depending on the particular local context. As we have seen in this volume, there are "Latina/os" in Canada, Israel, Spain, and elsewhere. Brazilian and Peruvian immigrants of Japanese descent living in Japan are *nikkejin*. The existence of self-proclaimed "Latina/os" in the non-US-based Latin American diaspora challenges the assertion by Suárez-Orozco and Páez that "[t]he very term *Latino* has meaning only in reference to the US experience. Outside the United States, we don't speak of Latinos; we speak of Mexicans, Cubans, Puerto Ricans, and so forth. Latinos are made in the USA."[11]

The notion of "making" Latinos refers here to the historical forces that have shaped Latinos in the US context: US economic and military penetration into Latin America and the resulting migratory displacement or "Harvest of Empire,"[12] following a demand for low-wage laborers in the United States; the growth of a diverse, multinational Latin American population; and that population's subordination and marginalization as racialized subjects.[13] Additional commonalities of language (Spanish) and religion (Catholicism) have linked the diaspora in their increasingly varied destinations throughout the United States.[14]

Although the experience of colonialism among US Latina/os has been particularly critical in shaping their formation as a diasporic community, as previous chapters have shown, migrants moving between Latin American countries and overseas have shared similar experience of labor exploitation, inequality, and racialization as they live and work as vulnerable minorities. Indeed, those similarities have most likely contributed to the use of the term "Latina/os" by Latin Americans in the non-US diaspora to refer to themselves in places such as Canada and Spain, Jordan and Italy.[15]

This volume's authors have differing opinions on the origins, emergence, and use of a pan-ethnic Latino identity in host countries. Massey argues—drawing on the case of the United States—that the potential for a Latino identity is "greatest when the Latino population is large and diverse," there is a significant "cultural and linguistic distance between the destination country and Latin America, greater exposure to processes of exclusion and discrimination, and greater economic exploitation at the hands of natives." Yet, in contrast, Canada's relatively small Latino community has organized and identified itself as Latinos in cities throughout the country. In their study of Spain's Latin American diaspora, Dyrness and Sepúlveda argue that young Latin American migrants develop and exhibit complex identity formations that belie simplistic linear assimilationist paradigms. In Madrid, for example, Latin American transnational migrants (Dominicans, Ecuadorians, Peruvians, etc.) maintain relations and contacts not only with family in their home countries but also in the United States, furthering the transnational cross-fertilization of ideas, artistic styles, labels, and other cultural influences.

The naming of Latin American's diasporic community is further complicated by the conditions of their migration, why they left their original homes, and how they arrived at their destinations.[16] As we have seen throughout this volume, socio-juridical terms such as immigrant, migrant, transmigrant, exile, and refugee each emerge from different historical contexts and carry with them a host of legal and extralegal constraints on rights and national membership. Most often determined by an individual's labor, political status, and length of stay in the host country, these terms change over time and can vary among members of one family. Additional terms abound for migrants who enter countries without legal authorization, so-called illegal, clandestine, or undocumented migrants. Whereas "illegal" and "clandestine" convey the notion of criminality, "undocumented" ignores those migrants who originally entered a country with legal documentation or carried falsified documents. Participants at the International Symposium on Migration, held in Bangkok in 1999, recommended the term "irregular." "Irregularities in migration can arise at various points—departure, transit, entry and return—they may be committed against or by the migrant."[17]

Additionally, an individual's legal categorization can itself shift depending on which government department is doing the classification and when. Comparing and contrasting the chapters by Roniger and Casillas, we note the tension between the terms "exile," "refugee," and "economic migrant." Each term has a particular relationship to direct or indirect forced displacement by the state and the related conditions of admission in a host country. One distinction drawn between refugees and migrants is that migrants do not face the threat of permanent harm or death. It can be, therefore, very difficult to determine at what point economic hardship and exploitive labor systems force people to flee a country because of a fear of death, a governing factor for receiving refugee status in many countries. As Catherine Nolan-Ferrell asks, "if parents watch their children die of malnutrition because of economic marginalization, does this push them into the category of refugee?"[18]

Furthermore, as Armony illustrates in his chapter on Latino Canadians, immigrants—especially newly arrived communities—are often categorized as emergent ethnic minorities. With varying relationships to and degrees of incorporation into the nation-state, immigrants and minorities have a range of representations and responsibilities in political systems.[19]

This volumes' authors examine the persistent, intersecting themes of labor, race, and nation-state formation that frame the transnational movement of Latin(o) Americanos. Although a nation-state focus is critical for understanding key areas of the migrant experience, such as immigration legislation, international migrants often move through more than one country, requiring a transnational approach to their study.[20] Yet while living and working transnationally is central to the experience of migrants, as Vior shows in his chapter on Bolivian agricultural workers in Buenos Aires, migrants also negotiate spaces "translocally," thinking and acting in terms of towns and regions. As Dick Hoerder argues, "Migrants move 'glocally'. Rather than pursue trans*national* strategies, they move across transregional, transcontinental, or transoceanic spaces and evaluate *life chances* in terms of *family economies* or *individual life-course projects and prospects* in shifting microregional or global economic frames."[21]

Aside from the case of Latin Americans in exile, this volume's chapters focus predominantly on the experiences of migrants leaving their countries of origin in search of labor opportunities. Through employer demand and strategic immigration laws, host countries encourage the arrival and maintenance of a pool of low-paid and vulnerable workers. At the same time, government officials, like those Margolis studies in Japan, are vigilant not to upset their country's dominant narrative of racial homogeneity.[22] As Adriana Kemp shows in an article related to her chapter with Rebeca Raijman in this volume, labor, race, and national membership are inextricably entwined in the migrant experience.

> [L]abour migration and citizenship [are linked] to racialisation processes in contemporary nation-states. . . . [There exists] the double moral standard that fuels the phenomenon of labour migrations globally: on the one hand, the increasing demand for and recruitment of a cheap and docile labour force in the guise of migrant men and women that pervades many neoliberal economies, and on the other, the strengthening of social and political barriers aimed at preventing their incorporation as legitimate members of the community.[23]

The movement of migrants across geopolitical borders challenges nations to reassert their legal and mythical notions of racialized citizenship. As we have seen in these chapters, race and nation are mutually constructed over time in relation to domestic and extra-national others: minority populations (e.g., indigenous and foreign communities) that upset the idea of national racial purity. Or as Micol Seigel argues, "race and nation must be understood together . . . for in our age these two categories are so profoundly intertwined that their relationship is constitutive of the meanings they both make."[24] Thus, for example, Casillas explains Mexico's enduring attempts to "*mestizar*" (misegenate) the indigenous population, "civilizing" them through a deliberate (and ultimately unsuccessful) process of encouraging the arrival of "white" migrants. As Sandoval demonstrates, the arrival of Nicaraguans in Costa Rica has upset many Ticos' sense of their country as an exceptional, white, middle-class nation and bastion of human rights. Similarly, the presence of Ecuadorians in Spain, Peruvians in Chile, and Colombians in Israel have all caused the host countries to reassert and fortify narrative and legal structures of exclusion. Having arrived at their destination countries, migrants face a host of obstacles to achieving legal status and membership. Despite these obstacles, they also have negotiated paths to belonging and engaging in community and political participation.

RECASTING DIASPORIC BELONGING

Belonging and Identity

> Dominican-born descendants of Haitian immigrants . . . seek acceptance as
> Dominican nationals on the basis of both their place of birth and the existence
> of an effective connection between them and the Dominican state (and their
> lack of connection with the Haitian state). Rejection of this claim by the
> Dominican state has placed tens of thousands of Haitian-Dominicans at risk
> of statelessness. (Martinez, this volume, p. 81)

This Haitian-Dominican example highlights the challenges and complexities of
belonging to a national political community for both the immigrant first generation and their second-generation children. With economic integration and contribution on the part of their parents' generation (as the first-generation immigrant
labor force), coupled with the birthright and cultural socialization of having lived
only in the Dominican Republic (DR), second-generation Haitian Dominicans'
claim to belonging to the DR seems to be a "reasonable expectation," as argued by
Carens.[25] And yet, as Martínez illustrates earlier, they continue to be on the verge
of expulsion and statelessness.

A central theme permeating all Latino migration case studies in this book is
the politics of belonging, a belonging that spans multiple localities and nation-
states. Each of these chapters demonstrates the varying and shifting scenarios
that migrants confront, thus illuminating the different dimensions and complexities of what it means to be in the diaspora.

The desire to belong is fundamental to the diasporic projects of building
new homes and communities, and creating new identities. Undergirding these
are the sociocultural practices and elements that migrants engage in and coconstruct in their new lands. We view the diaspora as an important socializing
agent for citizenship because, as Siu argues, "Being diasporic entails active and
conscious negotiation of one's identity and one's understandings of 'home'
and 'community'."[26] This goes to the core of establishing migrant communities
abroad. Siu defines "diasporic citizenship" as "the processes by which diasporic subjects experience and practice cultural and social belonging amid
shifting geopolitical circumstances and webs of transnational relations."[27]
Recent research has pointed out the benefits of transnational ties for immigrant youth in the areas of education, civic participation, and economic mobility in the host country.[28]

These chapters make evident that migration is both a source of struggle and
of possibilities. While conveying the multiple forms of discrimination, marginality, and oppression that migrants experience, these chapters also illustrate what
Rushdie calls "the great possibility that mass migration gives to the world . . . of
the transformation that comes of new and unexpected combinations of human
beings, cultures, ideas, politics, movies, songs." He writes, "mélange, hotchpotch,
a bit of this and a bit of that is how newness enters the world.[29]

Latino immigrants everywhere create spaces at the "border," spaces that are neither Spanish nor Dominican, neither Japanese nor Brazilian, reinforcing their bordered lives. Margolis poignantly demonstrates this cultural liminality for the *nikkejin*, Japanese people who emigrated from Japan and their descendants (aka Japanese Brazilians) and who have returned to Japan for work. She describes in this volume the multiple "cultural misunderstandings" between Japanese citizens and the *nikkejin*, such as cultural clashes with native Japanese arising from the fact that Brazilians often play loud music, barbecue on their balconies, do not keep appointments on time, or recycle properly. Because Japan does not have the same communal, cultural spaces that Brazilian Japanese were accustomed to, such as the *praça* (public square), they created new meeting spaces in front of grocery stores and "out in the streets." Such cultural practices caused much discord and misunderstandings among the native Japanese and their Brazilian relatives.

The social, economic, and legal conditions and analyses in these chapters point to the fundamental limitations of the modern liberal democratic state and its inability to welcome the immigrant other on a number of fronts. To say that the path to membership and belonging to the nation-state for immigrants and their descendants is fraught with multiple social and legal landmines is an understatement. Calhoun writes that "belonging matters . . . it matters as a feature of social organization. It joins people together in social relations and informs their actions. Without it the world would be a chaotic place."[30] And yet, Calhoun goes on to say, "liberal democratic societies have very little to say about belonging and so little capacity to recognize its importance."

Borrowing from Lowe, liberalism and the nation-state comprise contradictory sets of principles that argue for liberty and emancipation for the individual "within civil society," on the one hand, while simultaneously justifying social exclusion, exploitation, and dispersal/expulsion of the migrant subject, on the other. The marriage of racializing projects and nation-state formation and preservation allows the contemporary state to "safe keep and preserve" the nation through the exploitation of immigrant labor for its economic benefit and yet, at the same time, categorize and place migrant peoples "at various distances from liberal humanity"—Indian, Black, Negro, Chinese, immigrant, and so on.[31]

The enduring colonial difference maintained within the modern liberal state is all too evident in this volume's case studies. Martínez describes the contrasts between the profiting Dominican "growers and sugar mill owners" and the "overworked, starved, sick . . . sugar proletariat" working under dreadful conditions and "intolerable economic rights infringements." Sandoval lays bare the contradiction in Costa Rica between the imagery of a Nicaraguan migrant subject framed as the violent other and the fact that Nicaraguans have assumed the caretaker role for many Costa Rican elderly, children, and homes. Sandoval argues that the anti-Nicaraguan immigrant narratives in Costa Rica facilitate the disregard of international human rights agreements of which Costa Rica is a signatory. Moreover, Roniger, in examining the historical roots and institutional logic of exile, argues that "the recurrent use of territorial banishment reflects on the exclusionary nature of the nation-states in the region." He writes, "political actors and rank-and-file citizens have been forced time and again to leave their country of residence in order to escape repression, as they suffered the loss of civil and political rights or as they feared persecution or even the loss of life." (p. 232).

Social Costs and Consequences of Migration

> From the criminal network of delinquents dedicated to assaulting and robbing migrants, to the vast underworld of sex trafficking of women and child migrants, we see a plurality of underworlds that individually pose current or potential public safety problems and, when combined, constitute one enormous public security problem for all. (Casillas, this volume, p. 133)

For immigrants and their families the complicated process of entering and becoming new members of a national community is fraught with many social costs. As Casillas examines in his chapter, Central American migrants are exposed to any number of abuses along the southern Mexican border at the hands of criminal organizations, governmental officials, and even local private citizens. He adds, "In the context of Mexico, the concept of 'the Other' has not only been historically used to classify Mexico's indigenous population; it has also been used to classify undocumented foreigners . . . , fomenting a nationalistic fervor that serves as a pretext for taking advantage of migrants, who are widely seen as inferior and . . . unwelcomed within the national territory" (p. 118).

Race and racializing practices and discourses have also been at the forefront of dominant host societies' framing of the immigrant other. As Overmyer-Velázquez details in this volume, the historical emergence of Chile's racial constructions in the nineteenth century, as well as Chile's subsequent "racial orientation towards Latin Americans in general," continues to fuel xenophobic sentiment and actions in the present day. He writes of contemporary sensationalist television news shows depicting "Peruvian and other immigrants as contagion-ridden populations, prone to violence and social depravity" (p. 23).

In the case of Haitian immigrants in the Dominican Republic, obtaining legal citizenship "has always been made difficult by the anti-Haitian racism" (p. 81). The list of practices that Martínez calls "legally mandated exclusionism" includes arbitrary denial of birth certificates by agents of civil registry offices; the blocking of citizenship for children of undocumented immigrants; and "nationality stripping," the practice of removing previously acquired Dominican citizenship for Haitian Dominicans who have had valid papers their whole lives. Martínez laments that "a climate of potential threat has come to shadow even those Haitian-Dominicans who have legally possessed citizenship, assimilated culturally and moved up the social ladder" (p. 83).

The presence of immigrants in a new land invariably triggers and reveals the exclusivist and "purist" national narrative that defines who are "the" people of a nation and who are not. It is clear from the perspective of dominant populations that migrants are subjects who do not belong to the national narratives of past and present. They are a people whose past is not factored into the host nation's imaginary, which instead privileges racially supremacist notions of assimilation, integration, and progress. In their chapter, Dyrness and Sepúlveda examine the Spanish "integrationist narrative" that Latino immigrants must negotiate. They write, "Spanish educators and social workers we interviewed shared the view that ethnic association was equivalent to 'ghettos' and a threat to integration," and that "the centrality of conflict prevention in the integration discourse communicated the idea that immigrants could pose a threat if they remained visible; if they associated only with other immigrants and made visible displays of their ethnic identities" (p. 146). However attractive the assimilationist narrative of integration is to members of the dominant society, it fails to explain why many, in fact, need and reproduce ethnic, national, and cultural identities and distinctions. It obscures issues of inequality, discrimination, and oppression, and it glosses over, at a minimum, the exclusionary daily narratives and practices of the nation-state.[32]

For many immigrants, integrating into a new national community means negotiating complex cultural, linguistic, and racial elements that may or may not intersect with laws and governmental policies. These social vectors play out in formal as well as informal settings. As made evident from this collection of case studies, multiple lines of difference continue to challenge liberal democratic societies. Pollock et al. write that "late liberalism reveals ... a struggle at the heart of liberal theory, where a genuine desire for equality as a universal norm is tethered to a tenacious ethnocentric provincialism in matters of cultural judgment and taste." Rosaldo has called for a more expansive view of citizenship by advocating for recognition of a cultural citizenship, "which refers to the right to be different and to belong in a participatory democratic sense" and to have a voice and place in relationship to the other citizens.[33] The work in this volume builds on the ideas of difference, integration, and pluralism, but rather than focusing on benefits to host-country incorporation, the chapters also illustrate how the diaspora can be a resource for citizenship more broadly as immigrants come to terms with who they are in a new country, sometimes against all odds.

Civic and Political Participation

Set against the backdrop of limited and unrealistic integrationist narratives and, at times, hostile immigration policies and practices of host countries, the immigrants described in these chapters help us understand what citizenship, civic participation, and belonging can look like from the bottom up. Rather than viewing ethnic or home-nation belonging and identity as separate from civic engagement, migrants themselves demonstrate how belonging and identity can be multiple and "beyond the parameter of a single nation-state," and still be particularly useful for civic participation and development in the host country.[34]

In the Argentinian context, Vior's chapter illustrates the various ways the Bolivian immigrant community has engaged in cultural and commercial production in what is known as the "Bolivian territory" within the Buenos Aires metropolitan center. In this "Bolivian territory" one finds restaurants, soccer leagues, civic associations, magazines, radio stations and different types of retail stores, as well as *bailantas*, popular feasts where people come to eat and dance communally. From the perspective of members of dominant societies, immigrants' cultural forms of belonging and production seem to be a reproduction of traditional cultural practices from the immigrants' home country. What many fail to see is that these forms and practices also serve as social and civic infrastructure to support immigrants and help them thrive in their *new* home, which allows immigrants to negotiate the novel context through social and cultural expressions and eventually to engage in the political arena.

The studies in this volume also explain how Latinos are not mere victims of globalization, but rather subjects deploying agency within severe social and structural constraints. They utilize their intellectual, sociocultural, and political resources to construct new identities and spaces that transcend physical and social boundaries which cannot be reduced to one country or ethnicity. In many cases presented here, we see Latino migrants creating spaces of belonging and civic participation, all the while struggling against antagonistic local residents, constraining national immigration policies, and xenophobic politicians.

In Israel, for example, the state "deprived [Latinos] of social status, prestige, and power in the occupational and social spheres, and also of more traditional support structures" (p. 195). Thus, Latinos "search for alternative spaces to meet their needs, maintaining ties with communities back 'home', as well as articulating their own sense of community in the new country" (p. 195). They have done this, Kemp and Raijman argue, by creating religious and social activities (dance and soccer clubs) that came to serve as the "backbone of an emergent and distinct community" (p. 195).

Elements of civic participation in Latino diasporic communities can be seen in the processes of creating new spaces of belonging and community participation. According to Putnam (2003), these emerging social groupings and their threads of belonging are the building blocks of a more robust civic engagement and participation. Putnam contends that "society as a whole benefits enormously from the social ties forged by those who choose connective strategies in pursuit of their goals."[35] Valadez adds that the "ethnocultural group rights and conceptions of identity on which they partly depend will and should continue to be of significance for theories of governance in the global era."[36]

Understanding how diasporic communities mediate membership and social belonging from the bottom up helps us, as Benhabib et al. argue, to avoid the false dichotomy that forces a choice between the nation-state and other forms of attachments (whether they be to ethnocultural groups or larger federal states).[37] Examining the multiple, diverse experiences of the Latino diaspora in the hemisphere and around the globe allows us to go beyond well-worn mental maps to forge new ways of thinking and analyzing the cultural production of Latino belonging.

DECENTERING LATINO
AND LATIN AMERICAN STUDIES

The contextual and terminological overlap between the US Latina/o and Latin American migrant experience challenges us to reconsider how and where we study the global Latin American diaspora. Traditional Latino and Latin American Studies approaches have been too limited and, as García argues, require a "fuller recounting of the history of Latin American/Caribbean peoples" (p. xxii). This volume attempts to bridge these two sites of knowledge production by reorienting Latina/o Studies outside of a (North) American locus and Latin American and Caribbean Studies beyond the hemisphere, integrating and decentering traditional ethnic and area studies approaches.

The scholarly community has yet to rigorously unite these two approaches. As a prime example, the principal professional organization in the field, the Latin American Studies Association (LASA) has two related sections that rarely purposefully bring their panels into conversation with one another: Latina/o Studies and International Migrations. Established in 1997, The Latina/o Studies Section of LASA "formalized the academic study of the interactions of various Latin American populations in the United States."[38] LASA only recently (in 2013) included a section dedicated to international migrations. The International Migrations section sponsors papers and panels on migration in the Americas, including studies of Latin American communities in the United States.[39]

William Robinson forcefully argues the point:

> To consider inquiry into the reality of U.S.-based Latino/a populations as "Latino/a Studies" and inquiry into that reality south of the Rio Bravo as "Latin American Studies" is patently absurd. But it is more than that: it is epistemologically bankrupt and politically disempowering. It renders invisible to "Latin American Studies" the 40 million Latinos/as in the United States and cuts them off from the larger reality in which their lives are grounded at a time when our struggles and fates are more than ever shaped by our engagement with global-level processes and structures.[40]

Perhaps one reason for this absence of dialog can be found in the work by Silvio Torres-Saillant, where he points to the lack of critical attention to racism in Latin America among US-based Latina/o studies scholars. He argues that coming from a position of relative privilege of expression and resources, US Latina/o Studies scholars visit Latin America and the Caribbean to culturally recharge but then leave their critique of racial inequality behind. He writes, "Latino and U.S.-based Hispanic scholars writing and speaking from American university settings about race and ethnicity in Latin American and the Caribbean . . . have to show moral consistency as manifested in the willingness to oppose racism wherever it occurs."[41]

The hemispheric scholarly imbalance also exists in Latin America. Latina/o Studies scholarship, especially in Spanish or Portuguese translation, is in scarce supply, reinforcing the knowledge gap between north and south. Although admirable efforts have been made with considerable resources to translate works from Latin America in Spanish and Portuguese into English for US-based readers,[42] attempts at the opposite project have only rarely emerged in Latin America.[43]

Walter Mignolo's examination of the intellectual and institutional projects of Latin America's *Pensamiento Crítico* and Latina/o and Latin American Studies in the United States provides insight into how this volume's authors integrate these approaches in their study of the Latin American global diaspora. Mignolo argues that "Pensamiento Crítico, defined as 'knowledge production or social and philosophical thought in Latin America,' tends to investigate problems while Latin American Studies tends to study objects". On the other hand, Latina/o Studies shares a similar orientation toward research with Pensamiento Crítico since "scholars involved in these projects will be more interested in producing knowledge directly related to the problems of their respective communities".[44] Pedro Cabán offers a compelling examination of the relationship between Latin American and Latino Studies and their unique approaches to studying marginalized populations.

> The field of Latino Studies occupies a distinct niche in the academic hierarchy and is characterized by a profoundly different set of analytical and political concerns. Latin American Studies was a top-down enterprise promoted by government agencies, university administrations and large foundations. In contrast, ethnic studies programs were interested in studying the "Third World" within the United States and *linking these studies to the "Third World without."*[45]

Mignolo underscores the importance of the "geopolitics of knowledge" and asks the questions, "Who is producing knowledge/understanding? Where? Under what conditions and to what end?" This place-based orientation of knowledge production is critical for understanding what kinds of questions are asked by scholars and why.[46] The authors in *Global Latin(o) Americanos*, writing from different geopolitical and disciplinary locations, share this critical approach to investigating problems and draw on insights from both the Latina/o Studies and Pensamiento Crítico traditions in their work. Bringing scholars together from the global South and North in this collaborative volume allows for a critical "epistemic and political intervention" and provides a model for similar academic exchanges in other world regions.[47]

CONCLUSIONS

In examining the global Latin(o) Americano diaspora, this volume's authors contribute to theoretical and methodological developments and debates that seek to better understand nation-state formation, diasporic citizenship, transnational and civic subjectivities, workers' rights, new racial paradigms, legal systems, and education. Building on scholarship in area, ethnic, and migration studies, *Global Latin(o) Americanos'* original, interdisciplinary chapters examine how, in their diasporic experiences, migrants themselves engage and negotiate these multiple conceptual frames. Yet more needs to be known about the transnational practices and identities of global Latin(o) American migrant communities outside of the United States. Here we suggest some avenues for future research.

Although touched on in some of the chapters, it will be important to broaden the comparative analysis of different diasporic experiences and learn more about the relationship between internal migrants and immigrants. For example, what has been the dynamic in Argentina between recently arrived Paraguayan and Bolivian migrants and more established migrant communities from Europe? Similarly, how have Latino migrants in Europe interacted with other minority populations from places such as Poland and Turkey? How have governments responded to these types of multinational and cultural encounters?

If the global Latin(o) Americano diaspora continues to grow and migrate to non-US destinations, how will migrants impact political, economic, social, and cultural conditions in their countries of origin? How will Latin American governments faced with continued emigration sustain their particular nation-state ideologies and narratives?

Maylei Blackwell's scholarship points to another dimension of the global Latin(o) Americano experience that should be pursued. With a focus on cross border and transnational dialogues among indigenous women activists and their role in reshaping local ideals of justice as well as national and international policies, Blackwell points to the enduring existence of indigenous "migrants" in Latin America. Negotiating colonial and then national territorial impositions, indigenous groups have long crossed and lived along borders. In addition to creating solidarity networks across the US border, contemporary indigenous Latin Americans move and work throughout the region and have fostered transoceanic ties as well.[48]

Most important, we need to hear more voices from members of the global Latin(o) Americano diaspora themselves. As activist scholars, one way to support this is to work in solidarity with migrants by following the lead of the professional scholars and indigenous and Afro-Latin knowledge producers in the Other Americas/Otros Saberes Collaborative Research Initiative of the Latin American Studies Association. The Other Americas/Otros Saberes project brings together "civil society knowledge producers with university-based researchers who have similar areas of expertise, allowing both groups to reap the benefits of collaboration."[49] As communities of global Latin(o) Americanos grow and become more established in areas around the world, expanding our knowledge of the historical conditions of their displacement, transnational migration, and integration will help us understand how to best accompany migrants in their struggles for rights and membership in their new homes.[50]

NOTES

1. Nicole M. Guidotti-Hernándeza, "Dora the Explorer, Constructing 'Latinidades' and the Politics of Global Citizenship," *Latino Studies* 5 (2007): 209.

2. Global-Latino-Fest, accessed June 3, 2015, http://latinoculturalcenter.org/?attachment_id=26

3. In her work, Juana María Rodríguez, defines Latinidad as "a particular geopolitical experience but it also contains within it the complexities and contradictions of immigration, (post)(neo)colonialism, race, color, legal status class, nation, language and the politics of location." Juana María Rodríguez, *Queer Latinidad: Identity Practices, Discursive Spaces* (New York: NYU Press, 2003), 307.

4. Nancy Raquel Mirabal and Agustín Laó-Montes, eds., *Technofuturos: Critical Interventions in Latina/o Studies* (Lanham, MD: Lexington Books, 2007), 3.

5. Mirabal and Laó-Montes, *Technofuturos: Critical Interventions in Latina/o Studies*, 14.

6. For a concise overview of Latin America's complex interaction in world history, see William Sater, "Joining the Mainstream: Integrating Latin America into the Teaching of World History," *Perspectives on History* (1995).

7. Marca Peru, accessed on July 10, 2015, http://nacional.peru.info/en/content/PeruBrand. See also "Loreto, Italia: Campaña Nacional de la Marca Perú 2012," accessed on July 10, 2015, http://www.youtube.com/watch?v=zYcGSiHf6JE

8. These works exemplify two Latin American cultural forms, music and food, that are part of global circuits of production, distribution, and consumption. Michelle Bigenho, *Intimate Distance: Andean Music in Japan* (Durham, NC: Duke University Press, 2012); Frances R. Aparicio, *Listening to Salsa: Gender, Latin Popular Music, and Puerto Rican Cultures* (Middletown, PA: Wesleyan University Press, 1998) and Jeffrey M. Pilcher, *Planet Taco: A Global History of Mexican Food* (New York: Oxford University Press, 2012). See also the example of the Latino Americando Expo in Milan, Italy, started in 1991 for "lovers of music, dance, cuisine and way of life in Latin America," accessed August 21, 2015, http://www.expo2015.org/en/events/all-events/latinoamericando-2014-latin-america-in-milan

9. Jorge I. Domínguez and Ana Covarrubias, eds., *Routledge Handbook of Latin America in the World* (New York: Routledge, 2014).

10. For examples, see the China-Latin America Finance Database at Boston University, accessed on July 10, 2015, http://www.bu.edu/pardeeschool/research/gegi/program-area/chinas-global-reach/china-latin-america-database/ and the Leonel Fernandez Center for Latin American Studies at the University of Jordan, accessed on July 10, 2015, http://lfc.ju.edu.jo/Home.aspx

11. Marcelo M. Suárez-Orozco and Mariela Páez, *Latinos: Remaking America* (Berkeley: University of California Press, 2008), 4.

12. Juan González, *Harvest of Empire: A History of Latinos in America* (New York: Penguin, 2011).

13. For a detailed definition of the origins of US Latinos, see David Gutiérrez, *The Columbia History of Latinos in the United States Since 1960* (New York: Columbia University Press, 2004). The case of Puerto Rico, as Jorge Duany argues, continues to belong to the legal US empire and should be categorized as a "transnational colonial state." Jorge Duany, *Blurred Borders: Transnational Migration between the Hispanic Caribbean and the United States* (Chapel Hill: University of North Carolina Press, 2011).

14. Following Cristina Beltrán, we note that despite these many commonalities, constructing a unified Latino-ness is both inaccurate and politically counterproductive given the diversity of national, racial, religious, and other subject positions of the Latin American diaspora in the United States. See Cristina Beltrán, *The Trouble with*

Unity: Latino Politics and the Creation of Identity (Oxford University Press on Demand, 2010).

15. The authors' research and fieldwork in Europe (Spain, Italy, and Denmark) and the Middle East (Jordan, Lebanon, and Israel) introduced them to the use of the term "Latina/o" among people of the Latin American diaspora.

16. We acknowledge that among the numerous factors involved in causing and sustaining migration, global climate change and social media deserve special attention, especially in recent decades. Recent studies that examine these areas include Russell King and Nancy Wood, eds. *Media and Migration: Constructions of Mobility and Difference* (New York: Routledge, 2013); Myria Georgiou, *Diaspora, Identity and the Media: Diasporic Transnationalism and Mediated Spatialities* (New York: Hampton Press, 2006); Dominic Kniveton, Kerstin Schmidt-Verkerk, Christopher Smith, and Richard Black, "Climate Change and Migration: Improving Methodologies to Estimate Flows," International Organization for Migration. MRS No. 33 (2008); Rafael Reuveny, "Climate Change-Induced Migration and Violent Conflict," *Political Geography* 26, no. 6 (2007): 656–673; Robert McLeman and Barry Smit, "Migration as an Adaptation to Climate Change," *Climatic Change* 76, no. 1–2 (2006): 31–53; Kathleen Newland, "Climate Change and Migration Dynamics," Migration Policy Institute, September 2011.

17. Piyasiri Wickramasekera, *Asian Labour Migration: Issues and Challenges in an Era of Globalization* (Geneva: International Migration Programme, International Labour Office, 2002).

18. Catherine Nolan-Ferrell, "Working for Citizenship: Guatemalan Refugees in Southern Mexico, 1980–1996," paper presented at Aquí y Allá: Migrations in Latin American Labor History Conference, Duke University, May 2014.

19. For an elaboration on the political philosophy of minority rights, see Will Kymlicka, ed., *The Rights of Minority Cultures* (Oxford: Oxford University Press, 1995).

20. For a discussion of the use of the transnational frame in labor history, see John French, "Another World History Is Possible: Reflections on the Translocal," in *Workers Across the Americas: The Transnational Turn in Labor History*, Leon Fink, ed. (New York: Oxford University Press, 2011); Julie Greene, "Historians of the World: Transnational Forces, Nation-States," in *Workers Across the Americas: The Transnational Turn in Labor History*, Leon Fink, ed. (New York: Oxford University Press, 2011); Neville Kirk, "Transnational Labor History: Promise and Perils," in *Workers Across the Americas: The Transnational Turn in Labor History*, Leon Fink, ed. (New York: Oxford University Press, 2011); Aviva Chomsky, "Labor History as World History: Linking Regions over Time," in *Workers Across the Americas: The Transnational Turn in Labor History*, Leon Fink, ed. (New York: Oxford University Press, 2011); Dirk Hoerder, "Overlapping Spaces: Transregional and Transcultural," in *Workers Across the Americas: The Transnational Turn in Labor History*, Leon Fink, ed. (New York: Oxford University Press, 2011); Vic Satzewich, "Transnational Migration: A New Historical Phenomenon?" in *Workers Across the Americas: The Transnational Turn in Labor History*, Leon Fink, ed. (New York: Oxford University Press, 2011); Mark Overmyer-Velázquez, ed., *Beyond la Frontera: The History of Mexico-US Migration* (Oxford: Oxford University Press, 2011).

21. Hoerder, "Overlapping Spaces: Transregional and Transcultural," 36; emphasis in original.

22. See discussion of race, nation, and immigrant narratives in Mark Overmyer-Velázquez, "Histories and Historiographies of Greater Mexico," in *Beyond la Frontera*: The History of Mexico-US Migration, Mark Overmyer-Velázquez, ed. (Oxford: Oxford University Press, 2011), xix–xlvi.

23. Adriana Kemp, "Labour Migration and Racialisation: Labour Market Mechanisms and Labour Migration Control Policies in Israel," *Social Identities* 10, no. 2 (2004): 268.

24. Micol Seigel, *Uneven Encounters: Making Race and Nation in Brazil and the United States* (Durham, NC: Duke University Press, 2010), 4.

25. Joseph H. Carens, *The Ethics of Immigration* (Oxford: Oxford University Press, 2013), 64.

26. Lok Siu, *Memories of a Future Home: Diasporic Citizenship of Chinese in Panama* (Stanford, CA: Stanford University Press, 2005), 11.

27. Siu, *Memories of a Future Home: Diasporic Citizenship of Chinese in Panama*, 5.

28. Patricia Sanchez, "Urban Immigrant Students: How Transnationalism Shapes Their World Learning," *The Urban Review* 39, no. 5 (2007): 489–517; Patricia Sanchez and G. S. Kasun, "Connecting Transnationalism to the Classroom and to Theories of Immigrant Student Adaptation," *Berkeley Review of Education* 3, no. 1 (2012): 71–93; Thea Abu El-Haj, *Unsettled Belongings: Educating Palestinian American Youth after 9/11* (Chicago: University of Chicago Press, 2015); Deborah Reed-Danahay and Caroline D. Brettell, *Citizenship, Political Engagement, and Belonging: Immigrants in Europe and the United States* (New Brunswick, NJ: Rutgers University Press, 2008); Alejandro Portes, L. E. Guarnizo, and P. Landolt, "The Study of Transnationalism: Pitfalls and Promise of an Emergent Research Field," *Ethnic and Racial Studies* 22, no. 2 (2007): 217–237.

29. Salman Rushdie, "In Good Faith," *Independent on Sunday*, February 4, 1990.

30. Craig Calhoun, "Social Solidarities as a Problem for Cosmopolitan Democracy," in *Identities, Affiliations, and Allegiances*, Sayla Benhabib, Ian Shapiro, and Danilo Petranović, eds. (Cambridge: Cambridge University Press, 2007), 286.

31. Lisa Lowe, *The Intimacies of Four Continents* (Durham, NC: Duke University Press, 2015), 6–9.

32. Calhoun, "Social Solidarities as a Problem for Cosmopolitan Democracy"; Ana Rios-Rojas, "Managing and Disciplining Diversity: The Politics of Conditional Belonging in a Catalonian Institut," *Anthropology and Education Quarterly* 45, no. 1 (2014): 20–21; Abu El-Haj, *Unsettled Belongings: Educating Palestinian American Youth after 9/11*.

33. Sheldon Pollock, Homi K. Bhabha, Carol Breckenridge, and Dipesh Chakrabharty, "Cosmopolitanisms," *Public Culture* 12, no. 3 (2000): 581; Renato Rosaldo, "Cultural Citizenship and Educational Democracy," *Cultural Anthropology* 9, no. 3 (1994): 402–411; William V. Flores and Rina Benmayor, *Cultural Citizenship: Claiming Identity, Space, and Rights* (Boston: Beacon Press, 1998).

34. Siu, *Memories of a Future Home*, 196.

35. Robert Putnam, *Better Together: Restoring the American Community* (New York: Simon and Schuster, 2003), 269.

36. Jorge M. Valadez, "The Continuing Significance of Ethnocultural Identity," in *Identities, Affiliations, and Allegiances*, Sayla Benhabib, Ian Shapiro, and Danilo Petranović, eds. (Cambridge: Cambridge University Press. 2007), 303.

37. Valadez, "The Continuing Significance of Ethnocultural Identity."

38. LASA Latino Studies Section, accessed July 3, 2015, http://lasa.international.pitt.edu /sections/latino-studies/?pg=1.

39. LASA International Migrations Section News, Vol. 1, Issue 1., August 2013, http:// lasa.international.pitt.edu/cmsAdmin/uploads/IM1.pdf

40. William I. Robinson, "Why the Immigrant Rights Struggle Compels Us to Reconceptualize Both Latin American and Latino/a Studies," *Forum, Latin American Studies Association* 38, no. 2 (2007).

41. Silvio Torres-Saillant, "Racism in the Americas and the Latino Scholar," in *Neither Enemies Nor Friends: Latinos, Blacks, Afro-Latinos,* Anani Dzidzienyo and Suzanne Oboler, eds. (New York: Palgrave Macmillan, 2005), 295.

42. For example, see Latin America in Translation Series coordinated and funded by the Duke University and University of North Carolina Presses.

43. See the forthcoming series of US-based works on Mexican migration to the United States, prepared in Spanish translation for a Mexican audience by the Voces del México de Afuera project at El Colegio de la Frontera Norte.

44. Walter Mignolo, "Capitalism and Geopolitics of Knowledge" in Juan Poblete, ed. *Critical Latin American and Latino Studies.* Vol. 12. U of Minnesota Press, 2003, 33.

45. Pedro Cabán, "The New Synthesis of Latin American and Latino Studies," in *Borderless Borders: US Latinos, Latin Americans, and the Paradox of Interdependence,* Frank Bonilla et al., eds. (Philadelphia: Temple University Press, 2010), 202. Emphasis in the original.

46. In their comparative, qualitative survey of scholars of Latin America based in Latin America, the United States, and United Kingdom, Mu and Pereyra-Rojas conclude that "Latin American scholars [based in Latin America] identify themselves as agents of change, motivated by a desire to solve problems and fulfill social needs in the region, whereas US/UK-based scholars see themselves mainly as experts in the field, driven by a desire to impact the knowledge about the region." Enrique Mu and Milagros Pereyra-Rojas, "Impact on Society versus Impact on Knowledge: Why Latin American Scholars Do Not Participate in Latin American Studies," *Latin American Research Review* 50, no. 2 (2015): 216.

47. Walter Mignolo, "Capitalism and Geopolitics of Knowledge: Latin American Social Thought and Latino/a American Studies," in *Critical Latin American and Latino Studies,* Juan Poblete, ed. (Minneapolis: University of Minnesota Press, 2003), 32–75, 33–34, 52–53. The entire edited collection provides a profound analysis of historical development, intersections, and contrasts of these different sites and productions of knowledge.

48. Maylei Blackwell, "Zones of Autonomy: Gendered Cultural Citizenship and Indigenous Women's Organizing in Mexico," in *Gender and Cultural Citizenship: Rethinking Knowledge Production, Political Activism, and Culture,* The Working Group on Gender and Cultural Citizenship, ed. (New York: Palgrave Press, 2009), 39–54.

49. Charles Hale and Lynn Stephen, eds. *Otros saberes: Collaborative Research on Indigenous and Afro-descendant Cultural Politics* (New York: School for Advanced Research Press, 2013).

50. Enrique Sepúlveda, "Toward a Pedagogy of *acompañamiento*: Mexican Migrant Youth Writing from the Underside of Modernity," *Harvard Educational Review* 81, no. 3 (2011): 550–573.

Bibliography

Abbot, Thomas. "The Two Worlds of Buenos Aires: Macri's Legacy of Inequality." Washington, DC: Council on Hemispheric Affairs (COHA), 2014. http://www.coha.org/the-two-worlds-of-buenos-aires-macris-legacy-of-inequality-2/

Abrajano, Marisa and Zoltan L. Hajnal. *White Backlash: Immigration, Race, and American Politics Hardcover.* Princeton, NJ: Princeton University Press, 2015.

Abu El-Haj, Thea R. "'I Was Born Here, but My Home, It's Not Here': Educating for Democratic Citizenship in an Era of Transnational Migration and Global Conflict." *Harvard Educational Review* 77, no. 3 (2007).

Abu El-Haj, Thea R. "Becoming Citizens in an Era of Globalization and Transnational Migration: Re-Imagining Citizenship as Critical Practice." *Theory into Practice* 4, no. 8 (2009).

Abu El-Haj, Thea R. *Unsettled Belongings: Educating Palestinian American Youth after 9/11.* Chicago: University of Chicago Press, 2015.

Abu-Laban, Yasmeen. "Liberalism, Multiculturalism and the Problem of Essentialism." *Citizenship Studies* 6, no. 4 (2002).

Actis, W. "Impactos de la crisis sobre la población inmigrada. Entre la invisibilidad y el rechazo latente." Paper presented at the "El desafío de las grandes ciudades en un contexto de crisis: Presente y futuro de los hijos de la inmigración," Madrid, October 8–9, 2013.

Adams, Michael. *Fire and Ice: United States, Canada and the Myth of Converging Values.* Toronto: Penguin Canada, 2003.

Adúriz, Isidro. *La Industria Textil en Argentina. Su evolución y sus condiciones de trabajo.* Buenos Aires: INPADE, 2009.

Agar, Lorenzo. "Inmigrantes en Chile, un desafío para la interculturalidad." *Novamérica* 115 (2007).

Agencia EFE. "Entra en vigencia el plan dominicano para regular extranjeros." 2014. Accessed June 2. http://feeds.univision.com/feeds/article/2014-06-02/entra-en-vigencia-el-plan

Aguado, Teresa. "The Education of Ethnic, Racial and Cultural Minority Groups in Spain." In *The Routledge International Companion to Multicultural Education,* edited by James Banks. New York: Routledge, 2009.

Agudo, Alejandro. "El 50% de inmigrantes de segunda generación se siente español." *El País,* May 13, 2013.

Alberdi, Juan Bautista. "Bases y puntos de partida para lo organización de la República Argentina." Valparaíso: 1852.

Alemán, Carlos Enrique. "Nicas belicosos: Nicaragüenses en la Guerra Civil de Costa Rica, 1948." *Anuario de Estudios Centroamericanos* 39 (2013).

Algazy, Yosef. "Targeting the Leaders: Civil Rights Organizations Are Delighted at the Activities of Local Leaders of Foreign Workers." Ha'aretz, August 6, 2001.

Amaral, Rubem Guimarães. "Perfil da Comunidade Brasileira no Exterior." Brasília Departamento das Comunidades Brasileiras no Exterior, Ministério das Relações Exteriores, 2005.

Americas Watch. *A Troubled Year: Haitians in the Dominican Republic.* New York: Americas Watch and National Coalition for Haitian Refugees, 1992.

Amin, Samir. "Mundialización y financiarización." In *Los desafíos de la mundialización,* edited by Samir Amin, 127–145. México: Siglo XXI, 1999.

Amnesty International. "República Dominicana—Carta abierta al Presidente Danilo Medina." 2014. Accessed June 3. http://www.amnesty.org/es/library/asset/AMR27/008/2014/es/b0f89c58-43df-4b81-a854-3ce51e02638b/amr270082014es.pdf

Anaya Gautier, Céline. *Esclaves au paradis.* La Roque d'Anthéron: Vents d'Ailleurs, 2007.

Anderson, Bridget, Matthew J. Gibney, and Emanuela Paoletti. "Citizenship, Deportation and the Boundaries of Belonging." *Citizenship Studies* 15, no. 5 (2011).

Angell, Alan. "International Support for the Chilean Opposition, 1973–1989: Political Parties and the Role of Exiles." In *The International Dimensions of Democratization. Europe and the Americas,* edited by Laurence Whitehead. Oxford: Oxford University Press, 1996.

Angell, Alan and Susan Carstairs. "The Exile Question in Chilean Politics." *Third World Quarterly* 9, no. 1 (1987).

Annoni, Danielle, Antonio Augusto Cançado Trindade, et al. *Os novos conceitos do novo direito internacional: cidadania, democracia e direitos humanos.* Rio de Janeiro: América Jurídica, 2002.

Anti-Slavery Society. "Migrant Workers in the Dominican Republic." *The Anti-Slavery Reporter and Aborigines' Friend* 12, no. 6 (1979).

Aparicio, Frances R. *Listening to Salsa: Gender, Latin Popular Music, and Puerto Rican Cultures.* Middletown, PA: Wesleyan University Press, 1998.

Aprile, Sylvie. *Le siècle des exilés. Bannis et proscrits de 1789 à la Commune.* Paris: CNRS Editions, 2010.

Arrate, Jorge. *Exilio textos de denuncia y esperanza.* Santiago: Ediciones Documentos, 1988.

Armony, Victor. "Des Latins du Nord? L'identité culturelle québécoise dans le contexte panaméricain." *Recherches sociographiques* 43, no. 1 (2002).

Asamblea Legislativa de la República de Costa Rica 2009. *Ley de migración y extranjería* 8764. San Jose.

Avinery, Schlomo, Liav Orgad, and Amnon Rubinstein. "Managing Global Migration: A Strategy for Immigration Policy in Israel." Position Paper, Jerusalem, Metzilah Center for Zionist, Jewish, Liberal and Humanist Thought, 2010.

Aysa-Lastra, María and Lorenzo Cachón. *Immigrant Vulnerability and Resilience: Comparative Perspectives on Latin American Immigrants During the Great Recession.* New York: Springer, 2015.

Báez Evertsz, Franc, and Wilfredo Lozano. "Los cambios de la inmigración haitiana y la polémica de sus cifras." *Revista Dominicana de Política Exterior* 1, no. 1 (2005).

Balderrama, Francisco E., and Raymond Rodríguez. *Decade of Betrayal: Mexican Repatriation in the 1930s.* Albuquerque: University of Arizona Press, 1995.

Baluarte, David C. "Inter-American Justice Comes to the Dominican Republic: An Island Shakes as Human Rights and Sovereignty Clash." *American University Human Rights Brief* 13.2 (2006). http://www.wcl.american.edu/hrbrief/13/2baluarte.pdf?rd=1

Bandieri, Susana. *Historia de la Patagonia.* Buenos Aires: Sudamericana, 2009.

Bar-Tzuri, Roni. *Foreign workers without permits that were deported in 2008.* Jerusalem: Research and Economy Department, MoITaL, 2009.

Barahona de Brito, Alexandra. *Human Rights and Democratization in Latin America. Uruguay and Chile.* Oxford: Oxford University Press, 1997.

Barandiarán, Javeria. "Researching Race in Chile." *Latin America Research Review* 47, no. 1 (2012).

Barone, Víctor. "Globalización y neoliberalismo: elementos de una crítica." *Consejo Latinoamericano de Ciencias Sociales (CLACSO), Documento de trabajo* 95 (1998).

Barr-Melei, Patrick. *Reforming Chile: Cultural Politics, Nationalism, and the Rise of the Middle Class.* Chapel Hill: University of North Carolina Press, 2001.

Barrientos, Nora. "Políticas públicas e identidades étnicas: la corporación nacional de desarrollo indígena." in *¿Hay patria que defender? La identidad nacional frente a la globalización* by Centro de Estudios para el Desarrollo. Santiago: Ediciones del Segundo Centenario, 2000.

Bartram, David. "Foreign Workers in Israel: History and Theory." *International Migration Review* 32 (1998).

Basch, Linda, Nina Glick Schiller and Cristina Szanton Blanc. *Nations Unbound: Transnational Projects, Postcolonial Predicaments, and Deterritorialized Nation-States.* Langhorne: Gordon and Breach, 1994.

Baud, Michiel. "Sugar and Unfree Labour: Reflections on Labour Control in the Dominican Republic, 1870–1935." *Journal of Peasant Studies* 19, no. 2 (1992).

Beckman, Ericka. "The Creolization of Imperial Reason: Chilean State Racism in the War of the Pacific." *Journal of Latin American Studies* 18, no. 1 (2009).

Behiels, Michael D. and Reginald C. Stuart, ed. *Transnationalism. Canada-United States History into the 21st Century.* Montreal: McGill-Queen's University Press, 2010.

Beltrán, Cristina. *The Trouble with Unity: Latino Politics and the Creation of Identity.* Oxford University Press on Demand, 2010.

Benencia, Roberto. "Apéndice: la inmigración limítrofe." In *Historia de la inmigración en Argentina,* edited by F. Devoto, 433–524. Buenos Aires: Sudamericana, 2004.

Benencia, Roberto and Marcela Geymonat. "Migración transnacional y redes sociales en la creación de territorios productivos en la Argentina: Río Cuarto, Córdoba." *Cuadernos de Desarrollo Rural* 55 (2005).

Benencia, Roberto. "Los inmigrantes bolivianos en el mercado de trabajo de la horticultura en fresco en la Argentina." *Cuadernos migratorios* 2 (2012): 153–234.

Bengoa, Jose, ed. *La memoria olvidada: Historia de los pueblos indígenas de Chile.* Santiago: Cuadernos Bicentenario, 2004.

Berg, Ulla and Carla Tamagno. "El Quinto Suyo from above and from Below: State Agency and Transnational Political Practices among Peruvian Migrants in the US and Europe." *Latino Studies* 4, no. 3 (2006).

Berg, Ulla D. "El Quinto Suyo Contemporary Nation Building and the Political Economy of Emigration in Peru." *Latin American Perspectives* 37, no. 5 (2010): 121–137.

Bernstein, Deborah and Shlomo Swirsky. "The Rapid Economic Development of Israel and the Emergence of the Ethnic Division of Labour." *The British Journal of Sociology* 33, no. 1 (1982): 64–85.

Bertranou, Fabio, Luis Casanova and Tomás Lukin. *La formalización laboral en Argentina: avances recientes y el camino por recorrer.* 2013. Accessed February 24, 2015. http://www.ilo.org/wcmsp5/groups/public/---americas/---ro-lima/---ilo-buenos_aires/documents/publication/wcms_228768.pdf

Bhattacharyya, Gargi. *Dangerous Brown Men. Exploiting Sex, Violence and Feminism in the War of Terror.* London: Zed Books, 2008.

Bielefeldt, Heiner. *Philosophie der Menschenrechte: Grundlagen eines weltweiten Freiheitethos.* Darmstadt, Germany: Wissenschaftliche Buchgesellschaft, 1998.

Bigenho, Michelle. *Intimate Distance: Andean Music in Japan.* Durham, NC: Duke University Press, 2012.

Bissoondath, Neil. *Selling Illusions. The Cult of Multiculturalism in Canada.* Toronto: Penguin, 1994.

Blackwell, Maylei. "Zones of Autonomy: Gendered Cultural Citizenship and Indigenous Women's Organizing in Mexico." In *Gender and Cultural Citizenship: Rethinking Knowledge Production, Political Activism, and Culture,* edited by The Working Group on Gender and Cultural Citizenship. New York: Palgrave Press, 2009.

Blancpain, Jean Pierre. "Los alemanes en Chile 1816–1945." Santiago: Hachette, Ediciones Pedagógicas Chilenas (EPC), Editorial Universitaria, 1985.

Blancpain, Jean Pierre. "Francia y los franceses en Chile 1700–1980." Chile: Hachette, Ediciones Pedagógicas Chilenas (EPC), Editorial Universitaria, 1987.

Bloemraad, Irene. "'Two Peas in a Pod', 'Apples and Oranges', and Other Food Metaphors: Comparing Canada and the United States." *American Behavioral Scientist* 55 (2011).

Bobbio, Norberto, Antonio de Cabo, and Gerardo Pisarello. *Teoría general de la política.* Madrid: Trotta, 2009.

Bonacic-Doric, Lucas. *Historia de los yugoslavos en Magallanes.* Chile: Imprenta La Nacional, 1855.

Bonilla, Alcira B. "Ética y multiculturalismo." In *Segunda Muestra Nacional de Filosofía, "La recuperación del sujeto a partir de la construcción de la identidad,"* edited by M. Lobosco, 20–27. Buenos Aires: Universidad de Buenos Aires, Ciclo Básico Comúnvir, 2004.

Bonilla, Alcira B. "Autonomía moral entre limones y colectivos: las "mamacitas" bolivianas en Buenos Aires." In *Un continente en movimiento: Migraciones en América Latina,* edited by I. Wehr, 143–158. Madrid: Vervuert/Iberoamericana, 2005.

Bonilla, Alcira. "La filosofía intercultural como traducción racional." 2006. http://www.ddhhmigraciones.com.ar/publicaciones/publicacioneshome.htm

Bonilla, Alcira. "Ética, mundo de la vida y migración." In *Sociedad y Mundo de la Vida a la luz del pensamiento Fenomenológico-Hermenéutica actual,* edited by R. Salas Astrain, 27–58. Santiago de Chile: EUCSH, 2007.

Bonilla, Alcira B. "El derecho humano a migrar y la transformación de la noción de ciudadanía." In *Transformaciones, prácticas sociales e identidad cultural,* edited by R. Arué, B. Bazzano, and V. D'Andrea, 773–788. Tucumán: Universidad Nacional de Tucumán, 2008.

Bonilla, Alcira B. "El mundo cotidiano de la vida y las ciudadanías interculturales emergentes." In *Alltagsleben: Ort des Austausch oder der neuen Kolonialisierung zwischen Nord und Süd,* edited by R. Fornet-Betancourt, 211–234. Aachen, Germany: Wissenschaftsverlag Mainz, 2010.

Bonilla, Alcira B. "Ciudadanías Interculturales Emergentes y vigencia de los Derechos Humanos." In *La Travesía de la Libertad ante el Bicentenario. IV Congreso Interoceánico de Estudios Latinoamericanos, X Seminario Argentino-Chileno, IV Seminario del Cono Sur de Ciencias Sociales, Humanidades y Relaciones Internacionales.* Mendoza: Universidad Nacional de Cuyo, Centro de Estudios Trasandinos y Latinoamericanos, 2010.

Bonilla, Alcira B. "Ética intercultural de los Derechos Humanos. Teoría y praxis de los derechos culturales." In: *XI° Seminario Argentino Chileno y V° Seminario Cono Sur de Ciencias Sociales, Humanidades y Relaciones Internacionales 'A propósito de la integración. Las ciencias y las humanidades desde una perspectiva crítica latinoamericana.* Mendoza: Universidad Nacional de Cuyo, Centro de Estudios Trasandinos y Latinoamericanos, 2012.

Bonilla, Alcira B. "Ciudadanías Interculturales Emergentes." In *La ciudadanía en jaque. II. Problemas éticos políticos de prácticas conquistadoras de sujetos,* edited by A. Bonilla and C. Cullen, 7–38. Buenos Aires: La Crujía, 2013.

Bonilla, Alcira B. and Eduardo J. Vior. "Mundo de la vida, ciudadanía y migraciones." *Cultura-Hombre-Sociedad. Revista CUHSO* 18.1 (2009).

Bonilla, Frank, Edwin Meléndez, Rebecca Morales, and María de los Angeles Torres, eds. *Borderless Borders. U.S. Latinos, Latin Americans, and the Paradox of Interdependence.* Philadelphia: Temple University Press, 2000.

Bonilla-Carrión, Roger and Carlos Sandoval-García. "Aspectos sociodemográficos de la migración nicaragüense en Costa Rica, según el Censo 2011." In *Costa Rica a la Luz del Censo 2011.* San José, 2014.

Booth, Rodrigo. "El paisaje aquí tiene un encanto fresco y poético: Las bellezas del sur de Chile y la construcción de la nación turística." *Revista de historia iberoamericana* 3, no. 1 (2010).

Bouchard, Gérard and Charles Taylor. "Fonder l'avenir Le temps de la conciliation. Rappor." *Commission de consultatation sur les pratiques d'accommodement reliées aux différences culturelles.* 2008. Accessed on June 27, 2009. http://collections.banq.qc.ca/ark:/52327/bs66285

Bougois, Phillipe. *Banano, etnia y lucha social en Centroamérica.* San José: DEI, 1994.

Bourassa, Carrie. "Colonization, Racism and the Health of Indian People." *Prairie Forum* 29, no. 2 (2004).

Brocker, Manfred. *Ethnozentrismus: Möglichkeiten und Grenzen des interkulturellen Dialogs.* Darmstadt, Germany: Primus, 1997.

Brooke, James. "Sons and Daughters of Japan: Back from Brazil." *New York Times,* November 27, 2001.

Brown, Anna and Eileen Patten. *Hispanics of Nicaraguan Origin in the United States, 2011.* Washington, DC: Pew Hispanic Center, 2013.

Brubaker, Rogers, ed. *Immigration and the Politics of Citizenship in Europe and North America.* Boston: Boston University Press, 1989.

Buenos Aires Ciudad. *Derechos humanos y pluralismo cultural. Observatorio de colectividades.* 2013. Accessed on September 10, 2013. http://www.buenosaires.gob.ar/areas/secretaria_gral/colectividades/?secInterna=162&subSeccion=513&col=38

Burgogue-Larsen, Laurence, and Amaya Úbeda de Torres. *The Inter-American Court of Human Rights: Case Law and Commentary*. Translated by Rosalind Greenstein. Oxford: Oxford University Press, 2011.

Cabán, Pedro. "The New Synthesis of Latin American and Latino Studies." In *Borderless Borders: US Latinos, Latin Americans, and the Paradox of Interdependence*, edited by Frank Bonilla et al. Philadelphia: Temple University Press, 2010.

Cademartori, José. "The Chilean Neoliberal Model Enters into Crisis." *Latin American Perspectives* 30, no. 5 (2003).

Caggiano, Sergio. "Riesgos del devenir indígena en la migración desde Bolivia a Buenos Aires: identidad, etnicidad y desigualdad." In *Amérique Latine Histoire et Mémoire. Les Cahiers ALHIM*, 2014. Accessed on February 15, 2015. http://alhim.revues.org/4957.

Calavita, Kitty. *Inside the State: The Bracero Program, Immigration, and the I.N.S.* New York: Routledge, 1992.

Calder, Bruce J. *The Impact of Intervention: The Dominican Republic during the U.S. Occupation of 1916–1924*. Austin: University of Texas Press, 1984.

Calhoun, Craig. "Social Solidarities as a Problem for Cosmopolitan Democracy." In *Identities, Affiliations, and Allegiances*, edited by Sayla Benhabib, Ian Shapiro, and Danilo Petranović. Cambridge: Cambridge University Press, 2007.

Cammarota, Julio and Michelle Fine. *Revolutionizing Education: Youth Participatory Action Research in Motion*. New York: Routledge, 2008.

Campos, Anyelick and Larissa Tristán. *Nicaragüenses en las noticias: Textos, contextos y audiencias*. San José: Editorial de la Universidad de Costa Rica, 2009.

Candelario, Ginetta E. B. *Black behind the Ears: Dominican Racial Identity from Museums to Beauty Shops*. Durham, NC: Duke University Press, 2007.

Canevaro, Santiago. "Experiencias individuales y acción colectiva en contextos migratorios: el caso de los jóvenes peruanos y el ingreso a la Universidad de Buenos Aires." In *Migraciones regionales hacia la Argentina: Diferencia, desigualdad y derechos*, edited by A. Grimson and E. Jelin, 285–324. Buenos Aires: Prometeo, 2006.

Cantor, Guillermo. "Entramados de clase y nacionalidad: Capital social e incorporación política de migrantes bolivianos en Buenos Aires." *Migraciones Internacionales* 7, no. 1 (2013).

Cardoso, Lawrence M. *Mexican Emigration to the United States, 1897–1931: Socio-Economic Patterns*. Tucson: University of Arizona Press, 1980.

Carens, Joseph H. *The Ethics of Immigration*. Oxford: Oxford University Press, 2013.

Carr, Barry. "Across Seas and Borders': Charting the Webs of Radical Internationalism in the Circum-Caribbean." In *Exile and the Politics of Exclusion in the Americas*. Edited by Luis Roniger, James N. Green, and Pablo Yankelevich. Brighton, UK: Sussex Academic Press, 2012.

Casillas, Rodolfo. "La labor humanitaria y los organismos civiles: la experiencia de los albergues y casas de migrantes, realidades y desafíos." In *Las políticas públicas sobre migraciones y la sociedad civil en América Latina. Los casos de Argentina, Brasil, Colombia y México*, edited by Leonir M. Chiarello. New York: Scalabrini International Migration Network, 2011.

Casillas, Rodolfo. "La construcción del dato oficial y la realidad institucional: La disminución del flujo indocumentado en los registros del INM." *Migración y Desarrollo* 10, no. 19 (2012).

Castells, Manuel. *La era de la información*. Madrid: Alianza, 1997.

Castells, Manuel. *La era de la información*. Madrid: Alianza, 1997.

Castillo, Julia and Jorge Gurrieri. "El panorama de las migraciones limítrofes y del Perú en la Argentina en el inicio del siglo XXI." *Cuadernos Migratorios: El impacto de las migraciones en Argentina* 2 (2012).

Cavieres, Eduardo and Cristóbal Alijovín de Losada. *Chile-Perú, Perú-Chile: 1820–1920. Desarrollos Políticos, Económicos y Culturales*. Valparaíso: Ediciones Universitarias de Valparaíso, 2005.

CBS. Press Release 159 on July 30, 1998.

CCDH (Centro Cultural Domínico-Haitiano). *Análisis de la situación de inmigrantes haitianos en la República Dominicana*. Santo Domingo: CCDH, 1997.

CCSS [Caja Costarricense de Seguro Social]. *Asunto: Respuesta a oficio SAFC-ASG2-095-12*. San José: CCSS-ACE-206-10-2012, 2012.

CCSS [Caja Costarricense de Seguro Social]. *Asunto: Sobre la atención a mujeres extranjeras embarazadas indocumentadas*. San José: DJ-959-2013, 2013.

CCSS [Caja Costarricense de Seguro Social]. *Asunto: Aclaración de directriz institucional sobre atención de mujeres embarazadas no aseguradas y/o indocumentadas*. San José: CCSS-GM-9033-5, 2013.

Cebrián, Belén Domínguez. "La Unión Europea pierde brillo para los inmigrantes de Latinoamérica." *El País*, June 5, 2015.

Cedeño, Carmen. "La nacionalidad de los descendientes de haitianos nacidos en la República Dominicana." In *La cuestión haitiana en Santo Domingo: Migración internacional, desarrollo y relaciones inter-estatales entre Haití y República Dominicana*, edited by Wilfredo Lozano, 137–143. Santo Domingo: FLACSO-Programa República Dominicana and Centro Norte-Sur/Universidad de Miami, 1992.

Centro Bonó. "Red de centros sociales jesuitas pondera aportes de la Ley de convalidación y naturalización promulgada por el poder ejecutivo." 2014. Accessed May 26. http://bono.org.do/red-de-centros-sociales-jesuitas-pondera-aportes-de-la-ley-de-convalidacion-y-naturalizacion-promulgada-por-el-poder-ejecutivo/

CESO, Centro de Estudios Económicos y Sociales. "La situación habitacional en la Ciudad de Buenos Aires." *Informe C.A.B.A. Nro. I*. 2015. Accessed on February 23, 2015. http://www.ceso.com.ar/tipo/producciones-ceso

Chaui, Marilena. *Cultura e Democracia: O Discurso Competente e Outras Falas*. São Paulo: Editora Moderna, 1981.

Chavez, Leo R. *Covering Immigration: Population Images and the Politics of the Nation*. Berkeley: University of California Press, 2001.

Chavez, Leo R. *The Latino Threat: Constructing Immigrants, Citizens, and the Nation*. Stanford: Stanford University Press, 2008.

Chile. *Country Reports on Human Rights Practices for 1985 (and for 1987)*. Washington: Department of State, 1986 and 1988.

Chile Visión Television (CHV). "En la mira." And "Invasión silenciosa." Aired June 22, 2011.

China-Latin America Finance Database at Boston University. Accessed on July 10, 2015. http://www.bu.edu/pardeeschool/research/gegi/program-area/chinas-global-reach/china-latin-america-database/

Chomsky, Aviva, "Labor History as World History: Linking Regions over Time." In *Workers Across the Americas: The Transnational Turn in Labor History*, edited by Leon Fink. New York: Oxford University Press, 2011.

Christiny, María Verónica Cano et al. "Conocer para legislar y hacer política: los desafíos de Chile ante un nuevo escenario migratorio." Santiago: Centro Latinoamericano y Caribeño de Demografía (CELADE) – División de Población de la CEPAL, 2009.

Clarke, Kamari Maxine. *Fictions of Justice: The International Criminal Court and the Challenge of Legal Pluralism in Sub-Saharan Africa.* Cambridge: Cambridge University Press, 2009.

Clementi, Hebe. *La frontera en América. Vol. 3 América del Sur.* Buenos Aires: Leviatán, 1987.

Cobos, Ana María and Ana Lya Sater. "Chilean Folk Music in Exile." In *Intellectual Migration: Transcultural Contributions of European and Latin American Émigrés,* edited by Liliana Sontag. Madison: Wisconsin, 1986.

Cohen, Yinon. "From Haven to Heaven: Changing Patterns of Immigration to Israel." In *Citizenship and Identity: Germany and Israel in comparative perspective,* edited by Daniel Levy and Yfat Weiss, 36–56. New York: Berghahn Books, 2002.

Collier, Simon and William Stater. *A History of Chile, 1808–2002.* Cambridge: Cambridge University Press, 2004.

Contreras, Dante. "Distribución del ingreso en Chile: Nueve hechos y algunos mitos." *Perspectivas* 2, no. 2 (1999).

Cooper, Elizabeth. "The Conundrum of Race: Retooling Inequality." In *The Caribbean: A History of the Region and Its Peoples,* edited by Stephan Palmié and Francisco A. Scarano, 385–397. Chicago: University of Chicago Press, 2011.

Cornelius, Wayne, A., et al. *Controlling Immigration: A Global Perspective* (2d ed.) Stanford, CA: Stanford University Press, 2004.

Corona, Rodolfo and Miguel Ángel Reyes. "Identificación, caracterización y cuantificación" In *Flujos migratorios en la Frontera Guatemala-México,* edited by Ma. Eugenia Anguiano and Rodolfo Corona, 5-35 México: INM, Colegio de la Frontera Norte, 2009.

Corrêa, Marcos Sá. "O Brasil Se Expande." *Veja,* September 7, 1994.

Couso, Javier. "Chile: The End of Privatopia?" *Berkeley Review of Latin American Studies* (2013). Accessed on July 8, 2014. http://clas.berkeley.edu/resea rch/chile-end -privatopia.

Dancourt, Oscar. "Neoliberal Reforms and Macroeconomic Policy in Peru." *CEPAL Review* 67 (1999).

De Cristóforis, Nidia. "El primer gobierno peronista y la llegada de inmigrantes españoles y exiliados republicanos a la Argentina." *Miradas en movimient* 7 (2012): 4–25.

De Genova, Nicholas. "Migrant 'Illegality" and Deportability in Everyday Life." *Anun Review of Anthropology* (2002).

De Genova, Nicolas. "The Legal Production of Mexican/Migrant 'Illegality'." *Latino Studies* 2 (2004).

De la Cuadra Luque, Luis. *Necesidad de la emigración europea a Chile: algunas consideraciones sobre su importancia, utilidad i la urgencia de formar una sociedad anónima con este objeto.* Santiago: Impr. Chilena, 1872.

Del Campo, Felix. *La inmigración europea en Chile: como servicio del Estado.* Valparaíso: Lit. e Impr. Moderna, 1910.

Del Carmen García A., María and Daniel Villafuerte. *Migración, derechos humanos y desarrollo.* Mexico: Universidad de Ciencias y Artes de Chiapas, 2014.

Del Castillo, José. *La inmigración de braceros azucareros en la República Dominicana, 1900-1930.* Santo Domingo: Centro Dominicano de Investigaciones Antropológicas (CENDIA)/Universidad Autónoma de Santo Domingo, 1978.

Del Castillo, José. "Azúcar y braceros: historia de un problema." *INAZUCAR* 6, no. 29 (1981).

Del Castillo, José. "The Formation of the Dominican Sugar Industry: From Competition to Monopoly, from National Semiproletariat to Foreign Proletariat." In *Between Slavery and Free Labor: The Spanish-Speaking Caribbean in the Nineteenth Century*, edited by Manuel Moreno Fraginals, Frank Moya Pons, and Stanley L. Engerman, 125–234 Baltimore: Johns Hopkins University Press, 1985.

Del Olmo, Margarita. Reshaping Kids Through Public Policy on Diversity: Lessons from Madrid. Madrid: Navreme Publications, 2010.

Del Orbe, Justino José. *Mauricio Báez y la clase obrera*. Santo Domingo: Taller, 1981.

Del Punta, Claudio. *Haïti Chérie*. Film. Directed by Claudio del Punta. Rome: Esperia Film – Arethusa Film, 2007.

Deputy Inspector of the Argentinian Federal Police (PFA). *Non-identified by the Trafficking Squad of the Argentinian Federal Police (PFA)*. June 8, 2013.

Descalzi, Ricardo. *La Real Audiencia de Quito. Claustro en los Andes*. Barcelona: Seix Barral, 1978.

Deutsch, Sandra McGee. *Las Derechas: The Extreme Right in Argentina, Brazi, and Chile, 1890–1939*. Stanford, CA: Stanford University Press, 1999.

Devoto, Fernando. *Historia de la inmigración en Argentina*. Buenos Aires: Sudamericana, 2004.

DH. Asunto: Otorgamiento del control prenatal a mujeres embarazadas extranjeras. San José: DH-MU-09-2013, 2013.

DH. Minuta de reunión. San José: DH-DNA-0018-2013, 2013.

Diario Oficial de la Federación. Mexico: Ministry of the Interior, 2011.

Diaz McConnell, Eileen and Edward A. Delgado-Romero. *Sociological Focus* 37, no. 4 (2004).

Dijkstra, A. Geske. "Technocracy Questioned: Assessing Economic Stabilisation in Nicaragua." *Bulletin of Latin American Research* 18, no. 3 (1999).

Dimitriadis, Greg. Series Editor's Introduction to *Revolutionizing Education: Youth Participatory Action Research in Motion*. New York: Routledge, 2008.

Dinges, John. *The Condor Years*. New York: The New Press, 2005.

Dixon, Paul. "Is Consociational Theory the Answer to Global Conflict? From the Netherlands to Northern Ireland and Iraq." *Political Studies Review* 9 (2011).

Domingues, Petrônio. "O mito da democracia racial e a mestiçagem no Brasil (1889–1930)." Diálogos Latinoamericanos 10 (2005).

Domínguez, Jorge I. and Ana Covarrubias, eds. *Routledge Handbook of Latin America in the World*. New York: Routledge, 2014.

Doña, Cristián and Amanda Levinson. "Chile: Moving Towards a Migration Policy." Accessed June 3, 2011. http://www.migrationinformation.org/Feature/display.cfm?ID=199

Doña-Reveco, Cristián and Amanda Levinson. "The Chilean State and the Search for a New Migration Policy." *Ignire-Centro de Estudio Política Pública* (2012).

Donato, Katharine, et al., "Continental Divides: International Migration in the Americas." *Annals of the American Academy of Political and Social Science* 630 (2010).

Donoso, Carlos and Jaime Rosenbiltt, eds. *Guerra, región y nación: La Confederación Perú-Boliviana, 1836–1839*. Santiago: Centro de Investigaciones Diego Barros Aran/ Universidad Andrés Bello, 2009.

Dorsinville, Max. "Accord sur l'embauchage en Haïti et l'entrée en République Dominicaine des journaliers temporaires haïtiens." *Revue du Travail* 3 (1953).

Drake, Paul. Foreword to *Victims of the Chilean Miracle: Workers and Neoliberalism in the Pinochet Era, 1973–2002*, edited by Peter Winn, xi. Durham, NC: Duke University Press, 2006.

Dreidemie, Patricia and Eduardo J. Vior. "Indagaciones teórico-metodológicas sobre la construcción de ciudadanía cultural de comunidades de origen inmigrante en la Provincia de Río Negro (Argentina)." *Antíteses* 4, no. 7 (2011): 319–339. http://www.uel.br/revistas/uel/index.php/antiteses

Duany, Jorge. *Blurred Borders: Transnational Migration between the Hispanic Caribbean and the United States*. Chapel Hill: University of North Carolina Press, 2011.

Dudy, Peter. *Menschenrechte zwischen Universalität und Partikularität: eine interdisziplinäre Studie zu der Idee der Weltinnenpolitik*. Münster: Lit, 2002.

Durand, Jorge and Douglas S. Massey. "New World Orders: Continuities and Changes in Latin American Migration." *Annals of the American Academy of Political and Social Science* 630, no. 1 (2010).

Dyrness, Andrea. "'Contra Viento y Marea (Against Wind and Tide)': Building Civic Identity Among Children of Emigration in El Salvador." *Anthropology & Education Quarterly* 43, no. 1 (2012).

Earl, Rebecca, ed. *Rumours of Wars: Civil Conflict in Nineteenth Century Latin America*. London: Institute of Latin American Studies, 2000.

Easton, David. "An Approach to the Analysis of Political Systems." *World Politics* 9, no. 3 (1957).

Easton, Stanley E. and Lucien Ellington. "Japanese-Americans." In *Countries and Their Cultures*. Farmington Hills, MI: Gale Reference, 2005. http://www.everyculture.com/multi/Ha-La/Japanese-Americans.html

Edelman, Marc. *Campesinos contra la globalización. Movimientos sociales rurales en Costa Rica*. San José: Editorial de la Universidad de Costa Rica, 2005.

Eisenstadt, S. N. "Collective Identities, Public Spheres, Civil Society and Citizenship in the Contemporary Era." *Marburger Forum: Beiträge zur geistigen Situation der Gegenwart* 7, no. 5 (2006): htpp://www.philosophia-online.de/mafo/heft2006-5/Ei_Col.htm

Eisenstadt, S. N. "Multiple Modernities: A Paradigm of Cultural and Social Evolution." *ProtoSociology* 24 (2007).

El Visor Boliviano. CABA. www.elvisorboliviano.com

Eller, Anne. "'All Would Be Equal in the Effort': Santo Domingo's Italian Revolution, Independence, and Haiti, 1809–1822." *Journal of Early American History* 1, no. 2 (2011).

Encina, Francisco Antonio. *Historia de Chile*. Santiago: Editorial Nascimento, 1949.

Ennis, Sharon R. Merarys Ríos-Vargas, and Nora G. Albert. *2010 Census Briefs: The Hispanic Population 2010*. Washington, DC: US Bureau of the Census, 2010.

Espino Del Castillo, Bernardo. "Combate al tráfico de indocumentados." In *Asuntos migratorios en México, Opiniones de la sociedad*, 5–28. Mexico City: National Institute of Migration, Ministry of the Interior, 1996.

Estrada, Baldomero. *Presencia italiana en Chile*. Valparaíso: Ediciones Universitarias de Valparaíso, 2005.

Estrade, Paul. *La colonia cubana de París, 1895–1898*. La Habana: Editorial de Ciencias Sociales, 1984.

European Commission. Accessed on February 26, 2015. http://ec.europa.eu/ewsi/UDRW/images/items/docl_35105_974253369.pdf

FEDEAR. *La inmigración argentina: una cuestión de Historia e Identidad*. Alicante: Casa de las Américas, Colección Seminarios, 2009.

Fennema, Meindert, and Troetje Loewenthal. *La construcción de raza y nación en la República Dominicana*. Santo Domingo: Editora Universitaria—UASD, 1987.

Fernández, Enrique. "La emigración francesa en Chile, 1875–1914: Entre integración social y mantenimiento de la especificidad." *Amérique Latine Histoire et Mémoire* (2006).

Ferrás, Graciela Liliana. "Ricardo Rojas: Inmigración y nación en la Argentina del Centenario." *Memoria & Sociedad* 2, no. 22 (2007): 5–18.

FitzGerald, David and David Cook-Martin. *Culling the Masses: The Democratic Origins of Racist Immigration Policy in the Americas*. Cambridge, MA: Harvard University Press, 2014.

FLACSO. *Encuesta sobre inmigrantes haitianos en la República Dominicana: Resumen de resultados*. Santo Domingo: FLACSO-Secretaría General and Organización Internacional de Migraciones-OIM, 2004.

Flores, William V. and Rina Benmayor. *Cultural Citizenship: Claiming Identity, Space, and Rights*. Boston: Beacon Press, 1998.

Fornet-Betancourt, Raúl. *Menschenrechte im Streit zwischen Kulturpluralismus und Universalität*. Frankfurt a.M./London: IKO-Verlag für Interkulturelle Kommunikation, 2000.

Fornet-Betancourt, Raúl and Hans-J. Sandkühler. *Begründungen und Wirkungen von Menschenrechten im Kontext der Globalisierung*. Frankfurt a.M./London: IKO-Verlag, 2001.

Fornet Betancourt, Raúl. *Crítica intercultural de la filosofía*. Madrid: Trotta, 2004.

Fouratt, Caitlin E. "Those who come to do harm": The Framings of Immigration Problems in Costa Rican Immigration Law." *International Migration Review* 48, no. 1 (2014).

Fox, Jason. "Little Burajiru: Brazilians of Non-Japanese Descent in Japan." Research Proposal, Department of Anthropology, University of Florida, 1997.

Franzé, Adela. "Diversidad cultural en la escuela: Algunas contribuciones antropológicas." *Revista de Educación* 345 (2008).

Freire, Paulo. *Pedagogy of the Oppressed*. New York: The Continuum Publishing Company, 1970.

French, John. "Another World History Is Possible: Reflections on the Translocal." In *Workers Across the Americas: The Transnational Turn in Labor History*, edited by Leon Fink, 3-11 New York: Oxford University Press, 2011.

Freston, Paul. "Pentecostalism in Latin America: Characteristics and Controversies." *Social Compass* 45, no. 3 (1998).

Fried-Amivilia, Gabriela. "The Dynamics of Memory Transmission across Generations in Uruguay. The Experiences of families of the Disappeared, Political Prisoners, and Exiles, after the Era of State Repression, 1973–1984." PhD diss., UCLA, 2004.

Fritzsche, Karl-P. *Menschenrechte: Eine Einführung mit Dokumenten*. Padeborn: Ferdinand Schöningh and UTB, 2004.

Fuller-Rowell, T. E., A. D. Ong, and J. S. Phinney. "National Identity and Perceived Discrimination Predict Changes in Ethnic Identity Commitment: Evidence from a Longitudinal Study of Latino College Students." *Applied Psychology* 62 (2013).

Gabaccia, Donna. "Is Everywhere Nowhere? Nomads, Nations, and the Immigrant Paradigm of United States History." *The Journal of American History* 86, no. 3 (1999).

Gamboa, Manuel. "El anticomunismo en Costa Rica y su uso como herramienta política antes y después de la Guerra Civil de 1948." *Anuario de Estudios Centroamericanos* 39 (2013).

Garcia, Michelle. "No Papers, No Rights." *Amnesty International Magazine*. 2006. http://www.amnestyusa.org/amnesty-magazine/fall-2006/no-papers-no-rights/page .do?id=1105216

García Castaño, F. J., M. Rubio Gómez, and O. Bouachra. "Immigrant Students at School in Spain: Constructing a Subject of Study." *Dve Domovini: Two Homelands* 41 (2015).

García Grenzner, Joana. "Indignant Feminisms in Spain: Placing the Body before Patriarchal and Capitalist Austerity." *Signs* 40, no. 1 (2014).

Gatica, Mónica. "Váyase donde Usted quiera, con tal que no se lo coman estos perros acá...! Memorias de trabajadores chilenos en el Noreste de Chubut." *Testimonios* 3 (2013).

Gazmuri, Cristian. *Historia de la Historiografía chilena (1842–1970)*. Santiago: Editorial Taurus y Centro de Investigaciones Barros Arana, 2006.

Geertz, Clifford. *The Interpretation of Cultures: Selected Essays*. New York: Basic Books, 1973.

Georgiou, Myria. *Diaspora, Identity and the Media: Diasporic Transnationalism and Mediated Spatialities*. New York: Hampton Press, 2006.

Gerber, David. "Forming a Transnational Narrative: New Perspectives on European Migrations to the United States." *The History Teacher* 35, no. 1 (2001).

Gibson, M. A. and S. Carrasco. "The Education of Immigrant Youth: Some Lessons from the U.S. and Spain." *Theory Into Practice* 48 (2009).

Gibson, M. A. and J. P. Koyama. "Immigrants and Education." In *A Companion to the Anthropology of Education*, edited by B. Levinson and M. Pollock, 391–407. Malden, MA: Wiley-Blackwell, 2011.

Gilbert, Jorge and Edgardo Enríquez Frödden. *Testimonio de un destierro*. Santiago: Mosquito Editores, 1992.

Gill, A., and Yossi Dahan. "Between Neo-Liberalism and Ethno-Nationalism: Theory, Policy, and Law in the Deportation of Migrant Workers in Israel." *Law and Government in Israel* 10, no. 1 (2006).

Gilroy, Paul. *The Black Atlantic: Modernity and Double Consciousness*. London: Verso, 1993.

Ginieniewicz, Jorge. "Latin American Canadians Rethink Their Political Spaces: Grass-Roots or Electoral Participation?" *Political Studies* 58 (2010).

Ginwright, S. "Collective Radical Imagination: Youth Participatory Action Research and the Art of Emancipatory Knowledge." In *Revolutionizing Education: Youth Participatory Action Research in Motion*, edited by J. Cammarota and M. Fine. New York: Routledge, 2008.

Global-Latino-Fest. Accessed June 3, 2015. http://latinoculturalcenter.org/?attachment_id=26

Globo. "A volta dos brasileiros que moravam no exterior." April 17, 2012. globotv.globo.com/rede-globo/profissao-reporter/v/a-volta-dos-brasileiros-que-moravam-no-exterior-parte-1/1908007/

Gobat, Michael. "The Invention of Latin America: A Transnational History of Anti-imperialism, Democracy, and Race." *The American Historical Review* 118, no. 5 (2013).

Gobierno de la Ciudad de Buenos Aires (GCBA). *Censo Nacional 2010: selección de cuadros de Población. Cuadros por comuna. Población total nacida en el extranjero por lugar de nacimiento, según sexo y grupo de edad. Año 2010*. 2010. Accessed on September 10, 2013. http://www.buenosaires.gob.ar/areas/hacienda/sis_estadistico/censo_datdef/cuadros_poblacion.php

Goldberg, Alejandro. "Trayectorias migratorias, itinerarios de salud y experiencias de participación política de mujeres migrantes bolivianas que trabajaron y vivieron en talleres textiles clandestinos del Área Metropolitana de Buenos Aires, Argentina." *Anuario Americanista Europeo* 11 (2013).

Goldberg, Barry. "Historical Reflections on Transnationalism, Race, and the American Immigrant Saga." *Annals of the New York Academy of Sciences* 645 (1992).

Golte, Jürgen and Norma Adams. *Los caballos de Troya de los invasores: estrategias campesinas en la conquista de la Gran Lima.* Lima: Instituto de Estudios Peruanos, 1987.

Góngora, Mario. *Ensayo Histórico sobre la noción de Estado en Chile en los siglos XIX y XX.* Santiago: Editorial Universitaria, 1981.

González, Daniel. "Cómo opera la patota que protege a los talleres clandestinos de ropa." *Tiempo Argentino*, August 28, 2011. Accessed on September 11, 2013. http://tiempo .infonews.com/notas/como-opera-patota-que-protege-los-talleres-clandestinos-de-ropa

González, Guadalupe. "Percepciones sociales sobre la migración en México y Estados Unidos: ¿Hay espacios para cooperar?" in *México, país de migración*, edited by Luis Herrera-Lasso M. Mexico City: D.F.: Center for Economic Research and Teaching, 2009.

González, Guadalupe, J. A. Schiavon, D. Crow, and G. Maldonado. *México, las Américas y el mundo, 2010. Política exterior: opinión pública y líderes.* Mexico City: Center for Economic Research and Teaching, 2011.

González-Enríquez, C. "Spain." In *European Immigration: A Sourcebook*, edited by A. Triandafyllidou and R. Gropas, 339–350. Farnham, UK: Ashgate Publishing Ltd., 2014.

González, Juan. *Harvest of Empire: A History of Latinos in America.* New York: Penguin, 2011.

Greene, Julie. "Historians of the World: Transnational Forces, Nation-States." In *Workers across the Americas: The Transnational Turn in Labor History*, edited by Leon Fink. New York: Oxford University Press, 2011.

Grimson, Alejandro. "La migración boliviana en la Argentina. De la ciudadanía ausente a una mirada regional." In *Migrantes bolivianos en la Argentina y los Estados Unidos*, edited by A. Grimson and E. Paz Soldán, 13–52. La Paz: Programa de las Naciones Unidas para el Desarrollo (PNUD), 2000.

Guidotti-Hernándeza, Nicole M. "Dora the Explorer, Constructing 'Latinidades' and the Politics of Global Citizenship." *Latino Studies* 5 (2007).

Gurak, Douglas T. and Fe Caces. *Migrant Networks: Mechanisms for Shaping Migrations and Their Sequelae.* Ithaca: Dept. of Rural Sociology, 1989.

Gustin, Delancey and Astrid Ziebarth. "Transatlantic Opinion on Immigration: Greater Worries and Outlier Optimism." *International Migration Review* 44 (2010).

Gutiérrez, David. *The Columbia History of Latinos in the United States Since 1960.* New York: Columbia University Press, 2004.

Gutiérrez, Joaquín. *Puerto Limón.* San José: Editorial Costa Rica, reimpresión, 1950.

Haaugh, Louise. "The Emperor's New Clothes: Labor Reform and Social Democratization in Chile." *Studies in Comparative International Development* 37, no. 1 (2002).

Hacher, Sebastián. *Sangre salada: una feria en los márgenes.* Buenos Aires: Marea, 2011.

Hale, Charles and Lynn Stephen, eds. *Otros saberes: Collaborative Research on Indigenous and Afro-descendant Cultural Politics.* New York: School for Advanced Research Press, 2013.

Hall, K. *Lives in Translation: Sikh Youth as British Citizens.* Philadelphia: University of Pennsylvania Press, 2002.

Hall, Stuart. "The Whites in Their Eyes. Racist Ideologies and the Media." In *The Media Reader*, edited by M. Alvarado and J. Thompson, 271–282 London: British Film Institute, 1981.

Halland, Matthew and Jonathan Stringfield. "Undocumented Migration and the Segregation of Mexican Immigrants in New Destinations." *Social Science Research* 47, no. 1 (2014).

Halperín Weisburd, Leopoldo. *Precariedad y heterogeneidad del trabajo en la Ciudad de Buenos Aires*. Buenos Aires: Universidad de Buenos Aires, 2012.

Han, Petrus. *Soziologie der Migration: Erklärungsmodelle, Fakten, Politische Konsequenzen, Perspektiven*. Stuttgart, Germany: Lucius & Lucius, 2000.

Haney, William. *The Price of Sugar*. Film. Directed by William Haney. New York: New Yorker Films, 2007.

Harris, Gilberto. *Emigrantes e inmigrantes en Chile, 1810–1915. Nuevos aportes y notas revisionistas*. Valparaíso: Universidad de Playa Ancha, 2001.

Harris, John R. and Michael P. Todaro. "Migration, Unemployment, and Development: A Two Sector Analysis." *American Economic Review* 60 (1970).

Haslip, Gabriel. "Crime and the Administration of Justice in Colonial Mexico City 1696–1810." Ann Arbor: University Microfilm International, 1982.

Hederra, Sergio Carvallo. *El problema de la inmigración en Chile y algunos países sudamericanos*. Santiago: La Universidad de Chile, 1945.

Herrera Carassou, Roberto. *La perspectiva teórica en el estudio de las migraciones*. México: Siglo XXI, 2006.

Herrera García, Adolfo. *Juan Varela*. San José: Editorial Costa Rica, 1939.

Herzog, Tamar. *La administración como un fenómeno social. La justicia penal de la ciudad de Quito (1650–1750)*. Madrid: Centro de Estudios Constitucionales, 1995.

Hierro, María. "Latin American Migration to Spain: Main Reasons and Future Perspectives." *International Migration* (2013).

Higuchi, Naoto. "Migration Process of Nikkei Brazilians." Paper presented at the International Symposium on Latin American Emigration at the National Museum of Ethnology, Osaka, 2001.

Hines, Barbara. "The Right to Migrate as a Human Right: The Current Argentine Immigration Law." *Cornell International Law Journal* 43, no. 3 (2010): 472–511.

Hoefer, Michael, Nancy Rytina, and Bryan C. Baker. *Estimates of the Unauthorized Immigrant Population Residing in the United States: January 2010*. Washington, DC: Office of Immigration Statistics, US Department of Homeland Security, 2012.

Hoerder, Dirk. "Transformations over Time or Sudden Change: Historical Perspectives on Mass Migrations and Human Lives." *Comparative Population Studies* 37, no. 1–2 (2012).

Hoerder, Dirk. "Overlapping Spaces: Transregional and Transcultural." In *Workers across the Americas: The Transnational Turn in Labor History*, edited by Leon Fink, 33–38 New York: Oxford University Press, 2011.

Hoetink, Harry. *The Dominican People, 1850–1900: Notes for a Historical Sociology*. Translated by Stephen K. Ault. Baltimore: Johns Hopkins University Press, 1982.

Hoffman, Abraham. *Unwanted Mexican Americans in the Great Depression: Repatriation Pressures, 1929–1939*. Tucson: University of Arizona Press, 1974.

Holloway, Frances. "A City with a Hidden Textile Industry." *The Argentina Independent*, April 2, 2009. Accessed on January 17, 2015. http://www.argentinaindependent.com/socialissues/humanrights/a-city-with-a-hidden-textile-industry/

Hondagneu-Sotelo, Pierrette. *Gendered Transitions: Mexican Experiences of Immigration*. Berkeley: University of California Press, 1994.

Ikegami, Shigehiro. "Brazilians and Local Industrailization in Hamamatsu: A Case of an Industrial City in Japan." Paper presented at the International Symposium on Latin American Emigration at the National Museum of Ethnology, Osaka, 2001.

INA. Respuesta a la nota del 20 de noviembre de 2012, respecto a su solicitud del ingreso de personas migrantes en condición migratoria irregular a los servicios del INA. San José: SGI-1041-2013, 2012.

INA. Respuesta a nota con fecha 19 de febrero de 2013. San José: SGI-153-2013, 2013.

INEC [Instituto Nacional de Estadística y Censos]. *Indicadores Demográficos 2013.* San José: INEC, 2014.

INEC [Instituto Nacional de Estadística y Censos]. *Encuesta Nacional de Hogares. Cifras básicas sobre fuerza de trabajo, pobreza e ingresos.* San José: INEC, 2011.

Informe Anual sobre Derechos Humanos en Chile, 2010. http://www.derechoshumanos.udp.cl/archivo/informe-anual/, 238

Instituto Brasileiro de Geografia e Estatística (IBGE). "Para IBGE, crise internacional atraiu mais imigrantes ao Brasil." April 27, 2012. noticias.uol.com.br/cotidiano/ultimasnoticias/2012/04/27/para-ibge-crise-internacional-atraiu-mais-imigrantes-ao-brasil.htm

Instituto Nacional de Estadísticas y Censos (INDEC). *Censo Nacional de Población 2010.* 2010. Accessed on September 9, 2013. http://www.censo2010.indec.gov.ar/CuadrosDefinitivos/P1-P_Caba.pdf

Instituto Nacional de Migración. *Dossier flujo de entradas de extranjeros por la frontera sur terrestre de México registradas por el Instituto Nacional de Migración.* Mexico: Instituto Nacional de Migración, 2005.

Inter-American Court of Human Rights. "Case of the Yean and Bosico Children v. the Dominican Republic, Judgment of September 8, 2005." *Refugee Survey Quarterly* 25, no. 3 (2006).

International Labour Office. "Report of the Commission of Inquiry Appointed under Article 26 of the Constitution of the International Labour Organization to Examine the Observance of Certain International Labour Conventions by the Dominican Republic and Haiti with Respect to the Employment of Haitian workers on the Sugar Plantations of the Dominican Republic." *International Labour Office, Official Bulletin, Special Supplement 66 (Series B),* 1983.

Interview with Rodríguez Elizondo. Jerusalem: March, 2000.

Interview with Gustavo Silva by Mario Sznajder. Santiago: August 2001.

Interview with MUDHA Staffers. Santo Domingo: May 22, 2002.

Interview with Mario Sznajder. May 2002.

Interview with Laurel Fletcher. New Haven: February 4, 2005.

Interview with Sonia Pierre. Connecticut: March 6, 2009.

Interview with Emilia M. May 23, 2011.

Interview with Víctor Paiba Cossios. Santiago: March 20, 2011.

Interview with Erika S. Santiago: February 20, 2011.

Interview with Rongier and Sznajder. July 11, 2013.

Interview with members of the Alameda Foundation, a Deputy Inspector of the Trafficking Squad of the Argentinian Federal Police (PFA), and H. Zunini, technical advisor at the Centro Demostrativo de la Indumentaria (CDI, Experimental Center for Clothing). June 2013.

Irizzary, J. *The Latinization of U.S. Schools: Successful Teaching and Learning in Shifting Cultural Contexts.* Boulder, CO: Paradigm Publishers, 2011.

Ishi, Angelo. "Searching for Home, Pride, and 'Class': Japanese Brazilians in the Land of the Yen." In *Searching for Home Abroad: Japanese Brazilians and Transnationalism*, edited by Jeffrey Lesser, 75–102. Durham, NC: Duke University Press, 2003.

Ishi, Angelo. "Social and Cultural Aspects of Brazilians in Japan." *IDB Migration Seminar: Migration and Remittances in the Context of Globalization: The Case of Japan and Latin America*. 2004. idbdocs.iadb.org/wsdocs/getdocument.aspx?docnum=556433

Jacobson, Matthew Frye. *Whiteness of a Different Color: European Immigrants and the Alchemy of Race*. Cambridge, MA: Harvard University Press, 1999.

Jara, Álvaro. *Guerra y sociedad en Chile*. Santiago: Editorial Universitaria, 1971.

Jedwab, Jack and Victor Armony. "Hola Canadá. Spanish is Third Most Spoken Language." *FOCAL Point* 8, no. 4 (2009).

Jesuit Service for Migrants. *Narrativas de la transmigración centroamericana en su paso por México. Resumen ejecutivo*. Mexico City: Jesuit Service for Migrants, 2013.

Jones-Correa, Michael. "Under Two Flags: Dual Nationality in Latin America and Its Consequences for Naturalization in the United States." *International Migration Review* 35, no. 4 (2001).

Joppke, Christian. *Selecting by Origin*. Cambridge, MA: Harvard University Press, 2007.

Kalir, Barak. *Latino Migrants in the Jewish State. Undocumented Lives in Israel*. Bloomington: Indiana University Press, 2010.

Kanstroom, Daniel. *Aftermath: Deportation Law and the New American Diaspora*. New York: Oxford University Press, 2014.

Kay, Diana. *Chileans in Exile. Private Struggles, Public Lives*. London: Macmillan, 1987.

Kazemipur, Abdolmohammad. *The Muslim Question in Canada. A Story of Segmented Integration*. Vancouver: University of British Columbia Press, 2014.

Kemp, Adrianna. "Labour Migration and Racialisation: Labour Market Mechanisms and Labour Migration Control Policies in Israel." *Social Identities* 10, no. 2 (2004).

Kemp, Adriana. "Managing Migration, reprioritizing National Citizenship: Undocumented Labor Migrants' Children and Policy Reforms in Israel." *Theoretical Inquiries in Law* 8, no. 2 (2007): 663–691.

Kemp, Adriana and Nelly Kfir. "Between State Biopower and Social Politics of Life: Documented and Undocumented Care Workers in Israel." *Social Problems* (2015).

Kemp, Adriana, Rebeca Raijman, Julia Resnik and Silvina Schammah-Gesser. "Contesting the Limits of Political Participation: Latinos and Black African Migrant Workers in Israel." *Ethnic and Racial Studies* 23, no. 1 (2000): 94–119.

Kemp, Adriana and Rebeca Raijman. "Christian Zionists in the Holy Land Evangelical Churches, Labor Migrants and the Jewish State." *Identities: Global Studies in Culture and Power* 10 (2003): 295–318.

Kemp, Adriana and Rebeca Raijman. "Tel Aviv Is Not Foreign to You: Urban Incorporation Policy on Labor Migrants in Israel." *International Migration Review* 38, no. 1 (2004).

Kemp, Adriana and Rebeca Raijman. *"Workers" and "Foreigners": The Political Economy of Labor Migration in Israel*. Jerusalem: Van-Leer Institute and Kibbutz Hamehuhad, 2008.

Kfir, Nelly and Adriana Kemp. "Struggling Between Routine and Emergency: Migrants' Legalization and Human Rights Activism in Israel." *Critical Sociology* (2015).

Khan, Aisha. "Africa, Europe, and Asia in the Making of the 20th-century Caribbean." In *The Caribbean: A History of the Region and Its Peoples*, edited by Stephan Palmié and Francisco A. Scarano, 399–413. Chicago: University of Chicago Press, 2011.

King, Russell and Nancy Wood, eds. *Media and Migration: Constructions of Mobility and Difference*. New York: Routledge, 2013.

Kirk, Neville. "Transnational Labor History: Promise and Perils." In *Workers across the Americas: The Transnational Turn in Labor History*, edited by Leon Fink. New York: Oxford University Press, 2011.

Klagsbrunn, Victor Hugo. "Globalização da Economia Mundial e Mercado de Trabalho: A Emigração de Brasileiros Para os Estados Unidos e Japão." In *Migrações Internacionais: Herança XX, Agenda XXI*, edited by Neide Lopes Patarra, 33–48. Campinas: Program Interinstitucional de Avaliação e Acompanhamento das Migrações Internacionais no Brasil, 1996.

Klein, Herbert S. *The Atlantic Slave Trade*. Cambridge: Cambridge University Press, 1999.

Klein, Naomi. *The Shock Doctrine: The Rise of Disaster Capitalism*. New York: Metropolitan Books, 2007.

Kleiner-Liebau, D. *Migration and the Construction of National Identity in Spain*. Madrid: Iberoamericana, 2009.

Klintowitz, Jaime. "Nossa Gente Lá Fora." *Veja*, April 3, 1996.

Kniveton, Dominic, Kerstin Schmidt-Verkerk, Christopher Smith, and Richard Black. "Climate Change and Migration: Improving Methodologies to Estimate Flows." International Organization for Migration. MRS No.33 (2008).

Koopmans, Ruud. "Partizipation der Migranten, Staatsbürgerschaft und Demokratie: Nationale und lokale Perspektiven." In *Strategien der Integration*, edited by M. Pröhl and H. Hartmann, 103–111. Gütersloh: Bertelsmann, 2003.

Koopmans, Ruud and Paul Statham. "Migration and Ethnic Relations as a Field of Political Contention: An Opportunity Structure Approach." In *Challenging Immigration and Ethnic Relations Politics*, edited by R. Koopmans and P. Statham, 13–56. Oxford: Oxford University Press, 2000.

Koyama, Chieko. "Japanese-Brazilians: The Transformation of Ethnic Identity in the Country of Their Ancestors." M.A. thesis, Department of Anthropology, University of Florida, 1998.

Kraler, Albert and Christof Parnreiter. "Migration Theoretisieren." *Prokla: Zeitschrift für eine kritische Sozialwissenschaft* 140, no. 35 (2005): 327–344.

Künnemann, Rolf. *Six Lectures on the Right to an Adequate Standard of Living (Food, Housing, Health, Social Security)*. Heidelberg: FIAN, 1996.

Künnemann, Rolf. *Nine Essays on Economic Human rights (1993–1997)*. Heidelberg: FIAN, 2002.

Kymlicka, Will ed. *The Rights of Minority Cultures*. Oxford: Oxford University Press, 1995.

Kymlicka, Will. *Multiculturalism: Success, Failure, and the Future*. Washington: Migration Policy Institute, 2012.

La Alameda Foundation. "Historia." 2015. http://www.fundacionalameda.org/2011/06/historia.html

La Nación. "Me venía preparando para atender algo muy complicado." August 27, 2011.

La Nación. "INA tramitará matrícula de estudiantes sin papeles." August 4, 2013. Available at http://www.nacion.com/nacional/INA-tramitara-matricula-estudiantes-papeles_0_1357864281.html

La Tercera, "Christian Espejo: 'Muchos peruanos lideran bandas de delincuentes'." Accessed on June 13, 2011. http://latercera.com/contenido/674_190106_9.shtml.

La Tercera. "Inversiones chilenas en Perú." June 6, 2011.

Lam, W. S. E. "Border Discourses and Identities in Transnational Youth Culture." In *What They Don't Learn in School: Literacy in the Lives of Urban Youth*, edited by J. Mahiri, 79–97. New York: Peter Lang Publishers, 2004.

Landolt, Patricia and L. Goldring. "Immigrant Political Socialization as Bridging and Boundary Work: Mapping the Multi-Layered Incorporation of Latin American Immigrants in Toronto." *Ethnic and Racial Studies* 32 (2009).

Landolt, Patricia, L. Goldring, and J. Bernhard. "Agenda Setting and Immigrant Politics: The Case of Latin Americans in Toronto." *American Behavioral Scientist* 55 (2011).

La Población Migrante Nicaragüense en Costa Rica: Realidades y Respuestas" Comunicación, Universidad de Costa Rica. Fundación Arias para la Paz y el Progreso Humano Apartado. San José, Costa Rica, 2000.

Larimer, Tim and Hiroko Tashiro. "Battling the Bloodlines." *Time*, August 9, 1999. http://www.time.com /time/world/article/0,8599,2054423,00.html

Larraín, Jorge. *Identidad Chilena*. Santiago: LOM ediciones, 2001.

Larson, Elizabeth M. "Nicaraguan Refugees in Costa Rica from 1980–1993." In *Yearbook. Conference of Latin Americanist Geographers*, pp. 67–79. Conference of Latin Americanist Geographers, 1993.

LASA Latino Studies Section. Accessed July 3, 2015. http://lasa.international.pitt .edu/sections/latino-studies/?pg=1.

LASA International Migrations Section News. Vol. 1, no. 1. August 2013. http://lasa .international.pitt.edu/cmsAdmin/uploads/IM1.pdf

Laski, Harold J. *Liberty in The Modern State*. New York: Harper & Brothers, 2014.

Latin America in Translation Series. Coordinated and funded by the Duke University and University of North Carolina Presses.

Latino Americando Expo in Milan, Italy. 1991. Accessed August 21, 2015. http:// www.expo2015.org/en/events/all-events/latinoamericando-2014-latin-america-in-milan

Lawyers Committee for Human Rights. *A Childhood Abducted: Children Cutting Sugar Cane in the Dominican Republic*. New York: Lawyers Committee for Human Rights, 1991.

LeGrand, Catherine. "Informal Resistance on a Dominican Sugar Plantation During the Trujillo Dictatorship." *Hispanic American Historical Review* 74, no. 4 (1995).

Leman, Marc. *Canadian Multiculturalism*. Ottawa: Library of Parliament, Parliamentary Information and Research Service, 1999.

Lemoine, Maurice. *Bitter Sugar: Slaves Today in the Caribbean*. Translated by Andrea Johnston. Chicago: Banner Press, 1985.

Leonel Fernandez Center for Latin American Studies at the University of Jordan. Accessed on July 10, 2015. http://lfc.ju.edu.jo/Home.aspx

Lerner, Ivonne. "Two Latino NGOs in Israel: Languages and Identities." Unpublished Manuscript, Tel Aviv University, 2014.

Lerner, Ivonne and Katz, Beatriz. "Spanish Teaching in Israel: an Overview." In *El español en el mundo*, 205–252. Madrid Plaza y Janés, 2003. http://cvc.cervantes.es/obref/ anuario/anuario_03/lerner_katz/

Lesser, Jeffrey. *Immigration, Ethnicity, and National Identity in Brazil, 1808 to the Present*. New York: Cambridge University Press, 2013.

Levinson, B. "Toward an Anthropology of (Democratic) Citizenship Education." In *A Companion to the Anthropology of Education*, edited by B. Levinson and M. Pollock, 279–298. Malden: Wiley-Blackwell, 2011.

Levitt, Peggy. "Redefining the Boundaries of Belonging: The Institutional Character of Transnational Religious Life." *Sociology of Religion* 65, no. 1 (2004).

Lieutier, Ariel. *Esclavos: Los trabajadores costureros de la Ciudad de Buenos Aires.* Buenos Aires: Retórica, 2010.

Lijphart, Arend and Carlos H. Waisman. *Institutional Design in New Democracies in Eastern Europe and Latin America.* Boulder, CO: Westview, 1996.

Linger, Daniel T. "Brazil Displaced: Restaurante 51 in Nagoya, Japan." *Horizontes Antropológicos* (1997).

Linger, Daniel T. *No One Home: Brazilian Selves Remade in Japan.* Durham, NC: Duke University Press, 2001.

Linger, Daniel T. "The Identity Path of Eduardo Mori." In *History in Person*, edited by Dorothy Holland and Jean Lave, 217–244. Santa Fe: School of American Research Press, 2001.

Llambias-Wolff, Jaime. "The Voluntary Repatriation Process of Chilean Exiles." *International Migration* 31, no. 4 (1993).

Lohmann, Georg and Stephan Gosepath, eds. *Philosophie der Menschenrechte.* Frankfurt a.M.: Suhrkamp, 1998.

"Loreto, Italia: Campaña Nacional de la Marca Perú 2012." Accessed on July 10, 2015. http://www.youtube.com/watch?v=zYcGSiHf6JE

López Sala, Ana M. "Derechos de ciudadanía y estratificación cívica en sociedades de inmigración." In *Una discusión sobre la universalidad de los derechos humanos y lainmigración,* edited by Ignacio Campoy, 129–151. Madrid: Dykinson/Universidad Carlos III, 2006.

Loveman, Brian. *The Legacy of Hispanic Capitalism.* New York: Oxford University Press, 2001.

Lowe, Lisa. *The Intimacies of Four Continents.* Durham, NC: Duke University Press, 2015.

Lozano, Wilfredo. *La paradoja de las migraciones: El estado dominicano frente a la inmigración haitiana.* Santo Domingo: Editorial UNIBE, Facultad Latinoamericana de Ciencias Sociales, Servicio Jesuita de Refujiados y Migrantes, 2008.

Lucko, J. "Tracking Identity: Academic Performance and Ethnic Identity Among Ecuadorian Immigrant Teenagers in Madrid." *Anthropology & Education Quarterly* 42, no. 3 (2011).

Lukose, Ritty. "The Difference that Diaspora Makes: Thinking Through the Anthropology of Immigrant Education in the United States." *Anthropology & Education Quarterly* 38, no. 4 (2007).

Luna, Félix. *Historia general de la Argentina.* Buenos Aires: Planeta, 1995.

Lundquist, Jennifer H. and Douglas S. Massey. "Politics or Economics? International Migration During the Nicaraguan Contra War." *Journal of Latin American Studies* 37 (2015).

Mahler, Kristen Hill and Silke Staab. "Nanny Politics: The Dilemmas of Working Women's Empowerment in Santiago, Chile." *International Feminist Journal of Politics* 7, no. 1 (2005).

Manjuk, Valerja, Stoyanka Manolcheva and Eduardo J. Vior. "The Politics of Otherness—Constructing the Autonomy of Political Subjects in the Migrant Minorities as a way of Reforming Western European Democracies." In *Rethinking Non-Discrimination and Minority Rights,* edited by M. Scheinin and R. Toivanen, 135–154. Helsinki/Berlin: Åbo Akademi University/Institute for Human Rights, 2004.

Manjuk, Valerja, Stoyanka Manolcheva and Eduardo J. Vior. "Bestandsaufnahme demokratischer Initiativen in der politischen Bildungsarbeit mit muslimischen Jugendlichen in Deutschland—Ein Forschungsbericht." In *Extremismus in Deutschland,* edited by Bundesministerium des Innern, 316–337. Berlin: Bundesministerium des Innern, 2004.

Mara, Luís. "Claroscuros de un exilio privilegiado." In *En México, entre exilios.* By Pablo Yankelevich. Mexico City: ITAM, 1998.

"Marca Peru." Accessed on July 10, 2015. http://nacional.peru.info/en/content/PeruBrand

Margolis, Maxine L. *Little Brazil: An Ethnography of Brazilian Immigrants in New York City.* Princeton, NJ: Princeton University Press, 1994.

Margolis, Maxine L. "Transnationalism and Popular Culture: The Case of Brazilian Immigrants in the United States." *Journal of Popular Culture* 29, no. 1 (1995).

Margolis, Maxine L. "Notes on Transnational Migration: The Case of Brazilian Immigrants." In *Negotiating Transnationalism,* edited by Mary Carol Hopkins and Nancy Wellmeier, 202–222. Arlington, VA: American Anthropological Association, 2001.

Margolis, Maxine L. "Brazilians in the United States, Canada, Europe, Japan and Paraguay." In *Encyclopedia of Diasporas,* edited by Melvin Ember, Carol R. Ember & Ian Skoggard, 602–615. New York: Kluwer Academic/Plenum, 2004.

Margolis, Maxine L. *Goodbye Brazil: Emigrés from the Land of Soccer and Samba.* Madison: University of Wisconsin Press, 2013.

Márquez, Jaime Valenzuela. "Indígenas andinos en Chile colonial: Inmigración, inserción espacial, integración económica y movilidad social." *Revista de Indias* 70, no. 250 (2010).

Márquez, Jaime Valenzuela. "Inmigrantes en busca de identidad: Los indios *cuzcos* de Santiago de Chile, entre clasificación colonial y estrategia social." in *América colonial: denominaciones, clasificaciones e identidades,* edited by Alejandra Araya Espinoza and Jaime Valenzuela Márquez. Santiago: RIL, 2010.

Marshall, Thomas H. and Tom B. Bottomore. *Ciudadanía y clase social.* Madrid: Alianza, 2007.

Martí, José. *Nuestra América.* Caracas: Fundación Biblioteca Ayacucho, 1977.

Martin, Bernice. "New Mutations of the Protestant Ethic among Latin American Pentecostals." *Religion* 25, no. 2 (1995).

Martínez, Oscar. *Los migrantes que no importan.* Mexico City: elfaro.net, 2010.

Martínez, Samuel. *Peripheral Migrants: Haitians and Dominican Republic Sugar Plantations.* Knoxville: The University of Tennessee Press, 1995.

Martínez, Samuel. "Indifference Within Indignation: Anthropology, Human Rights, and the Haitian Bracero." *American Anthropologist* 98, no. 1 (1996).

Martínez, Samuel. "From Hidden Hand to Heavy Hand: Sugar, the State, and Migrant Labor in Haiti and the Dominican Republic." *Latin American Research Review* 34, no. 1 (1999).

Martínez, Samuel. "The Onion of Oppression: Haitians in the Dominican Republic." In *Geographies of the Haitian Diaspora,* edited by Regine O. Jackson, 51–70. New York: Routledge, 2011.

Martínez, Samuel. "The Price of Confrontation: International Retributive Justice and the Struggle for Haitian-Dominican Rights." In *The Uses and Misuses of Human*

Rights: A Critical Approach to Advocacy, edited by George Andreopoulos and Zehra Arat, 89–115. New York: Palgrave, 2014.

Martínez Pizarro, Jorge. *El encanto de los datos: Sociodemográfica de la inmigración en Chile según el censo de 2002.* Santiago: Naciones Unidas, 2003.

Mason, T. and G. Delandshere. "Citizens Not Research Subjects: Toward a More Democratic Civic Education Inquiry Methodology." *Interamerican Journal of Education for Democracy* 3, no. 1 (2010).

Massey, Doreen. "A Place Called Home?" *New Formations* 17 (1992).

Massey, Douglas S. *New Faces in New Places: The New Geography of American Immigration.* New York: Russell Sage Foundation, 2008.

Massey, Douglas S. "The Real Hispanic Challenge." *Pathways* Magazine. Special Issue on "Hispanics in America: A Report Card on Poverty, Mobility, and Assimilation." Winter 2015, 3–7.

Massey, Douglas S. "Preface: The Great Divide between Spain and the United States." Preface to *Immigrant Vulnerability and Resilience: Comparative Perspectives on Latin American Immigrants During the Great Recession,* edited by María Aysa-Lastra and Lorenzo Cachón, i–iv. New York: Springer, 2015.

Massey, Douglas S. and Amelia E. Brown. "New Migration Streams between Mexico and Canada." *Migraciones Internactionales* 6, no. 1 (2011).

Massey, Douglas S. and Audrey Singer. "New Estimates of Undocumented Mexican Migration and the Probability of Apprehension." *Demography* 32 (1985).

Massey, Douglas S., Joaquín Arango, Graeme Hugo, Ali Kouaouci, Adela Pellegrino, and J. Edward Taylor. *Worlds in Motion: International Migration at the End of the Millennium.* Oxford: Oxford University Press, 1998.

Massey, Douglas S., Joaquín Arango, Hugo Graeme, Ali Kouaouci, Adela Pellegrino, and J. Edward Taylor. "Teorías de migración internacional: Una revisión y aproximación." *ReDCE* 10 (2008).

Massey, Douglas S., Jorge Durand, and Nolane J. Malone. *Beyond Smoke and Mirrors: Mexican Immigration in an Era of Economic Integration.* New York: Russell Sage Foundation, 2002.

Massey, Douglas S., Jorge Durand, and Karen A. Pren. "Explaining Undocumented Migration." *International Migration Review* 48, no. 4 (2014).

Massey, Douglas S., Jorge Durand, and Karen A. Pren. "Border Enforcement and Return Migration by Documented and Undocumented Mexicans." *Journal of Ethnic and Migration Studies* 41, no. 7 (2015).

Massey, Doughas S. and Karen A. Pren. "Unintended Consequences of US Immigration Policy: Explaining the Post-1965 Surge from Latin America." *Population and Development Review* 38, no. 1 (2012).

Massey, Douglas S. and Kerstin Gentsch. "Labor Market Outcomes for Legal Mexican Immigrants under the New Regime of Immigration Enforcement," *Social Science Quarterly* 92, no. 3 (2011).

Massey, Douglas S. and Kerstin Gentsch. "Undocumented Migration and the Wages of Mexican Immigrants in the United States." *International Migration Review* 48, no. 2 (2014).

Massey, Douglas and Kristine Espinosa. "What's Driving Mexico-U.S. Migration? A Theoretical, Empirical, and Policy Analysis." *American Journal of Sociology* 102 (1997).

Massey, Douglas S., Magaly Sánchez R. *Brokered Boundaries: Creating Immigrant Identity in Anti-Immigrant Times.* New York: Russell Sage Foundation, 2010.

Massey, Douglas, Rafael Alarcon, Jorge Durand, and Hunmberto Gonzalez. *Return to Aztlan: The Social Process of International Migration from Western Mexico*. Berkeley: University of California Press, 1990.

Matibag, Eugenio. *Haitian-Dominican Counterpoint: Nation, State, and Race on Hispaniola*. New York: Palgrave Macmillan, 2003. Are deleted Massey citations placed elsewhere or deleted altogether?

Matos, Carmen. "Haití expide documentos a sus ciudadanos el el país." *Hoy*, September 15, 2012. http://hoy.com.do/haiti-expide-documentos-a-sus-ciudadanos-en-el-pais/

Máximo, Luciano and Gustavo Faleiros. "Crise traz de volta ao país 400 mil 'expatriados.'" *EU& Valor Econômico*, May 24, 2010. http://www.vermelho.org.br/noticia.php?id_noticia=130037&id_secao=2

McLeman, Robert and Barry Smit. "Migration as an Adaptation to Climate Change." *Climatic Change* 76, no. 1-2 (2006): 31–53.

McSherry, J. Patrice. *Predatory States*. Lanham: Rowman and Littlefield, 2005.

Menjívar, Cecilia. "Liminal Legality: Salvadoran and Guatemalan Immigrants' Lives in the United States." *American Journal of Sociology* 111, no. 4 (2006).

Merriam-Webster. Dictionary Entry of "Jus soli." Accessed at http://www.merriam-webster.com/dictionary/jus%20soli

Mignolo, Walter. Introduction to *Capitalismo y geopolítica del conocimiento*, edited by Walter Mignolo, 9–53. Buenos Aires: del Signo, 2001.

Mignolo, Walter. "Capitalism and Geopolitics of Knowledge: Latin American Social Thought and Latino/a American Studies." In *Critical Latin American and Latino Studies*, edited by Juan Poblete, 32–75 Minneapolis: University of Minnesota Press, 2003.

Mignolo, Walter. *The Idea of Latin America*. Malden, MA: Blackwell, 2005.

Migraciones, globalización, y género en Argentina y Chile. Chile: Fundación Instituto de la Mujer, 2005.

Milet, Paz. "Chile-Perú: las dos caras de un espejo." *Revista de Ciencia Política* 24, no. 2 (2004).

Miller, Arpi. "'Doing' Transnationalism: The Integrative Impact of Salvadoran Cross-Border Activism." *Journal of Ethnic and Migration Studies* 37, no. 1 (2011).

Ministerio de Relaciones Exteriores, República of Chile. "Decree Law N° 1,094 OF 1975." Accessed on February 4, 2011. http://www.extranjeria.gov.cl/filesapp/ley_reglamento_ingles.pdf

Mintz, Sidney W. "Whitewashing Haiti's History." *Boston Review*, January 22, 2010. http://www.bostonreview.net/world/whitewashing-haiti%E2%80%99s-history

Mirabal Nancy Raquel and Agustín Laó-Montes, eds. *Technofuturos: Critical Interventions in Latina/o Studies*. Lanham, MD: Lexington Books, 2007.

Modolo, Vanina. "Participación política de los migrantes. Reflexiones sobre la extensión de la ciudadanía en Argentina." *Revista Mexicana de Ciencias Políticas y Sociales* 59, no. 220 (2014): 349–370. Accessed on February 6, 2015. http://www.scielo.org.mx/pdf/rmcps/v59n220/v59n220a12.pdf

Montupil, Fernando, ed. *Exilio, derechos humanos y democracia. El exilio chileno en Europa*. Santiago: Coordinación Europea de Comités Pro-Retorno, 1993.

Moore, Daniel. "Latinoamericanos en Suecia." In *Suecia-Latinoamerica: Relaciones y cooperación*, edited by Weine Karlsson, Ake Magnusson, and Carlos Vidales. Stockholm: Latin American Institute of Stockholm University, 1993.

Morad, Moshe. "Salsa and Falafel – Music and Identity among Illegal Latino Immigrants in Tel Aviv." 2005. Accessed July 2014. http://www.soas.ac.uk/research/rsa/journalofgraduateresearch/editon1/file58316.pdf

Mörner, Magnus. *El mestizaje en la historia de Ibero-América*. Stockholm: School of Economics, 1960.

Morrell, E. "Youth-Initiated Research as a Tool for Advocacy and Change in Urban Schools." In *Beyond Resistance: Youth Activism and Community Change*, edited by S. Ginwright, P. Noguera, and J. Cammarota, 111–128. New York: Routledge, 2006.

Moya, Jose C. "Immigrants and Associations: A Global and Historical Perspective." *Journal of Ethnic and Migration Studies* 31, no. 5 (2005).

Moya Pons, Frank. *The Dominican Republic: A National History*. New Rochelle, NY: Hispaniola Books, 1995.

Mu, Enrique and Milagros Pereyra-Rojas. "Impact on Society versus Impact on Knowledge: Why Latin American Scholars Do Not Participate in Latin American Studies." *Latin American Research Review* 50, no. 2 (2015).

Muñoz, Solange. "Peruvian Migration to Chile: Challenges for National Identity, Human Rights and Social Policy." Santiago: CLASPO Report, 2005.

Murillo, Hugo. "La controversia de límites entre Costa Rica y Nicaragua. El Laudo Cleveland y los derechos canaleros." *Anuario de Estudios Centroamericanos* 12, no. 2 (1986).

Nájera Aguirre, Jessica Natalia. "Trabajo extradoméstico de las migrantes guatemaltecas en Chiapas." In *Flujos migratorios en la Frontera Guatemala-México*, edited by Ma. Eugenia Anguiano Téllez and Rodolfo Corona Vázquez. Mexico City: COLEF-INM/Centro de Estudios Migratorios-DGE/Editions, 2009.

National Commission for Human Rights (CNDH) and the International Organization for Migration (IOM), ed. *Una vida discreta, fugaz y anónima: Los centroamericanos transmigrantes en México*. Mexico City: Centro Nacional de Derechos Humanos, 2007.

National Commission of Human Rights (CNDH). *Bienvenidos al infierno del secuestro. Testimonios de migrantes*. Mexico City: CNDH, 2009.

National Commission of Human Rights (CNDH), *Special Report of the National Commission for Human Rights on the Case of Kidnapping against Migrants*. Mexico City: CNDH, 2009.

National Institute of Migration. *Compilación histórica de la legislación migratoria en México 1909–1996*. Mexico City: Talleres Gráficos de México, 1996.

National Institute of Migration. *Flujo de entradas de extranjeros por la frontera sur terrestre de México registradas por el Instituto Nacional de Migración*. Center for Migration Studies, 2005.

National Institute of Migration. *Apuntes sobre migración*. Ministry of the Interior, Mexican National Institute of Migration, Center for Migration Studies, 2011.

Negra de el Faro, Sala, ed. *Crónicas negras desde una región que no cuenta*. Mexico City: Aguilar, 2014.

Newland, Kathleen. "Climate Change and Migration Dynamics." Migration Policy Institute, September 2011.

The New York Times. Public Statement Made by President Obama. *June 2, 2014*.

The New York Times. "Questions about the Border Kids." Accessed on July 15, 2014. http://www.nytimes.com/interactive/2014/07/15/us/questions-about-the-border-kids.html?_r=0

"Nicaraguan Migrants in Costa Rica Face Deportation" *Unbound,* https://www
.unbound.org/Stories/2015/January/NicaraguanMigrantsInCostaRica, accessed June 1,
2016.

Nolan-Ferrell, Catherine. "Working for Citizenship: Guatemalan Refugees in Southern Mexico, 1980–1996." Paper presented at Aquí y Allá: Migrations in Latin American
Labor History Conference, Duke University, May 2014.

Norambuena, Carmen. "Política y legislación inmigratoria en Chile 1830–1920." In
Cuadernos de Humanidades. Santiago: Universidad Santiago de Chile, 1990.

"Nuevo reglamento de extranjería" Departamento jurídico de la Vicaria de la
Solidaridad. Documento 002129.

O'Connor, Erin. *Gender, Indian, Nation. The Contradictions of Making Ecuador,
1830–1925.* Tucson: University of Arizona Press, 2007.

O'Neill, Ellis. "How Will Chile's President-elect Bachelet Tackle Immigration
Reform?" *The Christian Science Monitor,* December 16, 2013. Accessed on July 7, 2014.
http://www.alaskadispatch.com/article/20131216/how-will-chiles-president-elect
-bachelet-tackle-immigration-reform

Oliver-Smith, Anthony. "Haiti and the Historical Construction of Disasters."
NACLA Report on the Americas 43, no. 3 (2010).

Ong, A. "Cultural Citizenship as Subject-Making: Immigrants Negotiate Racial and
Cultural Boundaries in the United States." *Current Anthropology* 37, no. 5 (1996).

Onishi, Norimitsu. "Enclave of Brazilians Tests Insular Japan." *New York Times,*
November 2, 2008.

Organization of the American States (OAS). *International Migration in the Americas: Second Report of the Continuous Reporting System on International Migration in the
Americas.* Washington, 2012. Accessed on September 9, 2013. http://www.oecd.org/
migration/48423814.pdf

Ortega, Javier. "El test de los cojones, parte I." *La Tercera.* Santiago: 2001. Accessed
November 28, 2001. http://www.tercera.cl/especiales/2001/verdeolivo/capitulo01/test01.htm

Osiatyński, Wiktor. *Human Rights and their Limits.* Cambridge: Cambridge University Press, 2009.

Overmyer-Velázquez, Mark, ed. *Latino America: State-by-State.* Westport, CT:
Greenwood Press, 2008.

Overmyer-Velázquez, Mark, ed. *Beyond la Frontera: The History of Mexico-US
Migration.* Oxford: Oxford University Press, 2011.

Overmyer-Velázquez, Mark. "Histories and Historiographies of Greater Mexico." In
Beyond la Frontera: The History of Mexico-US Migration, edited by Mark
Overmyer-Velázquez, xix-xlvi. Oxford: Oxford University Press, 2011.

Padilla, Beatriz and Joao Peixoto. *Latin American Immigration to Southern Europe.*
Washington, DC: Migration Information Source, 2007.

Palacios, Nicolás. *Raza chilena: Libro escrito por un chileno i para los chilenos.* Valparaíso: Imprenta de Gustavo Schäfer, 1904.

Papillon, Martin. "Framing Self-Determination: The Politics of Indigenous Rights in
Canada and the United States." In *Comparing Canada: Methods and Perspectives on
Canadian Politics,* edited by Luc Turgeon, Martin Papillon, Jennifer Wallner, Stephen
White. Vancouver: UBC Press, 2014.

Pasqualucci, Jo M. *The Practice and Procedure of the Inter-American Court of Human
Rights.* Cambridge: Cambridge University Press, 2003.

Patillo-McCoy, Mary. "Church Culture as a Strategy of Action in the Black Community." *American Sociological Review* 63, no. 6 (1998).

Paz, Alejandro. "Discursive Transformation: The Emergence of Ethnolinguistic Identity Among Latin American Labor Migrants and Their Children in Israel." PhD Diss. Chicago: The University of Chicago, 2010.

Pedrosa, Fernando. *La otra izquierda: La socialdemocracia en América Latina*. Buenos Aires: Capital Intelectual, 2012.

Pérez Rosales, *Emigración, Inmigración y Colonización*. Santiago: Impr. De Julio Belin, 1854.

"Perfil Migratorio de Nicaragua" Organización Internacional para las Migraciones, 2013.

Pero, Davide and John Solomos. *Migrant Politics and Mobilisation: Exclusion, Engagements, Incorporation*. New York: Routledge, 2013.

Personal communication with Raquel Zuñiga. June 3, 2013.

Personal communication with Vera Machado.

Peru Instituto Nacional de Estadística e Informática, 2008. Accessed on May 25, 2011. http://www.inei.gob.pe/

Pescarolo, Alessandra, Luis Á. Fernández and Jaime Rierra R. *La gran depresión (1873–1896)*. Barcelona: Oikos-tau, 1991.

Petrozziello, Allison and Bridget Wooding. *Fanm nan Fwontye, Fanm Toupatou: Making Visible the Violence against Haitian Migrant, In-Transit and Displaced Women on the Dominican-Haitian Border*. Santo Domingo: Colectiva Mujeres y Salud, Mujeres del Mundo, Observatory Migrants of the Caribbean (CIES-UNIBE), 2012.

Pieroni, Geraldo. *Vadios e ciganos, hereges e bruxos—os degradados no Brasil colonia*. Rio: Bertrand, 2000.

Piore, Michael J. *Birds of Passage: Migrant Labor and Industrial Societies*. Cambridge: Cambridge University Press, 1979.

Pilcher, Jeffrey M. *Planet Taco: A Global History of Mexican Food*. New York: Oxford University Press, 2012.

Pizarro, Cynthia. "'Ciudadanos bonaerenses-bolivianos': Activismo político binacional en una organización de inmigrantes bolivianos residentes en Argentina." *Revista Colombiana de Atropologia* 45, no. 2 (2009). Accessed on February 6, 2015. http://www.scielo.org.co/scielo.php?pid=S0486-65252009000200007&script=sci_arttext

Pizarro, Jorge Martínez. "Exigencias y posibilidades para políticas de población y migración internacional. El contexto latinoamericano y el caso de Chile." Santiago: Centro Latinoamericano y Caribeño de Demografía (CELADE) – División de Población de la CEPAL, 2002.

Plant, Roger. *Sugar and Modern Slavery: A Tale of Two Countries*. London: Zed Books, 1987.

Pollock, M. *Colormute: Race Talk Dilemmas in an American School*. Princeton, NJ: Princeton University Press, 2004.

Pollock, Sheldon, Homi K. Bhabha, Carol Breckenridge, and Dipesh Chakrabharty. "Cosmopolitanisms." *Public Culture* 12, no. 3 (2000).

Portes, Alejandro. "Chapter 1: Economic Sociology and the Sociology of Immigration: A conceptual Overview." In *The Economic Sociology of Immigration: Essays on Networks, Ethnicity, and Entrepreneurship*, edited by A. Portes, 1–41. New York: Russel Sage Foundation, 1995.

Portes, Alejandro, and Kenneth Wilson. "Immigrant Enclaves: An Analysis of the Labor Market Experiences of Cubans in Miami." *American Journal of Sociology* 86, no. 2 (1980): 295–319.

Portes, Alejandro, and John Walton. *Labor, Class and the International System*. New York: Academic Press, 1981.

Portes, Alejandro and Robert L. Bach. *Latin Journey: Cuban and Mexican Immigrants in the United States*. Berkeley: University of California Press, 1985.

Portes, Alejandro and Alex Stepick. *City on the Edge: The Transformation of Miami*. Berkeley: University of California Press, 1993.

Portes, Alejandro, and Ruben Rumbaut. *Immigrant America: A Portrait*. Berkeley: University of California Press, 1996.

Portes, Alejandro, L. E. Guarnizo, and P. Landolt. "The Study of Transnationalism: Pitfalls and Promise of an Emergent Research Field." *Ethnic and Racial Studies* 22, no. 2 (1999).

Portes, Alejandro, Rosa Aparicio, William Haller, and Erik Vickstrom. "Moving Ahead in Madrid: Aspirations and Expectations in the Spanish Second Generation." *International Migration Review* 44, no. 4 (2010).

Portes, Alejandro, E. Vickstrom, and R. Aparicio. "Coming of Age in Spain: The Self-Identification, Beliefs, and Self-Esteem of the Second Generation." *The British Journal of Sociology* 62, no. 3 (2011).

Portes, Alejandro and R. Aparicio. "Investigación longitudinal sobre la segunda generación en España: Avance de resultados." Madrid: Fundación Ortega-Marañón, 2013.

Portes, Alejandro and Rubén G. Rumbaut. *Immigrant America: A Portrait*. Berkeley: University of California Press, 2014.

Poveda, D. "Literacy Artifacts and Semiotic Landscape of a Spanish Secondary School." *Reading Research Quarterly* 47, no. 1 (2012).

Poveda, D., M. Jociles, A. Franzé, M. Moscoso, and A. Calvo. "The Role of Institutional, Family and Peer-Based Discourses and Practices in the Construction of Students' Socioacademic Trajectories." *Ethnography and Education* 7, no. 1 (2012).

Pratt, Mary-L. *Ojos imperiales: literatura de viajes y transculturación*. Buenos Aires: FCE, 2011.

Press Conference on March 28, 2012. "La Ley de Migración en Costa Rica: A dos años de su entrada en vigencia. Promesas, realidades y desafíos." San José.

Prime Minister's Office. *Decision no. 2183*. 2010. Accessed on December 31, 2013. http://www.pmo.gov.il/Secretary/GovDecisions/2010/Pages/des2183.aspx

Prime Minister's Office. *Decision no. 3807*. 2005. Accessed on December 31, 2013. http://www.pmo.gov.il/Secretary/GovDecisions/2005/Pages/des3807.aspx

Purcell, Fernando, and Alfredo Riquelme, eds. *Ampliando miradas: Chile y su historia en un tiempo global*. Santiago: RIL editors, 2009.

Putnam, Robert. *Better Together: Restoring the American Community*. New York: Simon and Schuster, 2003.

Que Es? Accessed on May 20, 2011. http://www.que.es/ultimas-noticias/espana/201104101952-unos-62.000-peruanos-chile-pueden-efe.html

Quijano, Aníbal. "Colonialidad del poder, eurocentrismo y América Latina." In *La colonialidad del saber: eurocentrismo y ciencias sociales – Perspectivas latinoamericanas*, edited by E. Lander, 219–264. Buenos Aires: Ciccus/Clacso, 2011.

Radclifee, Sarah and Sallie Westwood. *Re-Making the Nation: Place, Politics and Identity in Latin America*. New York: Routledge, 1996.

Raijman, Rebeca and Adriana Kemp. "State and Non-State Actors: A Multi-Layered Analysis of Labor Migration Policy in Israel." In *Perspectives and Practices of Public Policy: The Case of Israel,* edited by D. Korn, 155–173. Lanham, MD: Lexington Books, 2002.

Raijman, Rebeca and Adriana Kemp. "Labor migration, Managing the Ethno-national Conflict, and Client Politics in Israel." In *Transnational Migration to Israel in Global Comparative Context,* edited by Sarah Willen, 31–50. Lanham, MD: Lexington Books, 2007.

Raijman, Rebeca, and Adriana Kemp. "The New Immigration to Israel: Becoming a De-Facto Immigration State in the 1990s." In *Immigration Worldwide,* edited by Uma Segal, Doreen Elliott, and Nazneen S. Mayadas, 227–243. Oxford: Oxford University Press, 2010.

Raijman, Rebeca and Ariane Ophir. "The Economic Integration of Latin Americans in Israel." *Canadian Ethnic Studies* 46, no. 2 (2014).

Raijman, Rebeca, Silvina Schammah and Adriana Kemp. "International Migration, Domestic and Care Work: Undocumented Latina Migrant Women in Israel." *Gender & Society* 17, no. 5 (2003): 727–749.

Rapoport, Mario. *Historia económica, política y social de la Argentina (1880–2003).* Buenos Aires: Emecé, 2005.

Ratekin, Mervyn. "The Early Sugar Industry in Española." *Hispanic American Historical Review* 34, no. 1 (1954).

RECONICI.DO. "Resumen preliminar de la investigación sobre personas afectadas por la Resolución 12/07." 2011. http://www.reconoci.do/images/stories/documentos/resumen-preliminar.pdf

Reed-Danahay, Deborah and Caroline D. Brettell. *Citizenship, Political Engagement, and Belonging: Immigrants in Europe and the United States.* New Brunswick, NJ: Rutgers University Press, 2008.

Reitz, Jeffery G. "Multiculturalism Policies and Popular Multiculturalism in the Development of Canadian Immigration." In *The Multiculturalism Question. Debating Identity in 21st Century Canada,* edited by Jedwab, Jack. Montreal: McGill-Queen's University Press, 2014.

República Dominicana. "Ley General de Migración, No. 285-04." *Gaceta Oficial* 10291, August 27, 2004: 5–46, http://www.seip.gob.do/Portals/0/docs/Migracion/ley.pdf.

República Dominicana, Oficina de la Presidencia. "Decreto No. 327-13." 2013. http://www.consultoria.gov.do/spaw2/uploads/files/Decreto%20327-13.pdf

República Dominicana, Tribunal Constitucional. "Sentencia TC/0168/13." 2013. http://noticiasmicrojuris.files.wordpress.com/2013/10/sentenciatc0168-13-c.pdf.

República Dominicana, Congreso Nacional. "Ley No.169-14." 2014. http://www.consultoria.gov.do/spaw2/uploads/files/Ley%20No.%20169-14.pdf

"Resolución 12-07 ¿Qué es?" Accessed at http://www.youtube.com/watch?v=Rukj6D1Oxvs

Reuveny, Rafael. "Climate change-induced migration and violent conflict." *Political Geography* 26, no. 6 (2007): 656–673.

"Revista a las revistas chilenas del exilio 1973–1990." 2006. http://www.abacq.net/imagineria/revistas.htm

Ribeiro, Valéria. "Crise reduziu envio de recursos de imigrantes brasileiros para suas famílias." *Comunidade News,* June 25, 2009. www.comunidadenews.com/brasil/crise-reduziu-envio-de-recursos-de-imigrantes-brasileiros-para-suas-familias-5073

Richards, Patricia. *Race and the Chilean Miracle: Neoliberalism, Democracy and Indigenous Rights.* Pittsburgh: University of Pittsburgh Press, 2013.

Richardson, Bonham C. *Caribbean Migrants: Environment and Survival on St. Kitts and Nevis*. Knoxville: University of Tennessee Press, 1983.

Ríos-Rojas, Ana. "Beyond Delinquent Citizenships: Immigrant Youth's (Re)visions of Citizenship and Belonging in a Globalized World." *Harvard Educational Review* 81 (2011).

Ríos-Rojas, Ana. "Managing and Disciplining Diversity: The Politics of Conditional Belonging in a Catalonian Institut." *Anthropology & Education Quarterly* 45, no. 1 (2014).

Riosmena, Fernando. "Policy Shocks: On the Legal Auspices of Latin America–U.S. Migration." *Annals of the American Academy of Political and Social Science* 630 (2010).

Rivas, Jaime. "Los que se quedan en el camino. Inmigrantes salvadoreños en Puerto Madero, Chiapas." PhD diss., CIESAS Occidente, 2013.

Rivera, Carolina. "El trabajo de niñas, niños y adolescentes guatemaltecos en el Soconusco, Chiapas." In *Migración, seguridad, violencia y derechos humanos en el sur de México y Centroamérica*, edited by Daniel Villafuerte and María del Carmen García. Mexico City: Miguel Ángel Porrúa, 2011.

Rivera, Jorge Riquelme and Gonzalo Alarcón Muñoz. "El peso de la historia - inmigración peruana en Chile." *Polis* 7, no. 20 (2008).

Robinson, William I. "Why the Immigrant Rights Struggle Compels Us to Reconceptualize Both Latin American and Latino/a Studies." *Forum, Latin American Studies Association* 38, no. 2 (2007).

Rocha, Cristina. "Triangular Transnationalism: Japanese Brazilians on the Move Between Japan, Australia and Brazil." *Journal of Intercultural Studies* 35.5 (2014): 493–512.

Rock, David. *Argentina 1516–1982 from Spanish Colonization to the Falklands War*. Los Angeles: University of California Press, 1985.

Rodó, José Enrique. *Ariel*. Valencia: Prometeo, 1900.

Rodríguez, Gabriel Cid. "Guerra y conciencia nacional: la guerra contra la confederación en la imaginario chileno, 1836–1888." PhD diss., Instituto de Historia, Pontificia Universidad Católica de Chile, 2009.

Rodríguez De Ita, Guadalupe. "Una mirada urgente al sur: los refugiados guatemaltecos en Chiapas." In *Chiapas: rupturas y continuidades de una sociedad fragmentada*, edited by Diana Guillén. Mexico City: Instituto Mora, 2003.

Rodríguez Elizondo, José. *La pasión de Iñaki*. Santiago: Editorial Andrés Bello, 1996.

Rodríguez, Juana María. *Queer Latinidad: Identity Practices, Discursive Spaces*. New York: NYU Press, 2003.

Rodríguez Villouta, Mili. *Ya nunca me verás como me vieras*. Santiago: Las Ediciones del Ornitorrinco, 1990.

Roer-Strier, Dorit and Orly Olshtain-Mann. "To See and Not Be Seen: Latin American Illegal Foreign Workers in Jerusalem." *International Migration* 37, no. 2 (1999).

Rojas Mira, Claudia. "La Casa de Chile en México, 1973–1993." In *Exiliados, emigrados y retornados. Chilenos en América y Europa, 1973 a 2004*, edited by José Del Pozo. Santiago: RIL Editores, 2006.

Rojas Mira, Claudia and Alessandro Santoni. "Geografía política del exilio chileno: Los diferentes rostros de la solidaridad." *Perfiles Latinoamericanos* 41 (2013).

Roniger, Luis. *Transnational Politics in Central America*. Gainesville: University Press of Florida, 2011.

Roniger, Luis. "La sacralización del consenso nacional y las pugnas por la memoria histórica y la justicia en el Uruguay post-dictatorial." *América Latina Hoy* 61 (2012).

Roniger, Luis. *Destierro y exilio en América Latina. Nuevos estudios y avances teóricos.* Buenos Aires: EUDEBA, 2014.

Roniger, Luis. "Represión y prácticas genocidas: El sustrato ideologico y discursivo de la violencia generalizada." In *La Guerra Fría y las Americas,* edited by Avital Bloch and Rosario Rodríguez. Mexico City: Universidad de Colima y la Universidad Michoacana de San Nicolás de Hidalgo, 2014.

Roniger, Luis and Mario Sznajder. *The Legacy of Human Rights Violations in the Southern Cone: Argentina, Chile and Uruguay.* Oxford: Oxford University Press, 1999.

Roniger, Luis and Deby Babis. "Latin American Israelis: The Collective Identity of an Invisible Community." In *Identities in an Era of Globalization and Multiculturalism: Latin America in the Jewish World,* edited by Judit Bokser de Liwerant, 297–320. Leiden, Netherlands: Brill, 2008.

Roniger, Luis and Mario Sznajder. "Los antecedentes coloniales del exilio político y su proyección en el siglo XIX." *Estudios Interdisciplinarios de América Latina y el Caribe* 18, no. 2 (2012).

Roniger, Luis, James N Green and Pablo Yankelevich, eds., *Exile and the Politics of Exclusion in the Americas.* Brighton and Portland: Sussex Academic Press, 2012.

Rosaldo, Renato. "Cultural Citizenship and Educational Democracy." *Cultural Anthropology* 9, no. 3 (1994).

Rossini, Rosa Ester. "O Retorno as Origens ou o Sonho de Encontro com o Eldorado Japonês: O Exemplo dos Dekassequis do Brasil em Direção ao Japão." In *Emigração e Imigração no Brasil Contemporânea,* edited by Neide Lopes Patarra, 104–110. Campinas: Programa Interinstitucional de Avaliação e Acompanhamento das Migrações Internacionais no Brasil, 1995.

Roth, Joshua Hotaka. *Brokered Homeland: Japanese Brazilian Migrants in Japan.* Ithaca, NY: Cornell University Press, 2002.

Rudolph, Christopher. *National Security and Immigration: Policy Development in the United States and Western Europe Since 1945.* Stanford, CA: Stanford University Press, 2006.

Rugh, Jacob S. and Douglas S. Massey. "Segregation in Post-Civil Rights America: Stalled Integration or End of the Segregated Century?" *The DuBois Review: Social Science Research on Race* 11, no. 2 (2014).

Ruiz, Olivia. "Los riesgos de migrar: La migración centroamericana en la frontera México-Guatemala." In *Nuevas tendencias y nuevos desafíos de la migración internacional; memorias del seminario permanente sobre migración internacional,* edited by M. Á. Castillo and J. Santibáñez. Tijuana: Colegio de la Frontera Norte, 2004.

Ruiz, Raúl. *Diálogo de exiliados.* Film. Directed by Raúl Ruiz. France: 1974.

Ruíz, Vicki L. "Nuestra América: Latino History as United States History." *Journal of American History* 93, no. 3 (2006).

Rumazo González, Alfonso. *8 grandes biografías.* Caracas: Ediciones de la Presidencia de la República, 1993.

Rushdie, Salman. "In Good Faith." *Independent on Sunday.* February 4, 1990.

Sabar, Galia. "The Rise and Fall of African Independent Christianity in Israel, 1990–2004." In *Transnational Migration to Israel in Global Comparative Context,* edited by Sarah Willen, 31–50. Lanham, MD: Lexington Books, 2007.

Sala Constitucional. *Resolución 2012011760.* San José: Corte Suprema de Justicia, 2012.

Saldívar, José David. *Border Matters: Remapping American Cultural Studies.* Berkeley: University of California Press, 1997.

Saldivar, José David. "Border Thinking: The Coloniality of Power from Gloria Anzaldúa to Arundhati Roy." In *Identity Politics Reconsidered*, edited by Linda Martin Alcoff, Michael Hames-García, Satya P. Mohanty, and Paula M. L. Moya. London: Palgrave-Macmillan Publishing, 2006.

Salgado, Eduardo. "Eles Fogem da Bagunça." *Veja*, July 18, 2001.

Salgado, Paula D. "El trabajo en la industria de la indumentaria: una aproximación a partir del caso argentino." In *Trabajo y Sociedad: Sociología del trabajo – Estudios culturales – Narrativas sociológicas y literarias.* Santiago del Estero, Verano, 2012. Accessed on January 28, 2015. http://www.unse.edu.ar/trabajoysociedad

San Martín, Ximena Zavala and Claudia Rojas Venegas. "Globalización, procesos migratorios y estado en Chile." In *Migraciónes, globalización y género en Argentina y Chile,* edited by Cristina Cacopardo, et al., 150–191. Santiago, Chile: Movimiento Por Emancipación de la Mujer MEMCH, 2005.

Sanchez, Patricia. "Urban Immigrant Students: How Transnationalism Shapes Their World Learning." *The Urban Review* 39, no. 5 (2007).

Sanchez, Patricia and G.S. Kasun. "Connecting Transnationalism to the Classroom and to Theories of Immigrant Student Adaptation." *Berkeley Review of Education* 3, no. 1 (2012).

Sánchez, Romina. "Aquí vivo y aquí quiero votar." *Noticias Urbanas*, July 13, 2013. http://www.noticiasurbanas.com.ar/noticias/aqui-vivo-y-aqui-quiero-votar/

Sandoval, Carlos. "Contested Discourses on National Identity. Representing the Nicaraguan Immigration to Costa Rica." *Bulletin of Latin American Research* 23, no. 4 (2004).

Sandoval, Carlos. *Threatening Others. Nicaraguans and the Formation of National Identities in Costa Rica.* Athens: Ohio University Press, 2004.

Sandoval, Carlos. "Costa Rica: Many Channels, Scarce Communication." In *The Media in Latin America*, edited by J. Lugo. Buckingham: Open University Press, 2008.

Sandoval, Carlos. "Narrating Lived Experience in a Binational Community in Costa Rica." In *Ethnicities and Values in a Changing World*, edited by Gargi Bhattacharyya. London: Ashgate, 2009.

Sandoval, Carlos. "De Calero a la Trocha. La nueva disputa limítrofe entre los gobiernos de Costa Rica y Nicaragua (2010–2012)." *Anuario de Estudios Centroamericanos* 38 (2012).

Sandoval, Carlos. "Presentación." In *Criminalidad y discurso en Costa Rica. Reflexiones críticas sobre un problema social.* Edited by Sebastian Huhn, 10-38. San José: Fundación Rosa Luxemburgo-FLACSO, 2012.

Sandoval, Carlos. "To Whom and to What Is Research on Migration a Contribution." *Ethnic and Racial Studies* 36, no. 9 (2013).

Sandoval, Carlos. "Public Social Science at Work: Contesting Hostility Towards Nicaraguan Migrants in Costa Rica." In *Migration, Gender and Social Justice*, edited by T. D . Truong, S. I. Bergh, and D. Gasper, 44–62. Amsterdam: Springer, 2014.

Sandoval, Carlos. *No más muros. Exclusión y migración forzada en Centroamérica.* San José: EUCR, 2015.

Sandoval, Carlos, Mónica Brenes, and Laura Paniagua. *La dignidad vale mucho. Mujeres nicaragüenses forjan derechos en Costa Rica.* San José: Editorial de la Universidad de Costa Rica, 2012.

Sartori, Giovanni. *La política: lógica y método en las ciencias sociales*, translated by Marcos Lara. México D.F.: Fondo de Cultura Económica, 1996.

Sartori, Giovanni. *La sociedad multiétnica—Pluralismo, multiculturalismo y extranjeros*. Madrid: Taurus, 2001.

Sasaki, Elisa Massae. "Dekasseguis: Trabalhadores Nipo-Brasileiros no Japão." *Travessia: Revista do Migrante* (1995).

Sasaki, Elisa Massae. "A Imigração para o Japão." *Estudos Avançados. Dossiê Migrações* 20, no. 57 (2007).

Sasaki, Elisa Massae. "Ser ou Não Ser Japonês?: A Construção da Identidade dos Brasileiros Descendentes de Japoneses no Contexto das Migrações Internacionais do Japão Contemporâneo." PH.D diss. Department of Social Sciences, UNICAMP, Campinas, São Paulo, 2009.

Sasaki, Elisa Massae. "Depois de duas décadas de movimento migratório entre o Brasil e o Japão." Paper presented at the Seminário "20 anos dos Brasileiros no Japão" at the Universidade das Nações Unidas, Tokyo, 2010.

Sassen, Saskia ed. *Global Networks, Linked Cities*. New York: Routledge, 2002.

Sassen, Saskia. *The Mobility of Labor and Capital: A Study in International Investment and Labor Flow*. Cambridge: Cambridge University Press, 1988.

Sater, William. "Joining the Mainstream: Integrating Latin America into the Teaching of World History." *Perspectives on History* (1995).

Satzewich, Vic. "Transnational Migration: A New Historical Phenomenon?" In *Workers across the Americas: The Transnational Turn in Labor History,* edited by Leon Fink. New York: Oxford University Press, 2011.

Sbarbi Osuna, Maximiliano. "Crecen las migraciones internas en Sudamérica." *Observador Global*. Accessed on May 2, 2011. http://observadorglobal.com/crecen-las-migraciones-internas-en-sudamerica-n21018.html.

Scardaville, Michael C. *Crime and the Urban Poor. Mexico City in the Late Colonial Period*. University Microfilms International, 1977.

Schammah, Silvina, Rebeca Raijman, Adriana Kemp, and Julia Reznik. "'Making it' in Israel? Non-Jewish Latino Undocumented Migrant Workers in the Holy Land." *Estudios Interdisciplinarios de America Latina y el Caribe* 11, no. 2 (2000).

Schissler, Jakob. "Menschenrechte zwischen Univesalismus und Kulturrelativismus." In *Der Bürger im Staat*, 26–30. Stuttgart, Germany: Landeszentrale für Politische Bildung Baden-Württemberg, 2005.

Schlögel, Karl. *Planet der Nomaden*. Berlin: Wjs-Verlag, 2006.

Schnell, Yitzhak. *Foreign Workers in Southern Tel Aviv-Yafo*. Jerusalem: The Floershaimer Institute for Policy Studies, 1999.

Schuller, Mark. *Killing with Kindness: Haiti, International Aid, and NGOs*. Piscataway, NJ: Rutgers University Press, 2012.

Segura, Olman. Meeting Request to Carlos Sandoval García. August 20, 2012.

Seigel, Micol. *Uneven Encounters: Making Race and Nation in Brazil and the United States*. Durham, NC: Duke University Press, 2010.

Semyonov, Moshe and Noah Lewin-Epstein. *Hewers of Wood and Drawers of Water. Noncitizen Arabs in the Israeli Labor Market*. New York: ILR Press, 1987.

Sepúlveda, Enrique. "Toward a Pedagogy of *acompañamiento*: Mexican Migrant Youth Writing from the Underside of Modernity." *Harvard Educational Review* 81, no. 3 (2011).

Sepúlveda, Enrique. "Viviendo en Madrid: Observaciones de una ciudadanía diversa y desigual." *Diagonal*, April 7, 2014. https://www.diagonalperiodico.net/blogs/fuera-clase/viviendo-madrid-observaciones-ciudadania-diversa-y-desigual.html

Serrano, Amy. *The Sugar Babies: The Plight of the Children of Agricultural workers in the Sugar Industry of the Dominican Republic.* Film. Directed by Amy Serrano. Miami: Siren Studios, 2007.

Servicio Nacional de Turismo. "Chile es tuyo." Accessed June 6, 2011. http://www .chileestuyo.cl/ or https://www.youtube.com/watch?v=5BKw2pdUU8w

Servicios de Colonización Inmigración: colonización--tierras fiscales, defensa fiscal indígenas. Santiago: Impr. y Enc. Bandera, 1903.

Shachar, Ayelet. "Whose Republic? Citizenship and Membership in the Israeli Polity." *Georgetown Immigration Law Journal* 13, no. 2 (1999).

Shain, Yossi. *The Frontier of Loyalty. Political Exiles in the Age of the Nation-State.* Middletown, PA: Wesleyan University Press, 1989.

Sheel, Sylvia Dummer. "Los desafíos de escenificar el 'alma nacional': Chile en la Exposición Iberoamericana de Sevilla, 1929." *Historia Crítica* 42 (2010).

Shklar, Judith N. *Political Thought and Political Thinkers.* Chicago: University of Chicago Press, 1998.

Sidekum, Antônio. "Multiculturalismo: Desafíos para la educación en América Latina." *Polylog. Foro para filosofía intercultural*, 2003. Accessed on September 28, 2004. http://them.polylog.org/4/asa-es.htm

Silié, Rubén, Carlos Segura, and Carlos Dore Cabral. *La nueva inmigración haitiana.* Santo Domingo: FLACSO, 2002.

Silva, Carolina and Douglas S. Massey. "Violence, Networks, and International Migration from Colombia." *International Migration* doi/10.1111/imig.12169/.

Sinai, Ruth. "Leader of Local Filipino Workers Faces Deportation." Ha'aretz, October 10, 2001.

Situation of Nicaraguan Immigrants in Costa Rica" Central American Human Rights Commission Report. San José, Costa Rica, 2002.

Siu, Lok. *Memories of a Future Home: Diasporic Citizenship of Chinese in Panama.* Stanford, CA: Stanford University Press, 2005.

Skuban, William. *Lines in the Sand: Nationalism and Identity on the Peruvian-Chilean Frontier.* Albuquerque: University of New Mexico Press, 2011.

Smith, David Michael. "The American Melting Pot: A National Myth in Public and Popular Discourse." *National Identities* 14, no. 4 (2012).

Smith, Romina. "Distrito Tecnológico: Parque Patricios se Transforma: ya se radic-aron 158 empresas." *Clarín*, September 8, 2013. Accessed January 13, 2015. http://www .clarin.com/ciudades/Parque-Patricios-transforma-radicaron-empresas_0_989301167 .html

Smooha, S. *Arabs and Jews in Israel. Vol.1. Conflicting and Shared Attitudes in a Divided Society.* Boulder, CO: Westview Press, 1992.

Solivellas, María Florencia Jensen. "Inmigrantes en Chile: la exclusión vista desde la política migratoria chilena." Paper Presented at *El III Congreso de la Asociación Latino-americana de Población, ALAP*, Córdoba, Argentina, 2008.

Solimano, Andrés. *Development Cycles, Political Regimes and International Migration: Argentina in the Twentieth Century.* Santiago: ECLAC, Economic Development Division, 2003.

Sousa Sansa, Boaventura. *Epistemologías desde el Sur.* Buenos Aires: CLACSO, 2009.

Spenser, Daniella. "Trabajo forzado en Guatemala, bracerismo guatemalteco en Chiapas." *Cuicuilco* 4, no. 12 (1984).

Stabili, Maria Rosaria. "Exiled Citizens: Chilean Political Leaders in Italy." In *Shifting Frontiers of Citizenship: The Latin American Experience,* edited by Mario Sznajder, Luis Roniger and Carlos A. Forment. Leiden: Brill, 2012.

Staab, Silke and Kristen Hill Maher. "The Dual Discourse about Peruvian Domestic Workers in Santiago de Chile: Class, Race, and a Nationalist Project." *Latin American Politics and Society* 48, no. 1 (2006).

Stefoni, Carolina. "Inmigración en Chile. Nuevos desafíos," in Stefoni, Carolina, ed. *Impactos y desafíos de las crisis internacionales.* Santiago, Chile: FLACSO, 2002.

Stefoni, Carolina. "Inmigración y ciudadanía: la formación de comunidades peruanas en Santiago y la emergencia de nuevos ciudadanos." In *El Quinto Suyo, Transnacionalidad y formaciones diaspóricas en la migración peruana,* edited by Ulla Berg and Karsten Paerregaard, 319–336. Lima: Instituto de Estudios Peruanos, 2005.

Stefoni, Carolina. "La migración en la agenda chileno-peruana. Un camino por construir." In *Nuestros vecinos,* edited by Mario Artaza and Paz Milet. Santiago: RIL Editores/Universidad de Chile, 2007.

Stein, Ernesto, et al. *The Politics of Policies: Economic and Social Progress in Latin America.* Washington, DC: Inter-American Development Bank, 2006.

Stern, Steve. *Reckoning with Pinochet: The Memory Question in Democratic Chile, 1989–2006.* Durham, NC: Duke University Press, 2010.

Suarez-Orozco, Marcelo. "Some Thoughts on Migration Studies and the Latin American Exodo." *Latin American Studies Association Forum* 37, no. 1 (2006).

Suárez-Orozco, Marcelo M. and Mariela Páez. *Latinos: Remaking America.* Berkeley: University of California Press, 2008.

Sznajder, Mario. " Legitimidad y Poder Politicos frente a las Herencias Autoritarias: Transicion y Consolidacion Democratica en America Latina." *Estudios Interdisciplinarios de America Latina y el Caribe* 4, no. 1 (1993).

Sznajder, Mario and Luis Roniger. "Exile communities and their differential institutional dynamics: A comparative analysis of the Chilean and Uruguayan political Diasporas." *Revista de Ciencia Política* 27.1 (2007).

Sznajder, Mario and Luis Roniger. *The Politics of Exile in Latin America.* Cambridge: Cambridge University Press, 2009.

Tabuchi, Hiroko. "Goodbye, Honored Guests." *New York Times,* April 23, 2009.

Takenaka, Ayumi. "The Japanese in Peru: History of Immigration, Settlement, and Racialization." *Latin American Perspectives* 31, no. 3 (2004).

Takenaka, Ayumi. "How Ethnic Minorities Experience Social Mobility in Japan: An Ethnographic Study of Peruvian Migrants." In *Social Class in Contemporary Japan: Structures, Sorting and Strategies*, edited by Hiroshi Ishida and David H. Slater, 221–238. Oxford, UK: Routledge, 2009.

Takenaka, Ayumi, et al. "Peruvian Migration in a Global Context." and Jorge Durand, "The Peruvian Diaspora: Portrait of a Migratory Process." Both in *Latin American Perspectives* 37, no. 121 (2010).

Takenaka, Ayumi and Karsten Paerregaard. "How Contexts of Reception Matter: Comparing Peruvian Migrants' Economic Trajectories in Japan and the US." *International Migration* 53, no. 2 (2015).

Taylor, Charles and Amy Gutmann. *Multiculturalism: Examining the Politics of Recognition.* Princeton, NJ: Princeton University Press, 1994.

Telles, Edward E. *Race in Another America: The Significance of Skin Color in Brazil.* Princeton, NJ: Princeton University Press, 2004.

Telles, Edward E. *Pigmentocracies: Ethnicity, Race, and Color in Latin America.* Chapel Hill: University of North Carolina Press, 2014.

Textile Aspects of Argentina. 2013. Accessed January 17, 2015. http://www.textile -future.com/dynpg/print_text.php?lang=en&aid=978&showheader=N

Thomas–Hope, Elizabeth M. "The Establishment of a Migration Tradition: British West Indian Movements to the Hispanic Caribbean in the Century after Emancipation." In *Caribbean Social Relations*, edited by Colin G. Clarke, 111–132. Liverpool: Centre for Latin American Studies, University of Liverpool, 1978.

Tomada, Carlos. "El combate contra el trabajo esclavo." *Página/12*, March 26, 2013. Accessed on February 24, 2015. http://www.pagina12.com.ar/diario/elpais/1-216619 -2013-03-26.html

Torres, Andrés Zahler. "¿En qué país vivimos los chilenos?" *Opinión.* Accessed June 25, 2011. http://ciperchile.cl/2011/06/06/%C2%BFen-que-pais-vivimos-los-chilenos/.

Torres-Saillant, Silvio. "The Tribulations of Blackness: Stages in Dominican Racial Identity." *Latin American Perspectives* 25, no. 3 (1998).

Torres-Saillant, Silvio. "Racism in the Americas and the Latino Scholar." In *Neither Enemies Nor Friends: Latinos, Blacks, Afro-Latinos,* edited by Anani Dzidzienyo and Suzanne Oboler, 281–304. New York: Palgrave Macmillan, 2005.

Trindade, Antônio A. Cançado. "La interdependencia de todos los derechos humanos. Obstáculos y desafíos en la implementación de los derechos humanos." Instituto Interamericano de Derechos Humanos, 1999. Accessed on September 27, 2004. http://www.iidh.ed.cr/BibliotecaWeb

Trueba, H. T. "Immigration and the Transnational Experience." In *The New Americans: Immigrants and Transnationals at Work*, edited by H. Trueba, Pedro Reyes, and Yali Zou, 55–78 Lanham, MD: Rowman & Littlefield, 2004.

Tsuda, Takeyuki. "Reality Versus Representations: Ethnic Essentialization and Tradition in Japanese Media Images of Japanese Brazilian Return Migrants." Paper presented at the meetings of the American Anthropological Association, Washington, DC, 2001.

Tsuda, Takeyuki. "Crossing Ethnic Boundaries: Nikkejin Return Migrants and the Ethnic Challenge of Japan's Newest Immigrant Minority." Paper presented at the meetings of the American Anthropological Association, New Orleans, 2002.

Tsuda, Takeyuki. *Strangers in the Ethnic Homeland.* New York: Columbia University Press, 2003.

Tsuda, Takeyuki. "No Place to Call Home." *Natural History* (2004).

UNESCO. *Statistical Yearbook.* Paris: Unesco Publishing & Bernan Press, 1997.

United Nations. *Universal Declaration of the Human Rights* (UDHR). 1948. http://www.un.org/en/documents/udhr/

United Nations, Department of Economic and Social Affairs, Population Division. *Trends in International Migrant Stock: The 2008 Revision.* 2009.

United Nations. "Human Development Reports." Accessed on May 24, 2011. http://hdr.undp.org/en/

United Nations Population Facts. "International Migration 2013: Migrants by Origin and Destination." Accessed on July 14, 2015. http://www.un.org/en/ga/68/meetings/migration/pdf/International%20Migration%202013_Migrants%20by%20origin%20and%20destination.pdf

United Nations. Post-2015 United Nations Development Agenda." International Organization for Migration, 2015. http://www.un.org/en/development/desa/population/migration/data/ estimates2/estimatesorigin.shtml

United Nations. Website of United Nations Department of Economic and Social Affairs Population Division: International Migration. New York: United Nations, 2015. http://www.un.org/en/development/desa/population/migration/data/estimates2/estimatesorigin.shtml

United States Census. "The Hispanic Population: 2010." http://2010.census.gov/2010cesus/data.

United States Census. "Facts for Features." Accessed August 8, 2015. http://www.census.gov/newsroom/facts-for-features/2014/cb14-ff22.html

Urquijo, José María Mariluz. *Ensayo sobre los juicios de residencia indianos.* Sevilla: Escuela de Estudios Hispanoamericanos, 1952.

Valadez, Jorge M. "The Continuing Significance of Ethnocultural Identity." In *Identities, Affiliations, and Allegiances,* edited by Sayla Benhabib, Ian Shapiro, and Danilo Petranović, 313–414. Cambridge: Cambridge University Press. 2007.

Van Dijk, Rijk A. "From Camp to Encompassment: Discourses of Transsubjectivity in the Ghanaian Pentecostal Diaspora." *Journal of Religion in Africa* 27, no. 2 (1997).

Vargas del Campo, Alberto. "Hacia una Política de Inmigración. Los inmigrantes económicos: Criterios para su elegibilidad," *Revista Diplomacia* 73 (1997).

Vasconcelos, José. *The Cosmic Race / La Raza Cósmica.* Baltimore: JHU Press, 1979.

Vásquez, Ana and Angela Xavier de Brito. "La situation de l'exilé: essai de généralisation fondé sur l'exemple de réfugiés latino-américains." *Intercultures* 21 (1993).

Vásquez, Juan Carlos. *El Visor Boliviano.* CABA, March 3, 2015.

Vásquez, Tania. "La migración peruana a Chile: El crecimiento de la comunidad binacional peruano-chilena." *Revista Argumentos* 8, no. 1 (2014).

Vega, Bernardo. *Trujillo y Haití, Volumen I (1930–1937).* Santo Domingo: Fundación Cultural Dominicana, 1988.

Veganzones, Marie-Ange and Carlos Winograd. *Argentina en el siglo XX: crónica de un crecimiento annunciado.* Buenos Aires: Centro de Desarrollo, Organización para la Cooperación y Desarrollo Económicos, 1997.

Velasco, Germán Martínez. *Plantaciones, trabajo guatemalteco y política migratoria en la frontera sur de México.* Chiapas: Government of the State of Chiapas-Instituto Chiapaneco de Cultura, 1994.

Verité. *Research on Indicators of Forced Labor in the Supply Chain of Sugar in the Dominican Republic.* 2012. http://www.verite.org/sites/default/files/images/Research%20on%20Indicators%20of%20Forced%20Labor%20in%20the%20Dominican%20Republic%20Sugar%20Sector_9.18.pdf

Veronis, Luisa. "Immigrant Participation in the Transnational Era: Latin Americans' Experiences with Collective Organising in Toronto." *International Migration and Integration* 11 (2010).

Vior, Eduardo J. "Migración y derechos humanos desde una perspectiva intercultural." In *Migración e interculturalidad. Desafíos teológicos y filosóficos,* edited by R. Fornet-Betancourt, 109–117. Aachen, Germany: Wissenschaftsverlag Mainz in Aachen, 2004.

Vior, Eduardo J. "Die politische Partizipation von Migranten stärkt die Demokratie – Fallstudie: die bolivianische Minderheit in Argentinien." In *¿Sin fronteras? Chancen und Probleme laeinamerikanischer Migration,* edited by Lena Berger, et al., 49–72. München: Martin-Meidenbauer-Verlag, 2007.

Vior, Eduardo J. *Migraciones internacionales y ciudadanía democrática: influencias de las comunidades de origen inmigrante sobre el desarrollo político en Alemania, Argentina y Brasil.* Saarbrücken, Germany: Editorial Académica Española, 2012.

Vior, Eduardo J. and M. del Carmen Cabezas. "Fundamentaciones pragmáticas y teóricas de la ciudadanía sudamericana." Paper presented at the IV Jornadas sobre Debates Actuales de la Teoría Política Contemporánea, Buenos Aires, 2013.

Warner, R. Stephen. "Immigration and Religious Communities in the United States." In *Gatherings in Diaspora: Religious Communities and the New Immigration,* edited by R. Stephen Warner and Judith G. Wittner, 3–34. Philadelphia: Temple University Press, 1998.

Wasam, Ruth E. *Unauthorized Aliens Residing in the United States: Estimates Since 1986.* Washington, DC: Congressional Research Service, 2011.

Webb, Alex. "Bitter Toil: Haitian Sugar Workers in the Dominican Republic." In *Documenting Disposable People: Contemporary Global Slavery,* edited by Mark Sealy, Roger Malbert, and Alice Lobb, 138–151. London: Hayward, 2008.

Wehrfritz, George and Takayama Hideko. "A New Open Door Policy?" *Newsweek,* June 5, 2000.

Wickramasekera, Piyasiri. *Asian Labour Migration: Issues and Challenges in an Era of Globalization.* Geneva: International Migration Programme, International Labour Office, 2002.

Wimmer, Andreas and Nina Glick Schiller. "Methodological Nationalism and Beyond: Nation-State Building Migration and the Social Science." *Global Networks* 2, no. 4 (2002).

World Council of Churches, Migration Secretariat. *Migrant Workers in the Dominican Republic: A Case for Human Rights Action.* Geneva: World Council of Churches, 1978.

World Council of Churches, Migration Secretariat. *"Sold Like Cattle": Haitian Workers in the Dominican Republic.* Geneva: World Council of Churches, 1980.

Wright, Thomas C., Rody Oñate and Irene Hodgson. *Flight from Chile: Voices of Exile.* Albuquerque: University of New Mexico Press, 1998.

Wright, Thomas C. and Rody Oñate Zúñiga."Chilean Political Exile." *Latin American Perspectives* 34, no. 4 (2007).

Wünderich, Volker. *Sandino en la Costa.* Managua: Editorial Nueva Nicaragua, 1989.

Wurgaft. "The Term of the Leaders of Foreign Workers is Very Short. Then Came the Deportation." Ha'aretz, May, 6, 2003. B-4.

Wurgaft. "Shalom, and Thanks for the Humiliating Treatment." Ha'aretz, April 5, 2004, B-9.

Yamanaka, Keiko. "New Immigration Policy and Unskilled Foreign Workers in Japan." *Pacific Affairs* 66 (1993).

Yamanaka, Keiko. "Return Migration of Japanese-Brazilians to Japan: The Nikkejin as Ethnic Minority and Political Construct." *Diaspora* 5, no. 1 (1996).

Yamanaka, Keiko. "Factory Workers and Convalescent Attendants: Japanese-Brazilian Migrant Women and Their Families in Japan." In *International Female Migration and Japan: Networking, Settlement and Human Rights,* 87–116. Tokyo: International Peace Research Institute, 1996.

Yamanaka, Keiko. "Return Migration of Japanese Brazilian Women: Household Strategies and the Search for the 'Homeland.'" In *Beyond Boundaries: Selected Papers on Refugeees and Immigrants,* edited by Diane Baxter and Ruth Krulfeld, 11–34. Arlington, VA: American Anthropological Association, 1997.

Yankelevich, Pablo. "Exilio y dictadura." In *Argentina 1976. Estudios en torno al golpe de Estado,* edited by Clara E. Lida, Horacio Crespo and Pablo Yankelevich. Mexico City: Fondo de Cultura Económica, 2007.

Yegenoglu, Meyda. "From Guest Worker to Hybrid Immigrant: Changing Themes of German-Turkish Literature." In *Migrant Cartographies: New Cultural and Literary Spaces in Post-Colonial Europe*, edited by S. Ponzanesi and D. Merolla, 137–149. Lanham, MD: Lexington Books, 2005.

Zapata Barrero, Ricard. *Ciudadanía e interculturalidad*. Barcelona: Anthropos, 2001.

Zolberg, Arisitide. Introduction to *From Immigrants to Citizens: Membership in a Changing World*, edited by T. Alexander Aleinikoff and Douglas Klusmeyer, 383–385. Washington, DC: Carnegie Endowment for International Peace, 2000.

Index

Page references for figures are indicated by *f* and for tables by *t*.